West dodge.

Castle grant.

The Heart

Of The

Continent

**Being the History
of Assiniboia —**

**the truly typical
Canadian community**

Written and Illustrated
by E. S. Russenholt

Published by
MacFarlane Communication Services
Winnipeg,   1968

Acknowledgements

We give thanks . . . to all who cooperated to produce this book — without 1 cent of public money — national, provincial or municipal.

We give thanks . . . to each contributor of material, criticism, advice and work; to our Assiniboia Chamber of Commerce for blazing the trail to publication; to the Hudson's Bay Company for permitting the author to research micro-film records in the Public Archives of Canada; and to historians who provided basic information, as listed in our selected Bibliography.

We give thanks . . . that we Westerners, like all Canadians, are born into trusteeship of un-matched national land-and-water resources; that crops of grass and trees and buffalo and humans and other living things — growing, multiplying, dying thru myriad centuries — bequeathed to us our vast fertile soil, which we are barely beginning to use; and our equally vital gold-mine of History, which we are barely beginning to explore.

We give thanks . . . that wakening awareness demands more than "a recitation of cliches sanctified by repetition" which, too often, passes as History; and that the incompleteness of this book challenges deeper digging into the History of Assiniboia, the "mother lode" of the History of our great Nor-West — which gives our Canadian nation Dimensions that span the continent; and the Destiny to use the resources of which we are born trustees, for the good of all Mankind.

E. S. RUSSENHOLT
"Happy Acres",
Assiniboia

Contents

Foreword

Herein is told:

something of the History of Assiniboia — the *truly typical* Canadian community.

Each community developing within the embrace of the vast lands and waters which History has entrusted to our Canadian nation, is *truly* Canadian.

Each community in Canada is *truly* Canadian — by whatever trails, across whatever distance of land and sea and time its people found their diverse ways to share in building our new Canadian nation.

Each community in Canada is *truly* Canadian — whether its people came to Canada from one or two or three of the 100 spots on earth whence venturesome souls dared plant their lives in Canada, that their children and all mankind should harvest fullest returns from the vast resources of our nation.

Nevertheless, a *truly typical* Canadian community must be built by people whom destiny has brought together — not via one or two or three temporary resting places — but from a majority of all the lands whence are assembled all the vital components of our Canadian nationality.

Such a rare phenomena is Assiniboia — the *truly typical* Canadian community.

To Kaysha —

partner in family, work and life —

this book is humbly dedicated.

PART 1

The Trail
Into The History
Of Assiniboia

CHAPTER 1

Blazing The Trail

A history of Assiniboia could date from 1811.

In 1811, Lord Selkirk buys from the Hudson's Bay Company 116,000 square miles of lands and waters in "The Heart of the Continent" of North America. Much of this area is occupied by an aboriginal tribe whom neighboring Indians call "stone-cookers" — in syllables that white men repeat as "Assinaboils", "Assiniboins" or "Assiniboines". These hunters heat stones in their open fires; and drop these into birch bark rogans filled with water and meat — until the water boils and cooks the meat. To white men, then, these "stone-cookers" are "Assiniboines"; and Lord Selkirk names his purchase: "Assiniboia".

To Assiniboia, Selkirk brings from Europe and Canada, 5 groups of people — to buy land from him; and to farm it. These settlers adventure on a long journey — thrilling and fearful. As weeks and months go by, they realize this is a long, long distance from their homeland! What they see — voyaging into "the Bay"; battling raging rivers through rock and forest; up the 300 miles of Lake Winnipeg; through the grassy marshes of Netley and along the wooded banks of the Red River to the Assiniboine — all this gives them little idea of this new land — except its awful immensity! What they see of natives, at "the Bay" and en route, does not re-assure them. What they hear from "the Company" men reflects the contempt and fear in which these hold the Indians. Old-timers squeeze the last bit of enjoyment out of telling the new-comers blood-curdling tales of savages who wait to scalp them! In the years that follow, much is learned about our Canadian Nor'-West; and the peoples who, successively, have been its inhabitants. There is so much more to be learned.

Lord Selkirk's "Assiniboia" embraces some 74 million acres —

including the Red River Valley and the Assiniboine basin. Half of it, south of the 49th parallel, will become part of the States of Minnesota, North Dakota and South Dakota. The northern half will form part of the provinces of Saskatchewan and Ontario — and Manitoba as far northward as Swan River.

None of the first settlers — and few Canadians of succeeding generations — ever learn the vast wealth of resources in this region. From its hub, at "the Forks" of the Assiniboine and Red Rivers — eastward, the Roseau, Rainy, Winnipeg and English Rivers and 15,000 interconnecting lakes, offer vast riches of fur — with vaster wealth of forest, power and minerals awaiting development. Northward, beyond gigantic musquash and waterfowl marshes, fish-filled lakes stretch 300 miles to even vaster marshlands and power-packed rivers pounding down a stairway of cataracts unequalled on the earth — to "the Bay" and the open sea. Westward of Lakes Manitoba and Winnipegosis, the finest beaver range ever trapped, merges into parklands and plains a-move with pasturing buffalo. Southward, communities exploding with expansion offer opportunity for trade.

Later generations will wonder, condescendingly, that pioneer communities suffer starvation in the midst of such plenty; but, with all their increasingly sophisticated technologies, will fail to realize this region's abundant potential, for more than a century.

To its native Indians — and the voyageurs and hunters who mingle with them — the lands and waters of Assiniboia open opportunity for men of shrewd and skillful hardihood to live in freedom and spacious independence. This area is destined to be one of the most richly productive in North America. For 150 years before 1811 — and 60 years thereafter — to the man who comes to trade for furs, the sole value of Assiniboia and all its people is: the number of beaver and other pelts he takes out, each fall. To the entrepreneurs in the Montreal and London counting houses of the fur companies, its value is measured by the profits extracted from the traders forwarding the furs.

Lord Selkirk sees a more vital value. Whether as humanitarian or real estate promoter, or mixture of both, he sees something of the vast productive potential which Canadians will only begin to realize 150 years later.

The real values of "Assiniboia" are "built-in" through the ages. Our History should, perhaps, glance backward to the closing years of the most recent Glacial Age. As the waters are released from the ice-fields by the sun's increasing warmth, they flow to the oceans, via streams and lakes. In time, a regimen of water flow is established, in balance with topography, climate and seasons. Water, the stuff of life, circulates in eternal cycle — falling as rain or snow; flowing over, and through, the land to the ocean; climbing sunbeams; riding the skies as cloud; and falling, again, upon the earth.

The cosmic pattern established, decrees that the earth-bound part of the hydrologic cycle shall place more than half the fresh water on our globe within our Canadian boundaries. (A resource unmatched; unrecognized!)

Year by year, the southern margin of the ice retreats, northward. On the surface so exposed to ages of sun and wind, heat and cold, days and seasons — primitive life emerges, to utilize the food supply. Deer and moose browse in the forests. Beaver and musquash feed in the marshes. Fish multiply in the abundant waters. Antelope and buffalo pasture the grasslands. Wolves pursue their predatory purpose, to keep all active and healthy.

The process is underway — via the cycle of birth, growth, mating, multiplication, death, decay and new birth — of mixing organic matter with ground rock-dust to create fertile, living soil. Thus, is stored up our second un-matched resource: Land.

Land and water, married, give birth to all our manifold material production.

One day, somewhere in the vastness of Canada's Northwest, primitive humans appear. For, perhaps, two hundred centuries, successive waves of mankind flow and ebb over this "Heart of the Continent" of North America. One of the early men to arrive in "Assiniboia" is the Mound Builder, coming up the valley of the Mississippi, and down the Red. Other hunters probably follow reindeer from Asia to North America, across Bering Strait, thousands of years ago. Successive groups, at wide intervals in time, plod the same general routes, south-eastward.

However such diversely fascinating speculations may be resolved, history records that — in the two centuries from 1617, when Louis Hebert's family begins Canada's first farm above Quebec, to 1812, when Selkirk Settlers come to Assiniboia — explosive movements of population and changes in the basis of Indian living tremendously influence the history of the aboriginal tribes; and, subsequently, of the European invaders.

When Canada is "discovered" (with the suitably recorded arrival of someone from Europe) some 50 Indian tribes already inhabit the country. Their hunting grounds cover the entire geography of Canadian lands and waters. Their numbers are scattered — an estimated 220,000 people over 4 million square miles. They speak a medley of dialects, grouped in 11 languages.

Some time before 1600, (by the white man's calendar) Cree Indians are located in northern Ontario and Manitoba, around James Bay; and along the Saskatchewan River. About the time that most of Champlain's party succumbs to its first winter in Canada, the Assiniboine tribe separates from the Sioux; moves down the Red River; and occupies land along the Assiniboine. By 1678, when white men freight the first grain on the Great Lakes, Assiniboine hunters are feeding, clothing and housing themselves by killing buffalo, in southern Manitoba and Saskatchewan.

In the days before they get steel tools, horses and guns, our Western Indians lure buffalo into strongly-built pounds; and, with spears, kill entire herds. The food is shared by all. Such "improvidence" is a dominant factor in preventing the emergence of a "superior" class among the Plains Indians.

Hardships, recurrent famine and accidents of migration shorten the Indian's life span. Infant mortality is appalling. Early missionaries record that "hardly one in thirty survives". With no milk to supplement the mother's, the Indian babe must be nursed until able to eat meat, at 2 years. Long periods of lactation lower the fertility of Indian women; and limit the size of families. Population is limited, further, by the terrible custom among warring tribes, of killing all sexes and all ages; and destroying entire camps — as completely as any atomic bomb.

The Indians in Assiniboia face their dominant check on increase, in the uncertainty of their food supply. (As do all living things.) For our Plains tribes, the buffalo provides staple food, clothing and shelter. The buffalo herds find abundant feed — by moving, ceaselessly, from pasture to pasture.

Each autumn, cows and calves pasture their way southward. The bulls move from the open plains into the parklands. On wind-swept slopes and ridges, their sharp hooves dig through the snow to the grass beneath. Cured on the stem, this grass provides Nature's finest fodder. Nature fits the buffalo, superbly, to survive Western winters. In a blizzard, domestic cattle drift down-wind; buffalo head into the storm! Buffalo (like horses in the wild) fight off their principal predators, the wolves, as cattle never could. In general, only old, sick or damaged buffalo, with a percentage of foolish young, feed the wolves. With returning spring, the cows and yearlings drift back to the Northwest. The productive cycle is resumed.

The buffalo survive, and multiply, by constant migration. Our Plains Indians follow the ever-moving herds. Here, on the hoof, is complete living — for the Indians who can take it. Life depends on keeping contact with this moving wholesale supply. Each Indian band must be ready to move at times and for distances determined by the buffalo! Campsites are chosen near ford or hill, where fuel and water are available for the women; and whence hunters have a commanding view for buffalo or enemies. The necessity for moving quickly, far and often, streamlines Indian possessions to what can be quickly packed and easily carried.

In summer, Plains Indians assemble in camps of 100 to 200 tents — for mutual security and sociability. The Woodland Cree build domed lodges some 10 or 12 feet high, covered with bark. Plains tribes use teepees — conical tents, 15 or 20 feet in diameter; covered with buffalo hides, scraped thin. Teepees, like all possessions, must be quickly portable. Privacy is unknown; hygiene unthought of. Perhaps it is just as well that camps move frequently!

When winter comes, tribes disperse in groups of 10 to 20 lodges. Camps are sheltered in ravines or along wooded streams. When a camp succeeds in luring buffalo into a "parc", or pound, food is abundant. All winter, the men hunt and trap for food, and for furs to wear and to trade. The eternal meat diet is varied, somewhat, with wild rice — collected each autumn in the eastern part of Assiniboia; and with maple sugar, made each spring along the Assiniboine.

General belief peoples the "Land of Spirits" — in the sky or somewhere in the far West — with the Great Spirit, creator of all. In time of trouble, all Indians try to enlist the help of the spirits, through prayer. To them, the spirit world is very close.

Missionaries in 1668, find the Lake Superior area well populated. But before white men "discover" the Northwest, some tribes disappear, probably westward. In the early 1700's the Ojibway (Chippewa or Saulteaux), from headquarters at Sault Ste. Marie, control the northern shores of Lake Huron and Superior and the adjacent woodlands of Ontario, Wisconsin, and Minnesota. Pressured by competing traders, they intensify their trapping and hunting — for more pelts. As their own hunting grounds are "skinned" — and trading posts leap-frog Westward — the Saulteaux push into Manitoba.

The Cree begin to get guns from traders on "the Bay" in the 1660's. So armed, they venture from their forest home; and push Westward, into the parklands and plains. A century before the first Selkirk Settlers arrive in Assiniboia, the Assiniboine tribe come down the Red; and occupy the Assiniboine Basin. Bands of Cree move out from the fringe of the "Strong Woods", to hunt buffalo; and become the "Plains Cree". They ally with the Assiniboines. Joined by more bands, and acquiring guns and horses, their swelling numbers spread — southwest to the Missouri; northwest to the Peace River; and west to the Rockies.

Down north on "the Bay", in 1735, the English fur Company begins the massive masonry of Fort Prince of Wales, by the Churchill River. This year, LaVerendrye comes west; and, in the East, Canada's farmers

produce 738,000 bushels of wheat. At this point in time the Indian
tribes which mill about Assiniboia are estimated to number: Cree,
50,000; Saulteaux, 3,500; Assiniboines, 15,000; Blackfoot, 20,000;
and various others, for a total of 120,000.

The Assiniboines, with increasing numbers of warriors, horses and
guns, expand steadily westward. They carry war to Sioux, Mandans,
Kootenays. With their Cree allies, they raid the Blackfoot. They range
all the Great Plains as their hunting grounds. By 1750, the Cree control
all of northern Manitoba, Saskatchewan and Alberta. They penetrate
the foothills into the Rockies. They push down the great Mackenzie
River, years ahead of its white "discoverer". With superior arms and
numbers, they drive Slave and Beaver tribes northwestward.

Half-a-century before Selkirk's first settlers come to Assiniboia,
(1750-60) our Plains Indians are relatively "free from want". In 1772,
Matthew Cocking reports them far superior to other tribes who trade at
York Factory. By 1780, they ride the crest of their strength in physique,
numbers and organization; and reach the peak of their economic upsurge. Great changes are afoot in their political, social and religious
lives. Left to themselves for a few more generations, they might develop
a civilization — pervasive, powerful and permanent. It is not to be. The
great upsurge which carries them to their highest peak, rides a tide
which swiftly wrecks their way of life; and destroys the Indian, himself!

The competitive frenzy of white traders' demand for furs drives the
Indians to excessive slaughter of wildlife. Trapping out their own hunting
grounds, the best-armed bands invade the territory of neighbors. Eastern
Iroquis, for example, "push out to reach beaver areas beyond Lake
Winnipegosis"; and, westward, from Assiniboia to the Rocky Mountains. The passion for trade goods (particularily rum) that triggers this
aggressive scattering of their numbers, signals their doom! Their belli-
cose arrogance terrifies successive generations in Eastern Canada; but
the Iroquois fail to utilize the mobility so effectively exploited by the
mounted warriors of the Cree, Assiniboine and Sioux. Their scattered
remnants are ridden down by western cavalry!

The booming fur trade opens new forts, further and further into the
Nor'West. "For some years, all these Indians were rich; men, women
and children were covered with brooches, wampum, beads; all was
finery and dress". By 1797, over-trapping denudes great ranges of
beaver — "the gold coin, with which what have become the necessaries
of life, are bought".

"As time went on, the Indians began to relinquish many of the habits
and customs and even the appearance they had presented, before the
advent of the white traders . . . Took on many of the outer characteris-

tics of the European. They brought in the spoils of the chase; exchanged them for necessaries which they no longer provided for themselves. . . . The tribes were in the pay of 'the Company', or lived on its bounty . . . All originality was lost".

Nevertheless, the Indian, when he keeps his native way, survives in our Canadian Northwest, as white men could not. Settlers from Europe bring with them food, clothing, seeds, livestock, steel tools. With his steel axe, a white settler fells in 30 minutes, a tree that takes several Indians a week to down, with stone axes and fire. Yet — for 200 years, white settlers depend on their homelands. In Assiniboia, successive generations of whites live on supplies freighted through "the Bay" and from Eastern and Southern settlements; and escape starvation with food provided by our Plains Indians — and their offspring. Once on his feet, any capable settler with seeds, livestock and tools of steel, can live off any fertile farm, permanently. His children — and his children's children — capitalize on the cultivated acres, herds, grain, buildings and communities which he, and neighboring pioneers, bequeath them. By contrast, each Indian band, in each generation, lives by its own effort. Steel knives and axes are the trade goods first in demand. These reach "the Heart of the Continent" long before the first farm settlers arrive. Obviously, the Indian in Assiniboia has one advantage. He knows the terrible extremes of climate; and how these must be survived — in ways which take white settlers many years to learn.

Once over their peak, the Plains Indians disintegrate with appalling rapidity. In 1749, officials of the Hudson's Bay Company report the number of Cree to be about 100,000. In 1800, the estimated number is 14,000! By 1810, Alexander Henry finds "only about 300 tents full of Cree, capable of furnishing less than 1,000 men".

When Selkirk's white families come to farm in Assiniboia (and people in Canada and the United States kill each other in a war as insane as any Indian foray for scalps) the Indian tribes ranging Assiniboia are: to the west and north, Cree: 20,000; westward, Assiniboine: 9,000; eastward, Saulteaux: 10,000; and southward, the Sioux (still able to muster 2,000 warriors). The Saulteaux occupy the Red River Valley. Chief Peguis and his braves "hunt about Pembina and Turtle Mountain"; and, after 1806, grow some corn along Netley Creek. Cree and Assiniboine are lured westward by Missouri River traders and their "fire-water".

As the Settlements grow along the Assiniboine River and the Red, the ancient Indian war — Cree and Assiniboine versus Blackfoot — rages on. But, whereas, in the days of their strength, Cree and Assiniboine harass the Blackfoot on their own ground, the Blackfoot (who keep free of the traders more successfully than do other Plains tribes) now chase their fading enemies right to "the Forks". As one Hudson's Bay Governor reports: "Those Indians who have least intercourse with the factories, are by far the happiest".

Horses appear in our Canadian Northwest, early in the 1700's. On the Plains, horses find conditions ideal, fodder abundant and predators few. Horse numbers multiply and spread rapidly — northward along the foothills; eastward, over the Plains and parklands. In 1754, Anthony Henday, exploring inland from York Factory, reports Blackfoot and Assiniboine well supplied with horses; and horses ranging wild and free over the Plains.

Before the horse, the Indian's most treasured possession is his teepee, made from some 20 buffalo hides. Once mounted, hunters kill buffalo so easily, the hides become almost worthless; and food is more than abundant. The horse establishes new standards of value. With horses, a brave buys wives, rank in the secret societies, medicine bundles, status! It becomes as honorable to steal horses as to kill and scalp the horse's owner! The impact of this new dynamic is a salient phenomenon in the history of Man. These scattered, foot-bound, hungry hunters, once in the saddle, become fully-fed warriors — possessing mobility for themselves and possessions; and daring forays of thousands of miles! The explosion in travel diffuses social, political and religious ideas. Where the tribe had been a loose grouping of scattered kindred bands, now Plains Indians, hunting over wide ranges, become close-knit tribal units.

Another dominant factor in the eruption of Assiniboia Indians before 1812, is the acquisition of steel tools, including the gun. Firearms come into the Nor'West with the earliest fur traders. In 1671, Radisson orders that the Company ships "Prince Rupert" and "Imploy" include in their cargo: 500 fowling pieces, with powder and shot. Apparently, subsequent annual "outfits" are similar. In 1685, 400 guns are aboard the ship to "the Bay". If "Company" shipments average 400 firearms annually, the total for the century before 1812, is 40,000 guns. The Nor'West Company annual trade probably exceeds that number. Even at 400 yearly, their total for the thirty years before 1812 would reach 12,000. Thus, imports of these two warring Companies for this period could total 52,000 guns. Others (like Astor) trade unknown numbers of guns into the Northwest.

Withal, it is certain that, when the early farm settlers come to Assiniboia, many thousands of firearms are in the hands of hunters who live by their skillful use — in the vast area centring on "the Forks" of the Assiniboine River and the Red. Considering the violent clashes of interests; the lack of understanding; and the absence of law — it is a miracle that the universal presence of arms threatens the lives of settlers on so few occasions.

Observations duly recorded — often far apart in time and locale; sometime contradictory — provide some outline on which may be sketched a picture of Indian life. In such a picture, the violent upheavals among our Plains Indians during the century before settlers come to Assiniboia, may be summarized in 4 successive generations.

The first generation of Plains Indians in that century (say from 1710 to 1735) learn to catch and ride horses. More and more hunters get guns, steel knives and axes. So equipped, they out-run the buffalo herds; and, with gratifying ease, harvest abundant food, clothing and shelter for their entire band. Life is vastly improved for all.

The second generation of the century under review (from about 1735 to 1760) brings the Horseback Economy into full gallop. The hunting grounds of every band expands, by hundreds of miles. On horseback, the hunters reach buffalo, wherever the herds may be. With guns they readily kill all they need — and more.

With tools of steel, the skinning and the meat-cutting is done in a fraction of the time formerly required. The Plains tribes face a new phenomenon: leisure! Soon, they scorn the hardships of grandfather's day, when families wander a-foot, carrying all their possessions on their backs. To prove their hardihood, young Indians turn their leisure to fighting, robbing, killing each other.

The next generation (the third of our century, covering the span from 1760 to 1785) lives a life as different from their grandfathers', as the auto is from the ox-cart! Our Plains Indians grow numerous, fat and arrogant. As in every affluent generation, young "hot-rodders" yearn to show their strength and daring. Horses and guns give them mobility and firepower. These basics are a potent stimulus to the buffalo hunt; and then, to war! Camp by camp, the tribes are infected with war fever. Bands divide their days between the hunt — and war on other tribes. Just like the "civilized" English, Spanish, French and Americans — our Plains Indians must prove their prowess in war. Our Canadian Nor'West is a blazing battlefield — from Assiniboia to the Rockies!

The fourth generation of our summarized century (1785 to 1810) sees the Plains Indians (other than the Blackfoot federation) become slaves of the fur trade. Competing traders blanket the Nor'West with fur forts; and — using steel tools, guns, gadgets (and more and more rum) as bait — drive the Indian families to slave for more and more furs; shackled with more and more debt; and more and more debauched with alcohol!

Then — smallpox sweeps the land with deadly devastation!

Sporadic outbreaks of smallpox in 1700 and 1733 are forerunners of terrible epidemics in the 1780's — which spread terror and death across our entire Nor'West. Indian bands near trading posts, weakened by rum, are wiped out. Once populous tribes are decimated. David Thompson reports three-fifths (others estimate 90%) of all Indians die!

Thus, before the first Selkirk Settlers reach Assiniboia, the way of life which the Plains Indians had built for themselves, with the components available to them — is totally wrecked by war, fur trade, rum and small-pox!

Nor does settlement stay these terrible attacks of smallpox. Prince Maximilian of Neuweid writes in 1832: "Prairie one vast field of death. . . . Covered with unburied corpses . . . Assiniboine, 9,000 in number . . . nearly exterminated". In 1836, again, smallpox smites the Assiniboine; and over "4,000 die". In the 23 years, 1835 to 1858, the Cree are reduced from 4,000 to 1,000. They never recover!

In addition to aborigines, numbers of other people live around "the Forks" of the Assiniboine River and the Red before 1811, when Lord Selkirk names "Assiniboia".

About 1750, says one historian, the Plains tribes "come into our history". Actually, Europeans invade the Indians; and, in our Nor'West, history sees a head-on collision between the mobile, hunting life of the nomad Indian and the European's drive for profit — first, from the fur trade; then, from permanent tillage of individually-owned acres; and, later, from fantastic booms in real estate, as increasing population multiplies land prices.

The Indian cannot comprehend personal "real estate". In his economic philosophy, all lands and waters belong (for use) to the band — or to neighboring bands. Refusing to surrender individual freedom in widely-organized action, Indians never achieve the degree of conformity which is the white man's price for material wealth.

Europeans first come to Assiniboia to get furs. Most traders have only contempt for the Indians who get the furs for them. Early fur trade profits are fantastic; and lure traders, even to their death.

As competition between traders waxes increasingly keen and deadly, more and more brandy is offered as bait. A gallon of spirits gets a trader many times more choice furs than the same weight in steel tools. In their frenzy for furs, traders exploit the Indian's frenzy for "firewater"! Entire families become slaves of trading posts "where liquor is dispensed to them by the keg". In the white man's drive for fur profits, natives are demoralized, beggared and robbed of resources (or even desire) to master swiftly changing conditions. Any fair statement of "Profit and Loss" for the fur trade, shows all the "Profit" to the fur-men; and, to the Indians: "Loss of everything!"

CHAPTER 2

Following the Trail

Since we define History as "the study of When and How, Who lived Where," our history of Assiniboia must consider all peoples of this region. The myth that "Discovery" is in the footprints, and "History" in the lives, of Europeans alone, lacks historical significance. However, there may be evidence that the first white men to visit "the Forks" are 8 Goths and 22 Norwegians, in 1362. White fur traders appear 3 centuries later.

The fur trade — wild, dangerous, deadly — reaps fantastic profits from the fashion in European capitals, which dictates that gentlemen of fashion wear hats made of beaver. Charles I, King of England, gives fashion the force of law, in 1638, by proclaiming his royal will that no material, other than beaver, be used in making hats for "Gentlemen". Each such hat costs more than 6 months' earnings of a skilled artisan. (Such is the power of the Hatter's Guild!)

When the first Europeans step onto the soil of Canada, there are an estimated 10 million beaver on the Continent. Breeding grounds support up to 50 beaver per square mile. With water and timber plentiful, they multiply rapidly. The very characteristics which guarantee their multi-plication, however, makes them easy prey for hunter and trapper.

In Canada, under French rule, fur trading is monopolized by the King's favorites. Officials share the profits. Despite all regulations, however, by 1700, one-third of the able-bodied men of New France range the forests, hunting for furs.

Any expert bushranger can pack his canoe with traps, ammunition and supplies; evade the police; and gain the freedom of the waterways and forests — to hunt, trap, trade and wander at will.

In 1731, LaVerendrye is at Grand Portage west of Lake Superior. He is duly licensed to explore; and to trade. In the next 17 years, he and his sons set up 8 forts in Assiniboia. Fort Rouge is built — and abandoned — by 1737. LaVerendrye records 10 Cree lodges at "the Forks" in 1738, as he passes up the Assiniboine River to locate Fort LaReine, near Poplar Point.

Free men — unsung, unknown — follow LaVerendrye before his trail is cold. Some may have preceded him. Many hope to go back to Quebec with a fortune in furs in their canoes. Thus, years before France cedes Canada to England, Canadians develop a growing fur trade in Assiniboia. Many wander westward to escape the graft-ridden subservience of New France, to the freedom of the wilderness. Never intending to return to the over-policed impositions of civilization, they merge into the native population.

In the world-wide war games of European rulers, the politicians in favor at the court of France decide that Canada is "expendable". French regiments and supplies are diverted to hold other places, which these grandees consider of greater worth. The people of Canada are thrown, almost entirely, on their own native resources. Despite the heroic defence by its habitants, Canada is forsaken; and surrendered by France to England. In the subsequent political poker sessions (called "negotiations") the politicians of Paris, again, pass up Canada; and, in preference, take back Guadeloupe, in the West Indies. The 619 square miles of Guadeloupe's 2 islands are, mostly, volcanic; but 92 square miles grow sugar, which makes superlative rum. It is an ideal little "empire" for a court favorite to operate by slaves, under the whips of rum-swilling officials. After all, to the grandees of France, Canada is but "quelques arpents de neige"; or, in the words of a later generation of the English Establishment: "a few miles of eternal snow!"

The terms under which France surrenders Canada allow all who wish, to return to France. Many go. Of the meagre number of regular soldiers allotted to Canada by Parisian politicians, 615 return to France. The Intendant, Bigot, under whose regime "the inhabitants were shamefully robbed and maltreated" is called to Paris. Officials, who regard their positions in Canada as banishment — made endurable by the opportunity to enrich themselves by graft and the fur trade; contractors, whose shoddy work undermines the defences of Quebec; merchants, whose sole interest in Canada is profits (already shrewdly banked in Europe); all these — and all their hangers-on — leave for France.

Who stays in Canada? The habitants, who love their land. These true Canadians share Champlain's dream of building, here, a great nation. The servants of Mother Church stay; their life-work is to serve the parishes, teach in the schools, nurse in the hospitals. Officials and merchants of small communities and some of the soldiers stay — to make Canada their homeland.

New-comers move in, to replace the departees. Highland Scots, following their crushing defeat at Culloden, in 1745, escape the barbaric reprisals inflicted by their English conquerors, by leaving Scotland; and seeking opportunity in North America. Numbers of these make their way to Canada; and some fight in the ranks of Canada's defenders. After 1760, some of Fraser's Highlanders settle along the St. Lawrence. A few pick up seigneuries from departing grandees, at canny bargains. Others are captivated by beauteous Canadienne — who happen to be heirs to vast holdings. As always, the winning army is trailed by predatory hordes, greedy to cash in on victory. Profiteers from England and her American Colonies, flood into Canada.

There is an exodus, too, from Canada — to Assiniboia! The old French fur trade — with its tangled regulatory impositions which shackle Canadians in Quebec for the profit of grafting officials — is swept away. Young habitants are free to join voyageurs and courier-du-bois in following their dreams to the great Nor'West. Many exchange the strictures of foreign military rule in the Colony for the lure of the wilderness. English and Yankee traders, to harvest the fur profits formerly pre-empted by the French King's favorites, set up shop in Montreal. The fur trade, with its promise of quick profits for hard work, engages many emigré Scots. All these — and the voyageurs hired by them — head Nor'West. Soldiers from English regiments — some discharged; some deserters — go along, looking for adventure and freedom "over the hill". West and north they wander, along the old canoe routes — to Assiniboia, "The Heart of the Continent". Among many traders, Alexander Henry paddles northwest from Sault Ste. Marie with 16 canoes, freighting $15,000 in goods and 52 men.

In addition to traders — and those just hunting and fishing and following their whims — old "Company" servants operate farms at Fort Alexander, Brandon House and other fur posts. More gravitate to "the Forks", year by year. By 1816, Miles Macdonnell, Governor of Assiniboia, reports: "Hundreds of Canadian free-men roam the Colony . . . have families with Indian wives".

The Canada surrendered by France to England in the 1763 Treaty of Paris, includes a vague vastness beyond the Mississippi, traversed by a superb network of waterways, centring in Assiniboia.

The first "Montreal Trader" to return to Assiniboia is Francois le Blanc. His canoe carries trade goods valued at $12,000, on credit from Isaac Todd and James McGill. (McGill later, invests some of his fur profits in his University). The rush of fur men back to the Nor'West is underway! Soon, canoe brigades for the interior are leaving Rainy Lake every August. They speed down Lake Winnipeg to the Saskatchewan River — paddling 40 strokes to-the-minute, 18 hours a day — often, in time to rugged, rollicking songs. The canoes for Fort Chipewayan must arrive before October freeze-up! It is recorded that in a race down Lake Winnipeg, Duncan McGillivray's men paddle 48 consecutive hours without leaving their canoes! An exhausted steersman falls overboard; and is hauled back into the craft. Guides cut chunks of pemmican and feed the paddlers, non-stop. These Canadian voyageurs are short, active, tireless men. Many suffer ruptures and spastic backs before they are 40. Most of them die before 50!

The fur trade plays a vital — and contradictory — role in our History of Assiniboia. It introduces the steel tools which help our Plains Indians to their meteoric rise; and brings the rum and smallpox which engulf these tribes in ruin. The fur trade gives birth to pioneer farming; and then, throttles farm Settlements by Monopoly. Finally, it adds to Assiniboia's population the men who, eventually, defeat the Monopoly; and, thus, open Canada's great Nor'West to fuller development.

Superficial observation may suggest that the building of Canada's scattered provinces into a nation is not economic — but political. More penetrating analysis reveals that fur trade profits first capture the interest of such men as Smith, Stephen, Kittson and Hill; and lead them, through a maze of political deviousness, to the greater profits in steamboats, railroads, land and finance; and, so, to a paying basis for political consolidation.

In the early 1760's, "James Findlay from Montreal" is reported in the Nor'West "with three canews"; and William Tomison, Hudson's Bay Company man, comes up the Severn River from "the Bay". By 1768, 4 trading posts are in business on the lower Assiniboine and Red Rivers — 43 years before the first farm Settlers come to Assiniboia. Matthew Cocking records in 1772: "Hudson's Bay Company trade is diminishing, by the Canadians intercepting natives on their way to the Settlements". The English Company is forced to extend operations inland. In 1774, Samuel Hearne, building Cumberland House, as the first of many Hudson's Bay Company forts, reports 60 canoes of free traders from Grand Portage. To man these posts, writes Douglas Mackay, "came men who accepted the country . . . could live and travel among Indians . . . find satisfaction in the new and unknown. Keen observers and keepers of good journals".

Beginning in 1712, "the Company" hires Orkneymen as servants at $30 annually, for 5 years. From 1775 to 1850, their numbers multiply.

On completing their "Company" service, these sturdy pioneers become Settlers — a solid corner-stone of the population of Assiniboia.

In 1778, Peter Pond, first known white man to cross Methye Portage to trade with the Chipewyans, brings "out" 8,000 fine beaver pelts. More important, he learns about pemmican! Pemmican re-shapes the fur trade; increases the range of the canoe brigades; and confirms Assiniboia as the hub of the entire fur industry — and of History's greatest inland waterway transport system.

Daring free traders and canny Montreal merchants organize the Northwest Company, in 1783. In this year, too, the area open to their operations is drastically reduced when, by the Treaty of Versailles, aggressive Yankee and appeasive English negotiators "set the Canadian border with the express intent of making it impossible for Canada to survive".

In the fur trade, increasing competition dictates more men, more posts. Pine Fort is built on the Assiniboine River, in 1785, 18 miles below the mouth of the Souris. Hearne, for the Hudson's Bay Company, builds Swan River House, in 1790; Souris River Fort, in 1793; and Brandon House, on the Assiniboine, in 1794. The Nor'Westers build Assiniboine House beside the latter, while Hearne is 1,000 miles westward, building Edmonton House. Men from "the Bay" push up the Albany and down the English Rivers, in 1793, into Assiniboia. By 1794, "there are 21 posts on the Assiniboine River." The Hudson's Bay Company main transport line, from York Factory to the interior, is re-routed via the Red and "Upper Red" (Assiniboine) Rivers. Every new "discovery", every trade route extension, every added trading post — increases the importance of Assiniboia — as centre of the water-transport system; and of the vital pemmican supply.

John Macdonnell (brother of Miles, who becomes Governor of Assiniboia in 1811) writes of his first voyage with a Nor'West canoe brigade, in 1793. Canoes are made of birch bark; 40 feet long, with 5-foot thwarts; and 4-inch boards, just below the gunwales, as seats for the paddlers. The seams in the bark are re-gummed daily. At portages, 4 men carry the canoe, while other crew-men trot across twice, each time carrying 2 90-pound pieces on a tumpline. Men need new moccasins, daily. From Rainy Lake, le vrais Hommes du Nord take over. Following small waters to Lake Winnipeg, they dodge the giant cataracts of the Winnipeg River. Macdonnell records: "18 May, 1795; carcasses of buffalo in the river . . . count . . . 7,360 drowned or mired". (In the flooding Assiniboine!) Three days later: "21 May, Fort Riviere la Souris . . . Five different oppositions built here last winter, all working against each other". Competition goes mad!

This same year, David Thompson, "from Lake Winnipeg, follows the Red and Assiniboine Rivers, locating all Nor'West Company posts". His great map, for the first time, plots the waterways; and shows how, from "the Forks", men canoe to all corners of North America.

The plains and parklands tributary to this "Heart of the Continent" support incredible herds of buffalo. That doughty old trader, MacDonald of Garth, writes of seeing buffalo "in such numbers that we often get our canoes amongst them; and shoot hundreds without need". Daniel W. Harmon notes: "Buffalo . . . Countless herds. Fear to lie down at night, lest trampled to death. Havoc by prairie fires. Cree, Assiniboines . . . need firearms, axes, kettles, knives. Lost use of bow and arrow. Chiefs eager to trade daughter to white man for rum." (Twelve years before the first Selkirk Settlers arrive!) Canadian traders supply steel traps, after 1795, to help the Indian get more pelts; keep him in debt to the trader; and, thus, trap the trapper, as surely as his fur-bearing victim.

Trade booms! Each spring, 200 canoes carry goods from Lachine to the Nor'West. Reaching Grand Portage, they represent an investment of $750,000. The fur harvest for 1800, for the Nor'West Company alone, includes 106,000 beaver and 31,200 other pelts. This Company employs from 1,000 to 2,000 men. Wages average $200 yearly, paid in goods at high profits. Youths, chiefly Scots, are apprenticed as clerks for their keep and $500 for 7 years.

Alexander Henry, Nor'West trader, on August 2, 1801, writes in his journal: "arrived at 'the Forks'. Sent on the canoe. Took the horse . . . by land up the Assiniboine three leagues to Grand Passage (near later-day Headingly) "Crossed . . . water up to our saddles". Again, "1804, 17 October, snow. I take my vegetables up: 300 cabbage, 8 bushels of carrots, 16 bushels onions, 10 bushels turnips, beets, parsnip, etc". And on October 20: "Take in my potatoes, 420 bushels . . . Indians have stolen at least 200 bushels more" (At his Pembina trading post). At most fur forts, big gardens grow vegetables; small fields produce grain; and livestock is raised for food. The basic ration for the thousands of fur-men is pemmican. The expanding army of voyageurs, clerks and traders hired by the battling fur Companies, multiplies the demand for this staple. Supplying the pemmican needed is the basic industry on which Assiniboia is built. On the income from pemmican, increasing numbers of Canadian, hybrid and Indian hunters live the life they love. Most of them earn additional income by trapping (yes, and trading) furs. Thus, at "the Forks", in 1803-04, trader Dorion assembles 14 packs of furs; being the pelts of 356 beaver and 76 wolves.

By 1804, the Nor'West Company canoe route is loaded with traffic — from Montreal via Fort William and "the Forks" to the Saskatchewan, Athabasca and Columbia Rivers. Corn, peas and pork feed the voyageurs to Rainy Lake. Wild rice varies the diet to Lake Winnipeg. Pemmican carries the brigades to the far northern posts — where white-fish and cariboo are plentiful.

Every spring, boat brigades freight pemmican down the Qu'Appelle, Souris and Assiniboine Rivers to "the Forks"; and on, to the great supply depot at the mouth of the Winnipeg River. Here, boats are burned; nails salvaged and taken back up-stream, to build more boats. Labor and lumber are cheap; iron is beyond price. Pemmican is vital. Any failure in the pemmican supply in Assiniboia, spells starvation for voyageur and trader in the field — and loss for the fur barons! Before any farm settlers arrive in Assiniboia, "the Forks" is recognized as the vital waterways and pemmican centre.

By 1806, the Nor'Westers operate 9 lake boats, 17 canot du Maitre and 97 canot du Nord. The canot du Maitre (or Montreal canoes) are 40-footers, with crews of up to 14 each, carrying 8,000 pounds to Fort William. The canot du Nord are 25 feet long; and, with crews of 5 to 8, freight 4,000 pounds, north and west from Fort William. One-third of the freight carried by these brigades is food for the crews. The pay-load averages 400 to 500 pounds per man.

On July 8, 1806, Alexander Henry enters in his log: "Four p.m. reach Assiniboine at Grand Passage . . . three leagues above the Forks . . . Raft over to north side . . . 8 p.m. camp at White Horse Plain". In 1807, returning from Fort William, Henry records: "Increasing number of free-men from Canada. . . 45 on Red River". "Worthless fellows", he calls them. For Henry's purposes, yes. They are their own men. Free men! In this year, however, comes one such free-man whose name is writ larger than Henry's own in our History of Assiniboia. It is: "Lagimondiere!"

Jean Baptiste Lagimondiere is one of those young Canadians who, about 1800, finds freedom, adventure and independence in the spacious Nor'West. After 5 years, he returns to his home in Trois Rivieres. His parents urge him to settle down, as a good habitant. It seems that he will; and, in April, 1807, he marries Marie Anne Gaboury. Soon, however, the Nor'West calls! Jean and Marie paddle for a full moon, to reach "the Forks". In the fall, they move to Pembina. There, on January 6, 1808, their babe is born; a daughter, Julie; first white child of record born in Assiniboia, or anywhere in Canada's great Nor'West. When spring wakens the waters, Jean Baptiste with his family, paddles west-ward. Four springs they follow the buffalo hunt; and 4 winters, return to Edmonton. In 1811, they move back to Assiniboia. Thereafter, their lives are woven into our History.

When the first of Selkirk's Settlers arrive at "the Forks" they camp across the Red River from the Nor'Westers' Fort Gibraltar, where "oak trees, split, form its enclosure. Within, the house of the partners, 2 houses for the men, store, smith, stable and ice-house with a tower". Good log houses — up to 64 feet long. In winter, 20 employees live here. A good solid establishment; nevertheless, in the ferocity of the ensuing fur wars, it is wrecked within 6 years.

The fur-men dominate the written history of their day in Assiniboia. On arrival, however, they find other white men in the area. Canadians have ranged the forests, westward from the St. Lawrence, for years. In the early 1700's, Lemoyne d'Iberville urges that settlers be prevented hunting with the Indians; for "when they are in the woods, they do not desire to become tillers of the soil". Increasing numbers of outlaw bush-rangers choose rather to adventure in the wilderness than to serve the King, tilling the soil — no matter how dire the penalties. With the passing years, more men drift from Canada to Assiniboia "than there is any record of". Many work with the fur Companies. Many remain free men.

When France surrenders Canada, the officials who control the fur trade, take their wealth to Europe. The voyageurs and servants who, for miserable wages, brought the furs to market, are abandoned — to the wilderness! Refusing to trade their rugged freedom for the regimented sophistication of over-crowded towns, they become "natives" of the wilds they love. Lacking capital to trade, they live by hunting, trapping and fishing. Selecting a site on stream or lake, within paddling distance of a trading post, each builds his snug log cabin; acquires an Indian wife; and slips into customs native to the country and its people. Quickly, each cabin is "home" to a family of half-wild children. It is observed, also, as early as 1749 by a man of 30 years "Company" service, that most of the children in the camps around the fur forts claim "Company" factors as fathers. Thus, throughout the Nor'West, appear multiplying numbers of new people — descendants of hunters, trappers, wanderers, "Company-men" who may hail from Canada, England, France, Scotland, Orkneys, Ireland, the American Colonies or any land on earth — and Indian mothers. These people of mixed parentage soon out-number all others in Assiniboia. In 1870, a census of the Settlements along the Assiniboine and Red, records some 1,500 whites; 500 Indians; and over 9,000 hybrids.

We can take issue with one authority, who states: "Indians have little influence on the Colony, good or bad". Actually, in providing mothers for most of our population, the Indian inhabitants of Assiniboia influence our History, inevitably and decisively.

The actual buying of land by Selkirk's Settlers from his Lordship, generates the first faint interest in land titles among the people of Assiniboia. For two generations, occupants hold their land by "grant" or lease from "the Company" or "by the custom of the country". This "custom" recognizes the right of the squatter to use land; and to sell any improvements made thereon, to a subsequent occupant. Such casual claims, later, are swept away; and land titles become a question of deep vexation.

By the Treaty of Versailles, in 1763, whatever title to Canada which can be asserted by France is surrendered to England. This Treaty, like many preceding it concerning Canada, deals with boundaries defined only vaguely — or not at all! Title is so questionable that, subsequently, successive "negotiators" transfer great regions of Canada to the United States.

These events may generate little interest in future days. It may be useful to note, however, that the attitude, which so readily arrogates to Europeans title to the property of non-Europeans, may have created most of the troubles suffered in developing our Canadian West; and, even after millions die in two World Wars, threatens the peace of the world — and every community therein.

Europeans, with naively naked (and highly profitable) arrogance, date "discovery" of any part of the earth from the first recorded appearance, there, of some European, who (as in duty bound) assumes ownership for his monarch. Such title is duly recognized by other nations of Europe (when convenient). Inevitably, all such titles rest — behind whatever facade of legality — upon the power of the claimants to kill each other. Thus, for centuries, ownership changes with demonstrated "gun-power!" The fur forts built on the shores of Hudson's Bay, for example, are taken and re-taken by gun-power. The Forts at Moose, Rupert and Albany, between 1668 and 1693, change ownership 3 times between fur Companies in England and France; Severn changes twice; and York Factory, from 1670 to 1714, 6 times!

Lord Selkirk buys Assiniboia, in 1811, from the London Committee of the Hudson's Bay Company. Members of this august body know little of the country they "sell"; and care less — except that from its unknown come furs which make them rich!

The title for Assiniboia which "the Company" sells to Selkirk (and which his Lordship plans to retail to Settlers) rests upon a title which King Charles II gives to certain of his favorites, in the "Honorable Company". Charles' sole claim is that some subject of his realm records his arrival on that part of the earth before subjects of other European monarchs so record. The title to half a continent, given to "the great Company" by the Merry Monarch, is protested and contested through

after years. Such contests — when between the "Gentlemen Adventurers" and their friends of the Establishment, and a few "colonials" lost
in the snows of Canada — can be decided (with whatever legal make-
believe) in only one way!

It is a different matter, however, when the title is challenged by aggressive representatives of the United States. In 1803, that vigorous young
Republic buys from Napoleon, for $12 million cash, whatever title
France claims to Louisiana, a vast vague area between the Mississippi
River and the Rocky Mountains. The purchasers promptly claim everything — northward through Minnesota and the Dakotas — to the 49th
parallel; and westward through Oregon. It becomes increasingly popular
in the United States to push claims for Canadian territory to the most
aggressive limits. Too often, those claims win! (The Establishment in
England judging, doubtless, that available gun-power can be more profit-
ably deployed elsewhere.)

In 1816, Lord Selkirk makes a deal with certain chiefs of some of
Assiniboia's Indians, whereby he purports to "buy" title to designated
lands along the Assiniboine and Red Rivers. Does his Lordship "buy"
this land from these Indians (after he has already bought title to all
Assiniboia from "the Company) because he believes that these natives
have some residual rights therein? Or does he make this "treaty" as
good public relations? Further: can it be seriously believed that Indians,
for the palty payments involved, "sell" this land in the same sense that
his Lordship thinks he buys it?

These questions may be asked, also, of later so-called "treaties" by
which our Canadian nation (after paying "the Company" for what is
ruled to be a valid title) feels obliged to extinguish some right which the
natives still retain in ownership.

Historically, title to any territory rests upon common acceptance of
such title. Conceivably, lawyers of half-a-dozen nations could make
claims to our Canadian Northwest, quite as legal as our own. The *real
title* to any land or water and the resources thereof, rests on something
entirely different from, and far more substantial than, legal verbiage —
or even gun-power. The final title to resources — and their ultimate
possession — goes to the owner who demonstrates better use of the
resources in question than any other owner would do.

Meantime, the question of our assuming title to our Canadian lands
and waters from the Indians who precede us in ownership, may not be
as completely settled as we are in the habit of thinking. History . . .
including the history of our Assiniboia . . . raises more questions than it
answers.

PART 2

Battlefield
For Fur

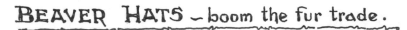

BEAVER HATS – boom the fur trade.

1770 DANDY

NAVY

CLERICAL

ARMY

CHAPTER 3

Savage Settlement 1811-19

In 1811, it is past mid-April when the ice breaks up on the Assiniboine River and the Red. At "the Forks", where the two streams merge, ice piles up in booming commotion; grinding giant blocks to slush, until the backed-up flood sweeps all ahead upon its muddy torrent.

May brings blazing sunshine. Snow disappears from plain and ridge; and from the timbered margin of creek and river. Crows overhead and crocuses in the tough prairie sod, announce that spring has come. Great "V's" of geese and clouds of ducks follow the ice, northward. Catkins burst on the swaying willows; and buds on the lacy branchlets of the elms. South of the Assiniboine River, people assemble from the scattered teepees and cabins which have been their winter homes, to gather the rising sap of the maples for sugar-making. At last, oaks and ash are tinted with the promise of another crop of foliage. Passenger pigeons pass over, in masses that dim the sun. Quickly, May is over-ridden by onrushing June; and the plains are a-wave with lush, new grass.

There is activity in the teepees outside Fort Gibraltar; and in the sheltering timber along Netley Creek. The Saulteaux families are preparing to move. From snug log cabins, scattered westward along the Assiniboine and southward along the Red, Canadian free-men, with their Indian wives and hybrid families, prepare to trek out to the plains. On the new grass, buffalo cows and yearlings graze their way northward. Bulls emerge from the parklands. The herds begin another summer of reproduction.

The hunters loiter. June is the month when the Nor'West Company canoe brigades bring their harvest of furs from the remote interior, to Fort William; and return with the year's supplies. Down the Assiniboine from the Souris and Qu'Appelle, brigades freight pemmican — to Fort Alexander, on the Winnipeg River. Each brigade, returning west and northward, takes its load of pemmican, to feed voyageurs and fur-men.

Meantime, this is the season for brief re-union with relatives and old friends; and exchanging news and gossip. With the voyageurs, perhaps 2,000 people gather around Fort Gibraltar. There are 20 or 30 Nor'West employees at the Fort; and, probably, 150 free-men, with native wives and children numbering, perhaps, 600. Indians — resident Saulteaux; and returning Cree and Assiniboines — may total 1,000. Fort Gibraltar, for a few days, is a hilariously busy centre.

Following the pattern of years, the brigades will soon be gone; the free-men, hybrids and Indians will scatter; and the fur-men at the Fort will settle back into their summer routine. This year, however, the voyageurs bring news from Canada more important than the supplies they freight. The Hudson's Bay Company is reinforcing its fur army; and bringing people to "the Forks" to start a farm Colony! It is unbelieveable! It is true!

In Scotland, after the rebellion of 1745, the clan system is destroyed. Many of a new generation of chieftains sell their clan lands for big-scale sheep farms; and clansmen who live, however miserably, on these holdings, are evicted.

Lord Selkirk learns about Assiniboia as early as 1801. His vivid imagination sees it as a site of a great settlement of his evicted countrymen. He buys shares in the Hudson's Bay Company; and pushes his idea of settlement. The sedate governing Committee is uninterested. However, when the aggressive Nor'West Company captures so much of the fur trade that Hudson's Bay shares lose two-thirds of their value, the Committee is forced to choose: give up the fur trade — or fight the Nor'Westers! William Auld, Hudson's Bay Company Northern Superintendent, on leave in London, and Colin Robertson, former Nor'Wester, urge the Committee to fight! A tentative decision to quit the fur trade, is reversed!

The Committee invites Selkirk to submit a plan for a Settlement "that will satisfy his aims while safeguarding theirs". In February, 1811, Selkirk submits his plan. Nor'Westers, led by Sir Alexander MacKenzie, buy shares in the Hudson's Bay Company; and fight Selkirk's plan by every means, fair and otherwise. The most furious meeting in the Honorable Company's long career approves Selkirk's proposal. On 12 June, 1811 (while the Nor'West brigades and local population are jollifying at "the Forks") the documents are signed and sealed which deliver Assiniboia to Selkirk; and appoint Miles Macdonnell its first Governor.

The written history of Assiniboia begins!

For a grant of land 5 times bigger than Scotland, a rough diamond of 74 million acres: 480 miles, north to south; and 560 west to east, Lord Selkirk pays $2.50 cash; and undertakes to provide the Company 200 servants yearly, while developing a farm Colony. Colonists must not trade in fur. Land will be available to retiring Company servants. All "subject to the rights of the Indians". Selkirk sees Assiniboia as the promise of a new life for myriads of outcast Highlanders and Irish.

The Nor'Westers see the Colony as a device of the old Company to destroy them! They fight savagely, cunningly, for their economic lives. Selkirk's recruiting agents — Colin Robertson in the Hebrides, Roderick McDonald in Glasgow, Miles Macdonnell in Ireland — make promises that stir the hopes of starving families. Then, hopes are dashed by tales of danger and death broadcast by the Nor'Westers. Nevertheless, on 26 July, 1811 — just 44 days after Selkirk gets his grant — some 125 Irish, Orkneymen and Scots rendezvous.

Port officials, relatives of Nor'Westers, encourage 20 men to desert. Miles Macdonnell orders the ship to sail, leaving behind supplies to be sorely missed at "the Forks". The 105 men packed aboard a rickety old ship, the "Edward and Ann," are all enlisted as Hudson's Bay Company servants. Some will be selected, later, to work for Lord Selkirk, in Assiniboia. The remainder, under Hillier, will go to "Company" fur posts. Miles Macdonnell has his appointment as Hudson's Bay Company Governor and Chief Magistrate of Assiniboia. He is, also, Selkirk's hired man in charge of the Colony. It is obvious to the Nor'Westers that all these people — Colonists and indentured servants, alike — are part of the Hudson's Bay Company army, aimed at their annihilation!

Miles Macdonnell, like a good commander, uses the weeks at sea to help the men train themselves to use firearms, for hunting and defence. They are raw and awkward. Hudson's Bay men and sailors treat them with contempt. On 24 September, 1811, after 61 days at sea, the emigrants land at York Factory.

The fur-men give the farm settlers a cold welcome. Fur-men are obsessed with the fallacy that farm settlement must hurt the fur trade. Hudson's Bay officials shut the gates of York Factory against the newcomers; and Miles Macdonnell must lead his bewildered charges 23 miles up the Nelson River. Under a high, wooded ridge, all hands work, however clumsily, to build huts for themselves, before winter grips the Northland.

Seven hundred miles southward, at "the Forks", the inhabitants who know the country and its climate, likewise, prepare for the winter.

Hunters return from the fall buffalo hunt, their creaking carts loaded with meat and robes. They trade some to the fur-men. The remainder will provide plenty for their families, all winter. Some of the Indian hunters set up their teepees near the Fort; others go to Netley Creek, to harvest their bits of corn. The hybrid families re-occupy the cabins they left in June. The free-men take their families back to their log-homes, scattered along the Assiniboine and the Red; and harvest whatever potatoes and grain are in their little fields.

The fur-men at Fort Gibraltar pile up cordwood, buy provisions and mocassins; and wait for winter. At many forts there are crops to harvest; and grain to thresh. Fur-men hate, despise and fear farming; but, at fur forts from Assiniboia to Edmonton and Athabasca, fields are tilled.

"At every fur trading post where livestock is kept and ground cultivated", writes Cowie, "A sturdy, reliable man gardens and farms in summer; and feeds cattle and hauls firewood with them during the winter". "These first Western farmers, at Nor'Wester forts, are old Canadian voyageurs. Around Hudson's Bay forts, retired Orkneymen till the fields. They are not rich in glamor — like hunters and voyageurs; not fat with profits — like the traders. But, by working sweat and stubborn shrewdness into expanding fields, they set the foundations of our Canadian West; and build substance and permanence into our history. They prove the fertility of our Western lands; and lead Selkirk to attempt his Settlement. They supply the Assiniboia settlers with seed grain and livestock, from fields along the Winnipeg and Assiniboine Rivers. The number of these pioneer farmers increases, as ageing hunters and voyageurs lay aside gun and paddle; and settle down to farm, with axe and hoe".

With crops in store; meat, pemmican and furs abundant; cabins repaired, windows covered with untanned skins scraped thin; and with fuel piled handy, fur-men, free-men and hybrids in Assiniboia look forward to a period of festivity and leisure. After New Year, they will be out on their trap lines, again. Now is the time for jollity and enjoyment.

On the Nelson River, the shivering new-comers exist on supplies from York Factory — grudgingly issued; and charged, plus profiteering mark-up, to Lord Selkirk's account. The winter is one endless quarrel — between Irish and Orkneymen. Insurrection splits the camp, until the mutineers are starved out. The breach between camp and Factory widens daily. The appointment of Macdonnell as Governor has side-tracked Auld, who bitterly criticizes both the Colony and its Governor. Reluctantly following orders to help the settlers, Company officers promote discontent and sabotage. Nevertheless, the settlers survive. They shoot game to add to their oatmeal rations; and so avoid scurvy.

By spring, they master axe and gun; and are eager for the next step in their great adventure.

In the Old Land, by mid-June, Selkirk's agents begin to assemble more recruits; some from the Highlands, others from Sligo. Selkirk appoints Owen Keveny to lead this second party to Assiniboia. Some settlers get special concessions. His Lordship grants Alexander MacLean 10,000 acres in Assiniboia; a dozen Merino sheep; and one year's subsistence for his family and servants.

Peter Fidler, Hudson's Bay Company factor, visiting in Ireland, tells Lord Selkirk how the Nor'Westers starve 15 of his men; and drive him from the Athabasca country. Angrily, Selkirk orders Hillier, who is to lead a strong Hudson's Bay party up the Churchill River: "Give them (the Nor'Westers) warning that the land belongs to the Hudson's Bay Company; and that they must remove from it . . . They must not cut any timber, either for building or for fuel. What they have cut should be openly and forcibly seized; and their buildings destroyed. They should be warned that they are not to fish in our waters; and if they put down nets, seize them as you would in England those of a poacher!" This is "strong medicine"! It is a startling assertion of absolute ownership of the lands and waters of the great Nor'West, by a few people in a foreign land 4,000 miles away.

Four thousand miles from Assiniboia, on 24 June, 1812, the good ship "Robert Taylor" sails from Sligo Bay — in company with two Hudson's Bay Company ships — carrying 120 settlers and "Company" servants under Owen Keveny and Dr. Thomas McKeevor. On 6 July, 1812, at York Factory, 700 miles from "the Forks", Governor Macdonnell, Dr. Abel Edwards, 6 Scots, 4 Orkneymen and 8 Irish embark in 4 flatboats on the Hayes River, for Assiniboia. Against the flooding current — along mud-banks and rocky cliffs, the settlers "track" their heavy-laden boats. Portaging around rapids, "sometimes a back-breaking day wins only a few hundred yards!" At Oxford House, Macdonnell recruits 4 more men, including an Indian guide, bringing his party to 23. Here, also, he buys — and takes aboard — a bull and a cow.

"August is laughing across the sky" when this vanguard of Selkirk's Settlers reaches "the Forks". The smiling wealth of trees, grass and flowers seems, indeed, the promised land. The party has travelled 728 wilderness miles in 55 days. One of them is Magnus Isbister, father-to-be of that famous son, A. K. Isbister. The new-comers camp with Hudson's Bay men, across the Red River from Fort Gibraltar. One record tells us there is no sign of hostility; another, that armed men, dressed in savage costumes, warn them they are not welcome!

Governor Macdonnell's journal records: "23 August, 1812, at Fort

Alexander, south side of Winipic River . . . Nor'West Company gentlemen put potatoes and vegetables into canoes". Big buildings and fields of wheat, oats and barley surround this post. Later, the Governor thanks the Nor'Westers for selling the Settlers potatoes, grain, cattle, pigs and poultry.

With a fine sense of the human tendency to honor dramatic ritual as the raiment of legality, Miles Macdonnell carefully plans and records a formal ceremony to register Lord Selkirk's title to Assiniboia. On Friday, 4 September, 1812, — with his officers under arms, a 2-gun salute and a flag-raising at exactly noon — he "takes seizin" from Hillier of the Hudson's Bay Company. John Wills, commander of Fort Gibraltar, and Alexander Macdonnell (cousin of Miles, the Governor) attend for the Nor'West Company. With due solemnity, "the conveyances are read, both in English and French . . . in the presence of all our people and several Canadians and Indians. The gentlemen drink toasts. The head is driven in a keg of rum for the populace".

Thus, 2 or 3 dozen fur-men and settlers announce (to themselves) that Assiniboia has new owners. Few of the Canadian free-men, Saulteaux, Cree, Assiniboine or those of mixed parentage among the "populace" who drink the keg of rum, know or care about the proceedings. No one tells them that this, their homeland, is being handed over, by a few recent invaders, to owners who have arrived even more recently. "The populace" whose lives centre at "the Forks" number, perhaps, 2,000 souls. They are multi-lingual. Only a minor fraction of them speak English or French; still fewer understand the legal verbiage. In fact, only "several Canadians and Indians" witness Macdonnell's assertion of title. Most of "the populace" are a month away on the plains, exercising real ownership of the land by harvesting its wealth in the fall buffalo Hunt.

Governor Macdonnell plants Selkirk's Colony in a loop of the Red River, 2 miles north of Fort Gibraltar, which he names "Point Douglas". The Governor wants grain planted this fall. Some settlers set to work clearing land; others dig the potatoes planted last spring by "Company" men. Fish and game promise abundant provisions. John Macdonnell writes: "Buffalo come to the fords of the Assiniboine. Plenty of sturgeon, goldeye, pike and whitefish. Catch forty while smoking pipe." These were "the staff of life" for countless former generations. If "settlers" are people who "become established in more or less permanent abode or way of life . . . Stay for some time . . . Cease from wandering" — this was home to a long succession of "settlers" — who knew the country and lived on its resources, for ages before Europeans ever saw Assiniboia.

Governor Macdonnell knows that fields around the fur forts grow crops of vegetables, grain and livestock; and that the Indians at Netley Creek have grown corn for years. He must find out how they do it. So, on October 4, he sows the Colony's first grain crop: 11 gallons of wheat, with a hoe! As he hacks the tough sod, he doubts the grain will grow. But he has to find out! (That crop fails. In the hard years that follow, the settlers try again — and again!)

Meantime, the "Robert Taylor" with the Settlers aboard, navigates a troubled course across the Atlantic. Mutineers plot to take the ship; sail her into a foreign port; sell the cargo; and divide the plunder. Fights erupt between the Irish and the Scots. Keveny enforces an iron discipline that raises howls about "brutality". Despite all, they arrive at "the Forks" on 22 October. Finding that the first party has gone to Pembina for the winter, they follow; and, 5 days later, "round a last bend in the River with flags flying, and a piper playing in the leading boat".

This party of 120 men (plus women and children) led by Owen Keveny, are genuine Settlers. From Ireland and the Hebrides they come, to make new homes in Assiniboia. In 4 months they travel 4,000 miles, to this new homeland. Their number includes pioneers like Andrew McDermot, John Bourke, John Cunningham, Francis Heron, Dr. Thomas McKeevor.

Far behind these Assiniboia scenes, Selkirk energetically pushes his plans. Colin Robertson, in Montreal, recruits Canadian voyageurs to fight the Nor'Westers in Athabasca. His Lordship urges improving the waterway; and building a highway, from York Factory to "the Forks". He offers to trade part of Assiniboia for land along such a road.

Through the winter of 1812-13, the first Selkirk Settlers share the rough, tough life of the natives. Discontent and self-pity lead 70% of the colonists to desert, eventually! During the winter, Settlers (or, more likely, "Company" servants) build a 35-foot schooner, the "Cuchillon"; and, in the spring, sail her down to "the Forks". Even this first winter, a school is opened in Pembina; Hugh Swords, a Hudson's Bay servant, teaches. In March, he "returns himself to labor".

The "Settlers" return to "the Forks" in mid-May. They sow grain on the little fields prepared the previous fall. Some seed has been brought from the British Isles; more is freighted from Fort Alexander, on the Winnipeg River.

Myriads of blackbirds and pigeons migrate northward, this spring, as usual. Each fall, their numbers fill the sky on their southward trek. Their passage threatens the crops. Farm families defend their fields with nets, guns and scarecrows. Men, women and children are on guard, in relays, night and day. The little fields must be fenced also, against invading wild animals.

Miles Macdonnell knows that livestock is vital on the embryo farms.

Four cows and a bull are bought from the Nor'Westers. Buffalo calves are tamed; and raised on cow's milk; but cross-breeding proves unsuccessful and is abandoned. During May, Peter Fidler surveys the first farms; 7 small lots at Point Douglas; and 100-acre lots with 10-chain frontage, northward along the west bank of the Red River.

On 28 June, 1813, Lord Selkirk sees sail from Stromness, some 90 carefully selected Settlers. Dr. Laserre is in charge, with young Archibald McDonald, second-in-command. This fine group proves a vital reinforcement to the farm families in Assiniboia. On the long voyage, however, fever takes Dr. Laserre, 5 Settlers and several sailors. The ship's master lands the Settlers, hurriedly, at Churchill, while Governor Macdonnell and Auld wait, with supplies, at York Factory. Auld sails to Churchill. On his orders, the Settlers re-embark. The ship runs aground. Again, the Settlers land. Carrying their sick 15 miles upstream, they build cabins in the woods; and prepare for winter.

These emigrants are strong and willing, but ill-prepared for Canada's winter. They cannot know until they experience the endless cold, what is needed in food, clothing and shelter. Scantily clothed and under-fed, they survive on oatmeal, ptarmigan and "guts!"

At the Settlement, Dr. Edwards accuses Governor Macdonnell of mismanagement, dictatorship and "fraternizing with the enemy" — the Nor'Westers. Auld and other "Company" officers criticize, ridicule; and erode the Governor's authority. On June 12, 1813, the Council of Assiniboia assembles for its first meeting.

Drought withers the crops. Grubs complete the ruin. Nevertheless, some of the seed wheat from Fort Alexander turns out well. One farmer, from 1 gallon sown, reaps 12½ bushels. Fish adds to the food supply. Buffalo hunting is the major occupation of Indians, free-men, hybrids and many farm Settlers. Pemmican is the first saleable return from the plains; the basis of the fur trade and Settlement; and the beginning of commerce in Assiniboia. In 1813, no new Selkirk Settlers come to "the Forks"; but there is a persistent drift of men from the St. Lawrence Valley, through the war zone, to the free Nor'West. Assiniboia changes substantially during 1813. Selkirk's Colony begins to look like a village. The weather is fine, week after week. The Settlers are mastering this new life. Working together building, farming and hunting, generates camaraderie. Settlers who winter at Fort Daer vie with free-men and hybrids, in hunting buffalo; and bring home meat and hides, in plenty. Neither of the two warring fur Companies has traders at Pembina, this winter. Dr. Edwards is at Churchill. Without the needling of conniving trouble-makers, quarrels are submerged in contentment. The Settlers conclude a good year, with a New Year's Eve party!

War between Nor'West and Hudson's Bay men — the inevitable outcome of unlimited competition for fur profits — engulfs the entire Nor'West. It centres on Assiniboia, the vital hub of pemmican supply and transport. Both Companies enlist more and more men — to fight each other. Every new recruit increases the demand for pemmican. This benefits the hunters located along the Assiniboine River and the Red, who live by killing buffalo and selling pemmican to both the warring Companies. Selkirk's Colony is ground like mincemeat between the two battling principals. Fur-men hate settlement! They believe (mistakenly) that farming must hurt their profits. Settlers, as people, do not enrage the fur-men; but, as farmers, they are to be eliminated! Further, to the Nor'Westers, the Selkirk Colonists are part of the Hudson's Bay Company; and a target for destruction!

All this explodes, when on 8 January, 1814, Governor Macdonnell proclaims that no person shall take provisions out of Assiniboia, for 1 year!

Miles Macdonnell may be driven to this drastic decision by humanitarian concern for the people in his charge, rather than by any prospect of profits for his employers, the Hudson's Bay Company. Starvation stalks his Settlers; and next summer will bring more new-comers to be fed. But this startling, stark and naive arrogation of absolute and total ownership is challenged! The Nor'Westers are stunned — incredulous — furious! For years they have taken pemmican from Assiniboia, to provision their canoe brigades which serve the entire Nor'West. Without this pemmican, their trade cannot live!

In Council, at Qu'Appelle, the people of mixed parentage declare that they share with the Indians the ownership of this great land, which the tribes have occupied since time unknown. They have mastered this country. It is theirs! Who is this later-comer, to deny their birthright? Assiniboia is the home of their buffalo Hunt, by which they supply pemmican to feed both Companies and the entire fur trade. The Settlers are free to take all they need. They claim the same right! Macdonnell's proclamation means, (to hunters and traders alike) that the Hudson's Bay men are to be fed; the Nor'Westers starved!

Reverence for legalized titles is strong. Auld tells Macdonnell that, among the Nor'Westers, Pritchard and Wills commanding Fort la Souris and Gibraltar, believe the Governor is right, but will not say so; others will fight! In a show-down, Auld reports, Selkirk's Settlers will desert Macdonnell! The Nor'Westers have similar information — via that Alexander Mclean on whom Selkirk showers such generous concessions.

This is the situation in late April. Shortly, Nor'Wester brigades from the Swan, Turtle, Souris and Qu'Appelle Rivers are due, bringing pem-

mican down the Assiniboine. The logistics of the fur trade require that
they deliver pemmican to the northern brigades at Fort Alexander, on
the Winnipeg River. To get there, they must go down the Red, under the
guns of Fort Douglas. The Governor's proclamation puts the people of
mixed parentage solidly against him and the Hudson's Bay Company —
and, hence, behind the Nor'West Company. These sons of voyageurs,
traders and free-men, by Indian mothers, cannot believe that men 4,000
miles away, who have never seen the country, can claim their native
land.

Hudson's Bay men, reluctantly, follow the new regulations, and
deposit their surplus pemmican at Fort Douglas. The Nor'Westers send
in no pemmican; they have no surplus. Sheriff Spencer leads a strong
party to Fort la Souris to commandeer pemmican collected there. John
Pritchard, post commander, refuses the Sheriff entry. Spencer's men cut
through the palisades; and carry off 400 bags of pemmican to the
Hudson's Bay fort at Brandon House. Spencer, then, seizes a Nor'West
pemmican brigade descending the Assiniboine. This is war!

Nevertheless, when the Nor'West brigades come down the Assiniboine
in June, the wintering partners parley with Macdonnell. Macdonnell's
concern for the Settlers is understood by men who know starvation.
Likewise, the needs of the brigades are recognized. Parley leads to
agreement. The Governor releases most of the Nor'West pemmican. The
Nor'Westers, next autumn, will provide 172 bags of pemmican for the
Settlers; and will send brigades to York Factory to get oatmeal for them.
The furs they carry to the Bay, will be taken to England on Hudson's
Bay Company ships — thus avoiding the war-torn Great Lakes. Loaded
with pemmican, the brigades sweep down the Red River — singing. It is
a good deal for all hands; but furiously repudiated by the Nor'West
partners from Montreal!

Meantime, successive parties of Selkirk's Settlers arrive at "the
Forks". They have wintered near Churchill. Company officials confiscate their gun-locks, so they cannot shoot "the Company partridge!" In
April, their gun-locks are restored. Those who survive the fever are on
their feet, again. On 6 April, 21 men and 20 women follow young
Archie McDonald over the frozen terrain, on the 180-mile trek to York
Factory, en route to Assiniboia. The men take turns breaking trail. The
women follow. A piper marches in the centre of the line. All pull toboggans, loaded with their possessions. Their guides and hunters take
"innumerable game" as they go. Hunters meet them with 200 partridges.
These folks from Kildonan, in Scotland, reach "the Forks" on 21 June.
The men are assembled; regaled with a ration of spirits; and issued
muskets, bayonets and ammunition. Their freight includes some brass

cannon, but no farm tools. Nevertheless, the new-comers set to work, and, with hoes and shovels, plant 300 kegs of potatoes and some grain.

In July, the Council of Assiniboia rules that hunters must not "run" buffalo; and thus, drive the herds away. This attempt to regulate the Hunt — to benefit both settlers and hunters — is defied by the hunters. The Indians have run buffalo for generations. The free-men and hybrid hunters have made pemmican their own little monopoly. They want to keep it!

On 2 September, the Governor brings 15 new settlers up from York Factory. Three houses, stabling for cows, sheep and hogs have been built — all enclosed within a strong stockade of oak logs, 232 feet square. The walls and roof of a two-storey "Government House", 64 feet by 22 feet, has been raised; two kilns of charcoal burned; 2½ acres of new land broken; and all the crops secured. A good season's work! Seeing the work of their hands, most Settlers are content.

Beyond the Settler's ken, however, fate works against the Colony. At sea, contrary winds and ship fever cause delay and death. Crops planted in the burnt-over soil, fail — all but the potatoes and turnips. Auld, Hudson's Bay officer, persistently blocks and undermines Governor Macdonnell.

Nor'Westers (and Hudson's Bay men, like Auld) work ceaselessly to drive Settlers out of Assiniboia. They tell terrible tales of Indian atrocities (though Assiniboia's Indians are never hostile); and make alluring promises of better lands and easier living in Canada.

Duncan Cameron, Nor'West commander at Fort Gibraltar, parades a parental concern for the Settlers. The upper echlons of Nor'Westers talk "annihilation!" Some Settlers begin to feel "at home" on their Assiniboia farms. But many give up hope. The land is too hard, the climate too harsh for them to bear! And there is the insistent, insidious line: move to Upper Canada, where land is free and life is easier. Captain Cameron will get us there. He is free with food, drink and sympathy. More and more Settlers visit him at Fort Gibraltar; nibble his bait; and swallow his propaganda! By September, Governor Macdonnell returns from "the Bay". The Settlers greet him with distrust, suspicion and fear; and the people of mixed parentage defiantly oppose him. In October, notices are nailed to the gateways of Nor'West forts, ordering the occupants out of Assiniboia! The enraged Nor'Westers decide that this Hudson's Bay Colony threatens their existence; and must be destroyed!

Selkirk's Settlers, for the first time, winter at "the Forks". Hunters go to Pembina; and bring home meat, in plenty. All are well-fed, safe and comfortable; but poisoned by Nor'Wester's propaganda! Miles Macdonnell, as Hudson's Bay Company Governor of Assiniboia and Lord

Selkirk's superintendent of the Colony, labors prodigiously in dual, interwoven, vaguely defined (and, perhaps, impossible) positions. He is down at York Factory, Company headquarters; and no sooner returns to "the Forks" than rumors of Sioux invasion call him to Pembina. In the Governor's absence, Cameron enlarges his fishing waters. With more and more Settlers in his creel, he plays his line before Hudson's Bay Company servants. Those nearing the end of their indenture, with money owing them, he promises: "get whatever you can out of their store. . . I will take any article . . . and pay you in Canada". He promises to buy the implements of Settlers who move to Canada; and give them free land. He has George Campbell, a Kildonan man, spread the rumor, house to house, that the cannon in Fort Douglas will be used to keep them all in the Settlement. They must get those guns to Cameron for "safe-keeping". Incredibly, an armed party enters Fort Douglas, on April 3; loads the guns onto a horse-drawn sledge; and delivers them to Cameron. He promptly trains the guns on the Colony! This affair, reeking of unbelievable connivance, indicates abject surrender to Cameron's propaganda. He increases the pressure, exploiting failure to provide a Presbyterian mininster. Hybrid hunters camp at Frog Plain. Galloping horsemen make nights hideous with Indian war songs and wild shooting. Raiders take isolated Settlers prisoner. Cameron spreads rumors of Indian massacre; and, at the same time, demands that Settlers surrender their muskets to him "in the King's name!"

Reports of these tragic days are fragmentary, biased and conflicting. It appears certain, however, that the lying propaganda, the stealing of horses, the smashing of farm tools and the everlasting harassment, lead to a "shooting war". Fort Douglas sentries on 8 May fire on a party, presumably Nor'Westers. On 10 June, there is an exchange of fire. Next day, again, Fort Douglas is under fire. A bullet whizzes by Dr. White, in the Governor's house. The garrison replies "with musketry and artillery". Three defenders are wounded. John Nolin dies when a swivel-gun explodes. Two officers are wounded. By 16 June, only 16 Settlers and 18 Hudson's Bay men are in Fort Douglas.

Miles Macdonnell, symbol of Hudson's Bay Company authority and the Colony's existence, to prevent further killings, surrenders himself to the Nor'Westers. From Fort Gibraltar they take him, prisoner, to Montreal — for trial! In the same brigade go 140 Settlers who desert him.

Of all Selkirk's Settlers, only 13 families "stand fast". Cameron, who has "bribed" and "bullied" 70% of the Settlers out of Assiniboia, now orders the 60 people remaining in the Colony — to leave forever! Dr. White becomes leader; and, with Peter Fidler, signs a "treaty" whereby all Selkirk's people abandon Assiniboia. Horsemen gallop through the fields; and fire the farmsteads. Those Settlers who determine to "stand fast", with Hudson's Bay servants, load what they can save into boats; and head down the Red River for Lake Winnipeg. They look back at their farmsteads, mill, fort, Governor's house, school — all raised by their hands — rolling away in smoke! Four Hudson's Bay servants remain, in the smithy, across the River. The fleeing flotilla (Settlers in boats; Hudson's Bay men in the "Cuchillon" schooner) makes its mournful way down Lake Winnipeg, to Norway House.

To the Selkirk Settlers, the destruction of their Colony on Red River, is overwhelming disaster. Historically speaking, however, this tragedy does not loom so large in the sweep of Assiniboia's development. If, as is suggested, more than 2,000 humans are "more or less permanently" settled around "the Forks" of Assiniboine and Red, and along the wooded banks of these Rivers and their tributaries, it is highly probable that many of Assiniboia's people are not even aware that one of the communities in the area has been cruelly obliterated. Certainly, among the Indians who gravitate to "the Forks", many old people have seen far greater numbers of people driven from their homes; robbed of all they possessed; and slaughtered, man, woman and child! To the hybrid people, some of whom participate as hired hands of one or other of the fur Companies, it may be a topic of gossip in the interlude between spring and fall buffalo Hunts.

Apparently, none of the "hundreds of free Canadians . . . with families by Indian wives" who (as Governor Macdonnell reports) live around "the Forks" and along the Assiniboine River, go with the deserting Selkirk Colonists to Canada; or with those who retreat to Norway House. Some of them may be hired by the battling fur companies; most of them, probably, remain "free men"; and pursue "the even tenor" of their lives: hunting, fishing, wandering in summer, back to their homes in winter. They love this land. They are settled here — permanently.

The deserters soon realize that they have been duped. George Campbell gets $500 cash and a free ride, for helping to destroy the Colony. The others are forced to paddle their own canoes to Upper Canada. They are "mad with rage". In 82 terrible days they reach their destination, 40 miles north of York (later, Toronto). Here, the Nor'-westers blandly disown them. In London, Lord Selkirk plans for more Settlers and a new Governor for his Colony. In June, 1815 — even as the deserters paddle eastward — new Settlers leave Scotland to replace them.

On 14 July, Colin Robertson, en route from Montreal to Athabasca, arrives at "the Forks". His journal records: "Ashore at Frog Plain. Walk to the Forks over the ruins of houses burned. A blacksmith shop all that remains of the Colony. Find 7 bags of pemmican, which I sent to the bottom of the river under Lagominieer". Robertson has no interest in the communities along the Red; and westward, along the Assiniboine — where live Lagimondiere and other free-men and people of mixed parentage. Ordered by Governor Thomas of the Hudson's Bay Company, he leads the Settlers from Norway House back to the Colony. His journal records: "The only families that accompany me back to the Settlement, (Mr. and Mrs. McLean and four children; Mr. and Mrs. Pritchard and one child; Pat McNulty and his wife and 2 children; widow McLean; Mrs. Gergman; Mrs. Kennedy". (A total of 16) "The servants that go with me to Red River are: A. McLean, Duncan McNaughton, Samuel Lamont, Michael Kilbride, Pat Clavey, Pat Corrigan, John Fowler, Norwegians Nels Mueller, Peter Ehat, Peter Isaakson and 12 Canadians. My officers are: Messrs. St. Germain, Pambrun and Holt with 2 Indian interpreters. With this corps I take my departure with the hope of re-establishing the Colony at Red River." On 8 August: "Leave Winnipeg House with 3 boats and 35 men, women and children.

On 19 August, Robertson and the returning settlers and Company servants, arrive at Frog Plain. Within a week, the farm families are harvesting the crops which, despite everything, yield 1,100 bushels of grain. These precious bushels are safely stored; and, under Robertson's energetic leadership, reserve provisions are accumulated. Six men go to Fort Daer, to get food, with 2 work horses. Robertson hires Lagimondiere, "with his excellent horses", to cart home the hay and the grain. Patrick Quinn is sent with carts "for wildfowl which Baptiste, our hunter, killed". Fort Douglas is re-built — to assure security, as well as abundance. On 13 October, Robertson leads a party of bold spirits, takes Fort Gibraltar; and recovers 2 field-pieces and 30 muskets. Satisfied, Robertson blandly restores the Fort to the chastened Nor'West Commander, Cameron.

News comes, with many new Settlers, on 17 October, that a new Governor, Robert Semple, is sailing up Lake Winnipeg. On this day, Robertson despatches Lagimondiere on a 3,000 mile footrace with messages to Selkirk in Montreal. Madame Marie Lagimondiere "leaves their snug cabin on the banks of the Assiniboine for Fort Douglas". On 3 November, Governor Semple and his advance party, reach Fort Douglas. Next day, 120 colonists and Company servants arrive.

Robert Semple is appointed Governor-in-Chief of Rupertsland for the Hudson's Bay Company, in May, 1815. Lord Selkirk makes him, also,

Governor of Assiniboia. His powers are clearly defined; and far exceed those of his predecessor. His staff includes Alexander Macdonnell, second Sheriff of Assiniboia; and two professional fighting men: Lieutenant Holt, late of the Swedish Navy; and Captain Rogers, ex-Royal Engineers.

Any truly balanced history of Assiniboia will make it clear that, when Robertson writes "a blacksmith shop is all that remains", he refers to Selkirk's Colony; that the Colony is one of a variety of communities in Assiniboia; and that its Settlers and Company servants are a fraction of the total population. That other settlers live along the Assiniboine River and the Red, Robertson notes only incidentally — as, on 4 September, he hires Lagimondiere and his horses; and, on 17 October, "Madame Lagimondiere moves her family from their cabin on the Assiniboine" to Fort Douglas. The record that the Lagimondiere family lives in that beautiful loop of the Assiniboine occupied by the St. Charles Country Club, in after years, is entirely probable. Certainly, if 2,000 humans live around "the Forks" in 1811, the number is above that total in 1815.

Lord Selkirk, in Montreal, writes to Colin Robertson: "The Nor'West Company must be compelled to quit all their intrusive possessions upon my land; and particularily their post at "the Forks". Nor'Westers get this letter when they capture Lagimondiere, as he races back to Assiniboia. At "the Forks", Colin Robertson, on 14 March, seizes the Nor'West Company packet, en route to Fort William; and, on 17 March, "with 11 volunteers" takes Fort Gibraltar, again! The captured Nor'West mail breathes fire and fight!

Holt and Rogers, Semple's mercenaries, are conspicuously contemptuous of natives; and eager to show them professional fighting. The schooner "Cuchillon", Lieutenant Holt reports, is fitted out as a "man-of-war"; and moored at the mouth of the Red, to intercept the Nor'West canoe brigades; and "give the scoundrels a drubbing." Such warlike preparations shatter any pretense that the Colony is an entity, separate from the Hudson's Bay Company; and convince Nor'Westers (and most of Assiniboia's people) that Colony and Company are a double-barrelled piece — loaded, primed and aimed at monopolizing the fur trade!

The Nor'west partners are divided. Few of the traders in the field are devoted to their Montreal agents, who "live high" on the hardships of the wintering partners. All are ready to fight against the Hudson's Bay Company; but war on Settlers, their own countrymen, is another thing. John MacDonald le Borgne writes: "Retribution is drawing nigh. We lost our friends by our selfishness." Robertson urges that Fort Gibraltar be dismantled to strengthen Fort Douglas. Semple vetoes such lawlessness. Nevertheless, a party from Fort Daer seizes the Nor'West post at

Pembina. This labels the Colonists aggressors, equally with the warring fur-men. The hybrid people swing to the Nor'West Company.

In May, rumor is rampant in Assiniboia that the annual Nor'West brigade is approaching from Qu'Appelle — "more like a war party than a fur brigade". On 8 May, these Nor'Westers capture the Hudson's Bay Qu'Appelle brigade — with furs and pemmican. Next, Fort la Souris is taken. On 31 May, Brandon House, on the Assiniboine, (Peter Fidler master) falls to 48 Canadians, hybrids and Indians in a well-executed cavalry manoeuvre. The leader of the victorious Nor'Westers is a young Scot-Indian, Cuthbert Grant. Assiniboia is a Battlefield for Fur!

As the May sunshine dries their fields, the farmers of the Colony — with locally-made plows and wooden harrows; drawn by lazy Indian ponies or ponderous oxen — sow their seed grain. They are more resolute than ever. No one, ever again, will talk them out of their land! Governor-in-Chief Semple is all energy and bubbly optimism, which advertise his uncertainty. He fails to understand how much of the Settlement's recovery is due to Robertson's shrewd knowledge of fur-men, free-men and hybrids. The Governor, Holt and Rogers call Robertson "Mr. Lofty". Rogers challenges him to a duel. John Bourke, "Company" store clerk, threatens him with a pistol. The breach widens daily, when the only hope is in unity. In summary, as W. L. Morton writes: "The definite policy and strong line of Robertson is giving way to impulse and vacillation on the part of Semple and his hard-drinking aides".

Robertson, prevented from saving the Colony, sails for York Factory, flying a pemmican sack at his masthead; and taking Duncan Cameron for trial in England. His journal records: "He (Semple) appears full of confidence — rather too much so. . . guided by the opinion of others".

By 10 June, Governor Semple decides to follow Robertson's earlier advice to dismantle Fort Gibraltar. The great logs are hand-spiked down; the best are rafted down the Red; and re-built into a strengthened Fort Douglas. All else is burned. Within 4 days, The Hudson's Bay Company and Selkirk's Colony have a re-inforced stronghold — the Nor'West Company, nothing!

Semple may not be, altogether, the "pompous ass" one historian describes him. He does ascribe extraordinary powers to his person and position. His arrogant, official superiority bars any understanding with such "lower orders" as Canadian free-men, Indians and people of mixed parentage who are the vast majority of Assiniboia's population.

The June days pass. The Nor'Westers from Qu'Appelle ride closer. Robertson had urged that, this year, the Settlers crop fields close around the Fort. Semple orders otherwise. Now, Settlers' families sleep inside the Fort, each night; and, each morning, the men go, warily, to work in their distant fields. Most of the free-men and hybrid families of Assiniboia are away on the spring buffalo Hunt. They will be coming home, soon, to sell pemmican and fresh meat to the brigades passing "the Forks".

On 17 June, 2 Saulteaux from the west advise Governor Semple that the Colony will be attacked! Chief Peguis offers the help of his 70 warriors. Semple haughtily declines. On 18 June, Cuthbert Grant leads 4 Indians, 6 Canadians, and 52 hybrids from Portage la Prairie. Is their purpose (as they say) to meet and supply the Nor'West brigade from Montreal, at Frog Plain? Or (as Hudson's Bay people say) to destroy the Colony? At Fort Douglas, there is tension, fear — and no plan for defence. On the afternoon of 19 June, the Governor rides through the Colony. A free-man (Bellegrade) asks him "Are you not afraid?" "No, I am not afraid", Robert Semple replies, "I have a paper I will read to them."

Cool shadows slant across the hot afternoon hush, when a shout from the Fort Douglas watch-tower brings the Governor, scurrying up. His spyglass shows some 35 horsemen, 2 miles off, riding northeastward toward Frog Plain. Tension explodes into panic! The Governor calls for volunteers, to go with him, "to see what these fellows want". Some 26 are issued muskets and ammunition — and no clear instructions. Sheriff Macdonnell is left in command of the Fort. Someone suggests taking a cannon. Semple says, "No". Marching northward, the party meets Settlers "running in panic". All the fur-men's lies about Indian atrocities, focus in this dread hour — to shatter morale! Among the nervous, jostling men, a musket fires! These "Company" hired men are untrained to arms; and, incredibly, are being led against men who live by the skilful use of their weapons!

The Hudson's Bay men meet a line of horsemen; and halt. The Governor orders Bourke to hurry back to the Fort for a cannon and more men. The Hudson's Bay men, on foot, retire slowly, toward the River. The Nor'West men, mounted, advance in a wide crescent. All are tense, nervous. Francois Boucher rides forward. Semple walks to meet him. Their voices rise. They shout! A shot! A volley! Another volley! The veneer of civilization dissolves in the stark primal fact of "kill or be killed". What really happens is lost, forever, in the "fog of battle". Within 15 minutes Governor Semple, 1 settler, 19 Hudson's Bay servants and 2 of the Nor'West party are dead. This is war! And "war is hell"!

Surviving Hudson's Bay men are pursued toward the Fort. Bourke, hurrying forward, fires his cannon — to cover the fugitives; then, to save the gun, gallops back. He escapes; but is wounded. For 2 days he hides; then, is taken prisoner.

John Pritchard survives — by the grace of an old friend. Late that night, Grant sends Pritchard to the Fort, to demand unconditional surrender. The people are terrified. Sheriff Macdonnell surrenders! All are held for 2 days at the Nor'West camp. Each is examined by Archibald Norman McLeod, Nor'West partner or Justice of the Peace, as suits the occasion. He sends Bourke, Pritchard, Pembrun, Corcoran, Hedon, Nolin and McPherson, as prisoners, to Fort William. Bourke is robbed; taken to Montreal; jailed, tried, liberated. He walks 22 days to reach Fort William. Again, he is arrested; taken to Canada; tried and acquitted. He gets backs to Assiniboia in 1819. The remaining Settlers and Hudson's Bay servants sail sorrowfully down Lake Winnipeg, to Norway House.

Like most such encounters, this clash between the warring fur Companies, is a tragedy of errors — including complete absence of understanding between various components of Assiniboia's population; and Semple's defiance of the tenets of leadership. Of all the tragic mistakes which culminate in Seven Oaks, perhaps the most tragic is the contempt in which the Governor and his "gentlemen" hold the free-men, Indian and hybrid peoples of Assiniboia. Europeans have found arrogance an over-powering weapon against other "lesser breeds". Against buffalo-hunters, it back-fires!

Lord Selkirk realizes that, in this war, his Colony — to live — must be able to defend itself. He enlists veterans discharged from mercenary regiments, after the War of 1812. Two days after Seven Oaks, he has hired Captains D'orsonnens and Matthy, 2 other officers and 104 other ranks of the disbanded Des Meurons and D'Wattville regiments; "with good reputation for efficiency and discipline. Men of respectable character, likely to make good Settlers" — also some Glengarry Fencibles; and 30 Iroquois canoe-men. Sir Gordon Drummond, Governor of Canada, details 7 regulars of the 37th Regiment, as Selkirk's personal bodyguard. Selkirk contracts to pay his men for the trip; and give them land in Assiniboia — or, if they prefer, free passage to Europe. Later, dour Alexander Ross declares them: "Germans, French, Italian, Swedish, etc., rough and lawless blackguards, bad farmers, quarrelsome, slothful, drunken". Through the wilderness to Assiniboia, these veterans freight 12 boat-loads of flour, pork, lard, corn, brandy and gun-powder — together with 6 cannon. On 16 August, they capture Fort William; and arrest Nor'West leaders.

William McGillivray's written account of the Seven Oaks tragedy is:

"a group of Indians and half-breeds had been peaceably passing Fort Douglas, on June 19, when Semple and his party emerged and without provocation made a wanton attack on them. . . . None of the Nor'West people had been within hundreds of miles of the clash!" Such blatant falsehood indicates the desperate competition which generates this fur-men's war. In this struggle for fur profits, there is neither honor or honesty. Human life is cheap. Owen Keveny, in late July, bringing calves from Fort Albany to "the Forks," is arrested by Archibald McLeod; released and re-arrested, again and again; and, finally, shot and stabbed to death. Lord Selkirk, repeatedly, begs both England and Canada to send troops to Assiniboia, to maintain law and order. Nothing is done. In London, the Hudson's Bay Company reigns supreme; in Montreal, the Nor'Westers.

At Norway House, the Colonists survive a hard and hungry winter. Some of them hire with the Hudson's Bay Company. Most of them determine to return to poverty, in Scotland. News that Lord Selkirk has taken Fort William re-kindles hope. Then comes news that, on 10 December, Captain Miles Macdonnell and Captain D'orsonnens, with John Tanner and 50 Des Meurons, Canadians and Indians follow the old Indian war road from the Savanne portage, Rainy Lake and the Rousseau River; and surprise and capture Fort Daer at Pembina!

1817 is a year of storms, early frosts and decisive events in the history of Assiniboia. On 10 January, in frosty moonlight, Captains Macdonnell and D'orsonnens, with 26 Des Meurons — having snowshoed through a blizzard from Pembina, behind a trail-breaking ox and cow — circle Silver Heights to Fort Douglas; scale the stockade; and capture its garrison of 16 Nor'Westers! The rising sun shows a new flag flying over the Fort. Free-men, hybrids and Indians look up, wondering.

Cuthbert Grant and 20 Metis, on 22 January, leave Qu'Appelle; and travel down the Assiniboine, to Point du Chene. They kill some Settler's cattle for provisions; sleep in the snow; and warm themselves in the houses of Canadian and hybrid friends, settled along the Assiniboine.

Grant and his men come down the Assiniboine, again, in mid-June — with provisions for the Nor'West brigades. Alexander Macdonnell, now Governor of Assiniboia, warns Grant to stay beyond the Grand Passage; and sends Laidlaw with 25 soldiers, Huester (who has deserted Grant) and Hudson's Bay man Louis Nolin, to arrest Grant. Laidlaw's party retires, judging it "impossible to attack the Metis camp, under a high bank". (Perhaps near the bridge, where later No. 1 highway crosses the Assiniboine River, west of Headingly.)

Selkirk arrives at Fort Douglas on June 21. The Fort cannon, manned by Des Meurons, thunder a salute. At last, His Lordship is actually in the Colony of his dreaming — a Savage Settlement where his Settlers build and rebuild homes that warring fur-men destroy.

In an obvious effort to lessen tension, Lord Selkirk permits the Nor'Westers to take pemmican down the Assiniboine and Red River, past Fort Douglas, on 3 July, for the Nor'West canoe brigades. Within 2 weeks, the Settlers are home from Norway House. It is so late in the season, they plant only a small acreage. The late grain is frozen; but a heavy crop of potatoes is harvested.

Lieut-Colonel Coltman and Major Fletcher, Canada's Commissioners, "to inquire into violence committed in the Indian territories" come up the Red River on 5 July, accompanied by Simon McGillivray and selected Nor'Westers. A guard of honor at Fort Douglas fires a 7-gun salute of welcome. Coltman ignores the compliment; and orders the flotilla upstream. Labouring to appear neutral, he sites his Headquarters midway between Fort Douglas and the site of old Fort Gibraltar. Then he advertises "whose side he is neutral on" by dining with the Nor'-Westers, as throughout the long trip!

Selkirk finds "Assiniboia a land of unbelievable goodness. Crops . . . in a vast circle . . . far beyond sight. . would repay fifty-fold, the hardy men who had crossed 200 miles of ice on Lake Winnipeg to plant them". All the livestock, including 60 horses, are gone. A few new horses are bought. The famous cow and ox, that broke the trail to re-capture Fort Douglas, are on a second experimental farm, laid out between Fort Douglas and "the Forks", with Laidlaw in charge.

Grant and his followers break camp at Grand Passage, up the Assiniboine, on 9 July; and head westward. Coltman overtakes the main body; and persuades them to return with him, to give depositions regarding Seven Oaks. Grant goes west. When his men of mixed parentage surrender to Coltman, his hopes for a "new nation" dissolve! (Not the first birthright traded for a mess of pottage!)

Commissioner Coltman finds it difficult to sift the mass of contradictory evidence by countless witnesses. It is said: "Coltman does not want the truth. He wants peace and quietness." Fletcher wants to play soldier, eat and drink. Both Commissioners appear antagonistic to Selkirk. Simon McGillivray, by arrogance and bullying, largely restores the dominance of the Nor'West Company in Assiniboia. Threats are broadcast that any who testify against the Nor'Westers must face their retaliation. Nor'West hired men invade the experimental farm; unyoke the Lac la Pluie cow and ox; and kill both before Laidlaw's enraged eyes. Such high-handed aggression may impress free-men, hybrids and Indians — but not the Colonists! They have learned their lesson. All know that a great battle is raging, high above their heads. Most Assiniboia Settlers — whether Selkirk Colonists, free-men or natives — want only to be left in peace to work out their own lives.

Among the varied components of Assiniboia's population, Selkirk makes an everlasting impression. His grand manner, military force, showmanship, and generous gifts hypnotize the natives. After consulting Assiniboia authorities and Coltman, Selkirk negotiates a "treaty", on 18 July, with some Indian chiefs for "title" to lands along the Assiniboine, westward beyond Portage la Prairie; and along the Red River. The Saulteaux, recent arrivals, assume full proprietorship. This antagonizes Cree and Assiniboine, occupants for generations. However greedily Selkirk's gifts are accepted by the Saulteaux, they do not "sell" these lands in the same sense that Selkirk assumes he "buys" them. Considering current antagonisms and subsequent disappointments, it may be that the place in Indian folklore which "the Silver Chief" is supposed to have achieved, is largely romancing by white men about their red brothers.

All Selkirk's Colonists are assembled, on 10 August, at Frog Plain. Here, Lord Selkirk tells them that the 24 families who lost their all in 1816, will have the only free grants to Settlers in the Colony. Lot 4 is allocated to the church; Lot 3 for a school. His Lordship orders that surveys proceed for roads, bridges and a mill. His veterans are settled across the Red from Fort Douglas. Beside them, Lagimondiere is alloted a homestead; and 10,000 acres is set aside for a Roman Catholic Mission.

By October, 1817, there are recorded in the Colony: 151 Scots, in 31 houses; 45 Des Meurons, in 31 houses; 26 Canadians, in 6 houses. A total of 222 people, in 68 houses. These may be 10% of Assiniboia's population. Strangely, no Irish are recorded — although many of the first of Selkirk's Settlers came from Ireland; and men like McDermot and Bourke, now completing their terms as Hudson's Bay servants, are leaders in the community.

The time comes for Selkirk to leave the Colony. Baggage is loaded on Red River carts — to be transferred, upon reaching the Mississippi, to river boats. His Lordship and party assemble; mount; wave; and ride westward along the north bank of the Assiniboine. At the Grand Passage, they wade the River; and turn southward for St. Paul. His Lordship is in Assiniboia 3 months, on his only visit to the Colony for which he dreamed so much; to which he gave so much; and which cost him so much — unto his very life!

In the communities scattered along the Assiniboine River and the Red, those Settlers who are going to Pembina for the winter, load their carts; and creak away. The Hunt comes home from the plains. Farm families bring in their hay; and stable their livestock. Fur-men fatten their dog-teams. Old-timers tell new-comers terrible tales of blizzards and freezing. Everyone "snugs in" for another Assiniboia winter.

Spring stirs with high hopes. Farmers get on the land early; and crop every available acre. Peter Fidler records: "this spring the cultivated fields are enlarged". Some Settlers are using plows made locally. Many still use spade, hoe and muscle to plant the seed. River fishing yields big catches. Buffalo are plentiful. The spring Hunt is highly successful. The hunters bring home perhaps 200 cart-loads of pemmican, meat and robes. All is distributed with joyous lavishness among the families of Settlers, free-men and hybrids who share in the Hunt. Farmers work over-time in their fields. Free-men sell some pemmican and robes to the traders; casually seed their patches of potatoes and grain; and take their ease. The hybrids fish — and celebrate their abundance. Traders balance their books; and order more trade goods. The Settlements buzz with "busy-ness"; and laze in well-fed indolence.

Crops come on wonderfully well. By mid-July, fields flourish with promise. Then: locusts — in clouds that strip leaf and life from every growing thing! Free-men and hybrids are already gone to the plains to hunt, trap and trade. Farm Settlers see their year's work ruined!

On 16 July, Pere Joseph Norbert Provencher and Father Dumoulin arrive at Fort Douglas, by canoe. Across the Red River from Fort Douglas they raise the first permanent Roman Catholic Mission — a log church, school and home — on the land granted by Selkirk. Mass is first celebrated on 1 November, 1818. With the priests come Canadian families from Quebec. The new-comers face a rugged life. Provencher writes: "The Colony . . . a picture of desolation. At the table of the Governor of Fort Douglas was neither bread nor vegetables. Only buffalo meat . . . and a little fish; no milk, no butter; often, neither tea nor sugar".

Settlers hired by the Selkirk estate, in September, begin ambitious buildings for another experimental farm, 4 miles west of Fort Douglas, north of the Assiniboine. Westward along this River, the cabins of squatters are multiplying. Orkney and native families are increasing the population of Orkneytown above "the Forks". The higher, drier ground; good timber; and the Grand Passage, where south and north traffic crosses the Assiniboine, beckon people westward. By October, their crops destroyed by grasshoppers, many farm families are with Indians, hybrids and free-men — hunting buffalo, westward from Pembina; and fishing on Lakes Winnipeg and Winnipegosis.

Unknown to its inhabitants, the south half of Assiniboia bought by Lord Selkirk from the Hudson's Bay Company, is taken by the United

States, on 20 October, when English and Yankee negotiators decree that, "the boundary from Lake of the Woods should follow the 49th parallel westward to the Stony Mountains". Thus, 30-odd million acres are confiscated from Lord Selkirk; the Hudson's Bay Company title is mocked; and the buffalo hunters see their traditional hunting ground taken by a foreign nation. Despite shifting political boundaries, however, Assiniboia remains the "Battleground for Fur".

Epidemics decimate Assiniboia's horse population. To get vital replacements, Archibald McDonald leads an expedition to the Missouri. He sets out, on 10 November, with 10 men, 3 horses and 2 carts loaded with trade goods. "Behind the Turtle Mountains" a blizzard buries all in snow. McDonald leaves his party, camped with the goods; and fights through the storm to Brandon House. There, he gets 5 sleds and 15 dogs. Returning to his camp, he finds his party gone; his goods carried off! He finds his property in the camp of some Saulteaux, who blandly tell him: "Your white men run when they see us in the woods. Maybe think Sioux". With his dog-teams, McDonald reaches the Mandans; trades his goods for 9 good horses and 170 beaver; and gets back to "the Forks" on New Year's Eve. The men who deserted him vow they were attacked — one says by 15; another, 50; and a third, 300 painted Sioux warriors!

As hunting (and contraband trading) prove more rewarding than farming, more Settlers join the free-men and hybrids in these "verboten" activities. Nevertheless, as winter wanes and sap wakens in the trees, the farm families prepare, once more, to cast their bread upon their fields along the Assiniboine River and the Red.

Pursuant to the report of Commissioner Coltman, the tight, pervasive Family Compact which operates Canada's government, rules that all parties to the fur war share guilt — but Lord Selkirk most of all! Symbolizing the London-based claimants to the entire Nor'West, he is hounded — to his death! For killing 22 men at one time, no one is really penalized. Naturally, "the fur trader's war flares up with all its old fierceness".

A new Governor — William Williams — takes command for the Hudson's Bay Company. He is a salty ex-Navy officer. He has a schooner built — decked, armed with light cannon; and carrying a crew, plus 20 of the soldier Settlers. Sailing merrily down Lake Winnipeg, the old soldiers welcome this change from farm work. At Grand Rapids, scene of so many such exploits, they ambush the Nor'West canoe brigades; confiscate fortunes in furs; arrest and rob the bourgeois; and send them to England for trial! In April Colin Robertson leaves Montreal with 19 Hudson's Bay Company canoes and 130 armed men — to battle for the fur riches of Athabasca!

The buffalo Hunt is Assiniboia's basic industry. The Hunt dominates the life of all the communities along the Assiniboine River and the Red. As buffalo shy away from the growing Settlements, the Hunt is organized to trail the herds, further and further southward and westward. Perhaps the free-men, hybrid and Indian hunters deliberately drive buffalo away from "the Forks" — to protect their own tidy monopoly for pemmican, tongues and robes!

Communication with the outside world is improving slowly. A letter from Lady Selkirk dated 28 April, at Montreal, is 46 days in transit, reaching Pere Provencher 13 June. Winter mail expresses, sometimes, are stopped by ice at Sault Ste. Marie; and letters sent in the spring arrive before those sent the previous fall! Postage through United States territory costs 25 cents for each sheet of paper. No envelopes, please, gentlemen!

This season, crops grow lush, heavy and green. Traders drive 52 horses from the Saskatchewan to Assiniboia. A bumper harvest is in the fields. It is never harvested! As promise verges on certainty — the fields are a-move with grasshoppers hatched from last year's larvae. They devour everything. Alive, they fill the air and smother fires; dead, their heaped up myriads stink! There is no grain to harvest; no seed for next year.

This fall, 18 new Settlers arrive from overseas. While Settlers are scattered for many miles along the Assiniboine River and the Red, the actual centre of Assiniboia is "the Forks". Scots are in St. John and Kildonan parishes. The Des Meurons veterans live beside the Seine. Canadian families gravitate to St. Norbert and St. Boniface parishes; and many are interspersed with the Orkney and hybrid families westward along the Assiniboine, to the White Horse Plain — and beyond.

Free traders are growing in numbers — and in annoyance to the big fur Companies. They operate "underground". The Companies have "spies behind every blade of grass"; and ruthlessly maintain their competitive dominance. Outstanding among the free traders is Andrew McDermot. Coming to Assiniboia, with Owen Keveny, in 1812, he completes his indentured service to the Hudson's Bay Company, this year; and, from his log cabin, launches his first merchandising venture. He buys a chest of tea; sews it inside a calfskin; and carries it, home to home, on his back. A superlative trader, he craftily eludes all Company men; and in this "Battlefield for Fur", he prospers, increasingly.

Alexander Ross

CHAPTER 4

The High and Heavy Hand 1820-1829

In the crackling frost of early January a line of men heads south from "the Forks", along the ice-bound Red. Dog-teams pull toboggans loaded with food for a long trip. These are Assiniboia farmers, on the hunt for seed wheat. They push southward — through icy sunshine and hammering blizzards. In 3 months they snowshoe 750 miles, to Prairie du Chien on the Mississippi River. Here, they buy 250 bushels of seed wheat. "As the long winter wanes, these Assiniboia farmers buy lumber; and build flat boats. When spring wakens the waters and opens the rivers, they load their 7½ tons of wheat on the boats — along with their snowshoes, toboggans and other gear — and head north. They fight their way up the ice-swollen Mississippi to Fort Snelling (where the city of St. Paul will later stand). They track upstream, against the current of the Minnesota, to Big Stone Lake. They portage their boats and cargoes to the headwaters of the Red — the River that carries them home! These pioneer farmers drive themselves over that 1,500 mile round-trip, to bring home wheat in time to seed. They get home in June. The wheat is planted. It grows and ripens. Well it might! Each bushel of that seed costs $20.00 in money — and courage and sweat beyond our ken."

Colonists are saddened, this spring, by the news that Lord Selkirk has died. Never robust, an urgent spirit drives him on — to burn out at 49! His ventures in helping the helpless, involve his estate in colossal debt. Our first Western Canadian real estate developer dies, broke! But — he wins for himself a place in our History that no other man can claim; that no controversy can undermine.

Settlements in Assiniboia begin to take shape, even before 1811. They spread from "the Forks", along both Rivers, far beyond the lots occupied by the families brought in by Lord Selkirk. With astonishly few exceptions, these communities live in harmony. This is the result, not of tight and efficient policing, but of the tolerant good sense of the people. The cruel war which twice wrecks Selkirk's Colony in Assiniboia is no game of "Settlers and Indians" — Scots against "half-breeds". It is competition run wild between two commercial outfits whose greed for profits over-runs the Settlements.

As Settlements grow, the buffalo Hunt becomes increasingly important — to all the people of Assiniboia; and, also, to the profits (and very existence) of the competing fur Companies. As the buffalo keep further away from Settlement, the Hunt increases its range and size. The spring Hunt in 1820 takes 540 carts out of Assiniboia.

Miles Macdonnell, the first Governor, shares the belief that Assiniboia includes the entire basins of the Assiniboine River and the Red, south, as well as north, of the 49th parallel. The Hudson's Bay Company sale to Lord Selkirk, so sets out; and the charter of "the Company" is accepted as verifying the validity of the grant. For years, Settlers from "the Forks" winter at Pembina, to hunt buffalo. Hunters of mixed parentage settle here; and from this centre, the Hunt pushes southwestward, to the Missouri Coteau. In 1818, the half of Assiniboia south of the 49th parallel is taken by the United States. The hunters settled at Pembina begin to move northward, to rejoin their kin around "the Forks". Loading families and possessions on carts, riding sturdy ponies and leading prized "buffalo runners," they drift down the Red River Valley, along the ancient trails that cross the Assiniboine at the Grand Passage; and locate along this River's northern bank, upstream from the cabins and cultivated patches which are the beginnings of the parishes of St. James, St. Charles and Headingley.

Increasingly, in these years, the people of Assiniboia are using York boats, rather than canoes. At York Factory and other "Company" depots on "the Bay", birch trees are scarce and stunted. Servants indentured from the Old Lands are not skilled canoemen, as are the Canadian voyageurs hired by the Nor'West Company. However, these Hudson's Bay servants remember the boats on the seas that hammer the Orkneys. They build strong, steady craft that become famous as "York boats". Like Viking long-ships, these are clinker-built. Each end is sharp; and raked 4 feet beyond the keel, to better navigate rocks and shoals. The standard York boat has a 28-foot keel; is 36 feet long, over-all; and of 8-foot beam.

The usual crew includes a bowsman, forward; a steersman, aft; and, amidships, six oarsmen manning long, heavy sweeps. Oarsmen sit by the starboard gunwale, facing the stern, with sweeps through oar-locks on the port side; and extending some 16 feet over the water. Between these, sit the oarsmen on the port side. At command, each oarsmen bends low; steps aft, pushing the inboard end of his sweep down and a-stern, swinging the outboard end clear of the water and far forward. Standing up and raising his arms, the rower drops the outboard end of his sweep into the water; and, stepping backward toward the bow, pulls a long, steady stroke that ends with him sitting, his arms high. This heavy drill — over and over — hour after hour — is slavery!

With a following wind, the crew hoists a big, square sail; and rests. Through shallows, they push the boat with long poles. Against swift, turbulent currents they "track" the heavy craft — with long lines pulled by the oarsmen, ashore; and the bowsman, aboard, poling the boat off rocks and shoals. Over portages, the boat is pushed on log rollers. Crews get plenty of practice. From Lake Superior to Lake Winnipeg are 53 portages in 657 miles!

All this is far from the quick, deft dip of paddles, 40 to-the-minute — to the rhythm of rollicking wilderness songs — with the relaxing forward swing that allows voyageurs to go top-speed for endless hours. The color-loving voyageurs decorate their canoes with bright designs. It is their delight to end a trip, wearing all their finery: gay-blazing shirts, flaming silk kerchiefs, multi-colored, finger-woven L'Assomption sashes — paddling at top speed, singing! A more vivid, picturesque tribe than bred by the heavy York boat; but, in the long sight, not so profitable. With historic inevitability, "slow and steady" wins the race between canoe and York boat — only to be replaced, in due time, by Red River cart, steamship and railroad. Meantime, the boat brigades give summer employment to, perhaps, 400 of Assiniboia's people.

Romancing about the great days of the fur trade can obscure actualities. The fact is: Hudson's Bay Company and Nor'West Company exist for one purpose: to pay dividends. Entrepreneurs in Montreal and London, credited with "building the fur trade" may be lauded as supermen. Actually, the fur trade is *built on* the resources of our Canadian Nor'West: the buffalo that provide food, clothing and shelter for hunters; beaver for their "cash crop"; and waterways for transport. The fur trade is *built by*: the "board-room" partners; the partners in the field; and the Indians, freemen and hybrids who live on the buffalo, harvest the beaver pelts and man the waterways. However the credit may be divided — among the few "counting house" partners who reap the fortunes; the more numerous working partners who endure hardships for lesser returns; and the myriad voyageurs, hunters and trappers who do the actual work for starvation wages — the sole purpose is to pay dividends.

The fur trade *does pay* — incredibly! The Hudson's Bay Company, during its early years of trading at Bay forts, returns annual dividends of

50% to shareholders in England. The Nor'West partners — despite the loss of great chunks of Canada's fur country given to the United States by "negotiations"; and troubles multiplied by war in 1812 — sometimes double their capital, annually! These fur barons wallow in wealth; reach into the Family Compact; and dominate courts and governments in Canada. Similarly, a few dozen shareholders wax rich and mighty; and, over longer years, exert a strong hand on the steering wheel of events in England.

Competition — intensified insanely — multiplies posts and payrolls. Before 1800, there are 21 trading posts on the Assiniboine River. By 1820, the Hudson's Bay Company has 76 inland forts; the Nor'Westers 97 — a total of 173 establishments (plus uncounted numbers of free traders) competing for the fur harvests of the Nor'West. Competition, run wild, explodes into open war! Costs rocket, as more and more men are hired — to fight each other.

The ferocity of the conflict increases with the numbers engaged. One hundred voyageurs, hired in Montreal by Colin Robertson for the Hudson's Bay Company, are starved out of far-away Athabasca, by the Nor'Westers. Another 120, led by Robertson to rescue survivors, are ambushed. Robertson is captured; escapes; is re-captured; escapes again; and goes to England. A Nor'West brigade, loaded with furs, en route to "the Forks," is ambushed and robbed at Grand Rapids. Nor'Westers promptly ambush and rob a Hudson's Bay brigade! The armies of the embattled Companies count thousands of men! Profits disappear — as proceeds are gobbled by multiplying costs.

There are other (and greater) costs. The driving greed which booms the fur trade, all too quickly decimates buffalo and beaver; and completes the ruin of those Indians who survive the smallpox — forcing traders to travel further to find fresh, unspoiled areas. Hundreds of freemen live, and raise their families, by manning the Hunts which feed both fur trade and Settlements; and by joining the brigades which freight supplies out to the great Nor'West and bring back the fur harvest, each season. It is killing work. The inland water transport, vital to both Companies, driven by the power of men's muscles, attains terrible efficiency — at cruel cost in men. By 1820, this system, centring on "the Forks" of the Assiniboine River and the Red, is the greatest inland water network the world has ever seen. The voyageurs who power it, often, are old men — discarded, replaced — at 40; and, before 50, dead!

The costs of delaying development of Assiniboia's manifold resources for the benefit of the fur trade, solely, are beyond calculation. However laudable the export of profits; and however beneficial the luring of adventurers into the Nor'West, the fur trade exacts a terrible price. The absentee shareholders of the fur Companies are alarmed only when net cash returns dwindle and disappear.

Responsibility for the fur war — and all its atrocities — must be focused at the autocratic peaks of the two fur Companies. The czars of these trading concerns make the decisions which lead to insane competition; free of any rules save those suggested by greed; and, inevitably, to war! The puny Colony on the Red and the penurious squatters along the Assiniboine are, at best, tolerated by both Companies; useful, maybe, if kept properly subservient to "the Trade".

Finally, from England comes the decree of Imperial Government, that such lawlessness end; and the competitors unite. This dictum of "the Establishment" may be hatched by the London Committee of the Hudson's Bay Company — as the only way to cut the ruinous costs of insane competition; and recover dividends which have disappeared. For the people of Assiniboia, Union replaces the destruction and death of the fur war with throttling monopoly. One substantial benefit is the addition of numbers of men now discarded by "the Company" who settle along the Assiniboine River and the Red. This year, 60 families of "Company" people come from James Bay.

The farm Settlers are proving the potential productivity of their lands. John Pritchard and his sons dig a field with spades; plant a bushel of wheat, kernel by kernel; and reap, therefrom, 74 bushels. Yes, this is "the good earth." Meanwhile, during the winter of 1820-21 the Settlers build a horse-powered gristmill. It grinds up to 15 bushels of wheat, daily. The mill-stones they make from limestone blocks, quarried locally. Governor Alexander Macdonnell reports to the London Committee, "I never saw better stones. No more millstones or grind-stones need be imported."

Rev. John West, Hudson's Bay Company chaplain, arrives at "the Forks", in October, 1820, the first Protestant minister in Assiniboia. He sets out, by dog-team, for Qu'Appelle on 24 January, 1821; and records vast herds of buffalo scraping the snow with their feet to eat the dried grass, beneath. Ten thousand are in view at one time. At Qu'Appelle, Indians come in, with provisions to trade. Many of them ride good horses, with saddles made of dressed skins, stuffed with buffalo wool; and with wooden stirrups. Their bridle is a thong of rawhide, with both ends tied to their steed's lower jaw. In February, West travels 80 miles to Pembina in 24 hours, by dog-cariole. Visiting camps on the plains, he sees hunters kill buffalo by crawling in the snow, pushing their guns ahead of them. "Buffalo meat is easier to digest than beef", he records. "The hungry traveller often eats many pounds just before he wraps in his buffalo robes for the night." By 22 February, West is back at Hayfield Farm. He writes: "Begin to think, like the Indians, that 100 miles is but a step. Drivers hurry their dogs, day after day, in trips of hundreds of miles. Most English half-breeds excel in this. Many Canadians are expert drivers and voyageurs. When tripping, they are all life — whipping their dogs barbarously, with appalling blasphemy. The Indians are corrupted by Europeans who . . . exceed in savagery — buying a woman with rum for the prime of her days."

On May Day, the river ice breaks up. Settlers, who wintered at Pembina, come home, down the Red, dodging ice flows, on rafts and dugouts made from big trees. The canny Scots bring dried meat and pemmican. Many others, less provident or more generous, have no food.

The land dries quickly. Fires sweep the plains — burning for days. This is the time for fishing. Sturgeon and catfish are caught in great numbers — weighing up to 100 pounds! Sturgeon feed the Settlement for a month; and supply lamp oil for the entire year.

The people who live along the Assiniboine and Red soon detect a basic change in their Settlements. A new power is making itself felt: the power of Monopoly. On 21 March, 1821, the two great fur Companies — at war for so long — effect a "Union". Actually, the English Company swallows the Montrealers. The old, steady-going Hudson's Bay Company digests the vibrant, dashing Nor'Westers. True, of the 53 Chief Factors and Chief Traders kept in the field, 32 are former Nor'Westers; but, in London, the English Committee rules supreme! Monopoly is absolute — free to rule — with a "High and Heavy Hand!"

Economic philosophers, one day, may examine our Canadian fur trade as a record of competition, absolutely free — limited only by the capacity of the competitors to ambush, rob, starve and murder each other; to destroy the resource they exploit; and to debauch the people who are their tools of exploitation. The pundits may examine, also, the absolute Monopoly which replaces wild competition; and may enunciate wise and contrasting conclusions based upon their examination.

The settlers of Assiniboia know little, and care less, about such things. Soon, they feel the tightening grip of the Monopoly which is to rule their lands and lives for a generation. Meantime, "Union" of the fur Companies multiplies Assiniboia's population. All "opposition" (sometimes 5 competitors at one site) are closed out. Fort William fades to a mere station. York Factory becomes fur trade headquarters. Two-thirds of all the hired men of the combined Companies are discharged. Many of these settle east of the Red River, where land is allotted them (as agreed when Selkirk bought Assiniboia). "The Company" loans some of them money for homes. Many Canadians and hybrids reinforce the Settlers already "scattered along the Assiniboine."

Peter Fidler's will, dated 16 August, 1821, bequeaths the library and scientific instruments of this great pioneer to the Governor of Assiniboia, for the use of the Settlers. His livestock goes to the Settlers, direct. In August, too, Nicolas Garry visits Assiniboia; and, at York Factory, on the 23rd, sees the landing of 170 Colonists from Switzerland.

In September Rev. John West, coming up from York Factory, marries Company clerk Thomas Isbister, to Mary Kennedy, the Chief Factor's daughter; and baptizes three of Andrew McDermot's children, at Norway House. A week later he overtakes the Swiss settlers. Several of their children have died. One of their boats has grounded; and another is wrecked, crossing Lake Winnipeg. Their food is low. They are eating owls and ravens! "At the mouth of the Red River," West writes, "Pigwiss gives us dried sturgeon." These clock-makers, musicians and mechanics are quiet, orderly and handsome people; but without experience in pioneering. They are kept over winter, by the Indians.

Locusts have destroyed the crops. Even to salvage what is left — "laborers are not obtained but at high prices — from $1 per day each." With a short out-turn from the farms, some of the Settlers must winter, again, at Pembina — to hunt buffalo. The provident and canny Scots are not in want. Among the Canadians, Des Meurons, Indians and hybrids of various parentages — degrees of improvidence and generosity send families to the plains for winter provisions.

By 1821, the organized buffalo Hunt has grown to be the body and soul of Assiniboia's economy. Everyone lives by the Hunt. In addition to the need for more food, new demands appeared. As so often in history, Assiniboia comes under the influence of far-distant events. The demand for buffalo robes multiplies. The new and booming industries of the United States find that the thick, tough hides make superlative belting. So long as water and steam provide the power for industry, every machine is driven by belts. The demand multiplies — and swamps the traditional fur trade. Hides, which had been a waste product, now bring income to Assiniboia hunters.

Spring and fall, hundreds of hunters with horses, oxen, carts and families venture forth on the Hunt. These hunters are a mixed lot. Some live by the Hunt, entirely. Others squat on a chosen site; build a cabin; cultivate a field or two; and go on the Hunt, more or less regularly. Some are full-time farmers, who take time off for the Hunt. Some are farmers' sons, or Company clerks, enjoying the Hunt as a holiday. Of many mixtures of many nationalities, they speak many and mixed tongues.

On the Hunt, they merge into a disciplined unity. In the 20 years following 1820, these Assiniboia hunter-farmers kill an estimated 650,-000 buffalo — an average of 32,500 each year!

This winter brings the threat of starvation. There are the 170 Swiss new-comers. The fall Hunt fails. There is little buffalo meat. From the grain saved from the locusts, seed must be kept for next year. The remainder is rationed, one pint of wheat per Settler per day. Some fish are netted through the ice. Few families have pepper, salt, flour or vegetables. The cold is terrible! Two men, bringing provisions, are frozen to death on the Plains. Some Settlers have tamed buffalo calves. These are slaughtered for food. An early spring is providential. Great flocks of geese, on 25 March, are greeted with joyous shouts.

On 5 April, reports reach the Settlement that the Sioux are moving north. Two boatloads of "Company" men and Settlers go to stop them at Pembina. The Sioux are an everlasting threat. One of their war parties attacks hybrid hunters; kill 2; and steal all their horses. By the end of May, farm families are working, overtime, sowing another crop with seed wheat brought from Fort Alexander; some supplied by "the Company" and some saved from last year. Food is still scarce. A Swiss gives a $25 watch for a bushel of wheat to eat. Another trades a snuff-box for a cat-fish.

On 20 May, 1822, George Simpson, newly-appointed Governor of "the Company," moves his headquarters into Fort Gibraltar — re-built; and re-named "Fort Garry." In June, a new Governor of Assiniboia appears: Andrew Bulger, ex-army officer. Following orders, he selects another "Council of Assiniboia." Settlers care little about either Governor or Council; but all rejoice that Alexander Macdonnell, Governor since August, 1815, is leaving. They call him "the grasshopper governor" — because he robs them, even more than the locusts do! Pompous and debauched, he and his gang of thieving favorites, use the Colony store (built in 1812 to supply tools, arms and oatmeal) to rob the Settlers by exorbitant prices and graft. John Haskett, agent of the Selkirk estate, comes with Governor Bulger. He promptly cuts debts charged to Settlers by 20%; wipes out interest charges; and orders more goods from England — to sell at 66⅔% above London prices. A "Company" store is opened in Fort Garry; and free-traders set up small shops outside the Fort.

A new day dawns when the "magnates" of the fur-trade "subscribe one hundred shares of $50 each" to promote the "Buffalo Wool Company." The numbers and ferocity of wolves that range Assiniboia make sheep-raising impractical. The new Company is to buy buffalo robes; build a tannery to make the hides into leather; collect the wool; weave the coarse hair into heavy coats and blankets for the fur-trade; and export the fine hair to English manufacturers of luxury woollens. John Pritchard is President and Manager. Success seems certain. Machinery, dyes and skilled workers are imported from England, High hopes dissolve in disappointment. The cloth produced refuses to take bright dyes; costs too much; and does not attract buyers. However, for a time, all — men and women; farmers and hunters — are working at big wages! Hunt and farms are neglected. Food becomes scarce. Prices sky-rocket! The Buffalo Wool venture fails . . . owing the Company $22,500! There are charges of mismanagement, waste and drunkenness. More remote factors fore-doom this early Assiniboia industry. Wool is the cornerstone of England's wealth. That market is sacred — unassailable! The venture does make money circulate, in Assiniboia.

This fall of 1822, the harvest is good. Stacks of grain rise on every farmstead. As winter advances, Settlers begin threshing. Yields are high: wheat and barley from 25 up to 30, 40, and even 50 bushels per acre.

In planning for a farming Settlement in Assiniboia, Selkirk recognized the vital place of livestock; and offered $4,000.00, plus $1,000.00 bonus for 50 heifers delivered at "the Forks." A Canadian, Roulette, "drifts" a herd 750 miles from Prairie du Chien; and sells them at good prices. Two succeeding herds are lost or killed. A fourth herd of 150 head, gets through from Illinois. In all, 300 cattle arrive during September. Settlers pay $150 for good milk cows; and $90 for good work oxen.

The new Council of Assiniboia appointed by "the Company" holds its first formal meeting on 24 December, 1822. Governor Bulger presides. Thomas Thomas, Alexander Macdonnell, Wm. H. Cook and John Pritchard attend as members. From this date, the Council of Assiniboia meets regularly. Governor Simpson, of "the Company," reports to superiors in London: "Nearly every member (of the Council) is hostile to Settlement — from the expense it entails and the continual fever in which the Colonists keep us. A great number of discharged servants, with their families, this season have gone to the Settlement, which will relieve our establishments greatly; but I imagine it will be necessary for us to assist many of them this winter." Gunn and Tuttle write: "The influx of families from the fur trade exceed in number the Colonists brought in from all quarters by his Lordship." Colville, head of "the Company" in England warns Simpson: "London will not tolerate any return to the old oppression of Selkirk's Colony." Unhappily, the Settlements will not throw off this "old oppression" for another generation.

Winter brings terrifying numbers of wolves into the Settlements. Singly, they skulk harmlessly. In packs, they kill horses, cattle and dogs

— right up to the farmsteads. This year, wildlife is scarce. This may be
the result of a decline in the productive cycle; or of wide-spread fires
set by Indian hunters, to protest Union of the fur Companies. Starving
Indians cook dead dogs and horses. Their children crack the bones for
marrow. It is a grim and ghastly winter.

Houses in the Settlements are built of logs. Those in the Selkirk
Colony and around Fort Garry are constructed, usually, on the Red
River frame pattern. Many, along the Assiniboine, are of the notched, or
dove-tailed corner construction introduced by Norwegian servants of
"the Company." All are fitted to withstand the cold and blizzards of
winter; the heat and storms of summer; and all the harsh conditions
imposed by this rugged land. New-comers to Assiniboia, from their
varied origins, bring useful customs, ideas and tools, which are changed,
adapted and harnessed with others devised on the spot, or borrowed
from neighbors. Thus, necessity invents new customs, ideas and tools,
native to this new and different land that all, together, are building.

Inevitably, if slowly, the first generations of Settlers recognize the
change in their lives. With subsequent generations, a new way of life
emerges — different from all its multiple origins — in customs, ideas,
outlook and even speech. This new way of life is native to Assiniboia
and our Canadian West. It demands that every Settler be expert in
farming, hunting, building. Within the homes, good wives work ceaselessly; dipping candles, baking bannock, cooking pemmican, spinning,
weaving, sewing, knitting. Withal, there is time for visiting, social gather-
ings and festivities, weddings and holidays. This year, a number of families come to Assiniboia, from Quebec.

Spring is backward in 1823. By 23 May, however, the Settlers are
seeding corn. (And clouds of blackbirds are gobbling the seed!) Passenger pigeons, by millions, visit Assiniboia on their northward spring
migration; and, again, as they move southward each fall. Great numbers
are bagged; and provide excellent food. At intervals, settlers turn fisher-
man; and join the natives in taking abundance of sturgeon, pike, pickerel
and goldeye. In 1823, an experimental farm is established by "the
Company." It is without "chick or cow;" but it makes plowing more
general.

In June, Governor Bulger leaves Assiniboia. A typical army officer, he
has restored order to the Settlements; and some dignity to the office. To
succeed him, Pelly is appointed Governor of Assiniboia. The real boss,
however, is George Simpson, Governor of "the Company". He closes the
Colony store, which has supplied Settlers since 1812; and makes "the
Company" store in Fort Garry the only lawful source of goods. "The
high and heavy hand" of Monopoly grips the business of supplying

goods, as well as the fur trade. (And, of course, increases the numbers of free-traders who dare dabble in both.) "The Company" introduces paper currency; and issues notes for 1 pound, 5 shillings and 1 shilling. Annual imports of goods and supplies to the Settlement exceed $100,000. Settlers of means and free traders import goods — paying "the Company" for freight, from London to York Factory — from $25 to $100 per ton.

In July, Cuthbert Grant becomes a "Company" clerk at $360 annually, for 3 years. Grant studies medicine in England the previous year; and has considerable medical skill and equipment. Life in Assiniboia is built on hard work. Nevertheless, there is time for enjoyment. Once their daily work is done, "Company" clerks mount their horses; and gallop over the open plains — shooting small game as they ride. Through the winter, the frozen Assiniboine and Red Rivers become a playground. Everyone races horses on the smooth ice. Wrapped in furs, couples and families drive for miles in the keen, bracing air.

Through these hard early years, farm fields are cleared with axes; and tilled with hoes. An increasing number of Settlers use plows. Grain is sown broadcast; harvested with sickles; and milled in stone "querns." The gun hangs in the Settler's home; and is carried, universally, to supplement farm output with meat and furs. Folks paddle the river highways between neighboring farmsteads and growing centres. During winter, cattle suffer heavily. Cold and blizzards; ravenous wolves; and, sometimes, hungry natives take their toll.

Settlements push westward, along the Assiniboine. This spring, with the blessing of Bishop Provencher, Cuthbert Grant begins the settlement of "Grantown" on the White Horse Plain. After English negotiators surrender the half of Assiniboia south of the 49th parallel to the United States, Canadian and hybrid buffalo hunters living around the Roman Catholic Mission at Pembina, begin to drift northward, to the Assiniboine River. Finally, most of them decide to move. Bishop Provencher writes: "This spring they are at the Forks, camping" along the Assiniboine. Before the spring Hunt, they locate at White Horse Plain.

"Grant is turning settler," Governor Simpson writes, "He is married to a daughter of Angus McGillis, a Settler worth $10,000 to $15,000. Has got land on the White Horse Plain on the Assiniboine, where he is joined by 80 to 100 families of half-breeds, all steady married men. Hitherto, the Metis lived by the chase; and, in consequence of the great demand for provisions, indulged their rage for dress, extravagance and dissipation; but domestic cattle are now getting so numerous that in two years there will be no market for the produce of their Hunts." (Sometimes, the Governor's assertiveness over-runs his usually keen judgment.) "Their pride and independence are such they will not enter the Company service."

The land which "the Company" gives to Grant (and takes away from him, years later) is on the Assiniboine River, above the Grand Passage, 12 miles west of "the Forks"; extending a further 6 miles westward; and 6 miles, northward from the River. Wood is plentiful for fuel, building and making Red River carts. South from the River are groves of maple where sugar is harvested, each spring. The broad-spreading plain gives a long, clear view of any Sioux war party that might strike from the south. It is a beautiful, useful and strategic site.

Grant is a Scot-Cree; son of a former Nor'West partner; born on the Plains; a true native. Throughout his active life he works and fights for the land and the life he loves; and for his people of mixed parentage. To these he gives his entire loyalty.

Throughout this writing we face the want of a word to name those people of our Canadian West who are born of mothers of Indian, and fathers of European, descent. "Half-breed" we discard; it stinks of derogation, contempt and hate; and is biologically inaccurate, since many leaders in the History of Assiniboia boast one Indian among, say, 8 great-grandparents, with the proportions changed in each successive generation. "Metis", in general usage, embraces only those hybrids whose fathers are Canadians who speak French; and omits all of 100 other paternities. In this sense, "Metis" excludes Cuthbert Grant, and, later, James McKay and John Norquay. With some misgivings, we use the name "hybrids" for all our people whose ancestry mixes European and aboriginals in whatever degrees.

Grant has a water-powered grist mill built on Sturgeon Creek. After floods wash out the project, he builds a wind-driven mill at Grantown. As hybrid hunters and voyageurs are discharged by "the Company" they gravitate from all parts of the Nor'West, to Grantown. This becomes the buffalo hunters' rendezvous. Each Settler gets a lot with river frontage, and 2 miles deep. Grant's home is a big log house near the west side of his seigneury. Eastward, are Angus McGillis and his sons, Francois Hall, Pierre Falcon, Alexander Breland. Westward, lots are reserved for the Mission that Rev. Picard Des Troismaisons begins with service in Grant's house; and which grows into the parish of St. Francois Xavier. Beyond, is Urbain Delorme, great plainsman, hunter and trader. If Governor Simpson has any pious hopes that these people will change from free plains hunters to settled farmers; lose their "pride and independence"; and serve the Company with subservient docility — he is disappointed! Grantown is peopled by a new breed: hunter-farmers, with time for trading, who, as their substance increases, become increasingly proud, independent, free — and misinterpreted!

Grant freights between Assiniboia and Norway House for "the Company"; and for himself. Grantown is his base for trading throughout the Souris, Turtle Mountain and Qu'Appelle country, which he knows so well. With a similar arrangement, of free trading while working for "the Company," Andrew McDermot locates at Pembina. Through such free traders winning furs away from the United States traders, for resale to "the Company", the Monopoly is to be maintained. McDermot, with a canny eye to the future, imports goods on "Company" ships for sale to the Settlers, "on the side."

Surveyor William Kempt in 1824 surveys the proposed winter road from "the Forks" to York Factory. This year, "the Company" buys from Assiniboia farmers, for shipment to Norway House: 10 tons of best flour at $5 per cwt; barley at $1.18 a bushel; 1,000 bushels Indian corn at $1.62; and 1,200 pounds of butter in kegs, at 25 cents per pound. Crops fail in 1824; but, when Governor Simpson promises to buy all "Company" needs from them, the farmers of Assiniboia expand fields and production. "This was no sooner done, however, than prices (of farm products) fall while every article the Settlers require is held at usual prices."

Assiniboia is now a separate colonial entity, administered for the Selkirk estate by "the Company." Behind its "front" of Governor and Council, Simpson is the real dictator. As the population of the Settlements increase, "the Company" appoints more Councillors; "but always, the paramount interest of the fur trade firmly in power." The machinery of Monopoly hums smoothly — with a "High and Heavy Hand" at the controls.

Among the fur-men forced by the Union to retire are: Donald Gunn, Thos. Thomas, Jas. Bird and others who contribute richly to the history of Assiniboia. Alexander Ross, who comes from the Pacific coast, earns the gratitude of posterity, as the first historian. For a time he serves as Sheriff; and builds his home, "Colony Gardens," into a show place. Replacing Rev. David Jones, Archdeacon Cochrane comes to Assiniboia, in 1825; and contributes beyond measure to this new land. Discharged fur-men, flocking to Assiniboia, increase the population to 1,500 white "people." (And several times that number of others!)

Ross writes: "The year 1825 is one of great enterprize among the Colonists. No less than 42 houses are built in a few months." Under Laidlaw, big buildings are raised at Hayfield Farm; and many workers hired. But there is "no ox to plow, no cow to give milk". A central mansion, that cost $3,000, is burned "in a drunken frolic." After years of work, waste and extravagance "every vestige of property on the farm disappeared."

Another herd of cattle gets through from the United States. However, with the "Buffalo Wool" boom ended, Settlers buy cannily. Cows sell for $30; the biggest trained yoke of oxen bring $100. "No country can produce finer heifers of 1 or 2 years old" writes Ross, "but after that age, they grow but little — the Settlers breeding them too young . . . But, while they diminish in size, they increase fast in number." This year, for the first time since Settlers came to Assiniboia, farmers admit harvesting a "really fair crop". Wheat seeded with hoes, returns 68-fold. Fields cultivated by the plow, return 44 times the seed grain.

Millwright Mitchell arrives from Scotland to set up a wind-driven grist-mill, which came with the early Selkirk Settlers; but was never erected. Its erection costs $7,500. Robert Logan, retired Nor'Wester, who looks after Selkirk's affairs in Assiniboia, buys the 100-acre site of Fort Douglas — with buildings *and the grist-mill* for $1,500! Logan soon has this first wind-mill in prosperous operation. Later, mills are built by local workman; average cost: $750.

This fall, the Plains are alive with mice. Armies of them destroy entire stacks of grain. But, buffalo are few and far away. Among the hunters, provisions run low. Cuthbert Grant, at Brandon House, is forced to kill horses and dogs to feed his people; and finally, abandons the place. The winter of 1825-26 is one of the most terrible recorded. Snow falls to record depths. Storms hammer the frozen land, endlessly. Indian and hybrid families starve in their winter camps. Cuthbert Grant snowshoes over the Plains with a rescue party; taking food by toboggan to starving hunters' families; and bringing in survivors. The known dead, from the brutal blizzards of December, number 33 people. The Assiniboine and Red are covered with ice six feet thick!

Meantime, "the Company" quadruples its capital stock — after a century at $519,000 — to $2,000,000; and declares 10% dividends, thereon. "The High and Heavy Hand" of Monopoly rakes in lavish profits!

The year 1826 is one of disaster for Assiniboia! The winter is the worst known. Blizzards, week after week, bury the Plains and parklands under 5 feet of driven snow. Buffalo, searching for forage, move far beyond their usual pastures. To find the herds, hunters range far and wide. Many of their horses perish. Those surviving are skin and bones. Horses, oxen, dogs are killed for meat, as a last resort. Without mounts and draft animals, hunters are imprisoned in the snow — some of them hundreds of miles from home. How many families perish and are never found, cannot be known. Some go mad before rescuers arrive. Others are frozen stiff. One mother carries her babe 125 miles in 3 days; and is found, frozen — a short quarter-mile from safety! Survivors eat their hides, moccasins! A man, his wife and three children are dug out of the snow, after 5 days without food or fire. The mother and 2 of the children survive. For days, the thermometer registers 45 below zero. By April, famine menaces Assiniboia. The Des Meurons veterans and the Swiss threaten mutiny. Only the Metis of Grantown have adequate provisions.

Suddenly, a warm wind blows in from the south. The snow melts! In one day (2 May), the Red River raises 9 feet! Within 2 days, water floods over the banks; and rises steadily. On 5 May, Settlers abandon their homes on the flood plain. Some escape with only the clothes they wear. Hurriedly, men man boats; rescue people, first; then livestock; and, finally, move furniture and grain. Often, rescuers are forced to chop holes in the roof of a flooded house; and, through it, take occupants aboard. Ice floes collide on the racing Rivers; grind along the banks; and shatter giant trees. Buildings drift, like boxes, on the racing currents. One home is swirled, flaming, down the current! The refugees flee — some to Logan's mill; some northward, to Stony Mountain and Bird's Hill; and many to the high ground, westward, along the Assiniboine River, Sturgeon Creek and Silver Heights.

Alexander Ross goes to the "banks of the Assiniboine. Here — on high ground, we find a dense crowd of people; and, among others, the rascally Des Meuron who, it is well-known, hardly possess an animal of their own — yet are selling beef all the time . . . On the delightful banks of Sturgeon Creek we roam, in peace and quietness, till the waters begin to fall. Provisions are scarce. Pemmican sells for 16 cents a pound; salt at $11.25 per bushel. The Des Meuron fed us on our own beef at 6 cents per pound. They, and others, help themselves." (Old soldiers never starve!)

Thunderstorms bombard the Settlement, on 10 May. A 3-day deluge of rain keeps the Rivers rising. Their level jumps 2 feet on 17 May! Indian villages in loops of the winding Assiniboine are trapped — and obliterated. "The people are engaged in prayer in the tents of the clergy at Stony Mountain, on May 21, when the camp takes fire!" With abundant man-power — and, certainly, plenty of water — the flames are quickly quenched.

For the first time in 21 days, the level of the Red River ceases to rise, on 22 May. River levels fall, slowly at first; then more quickly; and, on 27 May, recede 10 feet in 24 hours.

The flood of 1826 is (writes Archbishop Matheson) "higher than ever known by man; 17 miles wide and 35 feet above the common river level." Only one man has been drowned. Farm families find their home-steads "bare and naked." Ross tells us "Not a house was standing." He must refer to the Colony on the flood plain of the Red, not "the delightful banks of Sturgeon Creek" . . . where "we roam in peace" till the flood subsides. When he writes of wheat sown the third week in May, doubt-less, he has in mind little fields on this higher ground, westward. In the Colony, seeding begins on 14 June. On 2 July, farm families are busily planting grain and potatoes "as on every day since they returned to their homesteads." With water trapped in pools, a hot July brings out clouds of mosquitoes! Seed germination is explosive! Three days after sowing, green blades of wheat push above the soil!

After the flood, several hundred Des Meurons, Swiss and others forsake Assiniboia for the United States, Canada and Europe. They have never become really acclimated; and are replaced by "natives." Down the rivers from all the Nor'West, discharged "Company officers, with their families, come to Assiniboia." Some take land below Kildonan — and plant the parishes of St. Paul, St. Andrews and St. Peters. Other settle up the Assiniboine; and begin the parishes of St. James and Headingly. French-speaking Canadians and people of mixed parentages settle in the parishes of St. Boniface, St. Norbert, St. Vital on the Red; St. Charles, St. Francois Xavier and Baie St. Paul on the Assiniboine River. The area which will be the city of Winnipeg is home to the fami-lies of Andrew McDermot, Alexander Ross and Robert Logan.

Historically, floods have recurred, periodically, in the valleys of the Assiniboine River and the Red. They will continue to occur — until the regimen of water flow down the entire complex of waterways draining the Assiniboine-Red basin is brought under sensible and scientific man-agement.

More and more United States traders penetrate into Assiniboia — to buccaneer bigger and bigger shares of the fur trade. To protect "the Company" Monopoly against this mounting competition, Governor Simpson enlists "free" traders. Among others, he provides "Cuthbert Grant and Louis Giboche with goods to trade from Turtle Mountain to Qu'Appelle. They having it more in their power to harass our opponents than we could do with a formidable establishment." To further discomfit United States traders — and, perhaps improve relations with the people of Assiniboia — "the Company" announces that Settlers will be per-mitted to trade in furs, *if* they bring the pelts to "the Company" at Fort Garry. Further, Governor Simpson promises that "the Company" will buy from farmers all needed supplies which can be produced locally. Soon, the Company is fully supplied. Then, prices fall: flour from $4 to $2.87 a cwt; butter from 25 cents to 14 cents per pound; and cheese from 12 cents to 8 cents; while everything the settlers have to buy from "the Company," remains at usual high prices.

Alexander Ross leaves us a rugged critique on methods of handling (or mishandling) farm products in those days. He reports that the flour is inferior. There is no fanning mill to clean grain. Threshing is done by flails, on ice-floors. The wheat is ground when it is still frozen; and, presumably, with moisture content far above the "tough," "damp" or even "rejected," of later standards. The flour is packed in barrels made of green wood. There, it heats, sours, rots! Butter is brought to "the Company" store in open dishes, covered with towels or cabbage leaves. Good or bad, it is all thrown together; packed in green kegs; and shipped "hundreds, nay, thousands of miles; exposed for months to a burning summer sun". It arrives at remote posts anything but good dairy butter!

Governor Simpson decides to buy wheat to be milled "according to the Company's own liking." The price is fixed at 87 cents per bushel. The wheat is bought by measure, ungraded. There is suspicion of trickery. The crop is late and light. However, the Company buys 8,000 or 10,000 bushels. Then the trouble begins. With no adequate storage, the wheat is piled, 4 or 5 feet deep; and, with its excessive moisture content, bakes together. It is a compound of "wheat, smut, icicles, dried meat, mice, mice nests — heated together: a mass of impurity!" Against all advice, this mass is milled; and the flour shipped to "Company" posts! Ross criticizes the "slovenly habit of threshing grain on an ice-floor in the open air, chiefly by an indolent and wretched class of squatters who raise just sufficient to poison the good grain and destroy the market . . . The paupers of Red River — voyageurs, hunters, trip-men, fiddlers, idlers; and, last of all — farmers."

Ross' rugged writing does not stir up as much trouble in the Settlements as does the statement by Rev. D. T. Jones in the "Missionary Register" of December, 1827: "There is an un-Christian-like selfishness and narrowness of mind in our Scottish population — the most comfortable in our little community . . . The Orkneymen are far more promising. The half-breeds walk in godly sincerity."

Ross reports, in his combative style, that an Academy for Latin, Greek and Mathematics is "warmed into existence . . . Exclusively for the children of the Governor, Deputy Governor and Chief Factors — the great nabobs of the fur trade."

Under the stimulus of "the Company's" promise to buy supplies locally, and the influx of new people, more Settlers cultivate more acres. At White Horse Plain, Cuthbert Grant has 34 acres under the plow; Angus McGillis, 20. Grantown is a separate community, until newcomers, squatting along the Assiniboine, join those already settled on the

River's banks in what will be the parishes of Headingly, St. Charles and St. James.

Freighting for "the Company" takes many Settlers from their farms between seed-time and harvest. In York boat brigades, they navigate cargoes of furs down to York Factory; and struggle back to Fort Garry, with heavy loads of supplies. This is killing work. Strangely, it is done best by men who "Company" officials write off as "indolent" and "worthless."

Beginning in 1827, a succession of better harvests in Assiniboia put the farmers on their feet; and prove Western farming worthwhile. Assiniboia's output of wheat is a minute fraction of the 20 million bushels produced this year by the farmers of Canada. Nevertheless, the sale of 10,000 bushels to the Company, at 87 cents per bushel, puts substantial purchasing power in the hands of the Settlers. Although well-fed Company officials would sniff in derision at the thought, the day is coming when the despised farmers displace the fur-men and their restrictive Monopoly; and build the foundations of a far greater economy in the Canadian Nor'West.

Even with the growth in farm production, however, Settlements and fur trade still depend on the buffalo Hunt. It is worthy of report in the Fort Garry Journal, therefore, when on 5 May, Grant arrives at White Horse Plain from his trading station up the Assiniboine, with "3 bateaux loaded high with 50,000 musquash and other furs; and provisions, robes and leather." In July, "the Company" appoints Grant "Warden of the Plains," at a salary of $1,000 per annum. Thus, Simpson keeps Grant "loyal" to the Company; and uses him to defeat invading United States traders, increasing numbers of free traders in the Settlements and the menace of the Sioux. On every Hunt, Grant takes his medicine chest. When epidemic sweeps the country, he travels far and wide, to treat the suffering. No carbon copy is ever made of this original Assiniboia country doctor. The mission at Grantown is taken up by Rev. Jean Harper, in 1828; and called St. Francois Xavier, after the former mission at Pembina. Pere Harper wins the hearts of the buffalo hunters, by becoming an integral part of the Hunt.

Governor Simpson establishes a "new Experimental Farm on a rich and fertile spot on the Assiniboine River." It is provided with spacious buildings, parks, fields; cows of the best breed, a $1,500 stallion from England; and mares from the United States. Men and women are hired, in plenty; and plows, harrows, drills and other implements are imported. No expense is spared. The manager, McMillan, has been a good furman; but is no farmer. Science and system are conspicuous by their absence. Thousands of dollars are wasted by favorites in "cushy jobs."

After 6 years, the farm is sold. With grim and perverse satisfaction, Settlers watch this grand venture fail.

"The Company" is much more successful in promoting farming on the Pacific coast. French-speaking Canadian servants, discharged, are encouraged to settle in Oregon. Aggressive United States citizens are working to capture the Canadian Nor'West. "The Company" can well afford to invest in protection of its interests there. By 1828, the dividend paid to shareholders is 20%. As Governor-in-Chief, George Simpson is making Monopoly pay handsomely for his London employers.

Simpson is a man of boundless energy. By express canoe and on horse-back, he ranges, tirelessly, over the vast Nor'West; and eastern Canada, as well. He knows more about more of Canada, first hand, than any other man — before or since his time. The activities of this remarkable man far surpass "the call of duty." To his own marriage, 4 children are born. "Other children bearing the name Simpson — born of swarthy mothers in far-off posts", writes MacKay, "give rise to legendary tales of extra-marital relations on the heroic scale."

St. Andrews parish is established by Rev. William Cochrane down the Red River, at the Grand Rapids. Retired "Company" officials and servants, with their native wives, and children of mixed parentage, have the means to build well, live well and educate their children well. With substantial capital and wide experience in the country, the people of this community flourish "beyond all other English-speaking parishes."

To diversify farm production, Governor Simpson decides to promote flax and hemp-growing. With him, decision means action. Premiums are promised to growers. Hemp and flax of finest quality are harvested; and, after the premiums are collected by conniving favorites, left to rot! The costly flax mill never turns a wheel. Such ventures fail, perhaps, because the attention of the management is rivetted on the real gold mine: the fur trade monopoly.

Early Assiniboia farmers suffer from a "cost-price squeeze." "In 1829," writes Donald Gunn, "the Company reduces the price of produce to what suits their own interests." As increased production floods the market, limited by Monopoly, "the Company" introduces "delivery quotas," under which the owner of a farm sells 8 bushels of wheat; and a hunter or trip-man, 4 bushels. The price of "Company" land in Assiniboia is raised by 50%: from $1.25 to $1.87 per acre.

Settlements expand, along the Assiniboine River and the Red. Compared with Wisconsin and Minnesota, however, growth is slow, slow! Many Assiniboia Settlers declare that this is due to false reports circulated by "Company" men. In the interests of their Monopoly, zealots spread outrageously false accounts of the country.

CHAPTER 5

Cuthbert Grant

High Ground Westward 1830-1839

The Settlers who stay in Assiniboia after the 1826 flood, have built 204 new houses by 1830, with barns, paddocks and expanded fields. Sturdy, thrifty Orkneymen come as Company servants. When their indentured service is completed, they become Settlers. Families from the United Kingdom, as well as French-speaking Canadians, are moving in. Each year, also, sees people leaving for the United States. By 1830, however, Assiniboia has achieved a degree of security, prosperity and permanence. Already a new trade route to St. Paul, 400 miles southward, is developing. With new markets, free-traders take an increasing share of the fur trade, in defiance of "the Company" monopoly.

Pioneer farming in Assiniboia is hard work. The season is short; and operations hurried. Spring plowing begins early in May. Usually, grain is sown by 20 May, except barley. Wheat is the general crop. Fall wheat is tried; but fails. On a field "which sowed 10 bushels (probably 5 acres) the yield diminished until it produced only 52 bushels, with spring plowing", Alexander Ross reports. "I got it manured and plowed in the fall; and plowed it, again, in the spring. The season being favorable, I had 255 bushels on it. A neighbor, from 6 bushels sown, reaped 140 bushels. A field sowing 8 bushels (probably 4 acres) fallow for 2 years and plowed 3 times, produced 280 bushels!" From this year on, Settlers produce enough wheat to make plenty of flour for Settlements and "the Company". Hired help is hard to get, even at high wages. Indolent, awkward men demand 62 to 75 cents per day; women 25 cents to 37 cents!

Most of the houses along the Rivers are well-built. On the average, $300.00 builds a Red River framed log house, 20 feet by 30 feet in size. The best-built houses have shingled roofs; good, solid stone foundations;

and windows, doors and partitions, panelled and painted, or rough-cast with lime. A home, 40 feet by 50 feet, well finished, costs about $1,500.00. Of course, most of the squatter's homes up the Assiniboine River, are one-storey cabins. In St. Andrews parish, however, are several two-storey houses; some with galleries; and 2 with verandahs! Glass windows and outer doorlocks, luxuries hitherto unknown, are becoming common. Whatever their size, these homes, white as snow, look trim, neat, substantial and inviting. Solid stone structures are being built for officers and retired factors of "the Company".

After the warring fur-men bury the hatchet in Union, officers of "the Company" take complete charge in Assiniboia. "The Company" is the only source from which Settlers can buy supplies; and the only market to which they can sell products of the farm, the Hunt or the fisheries. "The Company" officers are "lords of all they survey". They can ride rough-shod over Settlers; and, too often, do so. Schooled in arrogance — with contempt for most; and responsibility to none of Assiniboia's people — they are arbitrary and harsh. Led by hard-driving Simpson, they fight to enforce their Monopoly. They stop supplying Settlers on credit, as has been the custom since Selkirk's time. All is on a strictly "business" basis. Supplies in "the Company" store are limited. Wealthier people are provided with what they want; those of smaller means are not. As a result, free-traders import supplies to meet the needs of the Settlers; and, outside Fort Garry, do an expanding business. From St. Francois Xavier to Kildonan, more and more free-traders supply goods; and trade in furs, in defiance of "the Company".

The mounting challenge to Monopoly rouses "Company" officers to increasing ferocity. Men are imprisoned; and homes searched by "Company" men who present no warrants other than their muskets and bayonets! Homes are destroyed. Furs are confiscated. All rights are sacrificed to the interest of the Monopoly. This "power-play" proves short-sighted; and results, inevitably, in the defeat of the Monopoly it is designed to maintain.

Governor Simpson orders that all supplies needed by "the Company" which are available from the Settlers, shall be bought in Assiniboia. The carelessness of some Settlers degrades the quality of grain, butter and meat brought to market. Carelessness by "Company" servants in handling, processing and packing these supplies further degrades the finished products. This drives "the Company" to import, from outside, provisions which could be plentifully supplied in the Settlements.

With characteristic energy, Simpson launches experimental farms to show the Settlers better methods of farming and marketing. It may be that the Governor's explosive forcefulness and violent likes and dislikes, invite the antagonism of Settlers rather than their co-operation. The very qualities which make him "the little Emperor" of the fur trade, make failure inevitable in his successive ventures into farming.

Life along the Assiniboine River and the Red flows in steady, slowly expanding, pace. June and July see most of the population away on the spring Hunt, with 820 Red River carts. The Red River cart has become widely used during the preceding decade. It is readily made and repaired from local materials, by any man who is master of axe, saw, auger and draw-knife. The hubs are short-sawn lengths of elm, which do not easily split. An axle of oak is chopped to the desired size; and shaved round at each end. The hubs are bored to take the rounded axle-ends. The axle-ends are bored for wooden linch-pins, which hold the hubs in place. Ash is boiled and bent into shape for felloes; and cut in proper lengths for spokes. The wheel rims are wrapped with wet rawhide or "shaganappie", which dries to make a tight, hard tire — if somewhat rough. The 6-foot wheels are decidedly "dished", to give resilience to the cart on rough, bumpy trails. The wheels may be bound together, covered with hides and used to raft across waters too deep to wade. Atop the axle, thin split strips of poplar provide a floor. On this floor, assorted sticks make a box, 4 feet wide, by 6 feet long and 3 feet deep. Two poles for shafts and an oxbow of ash, boiled and bent, complete a cart that can carry half-a-ton anywhere an ox can pull it. The Red River cart — used for tripping, hunting, freighting, everything — is the vehicle universal!

Making and repairing Red River carts is a vital part of the life of every Assiniboia community. Big-scale manufacture of this ubiquitious vehicle centres at Grantown — where elm, ash and oak are big and abundant. Local craftsmen become expert; and take pride in the consensus that the best carts that roll on the trails across the Plains and through the mountains are those made on the Assiniboine, at Grantown. The tonnage freighted on their wheels soon equals, then far exceeds, that carried on the waterways. Hundreds of men from the parishes on the banks of the Assiniboine River and the Red, go each summer — with York boat brigades to "the Bay" and the far Saskatchewans; and with Red River cart trains, to hundreds of trading posts on the endless trails that rut the vast Nor'West.

Unknown to "Company" men or Settlers, an event occurs on 17 July, 1830, which profoundly effects the history of Assiniboia. On this day, William Sublette camps 700 miles south of "the Forks", at a spot that will become Gering, Nebraska. He is leading the first wagon train across the United States plains. The great migration to Oregon — which is to rob Canada of that lush region; and to drain Assiniboia of many fine pioneer families — is underway!

By 1830, the hunters settled along the Assiniboine, east and west from White Horse Plain, are recognized as the major providers of the pemmican and meat on which fur trade and Settlements depend. These hunters include people of all races and nationalities — and mixtures thereof. However, the Metis — children of Indian mothers and French-speaking Canadian fathers — become dominant, particularily south from "the Forks" on the Red; and westward, along the Assiniboine. Native to the country, they multiply in number more rapidly than other groups. The necessities of the Hunt teach them the cohesive and disciplined strength of trained organization, on tactical patterns devised by Cuthbert Grant.

In July, Governor Simpson decides to close Upper Fort Garry, which is in dilapidated disrepair. Decked sailing sloops from Norway House cannot ascend the Red above St. Andrews Rapids. Therefore, Simpson determines to build a new centre, Lower Fort Garry, on a fine, high site below the Rapids; and 20 miles down the Red from "the Forks". This is to be a new headquarters for "the Company"; and the centre of government for Assiniboia. Construction is begun on 5 spacious, solid stone houses, offices, stores and shops — enclosed by a loop-holed stone wall with circular bastions at the corners. It is to be the most imposing fort on the Plains.

Two mills — one erected on the old Fort Douglas site and purchased by Alexander Logan; the second built for Cuthbert Grant at Grantown — have, for 6 years past, utilized the winds that fan the Plains to grind grist for Settlers and "Company". Now, with expanding fields and bigger harvests, an increasing number of mills are operating. "Moulter", paid the miller for gristing, is fixed at 10% of the grist.

The little fields of Assiniboia are no sooner sown, than hunters move out on their spring buffalo Hunt. This Hunt is to supply the pemmican and dried meat needed for themselves and for sale to other Settlers and "the Company". Actually, the Hunt is made up of 3 parties. One party moves westward from Pembina. Their captain, very often, is the famous Baptiste Wilkie. This group is small during the 1830's, since many of the Metis have moved to Grantown. Second, the hunters from St. Boniface and "the Forks" outfit at Fort Garry; and move, westward, to cross the Assiniboine 11 miles upstream, at the Grand Passage — recruiting, en route, the hunters of St. James, St. Charles and Headingly. Third, the White Horse Plain party follows Cuthbert Grant down to the Passage, and southward. The second and third parties — men, women, boys, girls, babes, dogs, horses, oxen, carts, — noise and confusion — move south and west, via the Pembina Hills. At a rendezvous, Mass is celebrated by Rev. James Harper. (After 1831, by Rev. Boucher). The Hunt is then organized for instant reaction to news of buffalo — or Sioux. A "Government" is set up, with definite and absolute powers. Everyone — hunter, farmer and visitor; white and hybrid; old and young — is detailed a specific role in total action. There is danger on every hand. Within the camp is jollity, friendliness, security and law. From the Hunt, each cart brings home 500 to 1,000 pounds of the pemmican, dried meat and tallow which feeds both fur trade and Settlements. The fall Hunt, each September and October, follows this familiar pattern. More of the total population share in the Hunt than in any other Assiniboia activity. Thomas Simpson writes, on 19 December, 1831, "The plains hunters have a very successful season. The quantity of provisions they have brought home is immense. G. Nolin, St. Boniface, Bourke, St. James — and all the old hunters, were out with the Hunt".

The keen, calculating eye of Governor Simpson sees, in the ocean of grass around "the Forks", boundless opportunity for raising sheep; and exporting wool. His bouncing energy suggests another try at a new industry. Several retired "Company" men of means agree. They form a joint-stock Company; and raise $6,000.00 to buy sheep. On 2 November, 10 horsemen, with 2 loaded Red River carts, head south on this mission. The Assiniboia farmers who went south to buy seed wheat, 12 years ago, trekked by snowshoes, toboggan and boat, vehicles of the fur trade. These sheep-buyers of 1832 are mounted on good saddle horses. Harnessed to their carts are tough, alert and lazy Shaginappi ponies. The Governor sends John Ray of "the Company" to supervise the business; and, also, Robert Campbell, who has come from Perthshire to help manage the Company's Experimental Farm. The Settlers send John Bourke. Ray — young and enterprising; but lacking the experience of Bourke — thinks the older man haughty and over-bearing. They quarrel. Bourke retires from the leadership.

There is no difference of opinion about the necessity for speed and action. Each morning, the party hits the trail by 3 a.m.; and push their horses till sundown. Camped, they take turns as sentry; and are up and away, again, before sun-up. A Sioux war-party trails them for 3 days; but are left behind. By saddle and cart, canoe and sled — and, finally, on foot — these Assiniboia farmers trek 1,800 miles in 63 days. On 3 January, 1833, they reach a river-town bursting with 10,000 people. This is St. Louis. Refusing to pay $1.87, each, for sheep offered in Missouri, Ray leads the expedition another 450 miles, to Kentucky. Here, in mid-May, 1,475 sheep are bought. John Ray counts out the $1.25 to $1.75 per head, in English money. The flock is counted; marked; and headed for home — "drifting" an easy 10 miles a day. On 3 June, they cross the Illinois River, at Peoria. The route traverses areas infested with spear grass. The sheep go lame; and sicken. Ten to 20 give up, daily. Their throats are cut; the carcasses left on the trail. The flock is halted; and sheared. The wool is sold. John Ray thinks the Yankee buyers try to cheat him; and has the entire clip burned! More sheep give out. One morning, 44 are killed! By July, only 670 survive; by August, 295. On 10 September, the drive reaches Pembina. The moccasin telegraph advises the Settlements. Within 2 days, boats from "the Forks" arrive with provisions; and take aboard 60 lame sheep. On 16 September, 1833, these Assiniboia farmers are back home, after travelling 5,000 miles, in 318 days. They deliver 251 surviving sheep to "the Company" Experimental Farm. Here, many more die. The leaders of the expedition are thanked by "the Company" — but censured by the Settlers. The "Company" refunds to the shareholders the amount each has subscribed.

Many writers record the difficulty of re-casting Indians into the European mould. Indians seem to have only contempt for the Settler's work, until results appear. Then they demand a share. There are differing opinions about how the Indians can be helped to work out their own destiny. Many fur-men and Settlers believe that they are best left to themselves. Others criticize that, after Indians are baptized, they "itch for blue coats, red belts and frilly shirts". When they start to church, they become bossy, petty, dishonest and selfish. They will sacrifice all for alcohol. It is left an open question.

The basin of the Assiniboine "being exceedingly poor in fur-bearing animals, having been overwrought during the opposition" writes Governor Simpson, "was unoccupied from 1824 until 1828". Brandon House is re-opened, for a time, under Chief Trader Heron, "with 12 free-men and Settlers — as a temporary post". Such hiring of free-men and Settlers by "the Company" indicates the close integration of fur trade and Settlements. This year, "the Company" buys from Settlers: barley at 50 cents per bushel; butter at 14 cents per pound; flour at $2.62 per cwt; 6,000 pounds pork at 5 cents. Gunn reports that, while "prices of farm produce were thus reduced," the price of goods in which the farmers are paid, varies from 100% to 400% above prime cost in London.

In far-away Oregon, events move dramatically to rob "the Company", and Canada, of this vast and wealthy region. In 1832, Captain Benjamin Bonneville arrives in Oregon, posing as a fur-trader. Actually, he is a United States Army secret agent — one of many, whose mission is to possess Oregon for the United States.

The population of Assiniboia in 1833, one authority states, is "less than 2,000". A census, the previous year, records 2,751. The discrepancy emphasizes the impossibility of taking any accurate "census" of early Assiniboia. Rather than cover all of Assiniboia, early census counts are limited to that fraction close to "the Forks"; and limited further, to only a fraction of all the humans who regard Assiniboia as "home". An unknown percentage of all who have homes along the Assiniboine, particularily, are far away for months on end. No official can know "whither they come or whither they go". Further, the term "people" appears, sometimes, to exclude the majority of humans who live in Assiniboia; and to include only those whose ancestry is of some European mixture. The nomadic life of our native Indians is too elusive for statistics. Hybrid descendants of Indian mothers and European paternity, by this time, may be the majority of all Assiniboia's people. Some of these are full, or part-time, farmers. Many more have cabins along the Rivers, which are "home" between trips with cart trains, boat brigades and the Hunt. Many lead lives no less nomadic and elusive than that of the Indian.

Of more importance in Assiniboia's history, distinctions seem to be developing, already, between the hybrid peoples of various paternities. Hybrids sired by Canadians from Quebec are fiercely proud to be Metis, Bois Brules. . . "the New Nation" — and to speak, mixed with their mother Indian tongues, the French of their fathers. To some writers, this makes them (along with other French-speaking Canadians) "the French". Hybrids of English, Irish, Scot or Ontario-Canadian paternity tend to develop the appearance, follow the customs, and speak the English of their fathers. Lacking cohesive one-ness, they dissolve into the general population. Canadians who use the French language call all these hybrids — together with all the conglomeration of nationalities that father them — "the English". Thus is planted, in the semantics of swaddling Assiniboia, a seed of division which grows to challenge our Canadian nationhood.

Governor Simpson leads in the formation of the "Red River Tallow Company". His plan is an enlarged blueprint of an idea outlined by Selkirk, years before. Under this plan, flax and cattle will be raised on grandly expanded scale. The road will be built from Assiniboia to "the Bay". Each fall, flax and market cattle will sail the 300 miles down Lake Winnipeg. At Norway House, flax will be loaded into sleds made from local timber. After the first snowfall, the cattle, yoked to the sleds, will begin the 400-mile trek along the winter road to York Factory. Way-stations at the end of each day's march will provide food, fodder and shelter. At York Factory, the flax will be stored; and the cattle fed hay until the marshes provide rich summer pasture. In the following September, the fattened cattle will be slaughtered; the meat and hides pickled; and the fat rendered into tallow. All will be loaded onto "Company" ships; and delivered to English markets. Costs from Fort Garry to York Factory are calculated at 87 cents per 100 pounds. Simpson foresees big profits, which, "in due time, may surpass the fur trade!"

Settlers are invited to buy shares in the Tallow Company; to be paid up in cattle — valued at $5.00 for each 1-year-old; $10.00 for each 2-year-old; and so on. In all, 473 cattle are subscribed. They are branded "TT": "Tallow Trade". In April, 2 men herd the cattle 10 miles to the Pine Hills. (Probably Bird's Hill). It proves early to put cattle on grass. On 6 May, these sparse pastures are buried under an 18-inch snowfall; and 26 cattle perish of cold and starvation! As pasture improves, the cattle do well. In July and August, great quantities of hay are stacked. In September and October, trees are felled; and the logs built into strong corrals, to safeguard the herds from wolves, at night. It is a hard winter. Weather of 45 degree below zero and deep snow, kill 32 cattle. Despite all defences, the wolves get 53! In this first year, 111 cattle — 23% of the entire capital — are lost! Nevertheless, the shareholders determine to carry on. There is courage, as well as enterprize, in Assiniboia! During the winter of 1833-34, work begins on the winter road to York Factory. Timber is cleared from the roadway; and a start made on building way-stations.

In June, a new Governor of Assiniboia, Alexander Christie, arrives. He supervises the re-building of Upper Fort Garry with stone. The new structure includes a 15-foot wall, 280 feet from east to west; by 240 feet north to south, with bastions at each corner. The plan proves too small. Soon, it is necessary to add a square of similar size to the north end of the stone fort — with walls of horizontal squared logs.

From St. Francois Xavier, Rev. Boucher retires to Quebec. He is succeeded by Rev. C. Poire. The mission now serves 424 people. A new chapel is built; and the first service, therein, is on Christmas Eve, 1833. An extension is added in 1834; and, from this date, births, marriages and deaths are registered, regularily.

The administration of Assiniboia is taken over, completely, by officers of "the Company". Hitherto, free-men and hybrid hunters have found ready buyers for pemmican at 4 cents a pound, on a seller's market. As "the Company" cuts the numbers of voyageurs — due to tightly organized Monopoly; and displacement of canoes by York boats, larger craft and Red River carts — the displaced men become hunters. The increased number of hunters produces more pemmican than the local market will absorb. The hunters, particularily the hybrid people, blame "the Company". Tension mounts; and, during the Christmas festivities

— explodes! When Thomas Simpson, great Arctic explorer, hits La Rocque for being insolent, the Metis are enraged. Surrounding Fort Garry, they angrily demand that Simpson be delivered to them. Governor Christie, with Chief Factor Cameron, Robert Logan and Alexander Ross go to the hunter's camp; make concessions; and tender presents and money to La Rocque. As the winter weeks pass, the Metis needs and demands increase; become more insistent. Many free-men and Metis families are far out, wintering on the plains. Those left around "the Forks", enjoying their leisure, find time to discuss and magnify disappointments and wrongs.

Early in the summer of 1834, the "TT" spread moves to better pastures. Good sheds are built. Hay is stacked in abundance. Alexander Ross is made superintendent of the operation. After criticizing the faulty management of other ventures, he now has his chance. His canny super-vision does reduce losses. In a disciplined routine, every night herdsmen drive the cattle into well-built shelters, within high-fenced corrals. De-spite all defences, however, 16 cattle are lost to the cold; and 20 to the wolves. "TT" surrenders! During the year the price of "Company" land is raised from $2.62 to $3.12 per acre.

In a deal that is kept secret for years, "the Company" buys Assiniboia from Selkirk's estate. The price, paid in stock, may have been $425,000 for the half of the original grant which escapes the clutches of the United States. Assiniboia has put Selkirk's estate in debt for, perhaps, twice that amount. Hitherto, the Settlements have lived — not under formalized laws — but by good faith, good sense and goodwill of the various communities of Settlers. Now, all are yoked, by imposition of absolute Monopoly, to the will of owners 4,000 miles away. By orders from London, Councillors are commissioned to assist the Governor; and Courts, laws and police are organized.

The "Company's" Council of Assiniboia first meets on 12 February. There are present: Sir George Simpson, as President; Alex Christie, Governor of Assiniboia; Right Rev. Bishop of Juliopolis; Rev. E. T. Jones, Chaplain to the Company; Rev. William Cochrane, Assistant Chaplain; James Bird, former Chief Factor; James Sutherland, W. H. Cook, John Pritchard, Robert Logan, Alexander Ross, Sheriff of Assini-boia; John McCallum, coroner; John Burns, medical adviser; Andrew McDermot, merchant; and Cuthbert Grant, Warden of the Plains. In a presidential speech, Sir George forecasts a population of 5,000 for Assiniboia!

The Council sets up a volunteer police force of 60 officers and other ranks. Sheriff Ross is commander, at $100.00 per year. Assiniboia is organized into 4 districts, each under a Justice of the Peace. For district

4, up the Assiniboine, Cuthbert Grant is Councillor, Magistrate and Sheriff. Governor Simpson writes: "We allow him $1000.00 per annum as Warden of the Plains, which . . . . affords us the benefit of his great influence over the half-breeds and Indians". A courthouse and jail are ordered built inside Fort Garry; to be paid for with duties of 7½% on all imports and exports.

Throughout the wide-spreading Settlement, the population is grouping itself into three parties: first, the "Company" with its Establishment of hired and retired officials, servants and hangers-on; second, and most numerous, the hunters and the hunter-farmers; third, the farmer-hunters and the farmers. Advancing another step toward common usage, too, is the semantic division into "the English" (the Establishment and the landowners); and "the French" (the hunters and the hunter-farmers).

With the coming of spring, free-men and hybrid hunters demand higher prices for pemmican; free export of robes and tallow to, and imports from, the United States. These demands are pre-emptorily denied!

The wolves which beset the Settlements are multiplied by the tonnage of buffalo meat left on the Plains by the Hunt, each November. By midwinter, this abundant food supply disappears. Hunger drives the wolf packs to ferocious excesses. Only when the countless buffalo herds and the great Hunt become memories, will the wolf armies which feed on them dwindle, so that cattle may winter in the open.

Observers tell of astonishing amounts of tea consumed in the Settlements; and of the even greater amounts used by Plains hunters and Indians. The Saulteaux make tea by dropping hot stones into a bark kettle filled with water; and, when the water boils, throwing in tea by handsfull! Ashes are strained out, through a mat of reeds. It is a rugged brew! The Company indents, annually, for 100,000 pounds of tea — twice the amount of tobacco used. One record tells of an Indian camp of 84 adults and children, using, during one winter — 3,580 pounds of tea! Four Red River cart-loads!

Rebuilding progresses at Upper Fort Garry. Lower Fort Garry is "Company" headquarters for a time; but living quarters, granaries, stores, courthouse and jail are built in the Upper Fort. Hunters and traders gravitate to "the Forks". There are other stone buildings in the Settlement, including 2 Protestant churches, the Roman Catholic Cathedral and some fine houses built by retired "Company" servants.

Many Scot Settlers resent the fact that they have not, yet, got their own minister. This may be the reason that, this year, 114 of them emigrate to the United States — taking with them herds of cattle and other valuable property.

The year 1836 is a twelve-month of disturbance and disappointment. As usual, spring-time means sugar-making; while hay-making occupies the late summer. The Settlement is steadily expanding. Farms are scattered along the Red River, south to Pembina; and along the Assiniboine, westward toward Portage la Prairie. The number and size of fields increases on high, dry spots cleared within a mile or two of the Rivers. Development is not so rapid, however, as on the Pacific Coast. Settlers around Fort Vancouver, this year, grow over 42,000 bushels of grain and potatoes.

The first petty jury on 28 April, 1836, convicts Louis St. Denis of theft; and sentences him to be flogged. Settlers, free-men and Metis are outraged! They chase the flogger, until the police rescue him. Thereafter, no one will be flogger — except when masked; and within the protection of the prison walls! One authority writes: "The working of the Council at Fort Garry provokes the first desire of the people for self-government".

Free-traders, for years, have imported goods from England on "Company" ships, to sell retail. As agitation develops against the Monopoly, "the Company" restricts such imports. This is quite within the Monopoly rights of "the Company"; and puts those interferring free-traders in their obviously subservient position! Also, it frustrates the rebellious among the Settlers. It must be, however, that History enjoys its own Glooscap jokes; for, as so often happens, hardship uncovers a blessing in disguise. Enterprising free-traders, denied use of "Company" ships, blaze trails to Fort Snelling, some 400 miles to the south; and, on those trails, with Red River carts, open an expanding trade with the "outside".

Surveyor George Taylor this year begins the "Old Settlement Belt Survey". In the next 8 years, Taylor surveys 1,542 River Lots along the Red, from Selkirk to St. Norbert; and, along the Assiniboine, westward through the parishes of St. James, St. Charles, Headingly and St. Francois Xavier. No further surveys are made until after Confederation. On this survey, only base lines near the river are established. On those, the width of each lot is fixed. The rear line of the lot is, approximately, 2 miles back from the river front. Most of these River Lots are 12 chains (792 feet) in width — each being a holding of approximately 200 acres. Each owner has the exclusive right to cut hay on the 2 miles beyond his River Lot. This survey is a sure indication of the mounting interest of settlers in lands, for a dozen miles up the Red — and for 3 times that distance up the Assiniboine, where "high ground, westward" is above recurrent floods; and offers dry land for cultivation. Families already living along the Assiniboine, exercise "squatter's rights"; and lay claim to the newly-surveyed River Lots.

This year, June blankets the fields with snow. Intense cold freezes the river margins. On 19 August, hard frost kills any hope of a harvest. October is cold, drizzly and frozen. The fall Hunt fails. Fall fishing for sturgeon is bad. Then, November turns mild. Farmers plow their fields. No snow falls until after the New Year. The drought has begun, which is to span the next 10 years.

Two young women move onto the stage of Assiniboia's History, in early 1837. One in the gilded coach of Empire; the other on snowshoes. One, acclaimed by all the pomp and power of a conquering people, in the forefront of world leadership; the other, hearing only the harsh croak of a raven or the jumpy flight of a whiskey-jack, overhead; and, underfoot, the crunching raquettes of 2 dozen pioneers, trekking through the Canadian wilds. One is England's Queen, Victoria, beginning her long and glorious reign; the other is Mary, slight young bride of Oliver Gowler, who snowshoes from York Factory to Norway House — with her husband and a party of Lincolnshire farm families, on their way to build new lives in the unknown vastness of Assiniboia. Which contributes most to Canada, who can say?

The governing Committee of "the Company", in far-away London, dictates another experimental farm at "the Forks". Carefully selected farmers are indentured as "Company" servants; and brought across the sea to operate this new venture. Landed on the rock-bound coast of "the Bay", in the late fall, they survive the endless winter at York Factory. By early April, food runs short. The new-comers must snowshoe 300 frozen, wilderness miles to Norway House, to keep alive. Inexperienced and clumsy on their strange foot-gear, they flounder, mile after mile, day after day — over deep snowdrifts, rocky ridges, frozen waters, and around raging rapids. As they master the sliding lope of the raquetteur, each day they cover more miles; but each night are exhausted. Little Mary Gowler cannot keep up with the marching line. She starts out ahead, each morning; shares hot soup with the others at noon; and struggles after the party, until, in the settling northland twilight, Oliver comes back to help her over the final mile. Mary Gowler, and the other "tenderfeet" to this hard land, make that trek on sheer courage — pioneer courage!

When the ice moves out from shore, they voyage another 300 miles, in open boats, up Lake Winnipeg and the Red River, to report for work. Years later, the story is told that the slight little bride is Mary, daughter of Lord Braybrook; and her husband, Oliver Gowler, the butler with whom she is determined to share her life! In this party, too, are the Goods, the Kirtons and others whose names are writ large in the pioneer work which builds Assiniboia — a new community in our new Canadian nation.

Captain George Marcus Cary is sent — with little experience and a high salary — to supervise these 13 families of workers in operating the new experimental farm. On 80 acres of fertile river bottom, east of Fort Garry (known as the "Red River flats") a grand farmstead is established, with costly, imported implements. The Captain and his staff raise barely enough to feed themselves. The sole benefit to the Settlers is: the lesson that scythes are better than sickles, for harvesting grain! These "Company" farms suffer from troubles which appear to beset most efforts to put farming on a "big business" basis — from the days when vast slave estates in Africa accelerate the fall of the Roman Empire, down to the present. Cary is known as a theorist — and a thorough gentleman. He works manfully for 10 years, to make the farm useful to the Settlement.

In Assiniboia, Alexander Ross tells us: "Nature is luxuriant during June, July and August. In spring and summer, clouds of mosquitoes and bulldogs attack anyone who leaves the roads. Most of these pests disappear in August and September. Black houseflies cover everything, all the time." "The Forks" is the hub of Settlement; and divides people of European origins from those who have come from Canada; Indians; and hybrids. Here are seen the "Company" officials — with their beaver hats, broadcloth, silk and carpeted mansions. Canadian free-men wear a blue capote, with a red sash over it; and corduroy trousers. Metis wear the same, but with sash under the capote. Metis women are slender, mild and sedate; taller than the men; and comely. They wear gaudy shawls and a blanket. They marry young; and, at 30, look old.

The habit of the hybrid people of sharing all they have — reduces all to misery. In spring-time, the Settlers from Europe work day and night, to seed their fields. Canadians fish. Metis go hunting. They live a "ragged life". Canadian homes are clean. Metis houses are bare. All ages sleep on buffalo robes. All visit, gossip, smoke tobacco and drink tea. Those who have good horses and fine carioles are in their glory. They love bluster and banter. The children are raised on meat and tea. A Metis family squats on the bank of a stream or lake; clears a few acres to plant potatoes and grain; builds a cabin; uses the timber; and, in 1 year or many, moves on. The custom of the country entitles the squatter to collect from a successor a fair price for improvements made. The people of mixed parentage speak mixtures of the various Indian dialects and the tongue of their fathers; together with some French and some English. A local dialect is taking form, to be known as "Bungay".

From the Middlechurch, southward, Scot Settlers have good homes; and abundance. Each man stays at his own work. Each woman is in her own kitchen. Young Scots, however, are copying the Canadians — driving on the river-ice in winter "Like Jehu!" Some even "enter church, whip in hand, and pipe sticking in their pocket". During the winter, carioling is the universal pastime of the population. (A masterly picture, this — as revealing of Ross as of the Settlements).

The shareholders of "the Company" in far-away England, can be well satisfied with the operation of their Monopoly, on all fronts. In May, 1838, the Imperial Government guarantees renewal of their licence until 1859. The trade returns dividends of 25% — on the stock which has been split 4 to 1. Satisfactory. Quite so!

The reluctant development of Assiniboia under dictatorial Monopoly is a sorry contrast to the westward rush in the United States. Flexing their strength (to which they admit no limit) empire builders agitate for a railway to the Pacific. Financial panic and depression during 1837 and 1838 puts the brake on business in the eastern part of the Republic — but accelerates the exodus westward. New routes opened, and new posts built by fur traders, promote settlement. In the Pacific Northwest, Astor's American Fur Company works openly, with U.S. officials under cover, to take over the country by occupation. In Oregon, missionaries and settlers from eastern United States urge Congress to take possession, forthwith.

"The Company" does develop extensive farms; and encourages retiring servants to settle in Oregon. The efforts of privileged Monopoly
prove all too puny, however; and are swept aside by the on-rush of populous multitudes, determined to take possession — for themselves; and
for their new nation. The certainty that Oregon shall be lost to Canada,
is already taking shape.

Later generations will never know the menace of fire to the pioneer
families of Assiniboia. A spark from pipe or gun can set the autumn-
dried grass a-blaze with fires that roar down the winds for weeks —
encircling whole Settlements in an ocean of flame. Families, overtaken on
the Plains, are burned to death. Settlers, Indians, horses, cattle, buffalo
— are over-taken; and left, blackened cinders, when the flames sweep
on!

On 13 March, 1839, the name "Assiniboia" is re-confirmed by "the
Company" — "for that portion of the land within Her Majesty's colony
which had been sold to Lord Selkirk in 1811" . . . . and secretly bought
back.

To assert Monopoly, absolutely, the "Company" appoints Adam
Thom, "Recorder of Rupertsland" and judge in Assiniboia, at the
princely salary of $3,500.00 yearly. Thom is that type of "strong man"
so beloved by Monopolists. Word has preceded him to Assiniboia that he
is antagonistic to Canadians who speak French. The majority of Assiniboia's population are suspicious of him before he ever appears. After
arrival, his attitude and actions confirm their suspicions.

Construction of Lower Fort Garry, on the Red River below St.
Andrews Rapids, is completed this year. Built from stone quarried from
the river-bank, the Fort covers a spacious $4\frac{1}{2}$ acres. It is an imposing
structure, dominating the Settlements and the vast wilderness beyond.
Within its solid stone walls, 60 Company servants: storekeepers, farmers,
carpenters, clerks, brewers and saw-mill men — are ruled in precise
discipline, tolled out by a bell. Sir George Simpson, Company Governor-
in-Chief, and his 18-year old Scot bride, for a time grace the Lower Fort
with their residence.

Throughout the United States, the writings of Washington Irving and
the lectures of Jason Lee are generating tremendous interest in Oregon.
Thomas J. Farnum, with his "Oregon Dragoons", heads overland; and
Jason Lee leads 51 settlers by sea to Oregon. A wave of acquisitive
fanaticism sweeps the people of the United States to the brink of war
with England.

CHAPTER 6

Louis "David" Riel

The Grand Passage 1840-1849

In February, Thomas Simpson returns to Assiniboia, after 38 months of difficult and daring exploration in the unknown Arctic. On the trip home, he drives his dog-team 1,900 miles in 61 days, including all stops. During the spring, this intrepid explorer enjoys his well-earned rest; and works on his report. Suddenly, mystery enshrouds him. On 5 June he leaves Fort Garry, headed for England, via St. Paul. He departs hurriedly. Nevertheless, 5 days later, this great traveller has covered only 47 miles. On 15 June, 2 of his companions are shot; 2 others escape on horseback; and Simpson himself, is dead! The story gains credence that he goes beserk; shoots his victims; and commits suicide. The truth will never be known.

Rev. James Evans passes "the Forks," to take up his work as Superintendent of several Methodist missions, further afield. He becomes famous as the inventor of syllabic writing of Indian languages. With his co-worker, Rev. Henry Birk (a Chippewa raised by the Steinhauer family) he casts type from melted down tea-chests; and prints hymns and scriptures on sheets of birch bark. These are bound into books which carry the message of Christianity to the Indian tribes. Whether Indians call Evans "the man who makes birch bark talk," certainly, his little printing press, at Norway House, is the first in the whole Nor'West.

With the "inevitability of gradualness", English, Scot, Orkney and Canadian settlers (and their varied offspring with Indian wives) "took up all the land between Upper and Lower Fort Garry. Also along the Assiniboine in the parishes of St. James, St. Charles and Headingly, on both the north and south banks."

This spring, for the first time, "The bells of the Roman Mission" call to "the boatmen on the river and the hunter on the plain." A 3-bell chime is installed in the tower of St. Boniface Cathedral. The 180-pound bell, which Lord Selkirk had given the Cathedral in 1820, is transferred to a new church in St. Francois Xavier.

The expanding Assiniboia Hunt — plus armies of hunters in the United States — drive the buffalo herds further and further west and south. The Sioux, robbed of their homeland by successive so-called treaties, likewise, are pushed toward the setting sun. Never slow to assert rights; nor to avenge wrongs — the Sioux fight to defend their hunting grounds. Every cart train, every rider, venturing south of the 49th parallel, is a target for their attacks. "The Hunt," organized around the Metis, under Cuthbert Grant, is disciplined in both defence and offence. Every camp is a stronghold. If a Sioux war party kills hunters, retribution is swift and sure. Louison Vallé and his son, while cutting up buffalo, are attacked by 12 Sioux warriors. The father is killed. The son escapes to camp. A vedette of 10 Metis pursues the killers; and shoots 8 of them — never leaving the saddle!

In mid-June, the multitudes who are going on the Spring Hunt from the banks of the Red River, outfit at Fort Garry; and move westward, along the north bank of the Assiniboine. Hunters from St. James, St. Charles and Headingly join the noisy rabble. The St. Francois Xavier party moves eastward. All ford the Assiniboine, at the Grand Passage; and head southward. Near the Pembina Hills, the various mobs rendez-vous. There are 620 hunters, 650 women and 360 boys and girls — with 1,210 Red River carts, 655 horses, 586 oxen — and 542 dogs! This Hunt represents a capital outlay of $109,000; and current expenses exceeding $52,000. (In Centennial dollars, these sums would be multiplied by 20!)

Quickly organized, the Hunt moves westward, to the Cheyenne River. The scouts find buffalo in abundance. From one single "run," 400 hunters return with 1,475 tongues. Cutting up the 1,475 carcasses is the work of women, after men strip the robes off the dead buffalo. The choice meat is cut into long strips; pressed by hand into quarter-inch thickness; dried on wooden frames; and tied into 60-pound bundles, for winter use. The remainder of the best meat is made into pemmican. Bones are split and boiled for marrow. The tongues are sold to traders — who salt and paint them with molasses, for sale in St. Paul, a delicacy to delight Eastern gourmets. After 3 exciting weeks, the loaded carts come squealing home — with 1,089,000 pounds of choice meat. Many times that tonnage is left on the open plains — for the wolves! Of the enormous amount of meat brought home, "the Company" buys a few tons, at 4 cents per pound. Far more finds its way to inviting United

States markets. The abundant balance assures food for months, to all and sundry.

Throughout the 1840's, settlers from the United States push into the Assiniboine valley. Free traders, from "south of the line" invade the territory hitherto sacred to "the Company;" defy its Monopoly; and trade with farmers and hunters for grain and livestock, pemmican and buffalo robes. Many leading Metis and Kildonan Settlers become free-traders; cart Assiniboia products southward; and freight home goods to trade to hunters and farmers. Famous among Assiniboia free-traders is Andrew McDermot. It is told that "he can speak Indian better than the Indians themselves . . . Run like a deer, and endure cold like an Eskimo dog." Born in Ireland, in 1790, Andrew arrives at "the Forks" in 1812, with Selkirk's second party of Settlers. He serves "the Company" 7 years; then starts his own store. A natural trader, his genial honesty and keen sense of values, make him Assiniboia's wealthiest man, by 1840.

Many people of mixed parentage (particularly those whose fathers are Canadians from Quebec) move from Pembina to St. Francois Xavier, 16 years ago. Now, increasing numbers of Metis gravitate to Pembina, again. There, they escape the Monopoly which so handicaps and annoys Settlers in Assiniboia. Paying no duties on imports or exports, they roam and hunt wheresoever and trade with whomsoever, they will. In Assiniboia, to enforce their Monopoly, "Company" men break into homes; confiscate private property; and take prisoners to York Factory to be deported to England! Even reprimanding its officials and payment of damages by "the Company" cannot prevent resentment, once kindled, flaming into passionate talk and violent action.

Improved communications are being developed, between Assiniboia and the outside world. There are regular mails to Fort William. The summer route follows Lake Winnipeg, Winnipeg River, Lake of the Woods, Rainy River and Lake to Fort William, and via the north shore of Lake Superior, to Sault Ste. Marie.

Buffalo hunting is bringing Assiniboia to world-wide notice. Florists, botanists and geologists come, to follow the game trails. Officers of the "Guards", titled men and wealthy sportsmen come to Assiniboia to "run buffalo" with native hunters. These expeditions, added to spring and fall Hunts, leave scarcely a workman in the Settlements to help sow and harvest crops. By contrast, settlement booms in Oregon. In 1841, on the Willamette River, 120 farms provide 35,000 bushels of wheat, plus oats, barley and potatoes; and 3,000 cattle, 2,500 horses plus hogs and other livestock. Assiniboia Settlers are making the long trip over the Plains and through the mountains, to the Pacific coast. This year, James Sinclair leads a party of 116 people to Oregon, with all their possessions, including horses and cattle. Sinclair — a Scot with a part-Cree mother; and a degree from Edinburgh University — is a leader among the native-born Settlers in Assiniboia, in their fight against Monopoly; has been subjected to cruel "Company" retaliation; but still hopes to "keep Oregon under the British flag." However, these farm families from Assiniboia are smothered under the numbers from eastern States. The spring of 1841 sees more than 500 immigrants at Independence, Missouri, en route to Oregon.

Governor Simpson, on one of his high-speed tours — with 18 mounted men and spare horses for each — overtakes the party from Assiniboia, between Fort Carlton and Fort Edmonton. Simpson writes that they are "agriculturists and others, principally natives of Red River . . . 23 families, young and active. Each family has 2 or 3 carts, with horses, cattle and dogs. Men and lads in the saddle; covered vehicles carry women and children. In single file they extend over a mile. All healthy and happy, living in abundance; and enjoying the journey with the highest relish." Sinclair and his guide, Pierre Dumonais, plan to "proceed by the Saskatchewan and across the Kooteny portage." Characteristically, the "little Emperor" calls the men of the party to council with himself; and tells them to change their plan, and go by the Athabasca water route. Quite as characteristically, James Sinclair goes ahead with his own plan. His guides desert. He gets another: Mackipictoon, the Cree Chief, who leads them to Fort Vancouver ahead of the "galloping Governor". Simpson, in amazement, writes: "through a more southerly pass, shorter and better, so that even with families and baggage they cross in shorter time than we."

By enactment of the "Company" Committee in London, Assiniboia becomes a municipal district, bounded by a circle with a radius of 50 miles from "the Forks" of the Assiniboine River and the Red. While the area of Assiniboia is, thus, reduced to a fraction of its original size, the population is growing. One addition is the birth, this year, of Mary Ann Kirton, born in Kildonan. Her parents were among the 13 families who came in 1836, to operate "the Company" Experimental Farm, under Captain Cary. This babe is destined to become Mrs. Joseph Good, famous Assiniboia pioneer.

As more Metis move to Pembina, there is much visiting back and forth with kin, and friends. Some Assiniboia groups venture in their Red River carts beyond Pembina, to Fort Snelling. This expanding north-and-south traffic searches out the trail most useful to people more concerned with ease of travel than with time. The trail becomes well-marked, even well-travelled, from Fort Garry, westward, paralleling the north bank of the Assiniboine, to the vicinity of Headingly; and, there, crosses the Assiniboine at "the Grand Passage". From the Grand Passage, those shrewd and leisurely trippers cross streams flowing into the Red River, in their upper reaches, where grades are easier than down-stream. From earliest remembered and recorded times, north-south traffic follows this trail. The exact site of the Grand Passage is unknown to later generations. There are countless spots, from old Holy Trinity cemetery, east of Headingly, to the old Bremner farm, 3 miles upstream, where banks and river-bed offer fairly easy crossing. It is probable that cart trains use several of these. It is suggested that the route which offers the easiest grades, the driest ground and the best grass takes this age-old trail from the Grand Passage, southwest for some 24 miles, on a bearing of 230° from the First Meridian, to about section 16, in Township 8, Range 3; and, thence, south-south-east, at 160°, along the 800-foot contour shown on later topographical maps. In any case, the hub of east-west and north-south trail traffic, in the days before the River steamboats, is the Grand Passage.

This is a year of disaster for Canada, in the loss of strategic territory. By the Webster-Ashburton Treaty, on 9 August, British negotiators present Maine with a fist clutching northward, toward the St. Lawrence. Lord Palmerston calls it: "the Ashburton capitulation!"

Of more concern to Assiniboia and our Canadian West, is the march of United States settlers on Oregon. J. C. Fremont leads an expedition westward. His report (written by his wife, Jessie) generates tremendous enthusiasm. Business busts and panic in eastern States head people to the Pacific Nor'West in a flood, which will sweep away from Canada the lush lands of that vast region. By 1843, the boundary dispute becomes acute. In the spring, 875 settlers cross the Missouri, for Oregon. Throughout November and December they straggle into Fort Vancouver. Many of them owe their survival to Dr. McLaughlin, of "the Company". He provides them with supplies, advice and help. In return, he is robbed of everything — except his place in history!

The United States pioneers who, by their occupation and physical presence carry Oregon into the Union, are participating in one of the great mass movements of mankind's history. On 2 May, over 1,000 of them form a provisional government in Oregon. Strong feelings are violently expressed. Peter Burnett, later the first Governor of California, declares "with our trusty rifles we will drive out the usurpers". Canadians explored, settled and traded in Oregon before Burnett was born!

In Assiniboia, the pace of development lags; but a fine spirit of "togetherness" enriches pioneer life. When Mary Ann Kirton's mother dies, a neighbor, Mrs. Cunningham, takes the child. As she says, long years later — "Many families had children taken in, as I was. Later, Donald Polson and his wife adopted me."

Medicine is scarce in the Settlements. The use of some native remedies is learned from the Indians. Some medicines are supplied through York Factory, for the whole Nor'West. James Hargrave, at York Factory, writes Cuthbert Grant, on 5 September; "Dr. Gillespie has done his utmost to complete your order for medicine. It is forwarded in a case for Fort Garry."

A census of Assiniboia, taken in March, 1843, records a population of 5,143. There are 870 heads of families. Of this total, 571 (65%) are Indians or hybrids, 152 Canadians, 61 Orkneymen, 49 Scots, 22 English, 2 Swiss, 1 Welsh, 1 Italian, 1 Norwegian, 1 Dane, 1 German, 1 Pole and 1 from the United States. They live in 730 homes; an average of 7 persons per home. Their 1,570 horses, 3,894 cattle, 1,976 hogs and 3,599 sheep are housed in 1,219 barns. Their grain is ground in 18 wind-mills and 1 water-mill. No Irish are recorded, although John Bourke and Andrew McDermot, who came with Owen Keveny in 1812, are leading citizens of Assiniboia.

The number of voyageurs who live by the fur trade has decreased to a fraction of the thousands formerly employed. This results, first, from the union of the warring fur Companies; and, subsequently, from the displacement of canoes by York boats and Red River carts. Brigades of 4 to 8 York boats, each with a crew of 10, freight 1,000 pounds per man. Canoe brigades carry about 500 pounds per man. As trails are blazed to the south and Nor'West, "the Company" handles more freight by cart trains. A cart train can defend itself from attacking Sioux. Each cart carries about 1,000 pounds. One man handles four carts — with 4,000 pounds of freight. Also — whereas one-third of the freight carried by a canoe brigade is food for its voyageurs, cart trains are self-supporting. Prairie grass feeds the draft animals. Plains wildlife supplies the personnel with provisions. The "Company" pays freighters $4 to $4.50 per hundred pounds for the 500 miles between St. Paul and Fort Garry — "in goods at Fort Garry prices". More than 1,500 carts are employed, freighting between Assiniboia and St. Paul; and 500 more between Assiniboia and the Saskatchewan country. Thus, "the Company" employs 600 or 700 cart-men, in addition to 500 in the boat brigades. By extending credit to both voyageurs and cart-men, "the Company" keeps them bound by debt.

James Sinclair emerges as leader of those who oppose Monopoly. "Company" officials retaliate, by holding his shipments of tallow at York Factory, until they begin to spoil; and he must sell to the "Company" at whatever price they offer.

Norman Kitson, a Canadian born at Chambly, Quebec, opens a trading post at Pembina, where he is surrounded by Metis. From this headquarters, he weaves a growing business into the life of Assiniboia and of the Plains, southward to St. Paul. More and more Assiniboia Settlers venture into the one highly profitable enterprise; the fur trade. "Company" men battle, tooth and claw, to halt such invasion of their Monopoly. They shackle citizens with irons, in Fort Garry jail. They raise duties on imports of stoves and other necessaries. They cancel land titles. "The open and defiant free-traders came from St. Johns, Middlechurch, St. Andrews. They challenge the Monopoly of the Company" — with the indomitable courage which is the price of survival in Assiniboia.

Kitson may be the first to take Red River carts from Assiniboia to St. Paul. His 6 carts carry, southward, $1,400 worth of pelts; and freight, northward, $12,000 in merchandise. If Kitson leads the way, other and bigger cart trains follow on his heels. Freight rates, paid in goods at high markup, average 20 cents per ton-mile. Freighting outfits multiply.

At St. Boniface, is born Louis Riel. He is of mixed parentage; one of his 8 great-grand-parents being Indian. His father is "the miller of the Seine" and a free-trade leader. His mother is Julie Lagimondiere, daughter of the first white woman to adventure to the Nor'West.

The Sioux become increasingly hostile to hunters and freighters who invade their hunting grounds. Sioux war-parties kill Metis hunters from Assiniboia, again and again. Now the Metis strike back — killing 16 Indian warriors from 3 tribes. Sioux chiefs demand 4 loaded carts, to pay for the killing of their young men. Cuthbert Grant, the Warden of the Plains, sends his reply: "We defend ourselves — though you be as many as the stars; and as powerful as the sun."

The hunters of the plains are, now, the most important and most prosperous class in the Nor'West. The number of carts taking part in the spring Hunt increases from 540 in 1820, to 820 in 1830; and to 1,210 by 1840. In addition to the summer Hunt, from mid-June to mid-August, and the fall Hunt, through September and October, more and more hunters winter on the plains — to take buffalo hides for the expanding trade in robes and leather.

This summer, Lieut. Warre of the 14th Regiment, nephew and ADC to the Commander-in-Chief of the forces in Canada, and Lieut. Vavasour, Royal Engineers, pass through Assiniboia, posing as private citizens. Actually, they are on a secret mission: to assess "the capabilities of Oregon in a military point of view." They report that Sir George Simpson's "idea of transporting troops with stores through such country and the mountains quite unfeasible." The trails they so condemn are

those which Assiniboia hunters, traders and emigrants to Oregon trav-
erse as a matter of course. They lose 34 of their 60 horses, and under-
standably, believe such trails, "quite unfeasible".

The Council of Assiniboia, in June, imposes further restrictions to
enforce Monopoly. In a letter dated 29 August, 20 Settlers ask Governor
Christie to define their rights. The letter is signed by: James Sinclair,
Antoine Morran, John Dease, William Bird, John Spence, Atall Trot-
tier, Baptiste Farman, Baptiste LaRoque, Baptiste Wilkie, Alexis Goulet,
Peter Garrioch, John Anderson, Charles Hole, Louis Lontenre de
Batoche, Thomas Logan, John Vincent, William McMillan, Henry Cook,
Thomas McDermot and Joseph Monkman. The Governor replies in
"sweet words" — too vague to satisfy the Settlers. "The Company"
refuses to take any more freight for James Sinclair, whose name heads
the list. This is legal under the Monopoly. But — such action defeats its
immediate purpose; and, eventually, the Monopoly.

The stream of Settlers from eastern United States to Oregon becomes
a torrent. This spring, 3,000 cross the Mississippi River, heading westward. In March, the United States annexes Texas. In April, the dispute
with England over the boundary flares, again. Assiniboia's summer
Hunt is turned back at the 49th parallel, by United States cavalry.

The fall Hunt goes ahead — on the traditional hunting grounds.
Father Georges Antoine Belcourt, shepherd to the mission at St. Francois Xavier, writes: "Some (Metis) go into the interior; and live on deer,
moose and bear. Others keep to the rivers and lakes and hunt fur-
bearers, as well as buffalo. The result is that but one-third of our men are
available for the Hunt in the fall." Last summer's Hunt fails. The
hunters return with only one-quarter of their accustomed load.

For the fall Hunt, Father Belcourt arrives, on 12 September, at the
rendezvous, beyond Pembina. From a hill, he looks down on the camp
of 60 lodges, 300 horses and 100 oxen. He sees young hunters returning
to camp, loaded with game; children coming home from fishing; carts
loaded with firewood, spare axles, lodge poles, drying frames and hide
stretchers. On 14 September, the Hunt moves — between a second
party of Assiniboia hunters who are moving toward the mountains; and
a third, "in the Turtle Mountain and Souris River country." Their 213
carts move in three columns, at 200 yards interval. Each cart carries
long poles tied on top, for frames to cure meat and hides. Mounted men
range ahead. All re-unite at an agreed camp-site by sunset. These
plainsmen travel all day; and arrive, often after dark, at the chosen spot.
Shortly after camp is set up within the circular laager of carts, the Scouts
return. Two sleep on the prairie; and, in the morning, bring in a load of
fresh meat.

A herd of bulls is spotted. They pasture further apart than cows. The hunters trot to within 64 yards; then, quietly, walk their horses. At a signal, all charge! "The dense mass flees with surprising speed. Several fall with the first shots. Others, wounded and furious, stand at bay". After a 30-minute chase, the hunters return. When a herd of cows is seen, excitement explodes!

Under rigid discipline, the 75 hunters approach quietly within two gunshots. "Horses share the joy and ardour of their riders." Buffalo mass together, when attacked. To overtake the cows, hunters thrust through a solid phalange of bulls. This is dangerous. "Last year, an Indian, after his horse was knocked over, was tossed and re-tossed by an infuriated bull 20 feet into the air — caught each time on its horns."

Dangerous, too, are stray bullets flying in every direction, through the clouds of dust. The hunters fire with astonishing rapidity. Often, 3 buffalo are knocked over by a hunter within 100 yards. Some fire 5 times during a single chase. The hunter carries 3 or 4 bullets in his mouth. At full gallop, he pours powder into the muzzle of his gun; spits a bullet on top; strikes his gun-butt on the saddle, to force the round to the breech; primes his piece; and fires, point-blank, at the animal which his trained steed follows, by pressure of the rider's knees!

In the first chase, 160 cows are killed. The women and boys pitch camp close by. Next day, 177 are killed. On the third day, some riders rest. Those who go out, shoot 114 cows. Next day the harvest is 168 cows — a total of 628 cows killed in 4 days!

To dress the carcass, a hunter props the dead buffalo on its knees; and spreads the hind legs — so that the animal is supported on its belly. First, the petite bosse (a small hump about 3 pounds; and a prime delicacy) is taken off. Next, the hide is slit down the back and removed. The meat is butchered into 16 standard cuts. All else is left to the wolves. The tonnage of meat left to waste is appalling. The wolves multiply astonishingly; and, when this food supply is devoured, kill cattle, sheep and dogs; and threaten the entire Settlement. The hunters go to this hard work with will and skill. Many a hunter will kill and dress 10 buffalo in less than 10 hours, alone!

The meat is cut up by the women, into long strips; hung on pole frames to dry. The choice strips are rolled into bundles. The rest is pounded into powder on a hide, shovelled together with melted fat; packed into sacks made of the raw hides. This is the pemmican that feeds Settlers and fur-men; and is traded to both "Company" and free-traders. A cow makes about 90 pounds of pemmican and jerked meat. Ten cows are killed to make up a cart-load. Hides are stretched, scraped and dried by the women, to make parchment and teepees. Men crack and boil bones, to get the marrow for frying. The marrow from 2 cows, stored in a bladder, weighs about 12 pounds.

On 25 September, at the Cheyenne River, immense herds pasture — 30 animals per acre "as far as the eye can see." In pursuing a herd at full gallop — suddenly, horses, hunters and buffalo avalanche over a rocky cliff! Among the rocks and the hammering hooves, only one man is knocked unconscious; a couple of horses are lamed; and a few buffalo suffer broken legs. The thrown hunters spring to their saddles, again; and gallop after the Hunt!

The Hunt starts for home on 16 October. The carts carry the meat from 1,776 cows. At current prices, the harvest is worth $8,500; expenses total $1,000; net earnings are $7,500. Averaged among 55 hunters, this means: 32 cows killed; and $137.00 earned, per hunter. All are wealthy — for a time!

On 24 October, the carts break through the marginal ice; and splash across the shallow Assiniboine, at the Grand Passage. Within hours, all are safe at home; and working feverishly, to get ready for winter! No wonder Assiniboia natives — Indian, white and hybrid — love the Hunt: the hard, dangerous and thrilling basis of life in the Nor'West!

The year 1846 brings a succession of epidemics; in January, flu; in May, measles; in June, the bloody flux. From June to August, deaths average 7, daily. A total of 321 died. Of these, one-sixth are Indians, one-sixth, whites; and two-thirds, people of mixed parentage.

"Hayfield" ends its 10 years as an Experimental Farm. Before Captain Cary moves to Canada, he voices a suspicion — shared by many — that "Company" men are determined that the farm must fail; and the Settlement remain stunted. "Company" servants, after completing their indentured service, take up farming on their own; and prosper!

In May, the artist Paul Kane travels with a party of Metis, from "the Forks" to the Missouri River Coteau. Steamboats ply the Missouri, crowded with passengers on their way to the frontiers. This spring, 2,000 settlers leave Missouri River towns, overland, in the invasion of Oregon. Leaders in Canada are aware of the inevitable consequences. John A. Macdonald writes: "The United States is resolved to do all — short of war — to get possession of the Western territory." All over the United States, an election campaign screams the slogan "Fifty-four — forty — or fight!" Voters approve. The Mexican War, declared in May, whips people into combative ecstasy. War against England, for Oregon, appears inevitable, imminent! Fortunately for both countries, their representatives hastily compromise. The interests of Canada are sacrificed on the altar of appeasement. The United States gets all territory south of the 49th parallel. Vast regions, which the old French régime made part of Canada, are donated, by English negotiators, to the aggressive Republic.

Peter Garrioch, on 28 May, jogs along the trail up the Assiniboine River to "Mr. Belcourt's", in St. Francois Xavier. En route, he adds 8 names to a petition to be presented to Queen Victoria. This petition — signed by 977 Settlers — challenges the "Company" charter and Monopoly; charges mismanagement; and prays for freedom from "Company" tyranny.

In June, this petition reaches the Colonial Secretary, Earl Grey, through A. K. Isbister. The Imperial authorities, advised by "Company" friends, appear annoyed that "an element in Red River kept protesting against the Company, through Isbister." Another cause for annoyance is talk of reciprocity between Canada and the United States, following repeal of British preference for grain, flour and timber — and the resulting destruction of 75% of Canada's trade. These Canadian colonials are becoming much too vocal in their own affairs!

Governor-in-Chief Sir George Simpson re-doubles his urging that British troops be sent to Assiniboia. His argument is "Oregon." His purpose (probably) to overawe "agitators" among the Settlers. In any case, on 17 September — months after the Oregon crisis is resolved — 6 York boats arrive at "the Forks", carrying British troops. Landing at York Factory on 7 August, they come up the rivers and lakes to Fort Garry, in 41 days. The contingent includes elements from the 6th Regiment of Foot (Warwickshires), Royal Engineers and Artillery. Personnel totals 18 officers and 329 other ranks — plus 17 women and 19 children. The force moves under secret orders. Nine guns are included with supplies, munitions and equipment.

The Officer Commanding this expedition is Major John Folliott Crofton. He does not like Assiniboia — nor its people. He writes to his wife — "I am disgusted with the ill-bred and vulgar folks here. Dislike having them to our table; but am necessitated to be hospitable. The place is squalid. Homes of the best Settlers have heaps of dung and dirt about their doorsteps." The coming of the soldiers causes a flutter in those hearts which beat for "society" (at various levels). A more solid result may be the increased markets for supplies; and the increase of $75,000 in circulation of cash. Settlers welcome these benefits; but many are still suspicious that Sir George wants the troops, to back him in coercing Settlers who defy him and "the Company" Monopoly. The harvest is disappointing. The local grain crop cannot meet increased demand. Flour is freighted in, by canoes, from Canada for the garrison. Donald Gunn, Rev. A. Cowley, and others, experiment with new methods and seed.

In England, A. K. Isbister and 5 other men of mixed parentage, write to Earl Grey, Secretary of State for the Colonies, charging "the Company" with oppression. Naturally, such charges are denied. Naturally, too, the superior echelons in Government understand the upper echelons who control "the Company." They are friends; often, colleagues. They speak the same language. Quite different from those annoying colonists; from — where is it? "Assini — something"? Then, there is Major (now Lieut-Colonel) Crofton, who has just returned from that place. Capital fellow, Crofton. He agrees: these people must be kept in hand! Quite!

Small wonder that 570 Settlers petition the Legislative Assembly of Canada for action which shall free Assiniboia from the throttling grip of Monopoly. This petition, like those to the Imperial Government, apparently, fails! To circumvent "Company" regulations and censors — free-trader James Sinclair forwards his mail via the American Fur Company through Francois Reinville. Other Settlers take advantage of similar methods, to defeat the Monopoly.

With the Pacific Nor'West lost to Canada, Governor Douglas of "the Company" moves headquarters to Fort Victoria, on Vancouver Island. In amazing contrast to the flat failure of successive Company farms in Assiniboia, on the Pacific coast, under the dynamic management of Douglas, the "Company" operates 7 farms of over 3,000 acres; mines coal; saws lumber and ships it to San Francisco; and raises the price of land to $5.00 per acre.

While settlers in Assiniboia are isolated by geography and Monopoly, the people of Canada's 3 maritime provinces build ships in every cove and harbour. These ships carry timber to England; flour, potatoes, salt fish and lumber to New England and the West Indies; bring home rum and molasses in trade; and adventure to the goldfields of California and Australia. The free-traders and free-men of Assiniboia — in similar freedom and for similar distances — in their home-made Red River carts — roam the vast grassland ocean of the great Plains! Many a family drives away from their cabin on the Assiniboine in the spring; and, with slow-moving cattle, covers 3,000 miles, before returning in the fall.

A Red River Library is inaugurated, 30 September, 1848, by Donald Gunn in his St. Andrews Home. It is built upon the 500 volumes bequeathed by Peter Fidler; and a grant of $250.00 from "the Company". Fidler's bequest of scientific instruments expands the scope of Gunn's scientific studies.

The garrison of British regulars moves from Assiniboia. A storm of criticism in Canada and in the United Kingdom, impels "the Company" to say the right word to the right people in London to have the force recalled. The regulars are replaced by ex-soldier pensioners from Chelsea Hospital. Some 70 of these pensioners arrive in the fall. A second contingent follows. The Officer Commanding this force is Major Caldwell. The "Company" appoints him Governor of Assiniboia. "A slow-witted and irresolute man — he is not a success."

Use of rum by the "Company" raises a storm of controversy, which rages for generations. Sir George Simpson testifies before a House of Commons Committee, in London, that annual imports into Assiniboia average 5,000 gallons — 3,320 gallons for the inhabitants; and 1,660 gallons for "the Company", for "an occasional dram to Indians employed, or for provisions, where we cannot get them otherwise." Governor Pelly affirms that for "the troops" at Red River — the daily ration required annually "was upwards of 4,500 gallons", which would provide 50 quarts for each regular soldier; or, 120 quarts for each pensioner. Compensation, perhaps, for the low pay doled out to these men?

A census, taken in 1849, reports Assiniboia's population as 5,391. This is 248 above the 1843 total. Apparently, Indians are excluded; also, unknown numbers of families who have homes along the Assiniboine River and the Red — but who live much of their lives wandering far away. Nearly half the recorded population is under 15 years of age. Of 1,012 women over 15, only 135 are unmarried. Of the 5,391 people counted, 91% are of other than Selkirk Settler origin. Some 1,511 non-residents are noted — of whom 636 emigrate to the United States; and 875 live on the plains. Settlers cultivate 6,392 acres; and have 12,760 head of livestock. Barns and stables number 1,401. Outside the 745 houses stand 1,918 vehicles; nearly 3 Red River carts to every home! There are, in addition, 428 canoes. The 2,600 boys and girls are taught in 12 schools. Grain is ground in 2 water-mills and 18 wind-mills. Private subscriptions, exceeding $32,000.00, have built 3 churches of stone, 3 of wood and 3 meeting houses. Up the Assiniboine, Grantown is growing rapidly. In this community of hunter-farmers, in 16 years, population has trebled, to 914; and cultivated acres have doubled, to 526.

The battle of Settlers against Monopoly crescendos to a climax when "Company" men arrest William Sayer, son of an old Nor'West bourgeois, along with McGillis, Larone, and Goulet — for trading goods to Indians for furs. The trial is set for 17 May. This day marks a long mile in the history of Assiniboia — and of our Canadian nation. Louis Riel "the miller of the Seine", of French-Irish-Indian parentage leads Metis, who assemble at St. Boniface Cathedral, across the Red River (in boats supplied, probably, by James Sinclair) and march to the courthouse outside Fort Garry. Here they are joined by hybrid men from St. Andrews, Kildonan, Middlechurch, St. James, St. Charles, Headingly and St. Francois Xavier. One account reports "400 armed men surround the courthouse". Another: "377 guns were counted". One writer even calls this "the Red River Rebellion of 1849". Reference to "armed men" may serve to build up drama, until it is remembered that most of the farmer-hunters and hunter-farmers carry guns, habitually, in these days.

The Governor, Judge Thom and the Council of Assiniboia are seated, with due solemnity, by 11 a.m. After waiting an hour, the court asks the men of mixed parentage to select a leader to bring in Sayer, the first accused. James Sinclair and 11 others enter, with Sayer. Twenty men stand at the courthouse door. Yes, they are "armed"! And, in justice to the dramatic, let us hasten to add that the "Company" law-men are, likewise, "armed"; and the courthouse, itself, is under the cannon of the "Company" Fort! Sayer confesses trading with Indians for furs. The Court pronounces him guilty. Then Sayer proves that Herriot, a "Company" Officer, gave him authority to do so! The Court withholds sentence. The others are never tried! All leave the court-room — free men! As they emerge a shout goes up: "Le Commerce est libre! The trade is free!"

English-speaking, French-speaking, Indian-speaking — all rejoice. Tyranny is broken! Trade is free! The people are free, free to build their Settlement as their enterprise may dictate. True, the legality of Company ownership drags on for another 20 years. But from this day, Monopoly withers in Assiniboia. Adam Thom shrinks from "Recorder", or judge, to mere secretary of the Court. The Court, itself, loses authority.

Within 2 months, the British House of Commons begins an inquiry into the "Company". The learned law officers of the Crown, naturally, back the "Company". Earl Grey invites A. K. Isbister, and others, to appear against the Company, and to bear all the costs of a test case. Isbister is 27 years old; just getting started. He cannot command finances of such magnitude. Even after he visits Lord John Russell, on 30 September, 1849, it is ruled that the petitioners must pay all costs; and that the validity of the Company charter must not be questioned. This effectually side-tracks Isbister, since challenging the validity of the charter is his prime purpose. The Imperial Government refers the 2-year-old petition of 1847 to the Company Committee, in London. These worthies give their assurance that "everything is fine at Red River". What else *would* they say? Such Imperial manoeuvres are, now, mere shadow-boxing. In Assiniboia, for all practical purposes, the Monopoly is ended. While the "Company" police are still active, no further attempt is made to enforce Monopoly through the courts.

The French-speaking and English-speaking Canadian-Indians become more militant under new leaders — James Sinclair for the English-speaking hybrids; and Louis Riel for the French-speaking Metis. Demands are made that Adam Thom be retired from the court; and that 12 representatives of mixed parentage be appointed to the Council of Assiniboia, to make it representative of the vast majority of the population. In due course, Judge Thom is removed. Major Caldwell, Officer Commanding the Chelsea Pensioners, and the Company's Governor of Assiniboia, takes over as Judge. The Company "almost ceases to enforce their Monopoly claims".

Along with Thom and his court, the Council of Assiniboia is discredited. As Magistrate and Councillor, Cuthbert Grant sees his overall authority dissolve; and his pervasive influence disappear. Sir George Simpson and "the Company", having used him, now cancel his land titles; and discard him — thereby calling new and more dangerous leaders into battle.

The long fight against Monopoly awakens interest in land titles. Chief Factor Ballenden writes to Sir George Simpson: "Title deeds will, in the eyes of the Settlers, give value to that which they considered almost valueless — their land." Enterprising Settlers realize that the shattering of Monopoly will allow scope for individual initiative; and will release, for resource exploitation, energies which have been shackled by regimentation. Reports reach Assiniboia that change is astir, too, in Canada. Rioting mobs burn the Parliament buildings in Montreal; and a Manifesto is circulated, urging annexation to the United States!

Ancienne église de St.Charles (renversée en 1884 par la tempête)
Sketched from drawing in "Vie de Mgr Tache, O.M.I."

In Assiniboia, after the free trade victory, "discouragement and slow decay vanish." Farms and homes stretch for 50 miles along the Red River; and for 70 miles along the Assiniboine. A profitable export market has always beckoned beyond the boundary. Now, free of stifling Monopoly, "open trade with St. Paul develops." Free-traders expand their operations to cover the entire Nor'West. They deal, openly, in all products — including fur — in free competition with each other; and with "the Company". Fur still promises biggest, quickest profits. But "the Company" no longer tyrannizes life and development. Settlers are no longer fenced in by the dictates of "the great nabobs of the fur trade." Assiniboia is free — free to harvest vast and varied production from prolific lands and waters; and to become far more than a "Battlefield for Fur."

PART 3

Buffalo to Bushels

YORK BOAT
ON THE
ASSINIBOINE

Canadians and Bois Brules
encamped outside St. Paul, Minnesota, 1858.
(From an old engraving)

Archbishop Tâche

CHAPTER 7

Up The Assiniboine 1850-59

Monopoly is dethroned. In the fresh, exhilarating air of freedom, Assiniboia stirs with new life. The realization that "le Commerce est libre" revives dreams of this community — not as a foundling on the doorstep of "the Company", doomed to a pauper future by an embarrassed sire; but as a new-born opportunity for countless peoples to build a new life . . . . in a new nation.

Increase in population is slow. In Upper Canada the 95,000 inhabitants of 1814 multiply to 950,000 by 1851. In the same period, Assiniboia grows from, perhaps, 2,000 to 6,000. Ruthlessly selective distance, climate — and Monopoly — brake development. Nevertheless, settlers steadily spread out to build homes, particularily westward, up the Assiniboine.

Among older communities, St. Andrews, established under Rev. William Cochrane in 1829, continues to "flourish beyond all other English (speaking) parishes". Thereto gravitate retiring "Company" officials — with native wives, families of mixed parentage and substantial wealth. Along the high left bank of the Red River, overlooking the Rapids, they build for themselves "stately mansions" of native stone. (To stand for 100 years). Along the River Road these members of a select squirearchy drive in splendid carriages, drawn by spans of beautifully-groomed horses; and followed by spotted English coach dogs. At a private school, their daughters learn to curtsy and play croquet. Here they build a bit of old England — as truly as solid substance and fond memory can make it.

However, it is westward, up the Assiniboine, that expansion is most remarkable. George Taylor's Old Settlement Belt Survey, 15 years ago, laid out 1,542 River Lots — along the Red from Selkirk up to St.

Norbert; and up the Assiniboine to beyond St. Francois Xavier. Averaging 200 acres each, these surveyed lots cover some 300,000 acres.

Up the Assiniboine, Taylor's survey includes the holdings of many squatters. Abundant wood for fuel and buildings; unlimited hay for livestock; and the river providing a highway, summer and winter — attract hunters, hunter-farmers, farmer-hunters and farmers, alike. White men have roamed its pleasant reaches for generations. How many build snug log homes upon its wooded banks, nobody knows. Some use their cabins merely as headquarters between spring and fall Hunts, trips with cart brigades or "wintering out" on the plains. Others occupy these homesites permanently. Some clear and cultivate patches of potatoes and grain.

After the survey, some of these Settlers assert "squatter's rights" to the River Lots which they occupy. Many talk about securing title — but never do. After all, one can always trade "improvements" to someone else; and move to another pleasant place in this vast land of limitless meat and fur. How many come; settle; raise families; and move on — leaving no record but empty cabins and little over-grown fields, can never be known. The universal human hatred of imposed restraint; love of personal freedom; and the challenge of adventure, suggests that the number is greater than is commonly conceded.

Among the earliest parishes "up the Assiniboine" is St. Francois Xavier. Begun 24 years ago, by 1833 the 434 parishioners build a new chapel of oak logs. Rev. C. E. Poire holds the opening service, on Christmas Eve. Father Georges Belcourt and Rev. J. B. Thibault labour, successively, on the woodwork. Last year's census records 914 people in the parish. Almost certainly, many Indians and absentee hunters and voyageurs are missed. This year, 2 Grey Nuns come from St. Boniface to teach 80 Indian pupils at the Convent school.

Upstream from St. Francois Xavier the parish of Baie St. Paul is established by Rev. Georges Belcourt, for the Saulteaux Indians domiciled between Lake Manitoba and the looping reaches of the Assiniboine River. Company lands are allocated to the mission by Governor Simpson, at Fournier's Prairie. By September, 1833, a church, house and school are built. The following year, Angelique Nolin — one of 5 daughters of the Pembina trader, educated in eastern Canada — comes home to be the first school teacher. The mission is provided with oxen by Bishop Provencher. Some 30 Indian families seed plots of grain. Subsequently, Father Belcourt employs his command of Indian tongues to publish primer and catechism in Chipewyan.

Many of the servants brought to Assiniboia by "the Company" are Orkney-men. (Written "Orkanie"). On completing their indentured service, these sturdy pioneers take up River Lots — at first, along the Red; and, after the 1830's, up the Assiniboine. By 1843, they number more than any other group of whites in the Settlement, except Canadians. In 1848, lands extending above Armstrong's Point are assigned to the garrison of Chelsea pensioners. The increasing numbers of ex-Company Orkneymen leap-frog upstream. Some of them had tilled fields around the fur forts where they had been engaged. With their native wives, they build snug farmsteads, lush gardens and trim fields — up to Omand's Creek; and, on, westward. With the pioneer readiness for nick-names, this community is called "Orkneytown". By 1850, the number of its families call for a mission.

To fill the need, Rev. W. H. Taylor starts the Anglican mission of St. James, in November. The following spring, work begins on building the rectory, which is completed in 1852.

On a beautiful site on the left bank of the Assiniboine, some 2 miles above "the Forks", St. James church is built of stout oak logs. Settlers like Neil Henderson (who farms near the later site of Maryland bridge) fell and trim the timbers near Poplar Point; raft them down to the church site; and build them into a strong and solid structure. The new church costs $1,620 in money — plus volunteer labor beyond computing. The new parish is financed by "The Society for the Propagation of the Gospel", in England. Books, plate and cash come from generous donors in the Old Land.

Census-takers in early Assiniboia face an impossible task. Only a fraction of the population is "fixed". Officials of "the Company" and some free traders are locateable. A few families farm, full-time; and their numbers can be counted. By contrast, the majority of "Settlers" in Assiniboia are "at home" for only parts of each year. For unpredictable periods their whereabouts is uncertain, unknown. This is inherent in the hunting, fishing, tripping and trading which is their life.

After the two big fur Companies merge in Monopoly, hundreds of their discharged servants stream out of the great Nor'West to "the Forks". Many of them remember the beautiful Assiniboine River; and locate on its wooded banks, below White Horse Plain — among Canadian free-men who came a generation earlier. Metis families, drifting northward from Pembina toward Grantown, join them. The homes scattered along both banks become "the Village". When there are "some 50 families" in the community, Father Louis F. R. LaFleche, serving in St. Francois Xavier parish, organizes building of a log chapel, "where the Metis hunters worship on Sundays". The number of families steadily increases; and, in 1854, the mission becomes the parish of St. Charles.

Eastward from White Horse Plain, settlers on the north bank of the

Assiniboine raise a church of logs — on a grassy glade sheltered by a grove of towering elm, ash and oak. This is Holy Trinity. The rector is Rev. Griffith Owen Corbett. He arrives in 1851; and names the new parish "Headingly", after his former charge in England. He serves here, for 14 years.

Higher up the Assiniboine, new parishes take form. Archdeacon William Cochrane is a moving spirit in building these new communities. In 1851, St. Mary's of the Prairie is established as a parish centering on Portage la Prairie; and a school of local timber is built. St. Anne's parish is founded around Poplar Point; and St. Margaret's in the High Bluff district.

All this is done in defiance of Governor Simpson, of the still-powerful Company. He does not like new settlements built beyond his immediate control; they might be centres for free traders! But Cochrane goes ahead. He is as determinedly dedicated to the work of his Master as Simpson is to making profits for his bosses in London.

By 1850, some 6,432 acres are cultivated, along the Assiniboine River and the Red. The Settlers form an Agricultural Association. They want to grow better cattle. The herds are small. Only one farmer has more than 42 head. In our harsh climate, imported cattle weighing over 1,000 pounds — in a generation or 2 are producing oxen of barely 700 pounds. Here, the best ox can be bought for $30.00; and good cows for $20.00 a head. Few Settlers raise hogs. Sheep suffer heavily from wolves and dogs. Pork and mutton bring 5 cents per pound; beef 4 cents. Butter sells for 14c a pound; cheese, 10c; and eggs for 12c a dozen. Wheat, weighing up to 70 pounds per bushel, brings 87c; barley, 50c; oats, 37c; and potatoes, 58c per bushel. No farm output is exported. Production barely meets local needs. In winter, food prices rise 50%. Horses find a brisk market. A good horse brings $125.00. From 1850, onward, horses and cattle are "drifted" southward, to be sold at good prices in the United States. On our farms, most of the work is done by the family. Some farmers hire hands — at $100.00 per year; women workers at $2.50 a month; and day workers at 37c. In seeding, haying and harvest times, wages jump to 62c a day, plus food and a blanket to sleep on! Tradesmen, throughout the year, earn 75c to $1.25 per day. We have in the Settlements: 4 blacksmiths, 3 carpenters, 2 millwrights and 1 mason.

In the homes that face the Assiniboine River and the Red, life is simple. Candles, bannock, pemmican, spinning wheels and weaving looms are in every home. Debating societies and "sociables"; old dances and Red River jigs; chansons from Quebec and church activities are recreation for mind and body. Weddings, Christmas and New Year holidays are celebrations. Visits to Pembina or treks to St. Paul — by

Red River cart in summer and dog-sled in winter — are occasions to be remembered.

The year 1851 brings to Assiniboia outstanding men to minister to spiritual needs. Rev. Alexander Tache comes to the parish of St. Boniface. In September, Rev. John Black arrives; and, at long last, the Scot settlers have their own minister. The "Company" grants them land down the Red; and $750.00 in cash, plus $250.00 yearly. The congregation of 300 could be happier only if Rev. Black "had the Gaelic". Down the Red River, by canoe from Montreal, paddle two surveyors: Herbert L. Sabine and William Lonsdale. Through long, useful years both help many concerned in such temporal items as land titles.

In this year, too, an event — 500 miles away; and totally unknown to many of our people — gives new direction to the whole development of Assiniboia; and to the history of our Canadian West. This June, as usual, the summer Hunt takes hundreds of Assiniboia's people from their homes. With hundreds already away in cart brigades, this Hunt is smaller than formerly. The St. Boniface hunters, with Father Lacombe on his first trip to the Plains, rendezvous with hunters from Pembina. The combined parties total 318 hunters, plus women and children. On 16 June, they head westward. Meantime, some 67 hunters from Grantown — with their women and children in 200 carts; and accompanied by Father LaFleche — cross the Grand Passage; and head south and west. On 20 June, all rendezvous. The St. Boniface and Pembina hunters, believing that Cuthbert Grant betrayed them at Sayer's trial, hunt independently. Nevertheless, for mutual support, the two Hunts follow parallel routes, 30 miles apart.

Small Sioux war parties are driven off. On 12 July, the Grantown Hunt reaches the Missouri Coteau — separating the Assiniboine drainage basin from the Missouri. A scout patrol discovers a great Sioux camp. The Sioux pursue, and capture 3 of the scouts. The Sioux warriors number 2,500 or more. In the Grantown Hunt are 77 who can handle guns — counting 12-year old boys! Galloping Sioux attack the lines of carts. With trained precision, oxen and horses are whipped to a gallop; and, in a hollow beside a pond, the 200 carts of the Hunt wheel into a circle, shafts pointing outward. Quickly, this barricade is reinforced with the long poles carried for drying meat and hides. Women hurriedly dig pits beneath the carts; and drag the children into their shelter. The cart barricade gives little protection from fire. Its purpose is to fence out the Sioux horsemen; and to fence in the livestock. The men (and boys) dig rifle pits 70 yards outside the laager — to hold the attacking Sioux beyond range of the draft animals. If horses and oxen are killed, none of the Hunt shall ever see, again, their beautiful Assiniboine.

The Sioux attack, wave after wave. The hunters from their rifle pits shoot them as they come over the skyline. Father LaFleche mounts a cart in the laager — waves a hatchet; and shouts encouragement to his people. Mounted Sioux gallop around the cart-circle; charge in; shoot; and swerve away. Others creep through the grass to snipe horses and oxen. One by one, the hunters pick them off. The Sioux charge en masse — hoping to stampede the livestock. The riflemen shoot down this final, desperate onslaught. The sun sets. Night falls. The moon rises; and moves into eclipse. All watch, wondering. The 3 captured scouts break for freedom! Two of them reach the laager, shooting down pursuers at the gallop! The third, on a slower horse, is cut down — with 3 bullets and 67 arrows! A patrol of 30 horsemen discover a Sioux sneak attack; and gallop back into camp, through a gap left in the carts. The gap is shut. The Sioux, again, are beaten off. After 6 full hours of attacks, they withdraw; but keep war-whooping all night. Two Metis steal out of the laager; and gallop to warn the main Hunt.

The hunters decide to move and join the main Hunt. They know that such a manoeuvre demands discipline and skill. But, they are confident that, trained by Grant so many years, they can do it! Before dawn, the hunters mount; and move out in 4 companies. The vanguard rides a mile ahead. The rear-guard, 2 miles behind. One company rides on either flank. Within these mounted guards, the carts roll ahead in 4 columns, at 400 yards interval. All are alert, on signal, to wheel into their defensive circle. The cavalcade moves a mile — 2 miles — a full hour. Then, the signal! The Sioux are in hot pursuit. Promptly, the cart columns, at the clumsy gallop, wheel into a double circle, with the livestock inside. Quickly, the dismounted hunters dig their rifle pits, outside. From these pits, for 5 long hours, they hold off attack after attack! A thunderstorm deluges the battle in sheets of rain! Before it clears, the Sioux are gone! The vanguard from the main Hunt arrives!

In the two-day action, 3 Metis hunters are wounded and I killed; 12 horses and 4 oxen are killed. The Sioux lose 80 warriors killed; unknown numbers wounded; and 65 horses killed. "In Indian warfare, these are shattering losses". This defeat ends the long Sioux reign of terror on the Plains. The Sioux will rise, again and again; and will menace isolated groups. To avenge their own betrayal, they will massacre defenceless settlers. But, the Battle of the Grand Coteau removes the overhanging threat of Sioux attacks which would destroy Assiniboia. For the organization and training that win this vital victory, our people have to thank Cuthbert Grant.

The Sayer trial, in 1849, frees Assiniboia from the grip of throttling Monopoly. The victory of the Grand Coteau, in 1851, frees Assiniboia from the throttling grip of the Sioux over the trade routes, southward. On the modest stage of our affairs, these events rank as the Magna Carta and the Waterloo of Assiniboia's history.

1852 is "the year of the flood". Beginning 2 May, the Red River rises, steadily. In 5 days, it is 8 feet above the usual high-water mark; and rising another foot every hour. People along the Red and around Fort Garry get out and away, quickly. Bishop Anderson observes, on 8 May: "Those in church this morning are now moving. Long lines of carts are making for Stony Mountain, with their cattle". Bannerman "with his York boats, moves families, their belongings and cattle" to higher ground, where the refugees set up "tents of buffalo skins". In fine spring weather, the birds sing overhead; while, below, the surging waters submerge farmstead after farmstead. Within 10 days, half the Colony on the Red is flooded. The River is reported to be "6 miles wide, for 12 miles". Some writers report a "lake several hundred miles long and 12 miles wide" . . . and "men, women and children drowning". Such accounts are false fiction — and worse history! The flood attains its peak — 18 inches below the 1826 high — on 22 May. One man is drowned; but damage in the Settlement totals a staggering $125,000.00!

On 11 June, the leading boat brigade from Montreal passes "the Forks", west-bound to meet the fur brigades coming down from the Mackenzie River country. The flood is over. By the end of June, families return to their water-logged farmsteads. The just-completed St. James rectory houses Assiniboia families who seek its safety. St. James, itself, being 40 feet higher than "the Forks", is not inundated. Nor are the communities further up the Assiniboine, on still higher ground.

On this higher ground, many refugees from lower lands, wait for the flood to subside; among them, the Sinclair family. James Sinclair is emerging as a leading citizen of Assiniboia — in battling Monopoly; and in leading settlers to Oregon, hoping to keep that region in British hands. In 1850, Sinclair brings heavy horses and wagons from St. Louis, for the long, hard trip across the Plains. Back in Assiniboia, this spring, he moves up the Assiniboine; and for 2 months lives in tents — among hundreds who seek sanctuary on the high, dry banks of Sturgeon Creek.

After the flood, many Settlers re-locate on higher ground up the Assiniboine. Among others, Oliver and Mary Gowler leave their farm on the flood plain of the Red; and select land near Headingly. They buy River Lot 64; and, on the well-drained banks of Gowler's Creek, they sow their first productive fields. They develop a prosperous farm, with good buildings and fine livestock; and raise a fine family of good Canadian citizens.

The Camerons, also, are early pioneers in the Headingly community.

William F. Fortune buys land east of the Grand Passage. William S. Stevenson buys River Lot 61; and farms thereon for 61 years. John Taylor, born in St. Paul's parish 24 January, 1834, graduates, at 18, from St. John's College in "the year of the flood"; and, after teaching a mission school at Oxford Lake at $30.00 for a year, becomes the first teacher in the first log school in Headingly parish. Some Settlers from Red River parishes move up the Assiniboine to Portage la Prairie; and beyond. In addition to fertile land, they find plenty of sturgeon, pike, perch and pickerel in the River; and whitefish in Lake Manitoba.

Many facts combine to keep early farming near the rivers. One of the simplest is that sloping ground is, often, the best drained; easy to clear; and yields good crops. In fact, drainage dictates the location and size of cultivated fields in pioneer Assiniboia. Wider freedom and our improving economy, release a flood of travel and trade. The trails southward, blazed by the free-men who roamed the original Assiniboia; and deepened by "Selkirkers", in trips to Fort Daer, are made into cart trails by the Metis of St. Francois Xavier and Pembina, hunting, tripping and visiting back and forth. This summer, 1853, barley is freighted from Assiniboia to Pembina, where spring floods "wash out" farming; and confront settlers with starvation.

Maverick traders capture an increasing share of business, which, formerly, was sacred to the "Company". Free traders, like Garrioch and Sinclair, incur the anger and feel the vengeance of the imperious Governor Simpson. Andrew McDermot, in his shop north of Fort Garry, probably captures more trade from the "Company" than all the other free traders combined; but, with genial shrewdness, keeps the "Little Emperor's" favor. Free traders no longer smuggle, but trade openly, across the boundary; and by-pass middlemen, to deal directly with wholesalers in St. Paul.

Imports — in more sophisticated variety and multiplied tonnage — are paid for by exports which, now, in addition to furs, pemmican, buffalo tongues and robes, include horses and cattle. St. Paul offers an inviting market for the harvests from Assiniboia's farms, as well as from the Hunt. Even the "Company" now freights supplies to Assiniboia via St. Paul, as well as York Factory; and, from Assiniboia, supplies the Nor'West by trailways, in addition to waterways.

Other parts of the country are developing more rapidly than Assiniboia. The ancient citadel of Quebec looks down on shipyards, busy building vessels that sail the 7 seas. More than 3,600 river craft freight into, and out of, Montreal. Toronto is a city of 40,000 people. Booming trade and travel keep 1,149 vessels busy on the Great Lakes.

Historians stress the hard living in pioneer Assiniboia. The most graphic descriptions fall short of a true picture of these hardships. Herein is proved, again, the sublime and perverse optimism of the human spirit. "When it is dark enough, we see the stars". Tough living breeds vast capacity for enjoyment. When Cuthbert Grant's daughter is married, a cavalcade of men and women, young and old, rich and poor, crosses the Red River from St. Boniface; and rides merrily the 20 miles along the Portage Trail to Grantown. A roasted ox is the centre-piece for heaped-up tables. Dancing and feasting last for days. Father LaFleche, a "fine musician", inspires the orchestra. From all parts of the Settlement come the great, the near-great and those less well known — to pay their respects; and join in the jubilation. With Cuthbert Grant, himself, business is not good. He still holds the deep respect of his people; but, since 1849, not their friendship nor their trade. The leading Plains' traders are now Urbain Delorme and Pascal Breland, Grant's son-in-law.

The tonnage of wheeled traffic multiplies. Every owner of an ox and cart — whether hunter, hunter-farmer, farmer-hunter or farmer's son — aspires to be an "entrepreneur", relishing the freedom of individual enterprise; and eager to contract for freighting. For security against the still-menacing Sioux, they travel together in cart trains, organized like the Hunt. With supreme confidence in themselves and in the land of which they are natives, these voyageurs of the oceans of grass readily launch upon trips to any part of the great Nor'West. Treks of 1,000 miles to St. Paul and back; and for twice that distance between Assiniboia and the Rockies, are commonplace. With draft animals pasturing their way across the Plains, a cart train is "automotive", self-supporting. When, finally, they come home, all hands don their multicolored L'Assomption sashes and tie bright handkerchiefs around their necks or heads, as do the boat men. After a summer of hard "tripping", the cart people winter with hunters, in a "feast or a famine". Toward spring, they repair their carts; and, if ambitious, build 1 or 2 new ones.

Cart trains are "big business" in this decade. More than 1,500 carts freight between Assiniboia and St. Paul; another 2,000 between Assiniboia and the Rockies; and the "Company" keeps more than 1,500 carts busy all summer. Thus, freighting may employ 3,000 to 4,000 carts. To man these, requires 1,000 "voyageurs". The addition of wives and children may bring the total "cart population" to above 4,000 persons — two-thirds the total living along the Assiniboine River and the Red! The life of the cart brigade — outdoors, adventurous, dangerous and free — fascinates "natives" of Assiniboia — of Canadian, Scot, Irish, English and other paternity. A train may embrace 800 carts, 300 men, 1,000 women and children, 1,000 oxen, 300 horses and dogs unnumbered! For security and efficiency, these are divided into companies, each commanded by a Captain; all under a central "Government". Organization is detailed and discipline strict, under unquestioned laws.

At dawn, all hands breakfast. With deceptive speed and tremendous racket — horses are saddled; oxen harnessed to the carts; tents of scraped buffalo hides rolled; and all gear is stowed aboard the carts. At the command, "Marche", the carts roll out in long lines of hideous screeching. The train travels 2 miles an hour, until mid-afternoon. Then, the carts are wheeled into a giant circle — in a hollow, beside a pond. Livestock is turned loose, under the eye of mounted patrols, to drink and pasture. In the gathering dusk, oxen and horses are herded into the circle of carts; and all gaps closed. Already, tents have been pitched at one end of the enclosure. Before them, fires cook the evening meal. Afterward, there is singing; music, benediction by the padre; and the camp sleeps — secure in the knowledge that patrols and sentinels, with military precision, watch through the night.

In far-off Labrador, a young Scot is taking the first steps on the Trail of Destiny that will lead him to dominant positions in Assiniboia — in Canada — in the world. Donald A. Smith marries the daughter of the newly-arrived "Company" factor. Exiled for 20 years to remotest Labrador when Governor Simpson finds the bonnie lad enjoying tea with Mrs. Simpson, young Donald studies philosophy, political economy, medicine, history. He becomes known as one of the "best informed and most independent thinkers of his time". In that distant desolation, he experiments with farming and livestock; and with processing and exporting salmon, sealskins, seal oil, quartz, wild tea. Many offers come to him from United States, as well as Canada. He refuses all. With the surety of his own "second sight", he follows his Trail of Destiny — which is to make him, among other things, the most widely-known citizen of Assiniboia.

There are 8 parish schools in the Settlements; and, this summer, a day-school opens, up the Assiniboine at St. Mary's La Prairie, in Peter Garrioch's home. Adventure and independence call Settlers ever westward. Ten families from Portage la Prairie, including the Andersons, Whitfords and Houses, trek by Red River cart to Victoria, near Fort Edmonton.

Cuthbert Grant dies on July 13, 1854. He is buried at St. Francois Xavier. Cuthbert Grant is a true native of Assiniboia — born in the great Nor'West. He molds the Metis hunters into the force which frees Assiniboia of Sioux attacks. He leads the Nor'West party in the tragic clash between the servants of the warring fur companies at Seven Oaks; and, ever after, is feared and hated by Hudson's Bay people. Nevertheless,

"Company" officials use him for their business ends; and discard him when his influence wanes. Withal, Cuthbert Grant's contribution to development of our Canadian West exceeds that of many men who are more richly recognized.

The Crimean War, beginning this fall of 1854, multiplies demand for buffalo robes; adds to the returns from the Hunt; and increases the number of cart brigades freighting exports to the United States. The maze of trails which, from all directions and through times unknown, led to, and from, Assiniboia, are becoming more deeply marked by the cart brigades, along selected routes.

From "the Forks", the great east-west route follows the north bank of the Assiniboine, past Portage la Prairie; over low plains, creeks and ponds — some 500 miles to Fort Carlton, on the North Saskatchewan River; and, then, another 500 miles to Fort Edmonton. It is known, variously, as "the Portage Trail", the "Carlton", "Edmonton", or "Hudson's Bay Trail". From this main route, trails branch off. For example, the "Yellowquill Trail" leads from Portage la Prairie toward the mouth of the Souris River; and the "Pelly Trail" swings northward between the Mountains and the Swan River Valley. These old trails are deeply rutted over a great width. Each driver handles 4 carts. He drives the lead ox. The next, he ties to the rear corner of his cart, so that it walks in the rut (and dust) of the wheel in front of it. Each draft animal, in like succession, walks in the wheel-track of the preceding cart. Thus, the carts lumber ahead — spread out, in echelon.

The humble (and miraculous) Red River cart — which makes Assiniboia almost a community on wheels — freights more than trade goods. There is an even more vital exchange of ideas and news. At long last, the Councillors of Assiniboia (Company appointees in the robes of public office) open a post office in the home of William Ross. "Ross House" — begun in 1852; delayed by the flood and completed in 1854 — is Assiniboia's first official Post Office.

Exciting news reaches Assiniboia: about gold on the Fraser River; fires sweeping the plains; and the first railway train from Montreal into Toronto, sending eastern Canadians into a "Railway Frenzy". This year, 2,437 papers, 2,821 letters and 580 parcels pass through "Ross House" post office. Letters of ½ ounce pay (at the receiving end) 24 cents postage to U.K., Ireland, France or Australia; and 10 cents to Oregon, California and Canada. William Drever is appointed postmaster, at $30.00 yearly. Upon his resignation, Nathaniel Logan becomes postmaster; and later, James Stewart, a St. James school teacher.

John Taylor, teaching school at Headingly, marries Flora Campbell, daughter of Chief Factor Colin Campbell; and buys from the "Company" several hundred acres beside his school. Teachers of parish schools earn, usually, some $200.00 yearly. John Norquay teaches at St. John's for this salary; and A. C. Garrioch reports it "more than ample to meet expenses".

Overall growth might be more rapid, were it not for Settlers who, having come, are ready to leave — eager to seek greener pastures "over the next hill". James Sinclair leads another party of emigrants from Assiniboia to the Columbia River this year.

In 1856, Assiniboia's population is recorded as 5,126 people who share Indian parentage; and 1,565 who do not. They cultivate 8,806 acres. (Up 2,464 acres in 5 years). Due to the Crimean War, farmers with wheat to sell, find prices up to $2.50 per bushel. At the same time, interest rates jump from 4% to 8%.

Multiplication of cart trains benefits farming. The demand for draft animals widens the market for farm-raised horses and oxen. Beyond this, while the horses and oxen that power the cart brigades pasture their way through the summer, for six months of each year they must be fed hay — 3 tons per head to come through the winter in good working condition; 2 tons to exist. If 4,000 carts roll back and forth across Assiniboia, 8,000 to 12,000 tons of hay are needed to feed the draft animals over winter. More than half the men and boys of the Settlements are on the trails at haying time. Farm families can readily sell all the hay they can make. Women, as well as men — and girls, as well as boys — work in the hayfields. The scythed hay, as it dries, is gathered with home-made rakes; and carried, on home-made forks, to small stacks. Branches, bound together, are thrown over the stacks to keep the hay from blowing away. The hay "privileges", in the outer 2 miles of the River Lots have increasing value. Cattle raised on Assiniboia farms are herded to United States markets. At the same time, the booming market southward, calls for more and more of the buffalo hunter's production: meat, tongues and robes; and provides competition with the "Company", at better prices. Expanding trade, traffic and travel boom the manufacture of Red River carts. Some are made on the Red River; many at Portage la Prairie; but the centre of cart manufacture is St. Francois Xavier. It becomes an axiom that "the best carts on any trail are made in Assiniboia".

Here we record some doings of distant dignitaries which have some impact on our Assiniboia history. The degree of such impact is the answer to the question: is the dictum of those in the robes of power as basic in building communities and nations, as the work, thoughts and dreams of residents whose bread is soaked in sweat; and whose names never appear in public print — often, not even on gravestones? Despite the heraldry of published histories, pontificial pronouncements of the former, often, are mere acquiescence in situations already established, in fact, by the latter. For years, the people of Assiniboia have worked for freedom in trade; and for something better in government than the dictatorial tyranny of a commercial Monopoly. They remember the painful loss of Oregon — where so-called "negotiations" acknowledged the demands of the resident majority. They have tasted, since 1849, some measure of freedom. They want full rations! Hundreds have put their mark to petitions to Imperial authorities. These petitions and more clamorous demands by citizens of Canada, have been side-tracked. At long last, in London, a House of Commons Committee begins an inquiry into Assiniboia; its affairs; and its future. A. K. Isbister and Rev. G. O. Corbett, of Headingly, speak for Assiniboia. Isbister urges: "United States are fast peopling territory along the frontier; and they will have that territory from us, unless we people it".

In March, Imperial authorities order Captain John Palliser and Dr. James Hector, geologist, to survey Assiniboia and the British Nor'West; and to report whether this wilderness has, in fact, any value for England. Yielding to a barrage of petitions, the Government of Canada, appoints surveyor-engineer Simon J. Dawson and chemist-geologist Henry Y. Hind to explore, and report on, Assiniboia and the Nor'West; and the value of these lands and waters to Canada.

During June, Edward Ellice informs the Select Committee that "Company" profits over the last 17 years average 16.4% annually. A profit position worth protecting! "Company" representatives testify that Indians in Canada number 139,000; and recite the ancient fallacy that farmers and fur traders are incompatible. The Select Committee, in July, recommends a typical compromise, which protects the profits of their friends of the "Company"; acknowledges some rights for the people of Assiniboia; and grants the feasibility of Canada taking over and settling, Assiniboia and the Nor'West — upon cash payment satisfactory to "Company" shareholders in England.

The English exploring party, under Palliser and Hector, in July, arrive in St. Paul, by railway; and trek by Red River cart to "the Forks". By August, they are at Fort Ellice. The vanguard of "The Assiniboine and Saskatchewan Exploring Expedition" follows the old canoe route, westward; and arrives at "the Forks" on 4 September — 40 days out of Toronto. They locate the Dawson Road; and, for 2 years, follow the old trails — east and west — of the Red; and up the Assiniboine to the Saskatchewan River. Less welcome visitors are the locusts, which destroy the crops as far westward as Portage la Prairie.

A new church at Portage la Prairie is completed in 1857. It has taken 2 years to raise its 70-by-30-foot walls, 14 feet to the eaves; and to add the tower, thrusting 60 feet skyward.

The structure is built of native oak logs, hewn flat on two sides; clapboarded and white-washed; and roofed with shingles split from oak blocks. Families fashion their own pews from oak and poplar. At his store in Portage, Peter Garrioch trades provisions for the pelts, willow baskets, ladles and brooms offered by his Indian customers.

In October, Canadian troops arrive in Assiniboia. Ever since British troops are withdrawn, 10 years ago, Governor Simpson has pressed for a garrison at Fort Garry. Whether he actually wants a force to "keep the natives in their place" or to protect the interests of England, his urging that a garrison is necessary, finds the right ear. On 28 June, 120 all ranks of the Royal Canadian Rifles leave Quebec for Assiniboia. (Some reports say 700.) Down the St. Lawrence they sail; through Hudson's Bay to York Factory; and up the old waterway: Hays River, Lake Winnipeg, Red River to Fort Garry. It is a hard, 3-month trip. These Canadians, recruited at the call of the Government in London, learn something about the immensity of the lands and waters destined to be Canada. Under command of Major George Seaton, the Canadian Rifles stay until 1861. For the rest of their lives they tell of open prairie where you can plow for miles, with never a stone to dull your 'share. The challenge of the new land calls pioneers from Ontario — as, through 100 years, it has called men from the narrow St. Lawrence valley. Among others, John Higgins arrives in Assiniboia; and his partner David Young. With a fine span of horses, these enterprising merchants drive right to the Settler's door, with their mobile store of goods heaped on a pedlar's wagon.

Beside Fort Garry, the "Company" reserves 500 acres as a campground for the Plains' traders when they flock in each summer, to trade for fresh stocks of goods. Free traders are close neighbors. Andrew McDermot's 200 acres front on the Red River, along later-day McDermot Avenue. His northward neighbor is A. G. B. Bannatyne; and, next, the Ross property. This fall, Assiniboia farmers work till freeze-up to bring more acres into production. Up to 1857, they supply local needs. Now, suddenly, the garrison and exploring and prospecting parties — at "the Forks" for the winter; and collecting supplies for next summer — multiply demand for farm output.

Reports of massacres of settlers in Minnesota and Iowa recall terrible memories to older colonists in Assiniboia. Since 1850, the number of white people in Minnesota increases from 6,000 to 150,000! The Indians are submerged, robbed! The Sioux take the warpath!

In December, Captain Palliser and Dr. Hector meet Indians, who come to "trade at Fort Carlton" — but leave most of their furs with the free traders — who "winter among the Indians, with goods furnished to them by United States traders".

At Fort Ellice, also, Palliser meets 7 men, 3 women and some children, returning from Oregon, whence James Sinclair led them last summer. They tell how that intrepid leader is killed by Indians. They find Oregon "not up to expectations". They are wintering by hunting buffalo in the Eagle Hills. Next spring, they will get back home — to Assiniboia.

The life lived by Assiniboia's people breeds strong characters — with strong characteristics marking each component group. These never merge in a molten mass, to be stamped with stereo same-ness. Parentage, color and speech, outlook and habits mix in infinite variety. Many writers produce excellent histories, from the viewpoint of a particular component group. Few attempt to weave the viewpoints of all components into the fabric of a complete and balanced record. "To see orsels as ithers see us", we draw upon an international magazine dated December, 1858; and its report of an Assiniboia cart train in St. Paul. The writer, in his time and place, sees our people as: "wild, picturesque, with free, firm step; bold, yet graceful abandon of carriage; nobility of stature; and bronzed features." They wear a "chevelure that waves about their shoulders; dark, coarse blue coats, with enormous buttons of polished brass; sashes of brightest red; jaunty little caps; trousers of corduroy or dark woollen, if not elk or bison skin; and dingy moccasins".

"The various hues of their complexion, from dusky Indian with arrowy raven hair, through all the intervening tints of dingy browns, to the ruddy cheek and blue eyes of the fair-Gael, proclaim the intermingling of the Caucasian with the aborigine. Within the circle of their camp is heard a strange melange of languages, as diverse as their parentage — French, English, Cree, Ojibway — with mingled accent, soft and musical; abrupt and gutteral, in strange and startling contrasts".

Hudson's Bay Company officers, this scribe records: "live in all the barbaric dignity of the feudal barons; and rule, with no less despotic sway, over their courier-de-bois. There are times, when, released from all restraint, these men gather; and hold high revel, as reward for their excursions into the boundless wilds. Songs ring out. Wild tales are told. They dance with Indian maidens. The bowl goes freely around, till mirth grows fast and furious; and only the end of the night ends their mad debauchery".

"As the great wave of migration rolls up the Mississippi, the Red River hunters seek a new outlet for their furs — over the level prairies to St. Paul. This trade has increased from 1 or 2 trains of 30 or 40 carts each, to long, winding caravans of hundreds. 'Selkirkers' the Scots are called. They are gay, cheerful and sprightly; full of fun and frolic; fond of singing and dancing."

At the Settlements, farming engages about half the population, mostly European and Protestant. The Bois Brules and Canadians of Roman Catholic faith live by hunting. The life of the hunters is spent in the chase or in indolence and festivity.

"While supplies are plentiful, they are the gayest of the day. Dancing, gambling, drinking, song and amatory sports while the hours away . . . In the spring they go to work, preparing for the Hunt. A thousand hammers tell of building and repairing carts".

As a cart train arrives, this writer sees: "On every face, the effects of their long and toilsome journey. Man and beast walk wearily; and in silence. Oxen are gaunt and lean; while the heavy wheels incessantly creak and groan, as if speaking for the dumb oxen their unspeakable woes". Thus, we of Assiniboia are pictured, in the year 1858, by our brashly prosperous neighbors, 500 miles south of us.

About this time, the Hudson's Bay Company is swallowed (again!) by an "International Finance Society". The wizardry of Edward Watkins, in integrating these with the Grand Trunk Railway and the Baring interests, of London, may startle the world of finance. The people of Assiniboia know nothing of it, for years. It matters little that they do not. They are building homes, a community, a country. As History is: "the study of How and When Who lives Where", the real stream of our history is in the dreams and thoughts and work of men farming, hunting, freighting and building; and women, cooking, cleaning, spinning, teaching and raising families. Promoter Watkins and his ilk are merely froth thrown upward by the tremendous current of these happenings.

The cart trains freighting between Assiniboia and St. Paul now employ 6,000 carts! "With plenty of pasture, pemmican and game, these cart voyageurs are the happiest people on earth. Around their camp fires at night — within the security of their cart-encircled camps — they sing, fiddle, dance. With their priest to hold brief service morning and night and celebrate mass on Sundays, the trip-men and their families would trade their life for no other". Many of these families spend the entire summer on the trails; and winter in Assiniboia.

The "Company" now forwards goods by cart trains to 152 posts, 3,000 traders and 100,000 Indian hunters and trappers over the great Nor'West. Cart brigades, likewise, supply free traders, from "the Forks" to the Rockies. The trails that reach out to the farthest outpost are the veins and arteries; and the traffic they carry is the life-blood, of the economy of the vast Nor'West. The heart of the trailways network — as of the network of waterways — is Assiniboia. Freight tonnage has outgrown canoes, York boats. It is out-growing even the multiplying number of cart trains — and calls for steamships!

Professor Henry Y. Hind arrives on 2 June to complete "The Assiniboine and Saskatchewan Exploring Expedition". With 3 tons of freight, his party has traversed the old Nor'West canoe route; via Moose Lake, Fort Frances and Fort Alexander.

The Expedition heads West — with 4 surveyors and 10 "natives" (8 of them hybrids, 1 of Scot and 1 of French-speaking Canadian parentage). Five carts and 1 wagon carry 2 canoes, instruments and food for 3 months. Hind reports the Nor'West full of buffalo — and Indians. The Expedition reaches the confluence of the Souris and Assiniboine Rivers, 146 miles from "the Forks", on 24 June. "In constant fear of the Sioux. Swim horses across the river; and ferry baggage in canoes. Carts and wagon towed over". From the Souris to Fort Ellice, they encounter grasshoppers! "Cloud after cloud. Grass eaten uniformly one inch from the ground". Hind and his party are at "the Narrows" of Lake Winnipeg on 16 October. He records ravages of disease and war among the Indians.

The United States garrison at Pembina closes the boundary to the Hunt; but opens a market for grain and meat. New money in circulation quickens the pulse of local trade. World-wide financial stringency, following the Crimean War, by-passes Assiniboia. Cart trains now take $250,000.00 in furs, pemmican, robes and tongues to St. Paul; and freight home $1,000,000.00 in goods, annually.

The cart brigades end the dependence of transport on waterways; and capture this trade so completely that Governor Simpson abandons the route through "the Bay"; and has "Company" freight brought via St. Paul to Assiniboia — by Red River carts. Sharp business men smell the profits in freighting; organize cart trains; and harvest their share of profits.

With his razor-honed business sense and his knowledge of the benefits of Monopoly (to monopolists) Simpson backs Norman Kittson (Canadian turned American) in developing a freighting monopoly on the trails; and, soon, on the Assiniboine River and the Red. A few trader's shacks, north of Fort Garry, are the unlikely seed from which sprouts the city of Winnipeg. Settlers up the Assiniboine are sowing expanding fields — from which our Canadian nation harvests a booming West!

A party of Grey Nuns, led by Mother McMullen, arrives in Assiniboia in 1859. Their first group came, 15 years ago, with a canoe brigade from

Montreal. This party travels from Montreal to Sarnia by railway; then steamship to Detroit; railway to Chicago and Prairie du Chien; and to "the Forks" by Red River cart train.

St. Paul merchants — eager to share in the freighting to Assiniboia — pay Captain Anson Northup $2,000.00 to move his steamship "North Star" from the Crow Wing to the Red River. During the winter, the intrepid skipper has his vessel dismantled; hauled on sleighs 150 miles across country to Georgetown, on the Red; and there re-assembled. After months of Herculean effort, this pioneer vessel, re-named "Anson Northup", steams proudly down the Red River and, 4 days out of Breckenridge, arrives at Fort Garry on 10 June, the first steamship in Assiniboia! The Royal Canadian Rifles, in garrison at Fort Garry, fire a salute. Bells ring from the cathedral in St. Boniface and the church in St. James. From all the Settlements — for 40 miles along the Red; and 70 up the Assiniboine — young and old crowd to "the Forks" to shout their welcome. The merchants celebrate; they know that the coming of steamships means more trade over the counter and money in the till. Even the Indians whoop — unknowing that their way of life is doomed!

Observers record that the steamboat's whistle stampedes cows pasturing on the River bank. Cart oxen — pausing to grab bits of trail-side grass, before the driver's whip urges them on — cannot know that all this racket announces competition for the cart trains. On 17 June, the SS "Anson Northup" heads into the current of the Red — aiming to make Ft. Abercrombie in 8 days. Twenty-five excited passengers are aboard. The skipper sails in daylight only; and ties up to the bank, at sundown. There are frequent stops for wood. The puffing engines burn a cord every hour! The "Company" is not slow to cash in on the steamboat business. Governor Simpson secures an operating depot, at Georgetown. Scheduled stages between St. Paul and Georgetown bring Assiniboia within 12 days of Montreal, for mail and passengers.

The spring Hunt heads westward, keeping north of the 49th parallel (more or less). Each succeeding Hunt penetrates further westward. This year, the hunters range beyond the Cypress Hills to reach the buffalo herds. June brings the Earl of Southesk, with Governor Simpson, to Assiniboia. His Lordship hires 8 natives of Scot parentage; has a wagon and 3 Red River carts loaded with supplies (guns, tents, blankets, sugar, flour, tea, rice, biscuits, jam and buffalo tongues for his party; and 90 pounds of "coarse" tobacco, as Indian presents). With 15 horses, including 2 special buffalo "runners", his safari heads into the western wilderness; and is lost to sight, until freeze-up.

This summer, three parties of "Overlanders", some 60 in all, leave from Assiniboia for the Cariboo. A growing stream of Canadians (mostly from Ontario) surges westward. William Coldwell arrives; and W. H. Lyon. Henry McKinney builds a log shack into the "Royal Hotel". W. B. Hall comes as a surveyor; and stays to be an outstanding citizen. From south of the border, aggressive characters push into Assiniboia; and talk annexation to United States. James Wickes Taylor — commissioned by the United States Treasury, ostensibly, to report on a route, via Assiniboia, to the Cariboo goldfields — begins his operations in the Settlement. A genial gentleman, he accepts pay from the U.S. Government, U.S. Railroads, the "Company" and (in due time) the C.P.R. Migration from Assiniboia to the Pacific coast continues. According to Governor Douglas, "parties leave Red River in spring with cattle; and reach British Columbia the following autumn".

The River Lots along the south bank of the Assiniboine are being taken up by incoming settlers. Surveyor W. T. Lonsdale and Herbert Sabine, for home-sites, choose Lots 6 and 7; and, to make their homes complete, marry two daughters of the pioneer Cameron family. West of them lives Hon. William Tait, a native of Assiniboia. He and James Tait are recorded in censuses taken in Assiniboia 27 years ago. Jane Inkster and Robert Tait are married, last year. The James Tait family live in a big house beside the later site of Headingly bridge.

Long after freeze-up, the Earl of Southesk's party returns to "the Forks" by dog-team, leaving their horses and outfit at Fort Pelly. A prolific writer, his Lordship records: "lakes abounding with ducks" during the fall.

William Coldwell and William Buckingham (young adventurers in their 20's) buy second-hand equipment in St. Paul to launch Assiniboia's first newspaper — "The Nor'Wester". With their wives atop cart-loads of press, type, paper, etc., they arrive at Fort Garry. On 28 December, 1859, their first issue appears: to come out every 2 weeks. The "Nor'-Wester" becomes the final authority for Assiniboia readers, in all disputes. In its columns, Settlers at Portage la Prairie, are called "Portagees". Historians of the day report it fair, even to the "Company", which it attacks. Assiniboia now has a regular monthly mail; a regular trade route for unlimited tonnage to expanding markets, southward; and a regular newspaper!

Even farming feels the urge to expansion. "The Nor'Wester" reports, in its first issue: "Last year, the temporary presence of a couple of exploring parties and a few batches of fortune-hunters on their way to the Fraser River, almost created a famine. The price of wheat rose from $1.17 to $2.35 per bushel! Flour rose from $2.87 to $8.50 a cwt. (For a time). The "Company" buys most of the produce; but farmers need extended markets. Current prices are: wheat, $1.12 to $1.25 per bushel; flour, $5.00 a cwt; barley, 75c to 87c; oats, 62c to 75c; potatoes, 35c to 37c per bushel; beef, 5c to 6c per pound; buffalo meat, fresh, 4c; dried, 6c; and pemmican, 8c per pound".

During the 1850's, Canada's railway mileage is built from 66 to 2,065 miles. The cost — including profits and graft — reaches $150 millions.

In Assiniboia, the expansion in freighting by Red River carts exceeds even the railway boom in Canada! Inhabitants of Assiniboia accept distance as a condition of living in the vastness of this land. Life is nomadic. Communities scattered over the Plains, from Lakehead to Rockies, live by the network of trails; and the wheels that make them. Assiniboia, hub of the transport system — with most of its population on the Hunt, on the cart trains, or on the move — is "a community on wheels". The census of 1849 records 3 Red River carts in the Settlement for every home. As the 1850's hurry by, the number of carts multiplies, perhaps by 5! It is a paying business. One trip — Assiniboia to St. Paul and return; carrying 1,000 pounds per cart at 20 cents a ton-mile, pays the entire capital cost of the outfit, plus 108% net to the owner! In addition, driver's wages ($30.00 for 2 months) are paid in goods, at 100% profit. *It is a* paying business! The cart voyageurs, either as small owners or as hired men, operate on credit. This has been the custom for generations of hunters; and, now, for the trip-men who live up the Assiniboine, in St. James, St. Charles and St. Francois Xavier. Formerly, the "Company" provided the necessary advances — and reaped rich returns. Latterly, free traders, with sharp noses for profits, claim their share of this lucrative business.

Most successful of all the free traders — both in service rendered and rewards reaped — is Andrew McDermot. He lives in "Emerald Grove" — in front of his big windmill. His trading store is an immense barn — full of smells and goods! He is a brisk, little man of 60-odd years, with twinkling blue eyes, long red hair, (turning white); and boundless good humour. He claims to deal in "everything but second-hand coffins". Shelves, tables and floor are heaped with boxes, barrels, bales; buffalo hides, pemmican, moccasins, boots, chests of tea, boxes of tobacco, rice, raisins, loaf sugar — all mixed with kettles, skillets and fine bead-work done by Indian and hybrid women. A "mowing machine, recently imported" sits among bales of buffalo meat dried on the plains for export. His son-in-law, A. G. B. Bannatyne, operates a store next door. Both, from free traders, are becoming "merchants".

John Schultz

CHAPTER 8

Trade Through The Sioux . . . 1860-69

The hunter, cart voyageur, farmer-hunter or farmer who concludes a long season of hard work (by settling his debts and getting a pittance in cash) may be forgiven for celebrating. (As is the way of men who do the world's work, in all times and places.) In Assiniboia, now, he has a choice. He may begin either at Henry McKinney's log shack "Royal Exchange Hotel" or at the "Emmerling House", opened on the trail north of Fort Garry by the German-American pedlar, George Emmerling. Recently arrived from the United States, with 1 barrel of whiskey and 2 of apples, this entrepreneur lures his share of patrons; enlarges his hostelry; and provides headquarters for the few adventurers from south of the border, who become known as the "American party".

Trader Bannatyne leads his spring brigade of 600 carts southward, freighting 350 tons of fur, robes, pemmican and tongues to St. Paul. After putting up "for 30 years . . . with primitive windmills", the "Nor'Wester" reports, "on 28 May was erected the first modern steam flour mill." James Ross, son of Alexander, returns from study in Canada. He buys Buckingham's share of "The Nor'Wester"; and aims his scholastic brilliance against the Monopoly which still dominates Assiniboia; "the Company" which profits from it; and their Council, which administers it.

Lord Southesk writes that, at White Horse Plain, he sees men "dress in capotes of dark blue; leggins of same. Caps, the same — or of fur. A bright scarf around the waist. (The universal L'Assomption sash!) Female costumes generally dark, also. A shawl or blanket covers the head — or a silk kerchief — in rich contrast to the glossy black hair . . . Farms run from the riverside into the grass-clothed prairies. Fine trees border the stream. Looks more homelike than . . .the Red River near

Fort Garry". The hybrid offspring of white men from various parts of the world and Indian mothers are: "physically, a fine race — tall, straight, strong, active, enduring". He notes that hybrids of English or Scot parentage differ, somewhat, from those whose fathers are French-speaking Canadians. His Lordship doubts: "if a half-breed, dressed and educated like an Englishman, would seem at all remarkable in London Society. They build and farm like other people; go to church; recognize no chief (except for hunting); and, in all respects are like civilized men — not more uneducated, immoral or disorderly than many communities in the Old World". Among the hybrid people are frugal, thrifty families with settled habits; and others, improvident and nomadic. In fact, all degrees of all mixtures, as in all peoples.

News that Sir George Simpson dies in Lachine, on 8 September, wakens mixed feelings in Assiniboia. In the 27 years since Simpson moves to Montreal, his empire shrinks — until he is "the little Emperor", not of the vast fur trade; but of only "the Company" — which is become a chattel of manipulated finance; is losing the fur trade; has robbed its servants of cash and loyalty; and has sacrificed the respect and support of many people in the Settlements. The wounds inflicted by "Company" dungeons, shackles and bayonets under his imperious dictatorship, scar too many memories in Assiniboia to be soon forgiven — or ever forgotten. A new Governor is named by the "Company's" London Committee. His name is Dallas.

The first export of commercial wheat from this future "bread-basket of the world" is recorded in "the Nor'Wester" of 26 September. "Four sacks of wheat are on board ("The Anson Northup") for a farmer in Monticello, Iowa, who is charged $20.00 for its transport from Fort Garry to St. Paul." Up the Red River to St. Paul; down the Mississippi to Prairie du Chien; and 60 miles southward, this first Western Canadian export wheat is carried 1,000 miles, to be seeded in Iowa. Forty years earlier, Assiniboia farmers snowshoe to Prairie du Chien to buy seed. From 1860, on, they export! As some reward, perhaps, this year returns the biggest crop yet harvested in Assiniboia.

By 1860, millions of buffalo are being killed for their hides. The world's expanding steam-driven industries demand vast quantities of belting. Buffalo hides offer the cheapest source of the best belts. Thick-hided bulls, scorned in the pemmican Hunt, now mean money! With the new high-powered repeating rifle, whole herds are slaughtered; skinned; and left to rot. For each hide — sold for $2 or $3 — 5 buffalo are killed! Travellers record how, "in these early 60's, steamboats tie to trees on the river bank for a full day" — to avoid masses of buffalo crossing "as far as the eye can see."

Two thousand miles south-east from Assiniboia, on 12 April, 1861, Confederate guns fire on old Fort Sumter. The Union guns of the Fort reply. Their deadly diapason announces bloody war — to determine whether the United States is, in fact, "united." The thunder of those cannon determines, too, that the Nor'West shall remain Canadian. War diverts the tide of migrating manpower from its west-and-northward flow, to battlefields southward and eastward, whence only some return. From Minnesota, alone, 25,000 young men go to Union armies. Without war's intervention, some of these certainly would have over-flowed the border into Assiniboia. Even 1,000 families could have dominated the entire Nor'West; and, as in Oregon, brought this vast land into "the American dream." Thus, History moves mankind back and forth upon the earth, as pawns impelled by powers beyond our ken.

In the Maritimes and Canada, army, navy and government officials and high Tories favor the Confederate States. French-speaking Canadians keep their vision of Canada, within Canada's borders. English-speaking Canadians, generally, are against slavery; and 40,000 men from Canada go to fight in Union armies. Adventure calls unknown numbers to join the armies of the South. England sends 14,000 soldiers to the frontiers of Canada. Forty thousand Canadian militia drill — with rifles, shotguns, pitchforks! From all this, reverberations reach Assiniboia as rumors and news; and as cash returns — in higher grain prices; and demand for Nor'West horses!

New-comers from Ontario are, this summer, joined by E. L. Barber, son-in-law of Alexander Logan; and Alfred Boyd, who opens a store in St. John's. Dr. J. C. Schultz returns, to make Assiniboia his home. This giant redhead owns a drug store, at later Main and Water Streets. Actually, he does little doctoring. He applies his tremendous energies to more exciting (and lucrative) trade. A "polished orator", he gravitates to politics; organizes migrants from Ontario into the "Canadian party"; urges, first, that Assiniboia be a Crown Colony; then, fights for annexation to Canada. He wages booming battle against "the Company", as the obstacle on this trail. Dr. Robert Bown, a classmate, comes with Schultz. As Assiniboia's first dentist, he, too, finds trading and fighting "the Company" more exciting (and profitable) than tooth-pulling.

The Royal Canadian Rifles — garrisoned in Assiniboia since 1857, in August are withdrawn to Canada, to protect more valuable (or more voluble?) frontiers. Down the Red River and Lake Winnipeg they navigate, to York Factory; and thence, to Canada. Merchants are sorry to lose the payroll; and farmers the market, provided by the soldiers. An outstanding settler on the south bank of the Assiniboine is W. B. Hall. He sends to the Old Country for his bride. They are married in St. Paul. By stage, canoe, and, finally, by buggy, they come to Headingly. "From the Forks, Donald Cameron, son of pioneer farmer Hugh Cameron drives us". On River Lot No. 1, parish of Headingly, they build their home: "the Hermitage". Furnished, at first, with a table, 2 chairs and a chest for a sideboard, the "Hermitage" becomes a community centre, where friends gather to share the Halls' interest, experiments and achievements in horticulture.

Assiniboia buzzes with debate about the Government of Canada proposal of 15 April, that a road and telegraph line be built through the Nor'West to the Pacific; and the refusal of Governor Dallas to co-operate. The Governor is annoyed by the attacks of Rev. G. O. Corbett against "Company" mis-rule. The "Company's" Council of Assiniboia convicts Corbett of attempted abortion on his servant girl; and sentences him to 6 months in the "Company" prison. The "Nor'Wester" proclaims him a martyr. Many Settlers agree. On 20 April, "a few determined characters," led by school teacher James Stewart, release Corbett from prison. Stewart is promptly arrested; and jailed. William Hallet, John Bourke and other citizens, smash the jail door with a crowbar; and release Stewart. There, the matter drops. Dallas, "the Company" and their Council, have "lost face". The old days are gone!

Many "natives" of Assiniboia, whose old-time reverence for "the Company" places its officers above criticism (if not above suspicion) suffer a sad shock when news comes from London that new owners have re-organized "the Company"; and swept away the old Board. "Company" officers are stunned! Shock gives way to rage, as time reveals that the working officers of "the Company" have been robbed of any share in "the Company's" most valuable asset: land!

The first celebration in Assiniboia of the "24th of May, the Queen's birthday" is enlarged by "Overlanders", outfitting for their long trek to the Cariboo gold-fields. Two days later, "SS International" arrives at the Forks. Built for "the Company" at a cost of $20,000.00, she is 150 feet long; 33 foot beam; draws 42 inches of water; and is registered at 133 tons. Of her 200 passengers, 160 are young Canadians "come to pioneer an overland route to the Cariboo."

"Cariboo fever" is making ordinary citizens into "Overlanders". All over Canada West, parties are organizing. One party is coming from Canada East. Seven parties from United States and 1 from England are on their way! At "the Forks", the Overlanders buy horses, at $40.00 each; oxen at $25.00 to $30.00; carts, $8.00; harness of buffalo raw-hide, $4.00; flour, pemmican and other provisions. The lead party rendezvous, on 3 June, at White Horse Plain. Its 138 people include the Schubert family; husband, wife (Kitty O'Hare that was) and 3 small children. These 138 pioneers adopt rules; elect a Captain; and, on 5 June, with their 97 carts and 110 horses and oxen, begin their historic trek — from Assiniboia "overland" to the Cariboo! A week later, they are shooting ducks and catching fish at Shoal Lake. Their sturdy carts carry them far into the mountains; and are left at the limit of wheeled traffic. Three months and 3,000 miles later, the Schubert family is swept into Kamloops, on a raft. It is 3 September. Their fourth babe, a girl, is born next day!

The United States garrison at Pembina — added to Overlanders and new-comers — expand markets for farmers, hunters and traders of Assiniboia. Our dependent population is reaching the point where real shortage threatens, when crop, Hunt or fisheries fail.

Robert and Mrs. Tait (nee Jane Isbister) build one of the first brick houses, near Deer Lodge. Oak sash, doors and furniture; and walnut woodwork — are brought from St. Paul by Red River cart. In the latter 60's, Robert builds a steam grist-mill on the Assiniboine, in front of their home.

This summer begins a 6-year drought. In the years when 'hoppers devour every green thing, many families move to Lake Manitoba; and live on fish. They mix ground grain with fish-meal, to make fish rolls. At the salt springs, French-speaking Settlers make salt. Girls (with lads in attendance) spend long winter evenings "knocking barley"; pounding the grain in hollowed-out blocks of wood, with wooden mallets; and winnowing out the chaff. The cleaned grain is used in broth and soup.

This summer, fear of the Sioux prevents "SS International" coming down to "the Forks." On 18 August, Sioux take the warpath. Minnesota is drenched with blood! Cart trains are plundered. (In their money-making hurry, cart train owners forget the defence lessons taught by Grant!) Minnesota newspapers report: "some 500 cart trains, now in transit to Fort Garry, are waiting at St. Paul and St. Cloud, until protection can be given." (Shades of Grand Coteau!) After a succession of broken United States promises, the Sioux are desperate! An Indian agent tells Little Crow, Chief of the Sioux reservation: "If your people are hungry, let them eat grass." On this terrible 18 August, that agent is dead, his mouth stuffed with grass! The pity is that, as a result of such contemptuous arrogance, 2,000 white settlers are massacred; and 300 women and children held prisoners. The pity is, too, that brave warriors, fighting in the only way they know for some semblance of justice, must be annihilated. Battle-trained troops are hurried to Minnesota and the Dakotas. The Sioux are decimated! Some retreat westward to the Badlands — to fight, for 15 years. Some flee, northward, to Assiniboia.

A "Company" cart train is pillaged. Governor Dallas, and his Council of Assiniboia, get 1,183 signatures on a petition praying the Colonial Office for troops. The "Nor'Wester" gets signatures on a counter-petition, asking for the troops; but criticising "Company" administration. Both petitions, presumably, find their devious ways into the same waste-basket. James Ross asks the Council of Assiniboia for more pay as postmaster. The Governor, smarting under his stinging attacks, as "Nor'Wester" editor, fires Ross as sheriff, postmaster and Councillor! Henry McKinney is appointed sheriff; and A. G. B. Bannatyne is made postmaster, at double the salary paid Ross!

This year, the property which is to become famous as "Deer Lodge" is bought by its equally famous owner: James MacKay. The land comprises Lots 1252 and 1253 of the 1836 survey. In 1857, William Inkster buys Lot 1253 for $172.50. The following year, Alexander Porter pays the same price for Lot 1252. William Inkster sells both lots to James MacKay, in 1862; and both are included in River Lot 21, St. James Parish, on the later re-survey.

In June, the "International Finance Society" buys the Hudson's Bay Company for $7.5 million; and promptly re-capitalizes it at $10 million. The Gentlemen Adventurers are no more! News of this deal "profoundly shocks" "Company" factors and traders. They yell, "We have been sold like cattle."

James Stewart calls a public meeting in St. James, on 11 June, to form "a temporary government by the people — until the British Government shall take the place into their own hands." The idea of a temporary Provisional Government is neither new, nor the nightmare invention of inflamed minds. Many people — new-comers and natives alike — are honestly convinced that Assiniboia needs better government. Probably because most Assiniboia men are away, on the trail or on the Hunt, nothing comes of Stewart's meeting.

Sioux or no Sioux, Assiniboia's cart trains keep rolling. In St. Paul, a Bill of Lading, dated 23 June, is signed by Dr. Schultz for a "Train of carts, Capt. E. L. Barber — to H. McKinney at Fort Garry, he paying freight at the rate of one pound sterling ($5.00) per 100 pounds." With more and more cart trains freighting, hay to feed the draft animals over winter becomes an increasingly important item of local trade. A day is set for the start of hay-cutting, in July. An incredible tonnage of hay is needed; but vast reaches of grass are available. Mutual respect, goodwill and helpfulness are general. When prairie fires burn a family's hay, neighbors supply them. One day, McBeth's stacks go up in smoke. The next, neighbors put 100 cart-loads into his farmyard.

The windmills that grind our grain operate best with the prevailing northwest winds: (The Indian's "Kee-Way-den"). When winds fail, farmers take their grist to John Tait's water-mill on Park's Creek; or, later, to Robert Tait's new steam-mill at Deer Lodge. At Portage la Prairie, Garrioch builds a machine, powered by eight horses, to thresh during the winter. Settlers bring their loads of sheaves from miles around. This year, too, Archdeacon Cochrane imports a horse treadmill from St. Paul. It is taken from farm to farm, to thresh right in the farmer's stackyard.

Luckily, good health prevails. In most of the Settlements there are "no doctors, no knowledge of drugs; only Epsom salts, castor oil, Perry Davis' Painkiller; and, for open cuts, tobacco." Mrs. John Spence, Indian wife, is local doctor in the upper Settlements on the Assiniboine; and "one of the great women" of pioneer days.

After years of study and exploration in the Nor'West, Capt. Palliser reports to his Government, in England. He recommends against settling the great Plains; and against a road to span their vastness. "The time has now gone by for such a project", he affirms. "An astronomical boundary line has completely isolated the central American possessions of Great Britain from Canada in the east; and . . . from the Pacific coast in the west". Fortunately for Canada — and for the world — Nor'Westers neither read his report; nor believe his conclusions! They go ahead, building their country!

Assiniboia natives learn, with pride, that the University of London has conferred the degree of LL.B. on A. K. Isbister. Isbister publishes a steady stream of text-books for schools and teachers. In Assiniboia, pupils of all parish schools study the same spellers and readers as are used in England.

Portage la Prairie asks to be included in the Municipal District of Assiniboia. The "Company" Council of Assiniboia refuses. In June, John McDougall, missionary from near Edmonton, comes to Assiniboia, to buy supplies for his mission and carts and oxen to transport them. He reports meeting the Assiniboia "summer Hunt, with about 500 carts" near Fort Ellice. McDougall headquarters with Oliver and Mary Gowler. He buys oxen at $35.00 each; 4 "fine" milch cows, at $18.00 each; and flour at $8.00 per hundred pounds. The drought is now in its third year. Nevertheless, the Hunt is good; and food is abundant. The Red River is so low that "SS International" makes only one trip. The "Company" is forced to hire many extra cart freighters.

South of the border, Gen. Sully's force defeats the Sioux in a battle of many days. Some survivors come to Assiniboia. But, Saulteaux, Cree and Chippewas give the refugees no peace. Traders refuse them ammunition. Most of them return to the United States. Meantime, however, gangs of Sioux raid farms at Headingly and White Horse Plain, to get food.

Through a dry, dry summer, the 'hoppers destroy farm crops. "Red River Fever" sweeps along the Assiniboine River and the Red. It is virulent, infectious, contagious. Throughout the fall, fires blast the dead grass and bush into black desolation. Winter strikes with even more than usual severity!

William McTavish follows Dallas as "Company" Governor. He steps into rapidly changing conditions. Costs of operation rise sharply — as free traders defy "the Company"; and competition intensifies. The vagaries of the Hunt, on which the fur trade lives; higher wages demanded by trip-men and voyageurs (who enjoy the new experience of choice between all the jobs offered by traders, cart trains, steamships and overland travellers) all these cut into "Company" earnings; and whittle the dividends of shareholders in England.

Farmers in various of the Settlements, winter livestock along the Assiniboine, near Poplar Point. Fine weather brings spring early. On 6 April, a Kildonan farmer is driving his herd homeward. As they drift along the Portage Trail, through St. James, a springtime blizzard explodes! In the howling gale and smothering sleet, the cattle scatter, helter-skelter! After 3 days, the storm abates. The farmer finds several of his cattle smothered under the snow that fills Omand's Creek to the brim! The summer that follows, is one of blistering drought.

The Assiniboia Hunt goes on, in expanding scale. "The Nor'Wester" of 8 June, 1865, reports: "The able-bodied population . . . has left . . . and it will be nearly 2 months before. . . they return. We are a nomadic race. Hundreds of men, women and children are off to the summer Hunt . . . Trip-men are away to the interior. One brigade of 150 carts is soon to start for Georgetown; and hundreds of carts are off to St. Paul" — to "trade through the Sioux."

Seven hundred miles south of Assiniboia, on 10 July, work begins on the Union Pacific Railway. Every mile is surveyed and built under military protection. The building of the "U.P." effects our history, profoundly. It splits the buffalo population of the continent into "south herd" and "north herd"; and upsets the pattern of annual migration for both. It brings thousands of men to slaughter the buffalo — for food, hides and "sport"; and hustles the day of extinction for the uncounted herds.

Dr. Schultz becomes sole owner of "the Nor'Wester", Assiniboia's only newspaper. Schultz "personifies violence". He damns "the Company" and their creature Council. Sued and jailed — for debt, he is released when 15 of his "Canadian Party" overpower the guards.

This fall, 200 gallons of whiskey is freighted to Portage la Prairie, in the wagons of 3 traders, known as "the Yankee boys". Promptly, comes the first outbreak of trouble between white citizens and Indians.

Archdeacon Cochrane resigns in June; and, with Colin Inkster, goes by cart brigade to St. Cloud; and on, to visit his son in Toronto. In late September he returns. At Westbourne, the Whitemud River looks inviting. He takes a swim, as he so often has done. The water is ice cold. Fever develops. On 1 October, 1865, this great pioneer takes the Long Trail. The Settlements are stunned! The funeral passes, mournfully, through the parishes — from his St. Mary's on the Prairie — High Bluff, Poplar Point, St. Francois Xavier, Headingly, St. Charles, St. James, St. John's, Kildonan, Middlechurch — to St. Andrews. Here he is laid to rest — at the end of 40 years devoted service to Assiniboia.

Rev. James Carrie takes over as rector of Holy Trinity Church, in Headingly. At St. Charles a new church is built. It stands east of the Convent, facing up the River. Fr. Lestance is the moving spirit in building this church and the first school in St. Charles. Confirmation, on 13 May, writes the following family names into Assiniboia's history: Bousquet, Swan, Caplette, Capisisit, Allary, Frederic, Ducharme, Jobin, McMullen, Cochrane, Bird and Bourassa. During the year, a new Presbyterian church is built in Headingly.

Up the Assiniboine, in May, a Saulteaux and one of "the Yankee boys" are killed in a fight. This fall, a Sioux kills a Saulteaux. Cattle and horses are shot by Indians. A Sioux kills a Sioux trader. Red Lake Indians attack and kill 4 Sioux around "the Forks." A hybrid, Demairais, kills a Saulteaux and is sentenced to hang; but authorities adroitly get him away — banished for life. All this prompts the organization of a police force of 100 volunteers.

Dr. Schultz tries for a seat on the Council of Assiniboia. The "Canadians", and some others, support him with a petition. When the "Establishment" black-balls him, editor Schultz thunders, in "the Nor'Wester" that "the Company" usurps the rights of the people! The fact that many agree gets Schultz little sympathy from Assiniboia natives.

The United States army is still Sioux-hunting. After 6 years of slaughter, no Indians range the region between Assiniboia and St. Paul. Trains of carts — and wagons — again travel the old Woods Trail. On the Plains Trail, from Fort Abercrombie to Pembina, a Minnesota newspaper reports: "not a human being, cabin or other mark of white or red man's appearance remains!" From Assiniboia, cart trains roll, without a break, to the far corners of the vast Nor'West.

The big event of 1867 is Confederation; and the news that the

British North America Act provides for the Nor'West joining the other provinces, in Canada. In the East, adding the Nor'West to Canada, is urged, loud and long, by William McDougall. Nor'West people voice varied ideas about union with Canada. "The Nor'Wester", of 13 July, affirms: "the land must be bought, when it is really acquired, from the Indians themselves." This appears reasonable; and well within the means of Canada — considering that Governments have handed out $130 millions to the Grand Trunk Railway! This year the United States buys Alaska from Russia for $7.2 millions — barely 5% of Canada's largess to Grand Trunk promoters!

In Assiniboia, 1868 brings moderation of the long drought; but the cumulative effects of 7 dry years is devastating. From Settlements up the Assiniboine comes news that Thomas Spence (recent arrival from Montreal; author of the "Indian" memorial to the Prince of Wales; and now a Portage la Prairie shop-keeper) sets up "The Republic of Manitoba" — with himself as President. Taxes levied to build a "government house and a jail" — wreck the "Republic". Shoemaker McPherson, of High Bluff, accuses the President and his cronies of drinking up the taxes at the local tavern. He refuses to pay; and backs up his words with a pistol! The Republic dissolves!

In the parishes along the Rivers, 9 Anglican clergymen are serving. St. James parish is the charge of Rev. Wm. H. Taylor, until this year, when Rev. W. C. Pinkham takes over. Dr. Schultz, to release his restless energies for other ventures, sells "the Nor'Wester" to his friend, dentist-free-trader, Dr. Walter R. Bown. Bown packs weekly issues with virulent attacks on "the Company". With "government weak", a contemporary records, "most settlers are law-abiding . . . and content . . . Not in accord with 'agitators' ". "The Nor'Wester" becomes the voice of the malcontents. Its abuse of "the Company" disgusts, "respectable" settlers. Nevertheless, while Bown is not a popular editor, he fights for self-government for Assiniboia.

The population of Winnipeg village is growing toward 200. Arrivals include James Ashdown, merchant; James Stewart, druggist; and William Chambers, who starts the Hingston Smith Arms Co. Dr. C. J. Bird moves in from Middlechurch. Among the few from the United States is John Wickes Taylor, who urges that England cede all North American possessions to pay United States claims arising out of the War between the States. Disciples of "Manifest Destiny" are sure, as a U.S. Senate report states: "The Northern Pacific Railway from Lake Superior to Puget Sound will seal the destiny of the British possession . . . They will be severed . . . Annexation will be a matter of time". Working with Taylor to grab Assiniboia are "General" Oscar Malmros, U. S.

Consul to the village of 200; and "Colonel" Enos Stutsman. Each of these men knows more about Assiniboia and its people than any of Canada's politicians ever take the trouble to learn. Only the perverse stubbornness of our people in loving this vast and vicious Nor'West, defies all logic of geography, economics and history, to keep Canada intact. But, as Wellington says after Waterloo: "It was a damned near thing!"

In Assiniboia, Settlements hug the Rivers; comfortable in rude prosperity; peaceful, law-abiding and loyal; with a strong, if silent, sense of community. Tidy farmsteads and fields along the banks; and, beyond, cattle pasturing on the rich grass, provide a fringe "of man-made beauty to the limitless carpet of prairie." This year, haying time sees mowing machines beginning to replace those back-breaking scythes. "Good feeling exists between all classes," writes Begg, "and more hospitable and happy people could hardly be found on the face of the earth than the Settlers of Red River in 1868-69." Then, in July, a cyclone wrecks many buildings. In August, "grasshoppers devour every green thing on the face of the land." The Hunt fails. The fisheries fail. Geese, ducks, prairie chicken disappear. It is the seventh year — when all wildlife follows the rabbits, in their "crash decline". Rudely comfortable prosperity dissolves in starvation! "The Nor'Wester" broadcasts a call for help! The Council of Assiniboia promptly votes $8,000.00 — in flour, and fishing and hunting equipment. "The Company" contributes $10,000.00. Generosity spans isolation; and contributions totalling $37,000.00 pour in from Canada, United Kingdom and United States.

A "relief committee" is organized. Settlers are hired to freight food from St. Paul; and take pay in provisions. Free traders — their freight refused by "the Company" — hire Settlers for their cart brigades. The Government of Canada approves the Dawson Trail, to link the Great Lakes and the Great Plains. On 18 September, Canada's Minister of Public Works, Hon. Wm. McDougall, orders John A. Snow to begin work on this road, at the western end. As yet, Canada has no right or title in this territory. Dawson and Hind survey it, with the consent and co-operation of "the Company". Snow and Mair barge in without even consultation. From the Minister down, all act as if Assiniboia is already part of Ontario; and they the arrogant owners!

The project is rushed, it is said "to provide relief work for Settlers." Few Settlers are employed. Some Metis are hired, to chop out and corduroy the right-of-way, through rock, timber and swamp. Their monthly wage, of $15.00, is paid in provisions from Schultz's store at Oak Point. (At 100% profit!) Most of the workers are from Canada and the United States. Enraged at the low pay and hard conditions, some

of these threaten to drown Snow. He testifies that the men hired in
Assiniboia are satisfactory; the trouble-makers are U.S. army deserters
and Canadians!

More and more new-comers are staking land. The great need is for
valid titles. "The Nor'Wester" publicizes the popular opinion that every
man has as good a title to his chosen acres as has "the Company" or any
"squatter". "You hold as much as you occupy". The custom of the
country has been for each family to use the land it needs; and, if and
when transferred, the new owner to pay for improvements. Now, this
custom is swept aside in a mad scramble for land. Canadians, Americans,
Europeans, even Metis from Montana, rush to stake claims. To
escape this melee; and, perhaps, to settle near better buffalo pastures,
Metis families begin to move from the Assiniboine River and the Red,
to the Saskatchewans.

In their hurry, some Canadians buy (?) land from Indians near Oak
Point; and eject the hybrid occupants, as illegal "squatters". The cry
sweeps the Settlements: "The Canadians have come to steal our homes!"
What else can a man think, who, bringing his family home after all
summer on the trail, finds his cabin and land in the hands of some new-
comer who claims the property? Too often, there emerges the sneering
contempt of new-come "white" men for the "natives" of Assiniboia, as
"miserable half-breeds". Chas. Mair writes home to Ontario, expressing
his contempt for the "half-breed" wives of leading Winnipeggers. When
he goes to get his mail, he is horse-whipped out of the post office, by
Mrs. Bannatyne! Letters reprinted in Eastern newspapers, which (like
Mair's) ridicule Assiniboia's people, invite hatred and distrust of all
Canadians.

Meantime, officials in Assiniboia live lavishly. "Above stairs"
guests are gorged with hospitality. Chas. Mair (recovered from his
horse-whipping) reports a dinner party in Fort Garry, on 27 November,
where all revel in: "oyster soup, whitefish, roast beef, roast prairie
chicken, green peas, tomatoes, gooseberries, plum pudding, blanc mange,
raisins, nuts, coffee, port, sherry, brandy punch . . . cigars . . . in
the heart of the continent . . . with Indian lodges within a stone's throw".

At this time, some 12,000 people live in Assiniboia. About 200 of
them live in 30 buildings, scattered along 2 muddy trails. There are 8
stores, 2 saloons, 2 hotels, 1 mill, 1 church, a small hall and a post
office. This is Winnipeg. Somewhere among these shacks are headquarters for the "Canadian party" and the "American party". The
spoutings of these "parties" spread fear among Assiniboia people —
Metis, "English half-breeds" and natives whose parentage includes no
Indian — that their lands will be taken from them; and they will be

menials to the "superior" people who are come to rule all "lesser breeds"!

Formerly, "Canadians" are those who adventure to Assiniboia from the St. Lawrence, as free-men or fur Company employees. Now, the new-comers from Ontario call themselves "the Canadians." Their views and propaganda, printed in "The Nor'Wester", smother observations and customs recorded only in the spoken word; and, "sanctified by repetition" becomes the basis of much of the "history" of these times. Some of these new-comers — aggressive, acquisitive — see this land as a vacant vastness awaiting their ownership. They recognize that natives of unquestioned "white" parentage have some rights; but have only contempt for all Indians and "half-breeds." Thus, a vociferous minority generates hostility and hate against all "Canadians". Regrettably, with such contempt becoming the fashion, many natives disown their Indian birthright, as a shameful thing. Assiniboia's people find themselves being divided into opposing groups.

In St. Charles parish, in September, Fr. Allard takes over as the first resident priest. Added to the parish records are the following family names: Hogue, Morrisette, Guiboche, Desjardins, Tobin, Mandeville, Capelette, Gaudry, Proulx, Braconnier, Bird, Laverdure, Shauteuse.

In December, Louis Riel returns to Assiniboia. Riel is one of Assiniboia's controversial citizens. A mass of material has been written of him. Much of it is better propaganda than history; and inflames rather than informs. Current writers are attempting to subject more complete records to more balanced analysis. Even so, studies by highly competent authors are marred, still, by nonsense about one group of human animals being "superior" to others. Perhaps 3 generations is too short a time for fires kindled by idealism, and fed by hate and selfishness, to cool — so that the ashes may be sifted (without burnt fingers) for all the evidence of history.

The secret sale of "the Company" in 1863, shocks and insults officials, as well as the people of the country, the real foundation of the business. Now, again, the Nor'West and its people are bought and sold "like a cattle ranch with the critters on it."

On 9 March, agreements are concluded, whereby Canada buys the Nor'West from a Hudson's Bay Company, sired by the Grand Trunk Railway and mothered by the International Finance Society. Canada is to pay the promoters: $1,500,000.00 cash; "reserves" around "Company" posts; and 7 million fertile acres. "The Company" retains all its trading privileges. The 12,000 people of Assiniboia — white, hybrid, Indian — are ignored! And out-raged! Incredibly, nobody in Canada even considers them. What about their farms? Will new-comers grab their land? Will religious freedom be lost? Will inflooding migrants smother the natives; and possess the country they pioneered?

To keep proper perspective, the events of these months must be related to the annual rhythm of Assiniboia's economy. In the clash of purposes and personalities so abundantly recorded, it is easy to forget that the daily life and work of the Settlements go on.

May begins the season's work. Farm families labor around the clock, to seed their fields. Dust from the harrowing of the last acre has not settled when some farmers and farmers' sons are away with 1 or 2 carts and oxen, to join a cart brigade. Farmer-hunters and the hunter-farmers hurry to finish seeding, before the Spring Hunt. Hunters repair carts, harness, tents; and get supplies. By mid-May the Hunt moves out to the Grand Passage; crosses the Assiniboine; and heads south and west. Cart brigades are already on the trails — some freighting furs and pemmican past Pembina to St. Cloud and St. Paul; some, westward, along the Portage Trail, with trade goods and supplies for "Company" posts and free traders, scattered over the Nor'West.

In June, the Hunt takes "all able-bodied men from the Settlement" as well as hundreds of women and children. Throughout the month, cart trains are returning from south of the border with merchant's goods. Other brigades are coming home to Assiniboia, with furs from the far Nor'West.

July is the time when free traders and trappers come from the Plains and forests to trade their furs; and, in their camps on "the Company reserve" beside Fort Garry, hold a few weeks high and noisy celebration! By mid-July, the cart brigades are home from St. Paul, with their cargoes of goods; and from the Nor'West with their loads of furs. About 15 July, too, farm families begin a month's work in the hayfields. Through the last days of July, the carts of the free traders and trappers, loaded with goods and supplies, screech their way along the trails southwest, west, and northwest — back to the fur country.

August welcomes home the spring Hunt; and soon, in the fall brigades, hundreds of carts are rolling toward St. Paul with furs and pemmican; and hundreds more, to the Nor'West with trade goods. September sends out the big fall Hunt; brings home the cart brigades from St. Paul and fur-loaded trains from the Nor'West; and sees farm families struggle to harvest the crops — handicapped by the shortage of workers.

The Settlements are home to some 12,000 people (give or take a few hundred Indians, travellers, and celebrating traders). Of this total, thousands are on the move for months at a time. When November ends fall work on the farms; and brings back the big fall Hunt, the population of Assiniboia is "at home" — excepting, only, those hundreds who elect to "winter out" on the plains and along the waterways.

The population may include 2,600 able-bodied men. During the summer, the cart trains may employ 1,500 of these. Another 600 or more, follow the Hunt. Perhaps 100 are on the steamships, the docks and in the warehouses. If 300 settlers are home on their farms throughout the year — cutting hay for the cart-oxen; and chopping wood for the steamships — we have a balance of only 100 officials, traders, teachers, priests, shop-keepers, editor, postmaster and craftsmen in Fort Garry and the village of Winnipeg. Of course, these 100 full-time inhabitants are at the hub of events. Many of them are recent arrivals from Ontario. Their names are featured in their newspaper and in records of public meetings, debates and councils; and pack the pages of our written history.

"The principle trail to the south crosses the Assiniboine at the Grand Passage", J. F. Robinson, Headingly merchant, advertises in "the Nor'Wester"; "The subscriber wishes to announce to the people of Headingly, White Horse Plain, Portage la Prairie that he has established a rope ferry across the Assiniboine at his place . . . It always is in good condition, when other roads are impassable". (How little advertising changes!)

William Dease, a leading Metis, calls a public meeting at the court house, on 29 July, to discuss the transfer to Canada. "Natives" suspect that Dease is acting for "the Canadian", Schultz; and do not attend.

In Canada, Hon. Wm. McDougall, Minister of Public Works, on 10 July, directs Col. J. S. Dennis to survey Assiniboia. Dennis warns: there may be trouble, unless claims of the people are settled. Nevertheless, he and his survey party ride the railway from Canada to St. Paul; and at St. Cloud, buy horses and wagons for the 450-mile trip to "the Forks." They pass hundreds of carts, freighting on this trail. On arrival, some of the surveyors stake land for future occupation (without regard to former owners; and although Canada has not yet taken possession of the country.) With the Dennis party is Major Boulton, late of the "British regulars".

On 28 September, McDougall is appointed Lieut-Governor of the Nor'West, at $7,000.00 yearly; and is instructed to proceed West, to superintend organization of the territory. Dennis sets up headquarters at Oak Point. Parties rush to survey Assiniboia into square miles "for immediate settlement"; and to fit these into the River Lots of the Old Settlement Belt Survey.

Suddenly — the survey stops!

On the base line running over the outer 2-mile "hay privilege" of the farm owned by Andre Nault, north of St. Norbert, surveyors lay their chain. They never pick it up! Eighteen Settlers stand on it. They are Metis. Among them is Louis Riel. He speaks for them. They challenge the right of Canada to survey the country, before Indian and Metis claims thereto are considered; and before individual titles, now recognized by "the custom of the country", are confirmed. The survey stops!

The Settlements seethe with talk of the "sell out" by "the Company;" and the invasion by Canadians. U.S. Consul Malmros writes from "the Forks", on 11 September: "the mass of Settlers are inclined to riot". Many native farmers, traders and trip-men, white, hybrid and Indian meet in Thomas Sinclair's home. All are angry. Their distrust is aroused by a few new-comers, who, Begg writes, "professing the cause of Canada, are really concerned with filling their own pockets. These men, when the survey begins, stake out big acreages . . . and boast they will be the owners when Canada gets possession." While dissatisfied and irritated, many "natives" are not yet ready to take action. They are uncertain what action they should take. The meeting registers no decision.

Meantime, many farmers and trip-men, with the few hunters now home from the plains, are coming to the decision that the only way to maintain their rights is to resist "the Canada's". Unfortunately, for Canada as for Assiniboia, Bishop Tache — universally revered, trusted and beloved — is in Rome. Rev. Georges Dugas, Rev. L. R. Giroux and Rev. M. J. Richot urge Riel to lead the resistance.

Prime Minister John A. Macdonald has been warned — in 1868 by Bishop Machray; and this year by Governor McTavish and Bishop Tache — that he must satisfy the just claims of the people of Assiniboia, or expect trouble! But Macdonald, Cartier and MacDougall all appear to regard Assiniboia's Settlers as savages to be ignored, rather than as citizens with rights to be respected.

The politician who has most fervently preached "the Nor'West" now proves how little he understands of its people; and the simple rights they ask for (and, in due course, get!) Wm. MacDougall is a "heavy" man — heavy-set, heavy-jawed, heavily pompous. On that 11 October when the survey of Assiniboia stops, MacDougall is at St. Cloud, Minnesota, waiting for his baggage to catch up. He travels like a conquering king to his kingdom — surrounded by job-holders and job-seekers, secretaries and servants; 60 wagons of baggage, 300 new Enfield rifles and cases of ammunition. His vice-regal party includes Miss MacDougall and servants; Capt. Cameron, his wife and servants; Dr. A. G. Jacques, Mr. Richards and Major Wallace. Charles Mair is there, too, with his wife, his friendship for the Lieut-Governor-elect and a Government job. And (lest these greats and near-greats soil their hands) there are "men" to pitch and manage camp.

Canada's Secretary of State, Hon. Joseph Howe, makes a flying visit to Assiniboia; talks to pioneers of all persuasions and parties; makes no public speeches; and attends no public functions. His entire effort is to generate assurance that Canada will deal fairly with all. On 18 October, Howe leaves for Canada. En route he meets MacDougall; and warns him of "uneasiness" among the Settlers.

Facing these problems, people around "the Forks" are unaware of an event of more ghastly significance. Smallpox sweeps the Indian camps — from the Plains to the Arctic; and kills 100,000 people — 8 times the total population of Assiniboia!

Those among the Metis who urge action, meet on 19 October in Rev. Richot's home. They organize on the familiar pattern of the Hunt; and elect John Bruce, President; with Louis Riel, secretary. Next day they form their executive: "Committee National de Metis". The "Committee" acts! Under the autumn-tinted trees, 40 men ride south of St. Norbert; and, on the Pembina Trail, erect "La Barriere". Riders deliver a letter from the Council to William MacDougall in Pembina, warning him not to enter Assiniboia without permission. Through the fateful months that follow, the majority of the people of Assiniboia insist that Canada negotiate with them. No more — and, certainly, no less!

On 25 October, the Council of Assiniboia meets. Two "Company" men — Dease and Goulet — are instructed to "collect as many as possible of the 'more respectable' of the French (speaking) community; and, with them, proceed to the camp of the party who intend to intercept Hon. Wm. MacDougall, to procure their peaceful dispersal". These emissaries of "the Company" duly report: "all classes hold that they have not been treated fairly, in not having been consulted; and that they have been sold as chattels". The Council of Assiniboia considers this report on 30 October. No French-speaking members attend. Judge Black presides: Governor Wm. McTavish being too ill. The Councillors present decide to dissolve. The last vestige of "Company" civil administration vanishes! The people of Assiniboia are without government!

On this date, Wm. MacDougall and his "conquering army" — staff, hangers-on and wagonloads of rifles and ammunition — arrive at Pembina. Despite the warning not to enter Assiniboia, MacDougall sends Col. Dennis to the Settlements to raise a force of Scots, English and their hybrid kin (who, combined, are fully half the population) to bring "himself" in triumph to his throne! Returning, Dennis reports: the English-speaking Settlers, although angry about not being consulted, will accept Canadian rule; but, they certainly will not fight their neighbors, the French-speaking half of the population, "with whom we live in friendship".

MacDougall and the "brass" of his army may be so greedy for the prize within their clutches, that they do not realize, or care, what the consequences can be, of arraying the people of Assiniboia against each other in battle. Fortunately, the canny natives have more sense; and a split is averted, for a time. Dennis tries again. Under pretense of surveying, he sends men to Portage la Prairie to raise the force he craves. Again he fails. Perhaps he begins to learn that, here, he is not dealing with the bar-room Fenians who made him look foolish at Ft. Erie, 3 years back — but with men who live, largely, by the guns they carry.

Wm. McTavish, "Company" Governor, advises MacDougall to remain at Pembina. Rumors sweep the Settlements like blizzards: "The English" are coming to burn the cathedral and convent! "The French" are raising Indians to make Riel a dictator! "The English" are bringing the Sioux to scalp us all! Riel is the tool of the United States! Although not head of the Metis Council, Riel is singled out, by "the loyal Canadian party" and MacDougall's frustrated flunkeys, as the arch-fiend causing all their troubles! J. A. N. Provencher and Capt. Cameron, of MacDougall's retinue, drive northward on the Pembina Trail, to "La Barriere". Mounted guards escort them back to the border.

On 1 November, the Metis Council musters its forces for a decisive step. Many hunters and trip-men are now home for the winter. These are men of action! John Bruce, president of their Committee (it is reported) reviews 500 men . . . "all bearing arms". Men in Assiniboia habitually carry arms, mostly old smooth-bore buffalo guns, with an effective range one-tenth that of the new Enfields. Next day, the Metis walk into Fort Garry — with its houses, workshops, store, jail, 390 rifles and 13 cannons — and take possession.

Dr. Schultz rages that "Company" officials connive at the take-over. Some of them may be "glad to see Canada and MacDougall in a jam". They, too, have been ignored. That they are "disloyal" is obvious propaganda. However, some of them may point out to Metis leaders, that the one thing the Schultz party lack is: guns. They can get none of MacDougall's Enfields. Metis guards watch them too closely. The Metis do not need the trade guns in Fort Garry. But Schultz may get them; and at one stroke, end all hope of negotiation with Canada! Its very nature brings all this under discussion by the Metis Council. The Council forestalls any such possibility — by occupying Fort Garry, themselves.

Realization that the Metis Council has taken possession of Fort Garry, fragments the people of Assiniboia into bewildered groups. For 2 generations, since the warring fur-men merge in 1821, Fort Garry has been the symbol, often of oppression — but always of stability. Now, stability explodes! Thought-pictures that mirror old beliefs and loyalties are blasted into smithereens, from which each individual must pick shatterings wherewith to build beliefs and loyalties, anew. Native Nor'Westers agree that Canada and "the Company" have traded them like cattle. They fear that "the Canadians" aim to take over the country they love — and have pioneered. Beyond this, many are uncertain — searching for what to believe.

Dr. Schultz yells "Rebellion"! (Against who, or what, is not clear!) The "loyal Canadian party" probably numbers 100, out of our population of 12,000. Of all Assiniboia people, they are, perhaps, the only organized "party". Young adventurers from Ontario come under the domination of Dr. Schultz' boundless enthusiasm, tremendous energy and volcanic patriotism. Among them are fine pioneers — and some extremists. These want Canada to take over the Nor'West, forthwith, from "the miserable half-breeds" and other natives. Most "Canadians" are among that fraction of Assiniboia's people who live at "the Forks", among the nomadic thousands who spend their lives on wheels. They control the press of Assiniboia; and have exclusive entre to that of Ontario. Some are professional men; and copious "ink-slingers". Their reiteration of "rebellion" fixes this word in our history. Actually, the "Red River Rebellion" never was!

The "American party", working out of George Emmerling's hotel, makes up for its infinitismal numbers with devotion to their Manifest Destiny. For example, J. W. Taylor learns more about our Nor'West — its resources, people and potential, than any other man of his day. They want our Nor'West for the United States. They have powerful arguments. In St. Paul, furs and pemmican bring twice Assiniboia prices, and goods cost less. Minnesota booms — partly on trade smuggled from Assiniboia. In United States, every man can hunt, trade and trip, free and unhindered. Canada should not deny the Nor'West people the right to decide their own future, by a free vote. (As, later, we urge for "backward" countries).

The English-speaking hybrids, who number about 5,000, are divided. Many of these, like the native settlers of all-white parentage, are former "Company" servants. They bristle in opposition to anyone other than "the Company", occupying Fort Garry. The same is true of many settlers along the upper Assiniboine.

The Metis — offspring of French-speaking Canadians and their Indian wives, numbering under 6,000 — are, likewise, divided. Many, like Chas. Nolin, are against Riel. Other wealthy Metis traders and farmers, like Pascal Breland, Wm. Dease and Joseph Hamelin, want no trouble. They are doing well with things as they are. (And didn't those Red River Metis turn against Cuthbert Grant?)

Those who do organize in the Metis Council, may respond, increasingly, to the leadership of Louis Riel. They insist upon the election of a Provisional Government, to negotiate with Canada, terms under which all will be satisfied to see the country transferred. Historians who enjoy emphasizing that their insistence is "backed by 500 Metis with arms" may overlook the fact that there are, probably, 5 times that number of men in Assiniboia "with arms".

The Metis Council — and most of the people of Assiniboia — want, first: confirmed title to the acres they occupy, whether by "Company" grant, or by "the custom of the country"; and, second, they want a recognized "place" in this great land, of which they are natives.

English negotiators who would readily die to prevent a foreign power possessing the smallest rocky tip of Cornwall, in "negotiations" give to the United States, Canadian territory with potential exceeding the entire British Isles! They love England; are part of it. Native Nor'-Westers, in like manner and measure, love Assiniboia. It takes years for new-comers to see — through flood and drought; storm and sunset — the limitless beauty of this vast land; and to feel part of its immensity. Some never do. "Many are called, but few are chosen" to be at home in the Nor'West. To those fortunate chosen, no other land on earth compares with this. The pioneers of Assiniboia earn their title to possession!

On 6 November, a group of Metis go to the "Nor'Wester" office. They want printed, invitations to English-speaking parishes to elect 12 delegates to meet with delegates from 12 French-speaking parishes, to insist that Canada negotiate with all the Settlers — the entry of Assiniboia into Confederation. Dr. Bown, "ye editor," is abusively decisive in his refusal to do any job printing for "miserable half-breeds". With equal decisiveness (and, we suspect, equal abuse) Bown is locked in his office — while his printers run off the required notices.

The 24 delegates are duly elected from all the parishes. They meet in Convention, on 16 November. The cannon of Fort Garry boom out a 24-gun salute. (Are the gunners "Company" servants?) "Meeting in a hostile camp", writes one reporter, "Nothing could be done without permission of Riel". Surely, that writer cannot know these men! For example, John Taylor sits in that Convention. Would any decision of his await anyone's permission? In the Convention, Dr. C. J. Bird, a native and former member of the dissolved Council of Assiniboia, helps frame a Bill of Rights. Some delegates want it sent to MacDougall; others to the Government of Canada. Without agreement, the Convention, on 1 December, adjourns to the 22nd.

At Pembina, Wm. MacDougall gets a letter from Hon. Joseph Howe, instructing him to "stay where you are". Governor McTavish now urges MacDougall to return to Canada; false friends have "misled him". On the other hand, "Friends of Canada" write, from Winnipeg: "The Company are with the rebels. Issue a proclamation. It will be responded to by 500 men".

After dark, on 1 December, Wm. MacDougall strides into Assiniboia! Hunched against a howling blizzard, by lantern light, he reads a "Queen's Proclamation", which he has forged; and returns to a warm bed in Pembina. Next day, he sends Col. Dennis to distribute his phony proclamation throughout the Settlements; and to enlist soldiers to "quell the insurrection". (MacDougall and his people must have their "rebellion"!)

One scribe tells that Dennis enlists and drills "English and Scot halfbreeds" at the Stone Fort and in Portage; and "the Canadians" in Winnipeg; but mentions no native white men. Dennis buys supplies, arms and ammunition. Indians, under Chief Prince, volunteer. (To get arms, ammunition and well fed, of course, they do!) "In each parish I formed a company of 50," writes Major Boulton. (1,200 men in 24 parishes — or 650 men in the "English" parishes and the village? How many "Companies" does the Major really form?)

Postmaster Bannatyne calls a meeting of the electors of Winnipeg for 26 November. How many of the village's 100 men foregather "all armed as customary" is not known. Riel and Schultz attend. It is proposed that "the Company" continue to govern; but reform. Riel agrees; but, by the end of November, is again urging a Provisional Government, elected by the people of Assiniboia.

Increasingly, Metis action is attributed to Riel. It may be that the buffalo hunters, home now, are urging him to stronger action. On 1 December, the Metis Council discusses contacting MacDougall. Word comes that Dennis plans to attack Fort Garry with his drilled companies. The Metis Council (or Riel) has "the Nor'Wester" and "the Pioneer" offices closed; and houses searched for arms. The drilling of companies of Indians and hybrids at the Stone Fort; and "the Canadians" in Winnipeg, consolidates most of the Metis around Riel.

On 6 December, the Governor-General of Canada proclaims amnesty to all who lay down their arms. Prime Minister Macdonald sends Col. de Salaberry and Fr. Thibault to tell the Settlers their lands and customs are safe. Privately, John A. writes: "We must construct a golden bridge (of bribery?) over which MacDougall can pass into the country".

In this day, when bribery is the currency of politics, politicians cannot believe that Riel, now emerging as leader of the resistance, with all his susceptibilites and faults, is dedicated, beyond influence by "gifts", to his purpose of forcing Canada to negotiate with Assiniboia's people.

Bishop Machray may see this; and writes to Col. Dennis that what is needed is "a very conciliatory attitude . . . from Governor MacDougall; and a plain setting forth of how the government is to be conducted . . . Generous consideration of grievances". Prompted by desire for the common good, this is an accurate appreciation of the situation. Howe writes, on 7 December, to MacDougall, giving the guarantees the people of Assiniboia want. Six weeks pass, before Donald Smith makes this information public.

Following instructions from Col. Dennis, "the Canadian Company", under Dr. Lynch, assembles at Dr. Schultz's house. (They say, to protect provisions stored there.) "This was a great mistake," writes one of them, Dr. O'Donnell. "Had they gone about their usual business, they would never have been attacked." The Metis surround the house, on 7 December; and capture 60 men "with arms". "All of this pays off for Schultz", O'Donnell avers. He is richly repaid for rebellion losses; makes fortunes in furs, land, telegraphs, railways; is knighted; and made Lieutenant-Governor and Senator.

Dennis still talks war! Failing to raise a force in the Lower Settlement, he writes MacDougall: "If the people were willing, they could muster arms enough to put down the half-breeds; but they won't do it . . . They are cowards!"

Meanwhile, the current of life flows on. Farm families have harvested a good crop; and are busy flailing out the golden grain. Some cattle are stabled for the winter; some are wintering along the Assiniboine, out Poplar Point way. Extra horses are turned loose, to fend for themselves until spring. Johnny Isbister marries Mary Bruce; and takes her to the snug cabin he has built on the Assiniboine, where golfers of a later day will often pause to view the beauty of the River. Mary makes moccasins for Louis Riel, who pays her in blankets, groceries and kindness. Mrs. Wm. Good (Mary Ann Kirton that was) had similar memories of the Metis leader. More people are settling up the Assiniboine. New family names added to the St. Charles Parish register during 1869 include: McNabb, Mackay, Piau, LeClerc, Viviers, Deschamps, Isbister, Smith, Swan, Grant, Turquotte, Hamelin, Allery, Inkster, Walsh, Shearer, Genthon, Posquet, Marion, McDermot, Van Dale, Sauve, Wilson, Williams, Ness, McMullen, Dease, Riel, Volas, Gladu, Millette, Taylor, Rachette, Falcon, Potras, Manzoni, Parenteau, McGilvery, Decette, Lawson, Sepisisit, Short, McLoughlin.

On 8 December, the Metis Council proclaims a Provisional Government. Next day, Bannatyne gets a proclamation from Dennis calling on "loyal" citizens to cease arming; and the party in arms to send a delegation to MacDougall. Four days later, Wm. MacDougall writes, inviting Riel to visit him. Riel ne responde pas. Perhaps the buffalo hunters on the Metis Council don't want their Secretary to meet the man Canada has sent to take over their country. On 10 December, Donald A. Smith is appointed Special Commissioner to Assiniboia: to inquire into the discontent; and solve the difficulties according to his best judgment. Within 3 days, he is on his way to Assiniboia — with guarantees of amnesty, of religious freedom and of land titles.

On 18 December, Wm. MacDougall leaves Pembina for Canada. Hon. Joseph Howe writes to him, on 24 December, condemning the "utterly illegal . . . reckless and extraordinary . . . proceedings of Col. Dennis". Alexander Begg, early Assiniboia historian, says that MacDougall's undoing is in "placing confidence in supposed friends; his total lack of any conciliatory spirit; and his overbearing manner". On Christmas day, John Bruce resigns as President of the Metis Council. Elected to fill his place is Louis Riel. Donald A. Smith, with his secretary and kinsman, Richard Hardisty, reaches Fort Garry on 27 December — 14 days from Montreal. Col. de Salaberry and Grand Vicar Thibault, also, arrive; and are lodged in the Bishop's House, in St. Boniface.

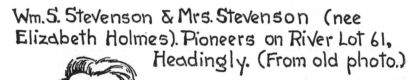

Wm. S. Stevenson & Mrs. Stevenson (nee Elizabeth Holmes). Pioneers on River Lot 61, Headingly. (From old photo.)

CHAPTER 9

Adams G. Archibald

Steamboat 'Round the Bend . . . 1870-1879

Donald A. Smith is 50 when he reaches Assiniboia. He commands wealth and power. He becomes, perhaps, the country's most famous citizen. With 33 years schooling in fur trade, disciplined study, persistent experiment and incisive observation, he knows the strength and weakness of white, Indian and hybrid; and the use of flattery, force, promises and bribery to harness these for his own purposes. He organizes a "Canadian" party among the French-speaking natives, "as instructed and furnished with means to do"; and, quickly, reports: "jealousy and distrust . . . among the 'French' party". Investing $12,500.00 in bribing those "whose assistance had been absolutely necessary", he "greased the way for a split in the Metis". Assiniboia natives believe that Smith tries, but fails, to bribe Riel; and, ever after, hates him with disguised and disciplined fervor.

Many Settlers talk of annexation to the United States; selling for higher, and buying for lower prices; and freedom to trip, trap and trade unshackled by Monopoly. Riel urges a Provisional Government elected by all the Settlers, to negotiate with Canada. Some historians rate Riel "a confused young man"; no match "for a man so skilful in deviousness" as Smith. This appears to be true. Nevertheless, history carries men and events upon its surging currents. Actually, through these swirling months of conflicting pressures and devious deceit, Riel — tossed amid tactics that disconcert and enrage his adversaries; and, perhaps, mystify himself — holds to his purpose to bring Canada to negotiate, with a tenacity which marks the zealot; and wins for the people of Assiniboia a negotiated entry into Confederation.

On the bitterly cold night of 9 January, some of the 60 men captured in Schultz's house, escape from the "Company" jail in Fort Garry. Most of them are glad to be brought back into the jail's warmth. Dr. J. C. Schultz, the vociferously "loyal Canadian" gets away. A master raconteur, his exploits become legendary, in many versions. One has him cutting a buffalo hide into strips; climbing through a window; and, in a waiting cutter, escaping in a blizzard. Some have him hidden in an ox-load of straw, coming to St. Andrews — where Rev. J. F. Gardner hides him in the parsonage attic. Others have him escaping on 23 January — using a knife smuggled to him by his wife in a pie, to cut the buffalo hide. The line breaks! He limps to Kildonan. Robert McBeath (like most natives, no friend of Schultz') "honors the ancient Scot law of sanctuary; and hides him". Some have him snowshoeing to Brokenhead and, with Joseph Monkman, to Canada. Others report him in Portage la Prairie, with Thomas Scott and Charles Mair, inflaming the Settlers. Dr. O'Donell — who, against his better judgment, is among the captured — writes that Dr. Schultz has a room to himself; and escapes "supposedly by letting himself down from a window", after 3 days in prison. He rides "in a dog cariole . . . most comfortable conveyance . . . to Ottawa". Somewhere in these versions, may be the truth.

The times vibrate with such stories. Begg (energetic Winnipegger; and prolific apologist for Smith) tells how canny Donald, to keep his "papers" from Riel, leaves them at Pembina. On 15 January, Hardisty goes to fetch "the papers".

A Riel man goes with him. "French" enemies of Riel have a party meet Hardisty to guard "the papers". On the vast plain, at dead of night, Riel meets this cavalcade; and "attempts to interfere". Lavielle and Riel wave pistols at each other. The combined parties, 60 horsemen, deliver "the papers" to Smith. Donald's report of this midnight melodrama — complete with waving pistols and Shakesperian declamations; thrilling and beautifully vague — stars Smith as the adroitly, modest "good guy'; and the villain: Riel!

Despite "practical imprisonment", Smith reports "frequent visits . . . from . . . influential and reliable men"; and that "one after another of Riel's councillors seceded from him". After "the papers" are delivered to him, Donald reports (again!) "Riel's men . . . now falling away from him". But "next morning . . . those who had seceded from Riel, were again on friendly terms with him".

On 19 January, from all the communities along the Rivers, 1,000 men assemble in Fort Garry. Donald Smith reads letters appointing him Canada's Commissioner to Assiniboia. Defying the cold, he talks, and the Settlers listen and question, for 5 hours. The Settlers reconvene the next day. Smith reads the Governor-General's Proclamation — never before made public in Assiniboia. Riel moves, and Bannatyne seconds, a resolution that 20 English-speaking and 20 French-speaking delegates be chosen from all the parishes — to meet on 25 January, to consider what is best for the country. There follow speeches — cheers — hand-shaking — unanimity!

The 1,000 who crowd Fort Garry in these meetings are, perhaps, 40% of all the men in the Settlements. Some "Company" officials attend; also free traders, now becoming "merchants"; and the "loyal Canadian" party and the "American" party. On every farm, someone stays home to do the work of every winter's day. Hundreds of families, "wintering out" on the plains, will hear of the meetings next spring, when they return to "the Forks". Meantime, homes along the Assiniboine and the Red buzz with the telling of what has been seen and heard; and with surmise of what it all can mean.

On 25 January, Thomas Scott escapes from the "Company" jail in Fort Garry; reaches Portage la Prairie; and, there, orates upon the sufferings of the prisoners and the fiendishness of Riel!

The delegates elected by the people of all the parishes along the Assiniboine River and the Red assemble in Convention on 26 January. As Canada's Commissioner, Donald Smith promises them that anything passed by this Convention will be considered in Ottawa. The delegates forthwith choose Louis Schmidt, Charles Nolin, James Ross, Dr. Bird, Thomas Bunn and Louis Riel, a Committee to prepare a "List of Rights". The Committee reports to the Convention, on 29 January, a "Bill of Rights" of 19 clauses. In a full week's debate, strong talk by these strong men, often explodes into angry dispute! With a zealot's scorn of compromise, Riel proposes that the transfer of the country be negotiated between Canada and the people of Assiniboia only — with "the Company" excluded! Despite recent shocking disclosures of shareholder's greed, reverence for "the Company" is still strong in the memories of Assiniboia natives — Indian, white and hybrid. This is reinforced by the presence and influence of Donald Smith. Riel's proposal is voted down — amid fiery exchanges between Riel and Smith's spokesman, Nolin.

On 7 February, after reviewing the Bill of Rights, Donald Smith invites the Convention to send delegates to negotiate with the Government in Ottawa. This is the word and action for which the people of Assiniboia have been fighting. It dissolves their troubles; and resolves their differences. In a generous gesture, a Committee confers with Governor McTavish of "the Company". He urges: "Form a Government, for God's sake; and restore peace and order". Thereupon, the Convention re-appoints the Committee which drew up the Bill of Rights, to decide . . . "the basis and details of the Provisional Government which we agree is to be formed". The Committee report is duly adopted. In a stormy midnight session, Louis Riel is elected President of the Provisional Government-to-be. Three delegates are chosen to negotiate in Ottawa: Judge John Black, Rev. M. Ritchot and Alfred H. Scott.

News that the Provisional Government is launched, triggers "great rejoicing". Bonfires and fireworks turn night into day! (The fireworks having been imported by Dr. Schultz, it is related, for the triumphal entry of the unlamented William MacDougall.) Law and order are re-established in Assiniboia. Unhappily, fate decrees otherwise.

On this day, 60 surveyors and other new-comers follow Scott and Boulton from Portage la Prairie — to release the prisoners from Fort Garry! They have few arms; and not even their next meal! At Headingly, fellow-Orangemen provide food and shelter from a blizzard. John Taylor, 2 Dennisons, 3 Morrisons, Magnus Brown, John Cameron, W. B. Hall and Mr. Farmer join the party — the latter being named Captain by the organizing Major Boulton. (Not for a long time are these "hotheads" forgiven by their neighbors!) News that the prisoners are being released, shakes Boulton's men with indecision. They meet in the Taylor home; and send William Gaddy to urge William Dease and the "legal French" to attack Metis homes; and, thus, draw men from Fort Garry! Gaddy, himself, is captured by Metis scouts. Meantime, on 11 February, the Convention ends; and delegates go home. Next day, the last prisoners are freed, after swearing to keep the peace.

Two days later, the blizzard has blown itself out. The night is clear and moonlit. The Portagees assemble at Headingly church. They decide to "advance"! (Where, and what for, who knows?) Ahead of them, rumors race rampant! At Kildonan, next day, they join 300 Canadians from Winnipeg, Indians from St. Peters and Settlers under Dr. Schultz. All bivouac in the church and school. The military mania of Schultz, Scott and Boulton leads to the first bloodshed! The camp vibrates with excitement. Norbert Parisien passes. Someone yells "Spy!" The Metis is grabbed; and penned up in the church. He is frightened! His captors, maybe more so! He gets loose; grabs a gun; runs for the wooded river-bank — his guards at his heels! At this tragic moment, young John Hugh Sutherland rides in, with the news that the prisoners are all freed. The terrorized Parisien — cornered — shoots! Sutherland is killed! His pursuers fell Parisien with an axe; bind his legs with a sash; and, with another sash around his neck, drag him, "like a toboggan" back to the church!

Donald Smith writes: "the rising is rash . . purposeless! Settlers bitterly complain of those who set it on foot". The instigators, doubtless shocked by their own action, decide to go home. The Portagees, for some reason, pass under the walls of Fort Garry. A troop of Metis herds them into the Fort. Some, like John Cameron and W. B. Hall, get home safely; but Magnus Brown and John Taylor, with 46 others, are jailed. Dr. Schultz is not among the captured. Boulton and Scott stick with their men. Boulton writes: "I was in a room by myself, with hand-cuffs and leg-irons". (Forged and used, hitherto, to enforce "the Company" monopoly!) This same day Parisien, escaping from the Stone Fort, is shot down by his guards!

At this bloody turn of events, Donald Smith is furious. Citizens who have retained their sanity, are appalled! A Metis Council court martial condemns 4 of the prisoners to be shot! Three of the condemned are reprieved; but Boulton's sentence stands. Young Sutherland's parents plead for Boulton. Donald Smith reports that *he* wins reprieve for the Major. Is Riel learning from that "master of deviousness?" Boulton is reprieved — but only after Smith agrees that his vast influence with the English-speaking parishes and the Metis in his pay, shall be used to have all parishes elect representatives to the Provisional Government, for which Riel has so consistently worked. Thus Smith has failed in any attempt he may have made to bribe Riel; has been forced to agree to the Bill of Rights and the Provisional Government; and now, again, serves his enemy. No wonder Smith hates Riel with everlasting hatred! Meantime, elections for members to the Provisional Government are completed in all parishes by 26 February.

In Fort Garry, none of Boulton's boys is happy to be in jail. The natives among them are canny enough to "roll with the punch". Some of them sympathize; and may even agree, with the Metis. Others are new-comers. Being of the "superior race", they are insolent and insulting to "the miserable half-breeds", whom they despise. Buffalo hunters, become soldiers pro tem, are not to be reviled and spat upon! They press for redress. Under mounting pressures, Riel makes a tragic mistake. The most violent of the prisoners is Thomas Scott. A court martial condemns him to be shot! Riel refuses all appeals for reprieve. On 4 March, Scott is executed!

The people of Assiniboia are stunned! The execution looses an epidemic of prejudices, lies and hate which infects all subsequent Canadian history; and invites politicians to exploit differences in language, the myth of race and the sanctity of religion for their own purposes and power. Rabble-rousers, writers, even historians, labor to load the guilt on Louis Riel. History demands a more just verdict. One later historian asserts: "The Government of Canada were entirely to blame for the Red River troubles". Even this is too narrow to be accurate. The moral and historical fact is: every voice raised in the Hymn of Hate shares the guilt!

Donald A. Smith leaves "the Forks" on 18 March. His habit of turning everything to account (for Donald) gets exercised, even en route to Ottawa. On the trail, he meets James J. Hill. Their minds mesh. Soon, with Norman Kittson, they set up a steamship monopoly on our Rivers. Thus begins an incredibly profitable partnership.

Assiniboia's 3 delegates to Ottawa leave on 23 March — with their Bill of Rights; and instructions that "The Northwest shall not enter Confederation . . . except as . . . the Province of Assiniboia".

Riel returns to "Company" officials the keys to their stores in Fort Garry, on 2 April — after negotiating a loan from the "Company" to the Provisional Government for $15,000.00 cash; and $20,000.00 in supplies. The "Company" store re-opens for business. Circulation of money quickens. Affairs, generally, settle into their accustomed course. Families who have wintered on the Plains, straggle homeward, along the muddy trails. Up and down the Rivers, hunters prepare for the summer Hunt. Farmers bring home the livestock they have wintered up the Assiniboine; round up their horses, that winter-long have ranged the bluffs and grasslands; and prepare to seed their fields. Life buckles the harness of routine upon the people of Assiniboia; and orders their days and hours.

Eastern newspapers bring news that a military Expedition is coming to Assiniboia. Imperial authorities sanction this move; and agree to send "regular" troops — on condition that, in the transfer of the country, Canada respects the rights of inhabitants; and pays 75% of Expedition expenses. On 3 May, "SS Algoma" steams out of Collingwood, bound for Fort William, carrying 100 boats, voyageurs, workmen and supplies for the Expedition. The "New Nation" advertises a giant lottery and a "grand target match"; and reports the laws of Assiniboia passed by the Provisional Assembly in its session, ended on 9 May.

Thursday, 12 May, 1870, is a big day for Assiniboia — bigger far for Canada. Canada's legislators, after months of evasion and tragic bungling, pass the Manitoba Act. The Act guarantees land titles to settlers; allocates 1.4 million acres for hybrid families and Selkirk Settlers; and satisfies demands of Assiniboia's people. Some historians record: "Riel has won!" This is what he has worked for. John A. smoothly "saves face" by cutting down the proposed big "Assiniboia" into a "Manitoba" embracing only 10% of the original grant to Lord Selkirk. With the dexterity which permits master politicians to face various ways, at once, the people of Assiniboia are told that the military Expedition is "one of peace — for the purpose, solely, of establishing law and order"; while, in Ontario, it is proclaimed a crusade to "crush rebellion" and to take vengeance on "Rebels"!

Col. Wolseley and his staff reach Fort William on 25 May, 4 days out of Collingwood. The "peace force" totals 2,331 men — including 92 officers, 1,951 other ranks, 274 voyageurs and 14 guides. Its elements string out, sometimes, over 150 miles of waters, rock and forest — inviting annihilation in detail, were any enemy so minded. The people of Assiniboia look forward to "the Expedition". Meantime, everyone is occupied with more vital affairs. Farming, freighting, fisheries, the Hunt employ all hands — except the few officials and merchants. The Provisional Government, elected by the people of Assiniboia assembles on 24 June; and accepts the Manitoba Act. Members anticipate terminating their care-taker role — on the happy day they turn over to Canada's representative. Unhappily, storms of hate and revenge blow the ship of State from this wise and rational course! "What might have been", had Archibald arrived to assume the powers of Lieutenant-Governor, ahead of the military, rather than 10 days later — is not to be.

On 15 July, the Manitoba Act comes into force. The vast lands and waters of Assiniboia become truly Canadian. Dr. Schultz ranges Ontario, orating that "Rebellion" must be quelled; and "Rebels" crushed! The men of the Expedition wallow through swamp, water and forest — 11 miles a day — toward Fort Garry. Soldiers and voyageurs man 30-foot boats, each freighting 14 men and 4 tons. Over magnificent lakes the boats carry the men; and, between, the men roller the boats. They build roads and bridges; raise and garrison block-houses; and even erect a hospital, at Rainy River.

Through July, the plains traders are at Fort Garry, trading for supplies. They "make their presence known with drinking, fighting, dancing, horse-racing, singing! But . . . never a murder!" With July, they are gone. The Settlements relapse into normal friendliness. "We have no banks, no insurance offices, no lawyers, only one doctor, no City Council, only one policeman, no taxes, nothing but freedom . . . We are tolerably virtuous and unmistakeably happy", writes Begg.

On 23 August, the vanguard of the Expedition rows up the Red River; lands at the Stone Fort; and, next day, passes the 27 buildings scattered around the junction of 2 muddy trails. Can this be Winnipeg? Where are the welcoming crowds of the enslaved people they have come to "liberate"? In extended order, the "regulars" — 350 all ranks from the 60th Rifles, Artillery and Engineers — approach Fort Garry, half-a-mile southward. When will the Fort's cannon and the sharp-shooting buffalo hunters begin to mow them down? The gates are open. The Fort is empty. Where is Riel? He had planned a ceremonious hand-over from the Provisional Government to Canada's representative. Bishop Tache convinces him that his presence may trigger trouble. He fades away; and invites an avalanche of contempt and ridicule for "cowardice".

The enslaved people — the murderous half-breed army — exist only in the hate propaganda peddled by Schultz and his ilk. The village street is deserted — not because of the drizzling rain — but because Assiniboia's people are about their work; with cart brigades on distant trails; on the fall Hunt; hustling to finish haying and begin harvest. Only a few officials and middlemen are in the village and the Fort.

Colonel Wolseley enters Fort Garry, accompanied by Donald Smith, who hurries to share his triumph. Ignoring the Provisional Government — elected by the people of Assiniboia; and recognized by the Government of Canada — Wolseley instates Smith as dictator. Within 3 days, the Ontario and Quebec battalions of Canadian volunteers begin to arrive. Two days later, on 29 August, the "regulars" head back to Canada, en route for England; and whatever duty the future may order. The Ontario Rifles move into quarters in Fort Garry; the Quebec unit at the Stone Fort.

Lieut-Governor Hon. Adams George Archibald arrives at "the Forks" on 2 September. Impartial and conciliatory (as Bishop Machray had urged MacDougall to be) Archibald agrees with Tache that it is "best that the leaders" in bringing Canada to negotiate, "not be found". Dr. Schultz is back in Assiniboia. He and his "loyal Canadians" — now reinforced by Ontario volunteers — demand vengeance! From a Winnipeg saloon. Elezear Goulet is chased into the Red River — and drowned! Investigation traces the crime to 2 volunteers. There it is "let rest". Francois Guilmette is killed in Pembina. Andre Nault is bayonetted; and left for dead.

A force of Mounted Police is formed, with 19 troopers under Captain Villiers, of the Quebec Rifles. These constables patrol southward to the boundary; and westward, along the Portage Trail. From "the Forks", continuous settlement extends, west to Portage la Prairie; north to St. Peters; and south to Ste. Agathe. Robert Cunningham and William Coldwell launch a new newspaper: "the Manitoban". In November, some eager promoter applies for a charter for a railway, to run from Lake Manitoba, through Winnipeg, to the nearest connection in Minnesota!

In late November, citizens go to the polls in Manitoba's first provincial election. It is a wild and woolly fight! Schultz and his "loyal Canadians" chant "revenge"! The natives and hybrids support Archibald, in re-uniting the population. Among the 24 MLA's returned, Dr. C. J. Bird, St. Paul's, is made Speaker. John Norquay — renowned for walking 60 miles to see his sweetheart in Portage; and, there, dancing through 2 pairs of moccasins — is elected for High Bluff. He serves 19 years! David Spence is returned to Poplar Point; Henry J. Clarke for St. Charles; Pascal Breland and Joseph Royal for St. Francois Xavier; and Louis Schmidt for west St. Boniface. John Taylor is elected in Headingly — but the new Attorney-General awards the seat to James Cunningham. Edwin Bourke is the first MLA for St. James; and J. Dubuc for Baie St. Paul. In Winnipeg, Donald Smith, with "Company" support, is elected over Dr. Schultz.

A census is taken in late 1870. Records are not complete. Inevitably, numbers are omitted, being on distant trailways and hunting grounds. The total population is recorded at 11,961; Indians, 558; "whites", 1,563; hybrids, 9,840 (being 5,757 Metis and 4,083 of English-speaking fathers). Of the "whites", 747 are "natives" born in the Nor'West; 294 in Canada; 125 in England; 240 in Scotland; 47 in Ireland; 69 in the United States; 15 in France; and 28 in other lands. These figures, show that the "parties", so highly advertised, exist mainly in the imaginations of those whose purposes they serve. Of the numbered population, 215 live in Winnipeg. In St. James, St. Charles and Head-ingly parishes, a count of 124 families, embracing 659 individuals, shows that 529 are native-born; 475 are hybrids, 158 whites and the remainder Indians. It is estimated that, westward, 60,000 Indians, 1,365 "whites" and 11,000 hybrids roam the Nor'West. (To the south, the population of Minnesota zooms to 439,706!) Family names prominent in this census, in St. James include: McDermot, Isbister, Turcotte, Smith, McKenzie, McKay, Gladu, Houle, Flett, Bourke, (of 26 members, 25 are born in Assiniboia) Genren, Fiddler, Hookey, Omand, Bierman, Welsh, Fowler, Land, Tait, Rowand, Pruden, Stodgell, Pinkham, Hallet, Bird, Good, Logan, Bruce, (all born in Manitoba); in St. Charles: Malette, Bracon-nier, Laverdure, Bird, Moricette, Falcon, Power, Dumas, Isbister, Good, Grant, Bannock, Murray, Adshead, Dubache. New families in the parish records this year include: Keplen, Thebault, Serres, Miller, Dumas, St. Benic, Goulet, Stevenson, Mogian, Ouelette, Durand, Lajimodiere, Sabye, Bremner, Atkinson, Villebrun, Brunault, McLeod, Mozine, Brown, Daignault, Nevielle, Delorme. In Headingly, the record of this census lists only 7 families: Cameron, Clouston, Stevenson, Dennison, Cook, Symerson and Gowler. Many pioneers, like the Taylors, are missing.

During 1871, the "white" population of Manitoba is doubled — with the coming of 1,500 immigrants, including the first band of Mennonites, in August. Then, there are 1,000 young Canadians with the Expedition. Unhappily, they have a deep hatred for most of Assiniboia's people; and a thirst for "vengeance" generated in 3 months battling the wilderness! Finding "Rebellion" (as pictured back home), non-existent, they feel cheated. Nevertheless, many fall under the lure of the Nor'West.

On 1 February, perhaps to mark the advance of civilization, fresh oysters are available for the first time in the Settlements. This month, too, citizens tender a grand ball to the officers of the Volunteers. The guest list of 119 (Winnipeg's population, now, is 241) includes: Hon. James McKay, Mr. and Mrs. Robert Tait, Mr. and Mrs. Andrew McDermot.

The first session of the Manitoba Legislature assembles on 15 March, in the home of A. G. B. Bannatyne, a spacious two-storey frame structure. Many of the 24 MLA's neither know, nor care, about "parliamentary procedure". Archibald's adroit manoeuvring keeps both Riel and Schultz in the background. The Legislature petitions the Government of Canada: "That the ridges . . . hitherto reserved as places of refuge . . . on occasion of inundation, be declared the inalienable property of the Dominion for the purpose". (The "aggressive young men" who have Winnipeg built on "the Red River flats" impose a legacy of flooding upon succeeding generations).

A great state dinner follows the opening of Parliament. A favored few wear evening dress. All Canadians dress "appropriately". Others wear native broadcloth capotes, with brass buttons, sashes and moccasins. "Most surprising" (to new-comers, perhaps) "is the ease of manner displayed by all".

In March, Sir William Butler reports wildlife scarce. His statement: "I travelled . . . Red River to Rockies without seeing one solitary animal in 1,200 miles of prairie" may indicate how excellent are the thousands of hunters who live by the wildlife Butler does not even see!

There are fights and near-riots, of course; but, since "soldier-men in barracks don't grow into plaster saints", the wonder is that disturbances are not more general. Freighting booms. Alloway Brothers and James Mackay have 400 horses and 6,000 oxen in their cart trains. Every spring, numbers of these go with the Hunt, to trade for buffalo hides. Buffalo are further away than formerly; but still are in vast numbers. In the valley of the Qu'Appelle, C. V. Alloway sees: "A million buffalo cross a ford . . . in 24 hours".

While new-comers bring different ideas in apparel, most natives of the Settlements wear homespun. Farm families raise their own sheep; shear, card and spin the wool. Some have looms. Others have weavers make their cloth. Furs are cheap. Fifty cents buys a beaver-skin. Buffalo robes cost $2.00 or $3.00. As traders become merchants, they import more women's clothing. John Higgins, with his wagon and fine horses, brings his store-on-wheels right to the settler's door. The half-dozen "merchants" at "the Forks" still deal, mostly, with the Indians. The only market for farm output is "the Company"; and most natives still deal at "the Company" store. Expanding trade and the soldier's pay, put new currency into circulation.

In mid-April "SS Selkirk" docks at Fort Garry — with 150 tons of freight and 115 passengers. Some of her crew of 32 are Metis, earning money to buy hunting ammunition. (Traders no longer supply them on credit, as in the old days.) To keep up with the rush for lands, the Government of Canada, on 12 April, votes $100,000.00 for surveys in the Nor'West. Anticipating multiplied population, the Manitoba Brewing Company calls tenders for a brewery to be built at Silver Heights. Alexander Begg, Secretary, urges farmers to grow barley.

On 21 April, 8 young men from Ontario scow down the Red River to "the Forks" — leading an army of homesteaders. They make the trip in 4 weeks: by rail, wagon and flatboat; camping ashore each night, amid snowbanks, mud, rain and wind. They catch fish and shoot ducks and prairie chicken, a-plenty. In this adventure, they invest $60.00 each; and, at "the Forks" sell the lumber in their flatboat at $70.00 per thousand feet! Immigrants flood westward. Families drive farm wagons all the way from Ontario. Most come by rail and steamboat — bringing livestock, implements and lumber. Winnipeg's boarding houses overflow. A "tent town" mushrooms!

Manitoba's Legislature ends its first session on 3 May, after passing 43 bills. Bill #2 requires that public accounts be kept in Canadian currency. Bill #15 legislates against pollution of rivers; and #35, against Canada Thistles. (Two problems which, ever since, grow worse!) The first School Districts are 11 parishes — including Headingly, St. Charles and St. James.

William Verity ships plows from his Ontario factory, by rail, to St. Paul; and, thence, by steamboat and Red River cart to Manitoba. These self-scouring plows prove excellent "sod-busters". Thousands of them break new fields; and reach the Rockies, years before the railway. As fields expand, horse-drawn drills supplant hand-sowing, on Manitoba farms. On 10 May, meteorological observations and weather forecasts begin in our Canadian West. The first "weather-man" for "the Heart of the Continent" is: Donald Gunn.

An Order-in-Council of 31 May, promises that "Settlers who improve land . . . in advance of a survey . . . will be protected". To the land-hungry, this means: "Anyone who stakes a claim, can hold it, against all comers!" Newspapers are flooded with notices, such as: "I have located, marked and staked . . . 160 acres . . . grant to John Miller (late of

Quebec Rifles) north of Assiniboine River . . . to the two-mile limit; and northward of land occupied by MacKenzie, Mackay, Tait and others".

South of the Assiniboine — where the Pembina Trail crosses Riviere Aux Islets du Bois — generations of Metis occupants have produced sugar, barley and potatoes; and found shelter, fuel and home-sites. While they are away with the Hunt or cart trains — new-comers stake their lands! Lieut-Governor Archibald averts battle, by inducing the Metis to give way. The homesteaders hold the land; and re-name the River: "the Boyne". Startling changes sweep the land. Settlers push beyond Portage la Prairie. Manitoba's "white" population booms to 25,228! Sixteen schools average 50 pupils attending. Manitoba's government grants $2,000.00 to a new Agricultural Society. By mid-summer, 13 survey parties are in the field.

This summer, Smith, Hill and Kittson complete their monopoly of River freighting. By rate-cutting, political and "legal" skullduggery, they ruin — and take over — competition; then — fix rates as they choose! These men, one historian records: "are rugged individualists and no nonsense about fair play to competitors". River steamboats operate on leisurely schedules. Vessels tie up, every 40 miles, to take on cordwood, collected by local traders. Often, passengers go ashore — to hunt, or stroll across short-cuts. The wood-yards become town-sites.

The issue of scrip for land, looses a flood of speculation. Swindlers get title to quarter-sections from hybrids (and discharged soldiers) for a few dollars — and lay the foundations of many Winnipeg fortunes. With money in their hands, Metis are briefly rich. Squandering their pittance of cash, they turn to the old ways. But all is changed! Trading, freighting, the Hunt — all are disrupted. Credit is denied. Traders, freighters, hunters are discarded. Whiskey traders are completing the wrecking of our Indians. For "whoop-up juice", they reclaim the rifles Indian hunters have just bought with a year's hunting. After a drunken orgy, 88 Blackfoot are reported killed! Even in the staid old "Company", field officers battle shareholders for a fair share of profits. Donald Smith, with his reputation as a negotiator won in Assiniboia, is chosen to confront the London Board. He returns with a new deal, which divides $535,000.00 cash, among the wintering partners; but excludes them from land profits (which, as Smith foresees, will far exceed fur profits). Of course, he who reaps most in money and advancement, is canny Donald Smith! Some of the "old guard" declare he "sold them out" for his own gain.

The dawn of 1 July is greeted by a 21-gun salute! People from all the Settlements gather to celebrate Manitoba's first Dominion Day. By noon, young and old are cheering horse races, football and cricket matches; or competing in running, jumping, quoits or climbing the greasy pole — for the $500.00 in prizes! Evening is illuminated by a torch parade; and a moonlight excursion on "SS Selkirk" (the "Manitoban" reports) is "largely taken advantage of".

The Board of Education forms St. James School District #7 on 2 July; and, next day, Headingly School District #8 — embracing the respective parishes.

Another newspaper, the "Manitoba Liberal", appears on 11 July. The editor, S. Mulvey, is "agin the government", entirely. On the 12th, editor Mulvey is parade master, when L.O.L. 1307 "walks", 80 strong. Surprisingly, historians largely ignore the Irish influence in Assiniboia's pioneer history. But, truth to tell, its many the Irishman knows that the fight betwixt Orangemen and Fenians decides the fate of our Canadian West!

The Manitoba Agricultural Society, at its initial meeting, on 1 August, elects G. B. Spencer, president; Hon. James Mackay, vice-president; W. B. Hall, second vice-president; Dr. J. S. Lynch, secretary; and John Taylor, treasurer. Parties of settlers, organized in "down east" counties, come "out west", over the Dawson Trail. Families stay at "the Forks", while menfolk locate homesteads. Then, all move in covered wagons, to settle new neighborhoods. Civilization, despite its high cost, spreads like a prairie fire. When it is known that Fonseca's store, in Point Douglas, has coal oil at $5.00 a gallon and glass lamps at $5.00 each, Settlers clear out the entire stock — and demand more!

On 21 August, Treaty #2 "extinguishes Indian titles" far beyond Manitoba. Historians write that Indians "imperfectly apprehend" these deals. For "selling" his country, each Indian gets $5.00 yearly; and a "gift for good behaviour" of $3.00 (which will buy, at current prices, 60 pounds of flour or 24 pounds of pork or 20 pounds of beef). Chiefs and councillors get uniforms, flags, medals. The Indians want two-thirds of their country for hunting grounds. (A feasible suggestion, since most of our Nor'West is unmanaged, 100 years later.) In a mania to make Indians farm, each band is "penned up" on a reserve, with some 32 acres per person (diminishing as numbers increase!) At best, these so-called Treaties are mere salve for our national conscience!

Ottawa is flooded with claims for "Rebellion Losses" — mostly from "loyalists", some of whom have left the country. Biggest claim is from Dr. Schultz — for $65,065.00. Judge Johnson comes to Manitoba; investigates; and reduces total claims to $85,755.95. The biggest slices go to "the Company" and Schultz.

August mails bring in 960 letters and 1,375 papers; and take out

1,019 letters and 196 newspapers. September sees the last Red River cart brigade sent by Winnipeg merchants to the United States. The first stage arrives in Winnipeg from Fort Abercrombie on 11 September; with 6 passengers; and is away on its return trip at 4 a.m. The owners, Blakely and Carpenter, have a Government contract for tri-weekly mails. Grace Church, Methodist, is dedicated on 17 September, by Rev. George Young. The Provincial Government votes $20,000.00 for roads. Roads are execrable! Even the Great Highway, westward to Portage and Edmonton, is a slithering streak of mud, snaking across the prairies between bluffs of oak, elm and poplar. Some of the myriad creeks are crossed by shaky pole bridges. A few of the countless mudholes are "corduroyed".

The first Provincial Agricultural Exhibition, held on 4 October, almost fails — because of a Fenian scare! On 5 October, "General" O'Donoghue leads 30 Fenians into Canada! They plunder "the Company" store at Pembina; and run when U.S. troopers appear. Dr. Schultz shouts that Fenian armies are pouring over the border — in another "Rebellion by the French"! On 8 October, Louis Riel and Lepine, with 200 Metis (organized as in the Hunt) volunteer to repel any invasion. Lieut-Governor Archibald thanks them publicly; and, thereby, incurs the wrath of the ultra "loyal".

Wild talk of "invasion" and "rebellion" sweeps the nation! On 21 October, 100 volunteers from Ontario and 100 from Quebec hurriedly head westward — to "quell another Rebellion". Ontario's Premier Blake offers $5000.00 reward for Riel, alive or otherwise. The Prime Minister of Canada says (in public) "I wish I could lay my hands on him". Privately, it is said, Macdonald sends $1,000.00 to Tache. The good Bishop maintains that the Government of Canada did promise full amnesty; but considers it discreet to get another $3,000.00 from Donald Smith (duly billed to the Government); and to induce Riel and Lepine, with $4,000.00 cash, to leave Manitoba for a year.

Donald Smith gets possession of Silver Heights on 28 October. This estate, comprising River Lots 17, 18 and 19, parish of St. James, was granted to Kenneth Logan in 1857; and transferred to John Rowand. It is now transferred to J. H. McTavish who, forthwith, transfers it to canny Donald. Were John Rowand living, he would have words for such goings-on!

The 200 Volunteers from the East arrive on 18 November. "Much to the satisfaction of our townspeople, who anticipate increased impetus to trade". This force crosses the Great Lakes in 3 days; transfers to boats; and, from the Northwest Angle, marches over rock, ice, frozen muskeg and prairie — to reach Fort Garry 28 days out of Collingwood.

This second Expedition finds no more "Rebellion" in Manitoba than did the first, in Assiniboia. However, troops remain in garrison for 6 years.

The shackles of isolation are broken. On 20 November, the telegraph line to Canada, via Pembina, is completed; and Lieut-Governor Archibald telegraphs to the Governor-General, Lord Lisgar: "The voice of Manitoba, collected this morning on the banks of the Assiniboine, will be heard in a few hours on the banks of the Ottawa. We may now count in hours the work that used to occupy weeks". Already, westerners talk of 300 million fertile acres, needing 25 million people! It is easy to forget that the majority of Manitoba's people, still, are hybrids. They share citizenship with the few "whites", in creating the vacuum-filling Provisional Government. They cast most of the votes which elect Manitoba's government. They provide Ministers; the Premier. Six of them draw up the Bill of Rights on which is negotiated Assiniboia's entry into Confederation. Their names — along with others like Mackay, Isbister and Norquay rank with any recorded in the history of our Canadian nation!

The Legislature of Manitoba meets in its second session, on 16 January; and, by a vote of 18 to 5, passes a resolution deprecating the action of Ontario's Premier Mowat, in offering a reward for Riel's capture. Lieut-Governor Archibald writes to Sir George Cartier, on 24 February, that "the people shall protect him (Riel) by an armed force against any attempt to arrest him. The difficulty is not with the people of the country, but among a small band of lawless men who infest the taverns of Winnipeg".

A meeting in Winnipeg, on 3 February, calls upon the Legislature for incorporation as a city. Feelings run high. Some urge that Winnipeg incorporate before some neighboring community does. Others fear taxation and real estate manipulation. Politics are violent! Dr. C. N. Bird, Speaker of the Legislature, is called to a patient, at midnight of March 8; and is mobbed, beaten, tarred and feathered! Even a $1,000.00 reward never discloses the perpetrators. At Silver Heights, the Manitoba Brewery Company, after heavy investment in buildings, begins operation. In April, the Selkirk Agricultural Society is organized, with A. M. Brown, John Taylor, W. B. Hall, John Fraser, Hon. M. A. Girard and Roger Goulet, directors; and James Stewart, Secretary.

A Winnipeg mob, on 24 April, burns Lieut-Governor Archibald in effigy. "The respectable people of the community" present this esteemed gentleman an address signed by 1,800 citizens. A man of great tact, Archibald assembles people of all political views at weekly dinners. At Headingly, Mrs. John Taylor dies, leaving 8 children motherless.

River traffic, disrupted by fear of the Sioux, is now resumed. "SS

Selkirk" arrives in port, on 10 May. Capt. Webber, takes his "SS Manitoba" up the Assiniboine, to Fort Ellice. The lumber industry booms! Millions of feet are sawn from logs floated down the Roseau River and the Red.

"The Company", on 27 July, has a great sale of town lots. Some 13 acres of their 500-acre reserve around Fort Garry brings $91,000.00. At this rate, their 500 acres is worth $3.5 millions! Sandford Fleming, engineer of C.P.R. surveys, with his party, on 1 August, heads west on the Portage Trail. At Silver Heights they see "gardens of astonishing wealth of vegetation. Morgan bought a farm for $2500.00; this year was offered $2,250.00 for the potatoes on it . . . . All the land along the Assiniboine . . . to 8 miles back, taken up." On 15 August, the party meets "Indians and half-breeds . . . with carts laden with buffalo hides and dried meat. Old men, women, children . . . all help. No carts but those of Red River could have stood . . . the boulders, ruts and holes".

The Dominion election is wild, even for 1872! Riel is nominated for Provencher; but, when Cartier loses in Montreal, John A. gets Archibald and Tache to persuade Riel to withdraw; and present Cartier with an acclamation. What Riel is promised, we can only guess. Election day is a major event in the Settlements along the Assiniboine. In Winnipeg, it explodes into riots — fights — burglared poll books, ax handles and pistols! The police chief is wounded. The militia is called out! This debauch of violence results in the election of Donald Smith in Selkirk; Robert Cunningham, editor of the "Manitoban", in Marquette; Dr. Schultz, in Lisgar; and, in Provencher, an acclamation to Sir George Cartier (courtesy of Louis Riel).

Our newspapers resume publication after being wrecked in the recent election. Prices of various commodities are advertised at: wheat, $1.25 per bushel; oats, $1.00; barley, $1.10, potatoes, 62½ cents; hay, $7.00 to $8.00 per ton; beef and lamb 12½ cents per pound; veal and pork, 20 cents. Average wages: carpenter, $3.50 a day; mason, $4.00; laborer, $2.50. The Hunt is going strong, again. This year, an estimated 2.5 million buffalo are killed in the Western States; and 1 million in Saskatchewan.

Local society buzzes with the excited news that a "real live Lord" has registered, on 7 November, at the Munro House. He signs himself "Lord Gordon Gordon". Affable, handsome, politely lavish with money (as to the manner born; sans vulgar display) he becomes known as a cultured aristocrat with vast ancestral possessions. He is an excellent shot; and indulges, to the full, his love of "sport". His Lordship engages Mr. Pentland, nephew of Mrs. Abigail Corbett, of River Lot 55, Headingly, as his "man". The touch of romance is added when Pentland weds the beautiful Miss Corbett, another relative of the widow.

Records of births, marriages and burials in St. Charles parish for 1872, list these family names for the first time: Martin, Schmitt, Boyer, Bourissa, Rickard, Metrara, Lesperance, Levate, LaPointe, Gariepi, Laviolette, Bruce, Pepin, Pruden, McPhillips, Moreau, Edmond, Gendron, Piednoir, Ridgedale, Lapierre.

Since earliest days in Assiniboia, winter is the time for jollity. Young and old, in sleigh-loads, drive miles to dances. Arriving at dusk, they stay till dawn. Drivers blanket and feed their teams. Then to the dance! After midnight supper; song and story — then, dance again! Finally, home to bed in, as a local scribe records: "comfortable, fur-laden Canadian sleighs. Canadian steeds with Canadian bells, whirl away on the crisp prairie road". It is good to be "Canadian"! "No one could be prouder than our Manitoba citizens, driving brightly caparisoned, well-groomed horses, encircled with sweet-sounding bells; hitched to finely shaped cutters and carioles furnished for comfort with robes made in the Settlements". It is good to be "Canadian" — in Manitoba!

The clamor for incorporation of Winnipeg employs indignation meetings, violent speeches, marches on the Legislature. A bill introduced, on 10 February, meets opposition. On second reading, the name is changed to "Assiniboia". Next day, "Assiniboia" and "Garry" are voted down; and the name amended to "Selkirk". The bill is laid over to the next session.

A flurry in land sales, is becoming a boom. At Headingly, John Taylor acquires 960 acres along the Assiniboine, plus 760 acres at White Horse Plain. After his first wife dies, Mr. Taylor marries Frances Jane Brown.

Manitobans are demanding "better terms" — including extension of boundaries northward, to the 60th parallel — increasing the area of the Province from 11,000 to 297,000 square miles. Ironically, the most vociferous are those who tried to force Assiniboia into Confederation without negotiation, at all! Action is delayed. The Macdonald Government is swept away in the Pacific Scandals.

"Granting scrip in lieu of actual land is a curse", writes Begg. Choice lands are grabbed by speculators; and held idle. Settlers are scattered; their energies wasted. Jealousies and hatreds die hard. Metis (and others) are cheated; and robbed! Peaceful hybrids are beaten, murdered! Lawlessness runs wild. Montana whiskey traders massacre 40 lodges of Assiniboines in the Cypress Hills; and go unpunished. On 23 May, the Parliament of Canada creates the Northwest Mounted Police; and sets up the first Northwest Council.

This spring, Lord Gordon Gordon has fine "sport" at the Brokenhead

River, shooting 1,500 partridges! Demand for buffalo hides triggers slaughter of the herds on an unprecedented scale. Dozens of brigades are on the Hunt. From a single brigade C. V. Alloway buys 21,000 hides for $3.00 or $4.00 each. He brings home, also, 3 buffalo calves — which are mothered by a cow at Deer Lodge.

Sir George Cartier dies. In the subsequent by-election, the voters of Provencher return Louis Riel, by acclamation. The Parliament of Canada votes 124 to 68, to expel him. The people of Provencher elect him, again!

In August, 880 Mennonite settlers arrive on "SS International and "SS Cheyenne"; and settle southwest of "the Forks". Survey parties cannot keep ahead of the land-hungry. Manitoba is booming! The mills of Macauley & Sprague and Banning & Dick work day and night, cutting lumber that is nailed into buildings — hot from the saw! It is getting too crowded for the freedom-loving Metis. Families leave their homes along the Assiniboine; and, with minds as mobile as possessions, move to the Dakotas, Montana and far up the Saskatchewan Rivers, to found Settlements like St. Paul de Metis.

On the spacious verandas of Deer Lodge, Lord Gordon Gordon — enjoying a visit with his friend Mackay — dozes through the afternoon of 2 July. Coming from nowhere, 4 men seize him; bind him on a buckboard; and gallop southward! The kidnappers work with the quick, unhurried sureness of policemen. They *are* policemen — from Minneapolis! James Mackay, called by servants, gallops in hot pursuit — after wiring Canadian customs officials at Emerson. These wait, with rifles; halt the galloping horses; free his Lordship; and arrest the Minneapolis policemen, who are whisked back to "the Forks"; and clapped into jail! The Settlements explode with excitement which, in turn, almost detonates an international crisis! The ensuing trial brings lawyers and governors from the United States; and sets the wires buzzing between Washington, Ottawa and London! The St. Paul "Pioneer" screams: "If the prisoners are not liberated, Manitoba should be wrapped in flames". Old buffalo hunters jeer at threats of invasion. Finally, tempers cool. The trial simmers out. Along the Assiniboine River and the Red, there is general sympathy for Gordon. When it comes out that he has outswindled those master-crooks, Vanderbuilt and Gould, right in their New York lairs, settlers admire, rather than blame, him!

His Lordship takes quarters in the home of Mrs. Corbett. He sues his kidnappers for a million; but goes off hunting and fishing. He spends, if not lavishly, certainly without stint. His British funds appear to be "inexhaustible". But why, always, at hand — a "brace of pistols"? In August, with 4 wagon-loads of arms, tents and supplies, Gordon heads westward. Attorney-General Clark brings him back, to face farcial charges of "stealing an awl, value 15 cents!" The trial is drawn out endlessly, in ways known to lawyers. He is jailed; released; re-jailed; released again. He "looks like a man hounded to death". Is someone blackmailing him for political purposes? Suffering from a heart ailment, nevertheless, Gordon loves to roam the marshes along the Assiniboine, where the shot that brings down one duck, raises a thousand more on the wing!

Ambrose Lepine, charged with the murder of Thomas Scott, on 22 December, is convicted; and sentenced to hang. Petitioned by 58,568 Canadians, the Governor-General commutes sentence to 2 years imprisonment; and loss of political rights.

A telegraph line and monthly mail are established by the Government of Canada, between Edmonton and Winnipeg. Civilization is invading the Nor'West. Nevertheless, old native customs persist. Winter, still, is the time for merriment. Christmas is celebrated with a full week of dances and feasting on pemmican, ducks, geese, venison, fish, buffalo tongues, dried plums, saskatoons. There is rough plenty for all!

Population is growing. Westward, along the Assiniboine, St. Charles parish writes new family names into the records: Boye, Vallette, Comtois, Richot, Aymond, Maloney, Tache, LaRiviere, Macdonald, Ryan, Rowand, Hughes, Beauchene, Bruneau, Williamson, McTavish.

Winnipeg's first civic election is held on 5 January, 1874. Voters number 308. In the election, 562 votes are cast for Mayor! F. E. Cornish, "flamboyant", aggressive and backed by "the Company" — is elected!

In the Dominion election, on 22 January, Manitobans elect: Donald Smith (this time as a Liberal), Dr. Schultz, Cunningham and Louis Riel. Schultz enjoys his vengeance, by having Riel expelled from the House! Frontier politics — lacking the refined viciousness of civilization — are violent with a rough jollity. A local scribe reports that, on this occasion, the Grits are sure of winning. They hire (and pay for) a band to lead a grand parade. Final returns, from Headingly, give victory to the Tories. *They* kidnap the band for *their* parade. The Tories have laid on, for themselves, a victory feast at Bannatyne's store. While they parade, the Grits take possession; and "lick the platter clean"!

January brings some French-speaking Canadian repatriates from Massachusetts. Native Nor'Westers cannot understand why Canadians from Quebec and Ontario go to the United States by thousands, when Manitoba calls!

One of the great Nor'Westers, during this time of transition from Buffalo to Bushels; and carts to steamboats, is James Mackay. He is a "big man" in every way, weighing some 350 pounds; and travelling by specially-built buckboard. At Deer Lodge, Mackay runs a big spread, with many servants, 2 cellars, 2 kitchens and hospitality for all! Hunter, trader, guide, politician and counsellor to Indian, hybrid and white, Mackay knows, and loves, his Nor'West. When his daughter weds Richard Power, "grand constable pour la Province de Manitoba", celebrations draw people to Deer Lodge from miles around — for days!

On 10 June, 217 men, with 244 horses — 13 days out of Toronto — join the 6 troops of North-West Mounted Police already assembled at Fort Dufferin. On 8 July, 274 "Mounties" ride out of the Fort, into the sunset. Ahead — native guides; and a ride of unknown mileage across the "lawless" Nor'West. Behind — 114 Red River carts and 73 wagons with native drivers, 142 cattle, 31 cannon, 93 plows, harrows, mowing machines, everything to make the Force self-supporting. Westward along the "Boundary Trail" the column winds its way. Before they reach the Cypress Hills, they meet the Hunt, returning to the Settlements — carts loaded with meat and robes. From the foothills, 2 troops double northeastward, to their Swan River Headquarters. Eleven posts are established at strategic centres. Law rides the Nor'West!

The final scene is enacted in the Gordon Gordon tragedy. In the twilight of an August evening, an official from Edinburgh, a lawyer and policeman present themselves to his Lordship, in Mrs. Corbett's home. They have a warrant for his arrest — for buying jewelry 6 years ago; and neglecting to pay for it. Gordon Gordon says, serenely: "Allow me to get my cap". He enters his bedroom. A shot! The policeman bursts in. The man called Lord Gordon Gordon is dead! All chance of discovering his real identity dies with him. Local scribes report him "driven to desperation by persecutors. He came to Manitoba with large sums of money. What became of this?" It is widely believed that the Attorney-General has blackmailed him. He is buried outside the churchyard. His wooden cross disappears. With the passing years and increasing population, the cemetery is enlarged; and enfolds his final resting place within its sacred precincts.

Rev. J. Hines, missionary travelling to central Saskatchewan, records that, from railhead to Winnipeg, 200 miles, takes 7 days by steamboat. In Winnipeg, he buys clothing, provisions, cooking utensils, implements, seed, oxen and carts. He hires a St. Peter's Indian, good with ax, scythe, pit-saw and plow. Three days travel brings them to Headingly; 4 more to Portage. Sixty miles in 7 days! At each halt, mosquitoes drive the draft animals wild! Oxen crowd into the campfire smoke. All night, "smudges" are kept going. Often an ox is "suffocated by mosquitoes and sandflies in its nostrils!" In the Qu'Appelle Valley, storms of "hoppers" cover the sun.

In a Manitoba election, on 23 December, Edwin Bourke is returned for St. James; and John Taylor for Headingly. Financial stringency dictates economy. Appeals to Ottawa bring no help. The Province, the Nation, the World, are gripped by depression.

Families along the Assiniboine enjoy driving and skating on the river ice. In the native tradition of winter exuberance, young and old flock to the first skating carnival held in Wilson and Bryden's new rink, at the foot of Post Office Street, on 4 February. The somnolent Selkirk Agricultural Society re-organizes, with W. B. Hall and John Fraser among the directors. Through a blizzard, on 2 March, Rev. George Clark drives to Headingly, to preside at a meeting of Good Templars. Wm. Tait and John H. McTavish are appointed the Nor'West Council. The Parliament of Canada confirms the long-debated amnesty (even to Riel, after 5 years of banishment) on 15 June, less than 6 months after expelling him from the House!

This year, 1875, 11,970 pioneers come to Manitoba. Many locate on the plains, slicing the tough sod with short-handled John Deere and Verity plows. Flour milling surpasses lumber as Manitoba's leading manufacture. Clouds of locusts devour the crops — destroying even the potatoes! The Hunt and fisheries fall far short of feeding the increased population. Freighting, grading on the Pembina railway and Government building, provide some relief work. The Government of Canada advances seed grain loans to stricken farm families. Hundreds of Metis move from their homes along the Assiniboine River and the Red to settle on the Saskatchewan and Beaver Rivers. There are still buffalo to supply their needs. Major A. G. Irvine, NWMP, reports riding from Fort McLeod through herds of buffalo — almost to Qu'Appelle. Some 4,400 Mennonites settle in southwestern Manitoba. On 11 October, 285 Icelanders arrive; load supplies onto house-boats; and coast down to "New Iceland" on the western shore of Lake Winnipeg. The young men and women walk back to Winnipeg; and find work — the men at $1.00 per day; the women at $4.00 to $6.00 per month. At their new settlement, "Gimli", pioneers build log homes — not on the Red River frame pattern; but, with logs laid horizontally and notched at the corners.

People living along the Portage Trail in St. James, St. Charles, Headingly and St. Francois Xavier can now use the regular stage operated by Michael Blake between Portage and Winnipeg. More and more settlers are locating south of the Assiniboine, westward to Oakville — and beyond. To meet the demand for lumber, Macauley's sawmill, this summer, cuts 3,340,000 feet. "Pretty good", chortles a proud citizen, "For a country where some people say there is no wood"! A sudden freeze-up ends the navigation season, catching many vessels in the ice!

Freight which cannot, now, be moved by steamboat, must be teamed. This gives much needed work through the winter. December sees Manitoba's first curling games for prizes, with the ancient irons.

School population increases, remarkably, with 4,782 pupils attending 50 schools: 91 at Headingly; 92 in St. James; 140 in St. Charles; and 443 in St. Francois Xavier. The Board of Education forms Sturgeon Creek S.D. #30, on 7 January, 1876, embracing parts of St. James and St. Charles, north of the Assiniboine.

Following destruction of last year's crop by the 'hoppers', there is a shortage of seed grain. In March, supplies are brought in from Minnesota. The long drought ends; and 5 years of heavy rainfall begin. Water levels rise. Steamboats navigate far up the Assiniboine.

The season's first train of 60 carts, screeches along Winnipeg's Main Street on 28 June, loaded with 2,050 buffalo robes worth $45,000.00. The awful music of their passing has scarcely stilled, when 670 bellowing cattle follow. This is a herd driven from Montana by T. J. Demers, for sale to inflooding settlers. Another party of 1,226 Icelandic immigrants arrives; followed by 400 more in August. A 5-year epidemic of "Manitoba Fever" — for land — has begun. It will bring 40,000 settlers. Barbed wire and improved farm implements expand acreage and earnings. Wheat may become a leading export!

Settlers from along the Assiniboine, visiting Winnipeg, by crossing the bridge at William and Main Streets, can see the new City Hall — with a theatre on its second floor; and its foundation (alas) in the treacherous bed of a prairie creek. In the corner stone is a copy of the first document printed in Assiniboia (now Manitoba) by Rev. G. O. Corbett, of Headingly, titled: "Some Reasons for a Crown Colony". On 28 July, Fr. D. Dandurand comes to St. Charles — to begin his 24 fruitful years as parish priest.

October sees Manitoba's first bumper grain crop safely in store. Farmers harvest an average 32.5 bushels of wheat per acre. In Ontario, crops have failed. On 12 October, R. C. Steele of Toronto, arrives — to buy good Manitoba hard wheat for seed. He wants 5,000 bushels. His offer of 85 cents a bushel fails to stampede the canny farmers of the Assiniboine and Red. Higgins & Young do buy, for him, some 857 bushels. Farmers cart it to the old landing at McMillan's mill. They are not excited about this shipment. They have exported wheat, southward, for 10 years. This is the first shipment to eastern Canada. The wheat is loaded aboard "SS Minnesota". The mist that hides the River from the dawn of 21 October, is pierced by the sounds of running ropes, clanking chains, shouted curses and the shrill whistle of the "steamboat 'round the bend", gathering way, heading south — just ahead of freeze-up. Transferred at Fisher's Landing, the wheat goes by rail to Duluth; by lake vessel to Sarnia; and rail to Toronto. The buyers, in addition to the 85 cents to producers, pay 35 cents a bushel freight; and sell the wheat to Ontario farmers, at $2.50 per bushel.

At Headingly, the Holy Trinity congregation see their new church consecrated by the Bishop of Rupertsland, on 16 November. Despite wintry cold, roaring stoves warm the building. This new church replaces the original, built in 1852. Rev. R. E. Washer, then Canon A. E. Cowley, are encumbents.

At last, Manitoba farming turns the corner — and heads for prosperity. In the Settlements, 10 mills are grinding 4,000 bushels, daily. Farmers along the Rivers have harvested 1,083,000 bushels of grain! After 7 years of debate and delay the "Hay Privilege", whereby Settlers claim the Outer 2 miles of their River Lots, is confirmed by the Government of Canada. The militia Battalion from Ontario, in garrison since '72, is relieved by local units. Merchants are sorry to lose the payroll. The Legislature of Manitoba establishes the University of Manitoba. The advance of civilization is apparent, further, in the transfer of prisoners from Fort Garry, on 2 February, to the new Stony Mountain Penitentiary.

Settlers are building new communities south of the Assiniboine. In February, tenders are called to carry mail, by stage, from Headingly to the Boyne Settlement. On 23 March, a meeting is called in Headingly School by John Taylor, MLA, and W. B. Hall, to discuss the creation of a rural municipality. Farm lands along the Assiniboine, all the way to Portage, sell for $2.50 an acre. Settlers see the steam tug "Prince Rupert" towing barges on regular trips to Portage and Brandon. This season, before 24 May, 77 flatboats dock at "the Forks", with 1,327 tons of freight. A July hurricane — smashing windows, chimneys and buildings; and uprooting trees and shrubs — inflicts widespread damage along the Assiniboine, and causes concern to "numbers of gentlemen who use small yachts" on the Rivers. Portage la Prairie now boasts 2 churches, a school, 20 business places and 300 people. Three Maritimers reach the confluence of the Minnedosa River and the Assiniboine; and, there, plant a "Nova Scotia Settlement", the seed from which grows the city of Brandon.

On 6 August, Settlers assemble at "the Forks", to greet the Governor-General of Canada and Lady Dufferin. The Governor's party lands from "SS Minnesota"; and, following a gala reception at Winnipeg's new City Hall, repairs to Silver Heights. Addresses, speeches and presentations introduce a "continuous round of entertainment" through the following weeks. On 29 September, in St. Boniface, the Dufferins drive the first 2 spikes in the railway to Pembina; and return, via the United States, to Ottawa. Ten days later, "SS Selkirk" steams into port, pushing barges carrying the C.P.R. locomotive, the "Countess of Dufferin", with caboose, flat cars and piles of ties for the new railway.

The railway boom bursts in Minnesota! Donald Smith, "Jim" Hill, Norman Kittson and George Stephen grab the St. Paul & Pacific Railway — bankrupt, mortgaged, forclosed, remortgaged — from Dutch bond-holders. These 4 Canadians acquire an equity of $28 millions by investing only $300,000 of their own cash! Hill, the builder, pushes construction; and succeeds in putting rails into Pembina in time to salvage land grants of 2.5 million acres. With the profits from these dealings, this group steps into the big league of finance and railways.

The flow of settlers of all origins into Manitoba, continues. Family names added to the St. Charles parish register, this year, include: Lamirande, Versailles, Bellisle, Kittson, Rochblanc, Lasuppi, Berard, Desjarlais, Gregoire, Houde, Hogg, Willet, Benister.

How the people of Assiniboia live in '78 is best told by themselves. John Taylor writes in his diary: "Tuesday, first day of January . . . fine. Service in the church. We had roast turkey, roast beef and plum pudding for dinner . . . Quite a number of calls: Rev. Washer, W. B. Hall, Mrs. Clouston, Douglas, Magnus and Wm. Brown, John Suther-land, Maggie Sutherland, Maggie Brown, Harry and George Pentland, W. A. Farmer, Fowler, Gifford, Joseph and Robert Tait, David Corbett and Malcolm Galbraith. After tea, we had a drive down as far as the island. Most extraordinary weather . . . Yesterday we drove up from Town all the way by the River."

"Wednesday, 2 January. Strong wind from the south. James Brown and I travel out as far as Woodlands, in search of horses . . . Stopped at McGambold's and had dinner . . . 3 or 4 miles further . . . found our horses. Made tracks for home. . . Had quite a snowstorm to face . . . Home at half-past nine, after a cold day's ride."

"Thursday, 3 January. Strong NW wind and cold. Snowing. About 2 inches of snow fell . . . a great help to the horses wintering out, as they have suffered . . . for want of drink. Called on Sandy Cameron, James Clouston, Mrs. Lonsdale and Alex Clouston".

"Friday, 4 January. A fine day. About half-past eleven, I was roused out of bed by Wm. Dennison who came to get cotton for his mother, who had just died . . . Mrs. Dennison has been laboring under insanity for the last 3 or 4 months. Mrs. and Miss Taylor were down to tea at Mr. Hall's". "Saturday, 5 January. A cold day; wind blowing strong from NW. Mrs. Dennison buried today. Wm. Slater and Herbert drove down to Tom Slater's. I kept the store in the afternoon. Sandy staid overnight . . . finding the weather too cold to face. Sunday, 6 January. Clear and cold. H. C. Taylor and Wm. Slater return from Baie St. Paul. To church this evening and hear a very good sermon".

"Monday, 7 January. Stormy . . . Wm. Hall called to see if I could lend him a horse. Tuesday, 8 January. Fine. Busy whitewashing the old kitchen. Government sent tickets for the opening of Parliament. Donald Cameron and Maggie Brown came. Wednesday, 9 January. Fine. Good meeting of Lodge in old kitchen; 11 of the brethren present."

"Thursday, 10 January. Down to attend Parliament. Room filled . . . James and Douglas Brown hitched their team into my bobsleigh and took Mrs. Taylor, Miss Taylor, Maggie Brown and myself along with them. Drove all the way on the ice. Lt-Governor Cauchon was trembling like a leaf, delivering his speech from the throne. Unwell. Speech short and did not promise much. Friday, 11 January. Sitting in the afternoon. Speech from throne discussed. Mr. Chenier moved adoption; and I seconded. Martin, Sutherland, Cornish, Luxton, Black, Lemay and Girard all had a speech to make. Western members all absent; and Mr. Mackay. Home with Willie Brown."

"Saturday, 12 January. Fine, Mr. Washer call; pay small bill for milk. Mr. Corrigan brought back hay rake. David Morgan married Irish Jim's stepdaughter. Busy cleaning harness, when James Cunningham, George Gray and Malcolm Galbraith called in; and invited me to go along to the wedding. Remained till about midnight. All seemed to enjoy themselves. A little misunderstanding between Pierre Lavalle and John Black ended in Pierre on the floor. Sunday, 13 January. Fine. Church twice. Mr. Lonsdale call in the evening.

"Monday, 14 January. Down to Town. Mrs. Taylor drove me down. Remain till Friday evening, in session. Nothing of importance occur. Drive up with Edwin Bourke . . . a lift up with James Isbister . . . and from there I walk. Peter was on his way (to get me) but home before him. Still fine. Wednesday, 23 January. To St. Boniface, to concert in aid of their hospitals. Very good. Music splendid. Never saw such a large organ as in their Cathedral. Its power is something astonishing. Sunday, 27 January. Never saw such a remarkable winter. Still using wheels . . . too little snow for sleighing . . . Parliament prorogued Saturday noon. Last session. Had an oyster dinner at Mochamps and some speechifying. Sunday, 3 February. Thawing. The Bishop hold confirmation for over 20. Johnny drive Mary down back to school. Chas. Bremner called this morning to pay balance of his school tax. Monday, 4 February. Fine . . . Annual school meeting . . . Alexander Clouston elected trustee. Tuesday, 5 February. Mr. Washer and lady call to borrow horse and cutter to drive down to Mrs. Gowler's. The old lady is very poorly. See 2 spring hawks and a blackbird. The little snow is disappearing. This evening, raining. David and Sandy's man . . . down to town with loads of grain. Wednesday, 6 February. Rain most of the night. . . To town to see about a school teacher. Rain all day; at 7 p.m. . . . snow. Lot of water on the River".

James Mackay's buffalo herd — kept at Deer Lodge in summer; at Baie St. Paul in winter; and fed hay, like domestic cattle — has increased from the original 5 calves to 16 head. In February, Col. Sam Bedson buys them; and drives them, via Winnipeg, 22 miles to Stony Mountain. That same night, they return to Deer Lodge — in a beeline, 18 miles! Next day, they are driven, again, to Stony Mountain. One calf, 3 days old, does the 62 miles through deep snow. These natives are fitted to live in Manitoba!

The Rivers break up in March. The "Prince Rupert" steams up the Assiniboine, on 1 April. Farm families along the Assiniboine wave at Billy Smith and his barges from Portage, coming down with 1,200 sacks of flour; and 5 tons of feed and potatoes. He docks at "the Forks", on 7 April. Already in port, is a barge unloading 6 tons of nitro-glycerin; half-a-ton of dynamite; and 7 tons of Volney powder — for work on the C.P.R.

"SS International" — having discharged her cargo of flour, pork, stoves, organs, furniture, horses, cattle, etc., on 8 April, loads from Bannatyne's warehouse the biggest water-born shipment of wheat ever to leave Manitoba. W. J. S. Trail consigns 2,788 bushels to David Dows & Co., New York, for export to Europe.

On 5 May a scribe records: "Higgin & Young bag, tie, address and ship on board "SS Selkirk" 2,100 bushels of wheat consigned to the Old Country, between 4 p.m. and 10 o'clock the next morning!" By 31 May, exports of Manitoba hard wheat reach an estimated 35,000 bushels! Seventeen steamships are operating on Manitoba waters. Another 18 are building. The "rush of immigrants daily is increasing". And, in the way of all living things, our great pioneer, James Mackay, heads West, to "the Happy Hunting Ground".

On 3 August, Donald Smith (after John A. calls him "the biggest liar I ever met" . . and who questions the word of 'the old Chieftain' on such an issue?) gets the running rights he wants, over the new Pembina-Winnipeg railway. Smith, Hill, Kittson and Stephen, re-name their bankrupt St. Paul & Pacific — the "Great Northern Railway"; and, by successive financial manipulations "cut among themselves a melon of $300 millions . . . on an investment of $300,000.00 . . while letting the public pay the cost," writes historian W. G. Hardy. (And while the Settlers . . who give value to the land and to the railways which live thereoff . . . "eat their bread in the sweat of their faces".)

The National election of 26 September returns Schultz, in Lisgar; Dubuc, in Provencher; and gives Prime Minister Macdonald an acclamation in Marquette. In Selkirk, Smith wins over Norris, by 9 votes. Norris demands a re-count. It is set for 3 October. Smith gets a re-count by Judge Betournay, on 2 October. By 3 October, the ballots are away to Ottawa! While voters of Headingly and west Winnipeg oppose Smith, "Company" officials and servants, including Metis in St. James and St. Charles, elect him.

Local newspapers feature Mr. Hall's display of "Totofsky apples as large as oranges" grown at Headingly. The Provincial Show opens, on 9 October, in Winnipeg. On 11 October, the Winnipeg Snowshoe Club organizes. Fanciers have formed a Pigeon Club, in St. James. In the pioneer tradition, Manitobans create their own entertainment.

The Davis Government resigns. Their policy of economy — having served its purpose and time — is swept away in the more exciting tide of "progress". Hon. John Norquay becomes Premier. He pledges roads, railways and bigger boundaries for the new Province. Norquay is a native leader. The subsequent election returns 6 opposition members; 2 independents; and 16 Government supporters. The MLA's elected to this third Manitoba Parliament include: J. A. K. Drummond, High Bluff; Andrew Bourke, Baie St. Paul; Louis Scmidt and Hon. J. Royal, St. Francois Xavier; John Taylor, Headingly; Alex Murray, St. Charles; and David M. Walker, St. James.

A return from Headingly school signed by John Taylor, secretary-treasurer, and A. C. Clouston, trustee, reports 71 children in the district. Of these, 27 boys and 32 girls attend school. Families represented on the roll are: Taylor, Sayer, Bremner, Smith, Cameron, Dennison, Hall, Lonsdale, Clouston, Tait, Simpson, Field, Lambert, Moore, Stevens, Corbett, Sutherland, Bewel, McLaughlin and Fidler.

John Taylor tells in his diary: "Tuesday, 12 November. Helping Browns thresh. Peter had my team. . . to town for a large wheel for their mill. Wednesday, 13 November. Peter start home before we got out of bed. Weather beautiful. Good skating. Thursday, 14 November. Hard frost at night . . . Flooring stable. Friday, 15 November. Fine. Indian summer. Saturday, 16 November. Beautiful. Winnowing wheat all day. Sunday, 17 November. Fine. To church, forenoon and afternoon. Out looking for calves. Monday, 18 November. Winnowing wheat. Gregoire and George go for 2 wagon loads of hay. Rain, snow — then cleared. Tuesday, 19 November. George and Alixis to Rockwood mill with 80 bushels of wheat. Old Dauphinais call to solicit my vote for coming election. To Bremner's in evening . . . Johnny out after horses. Thursday, 21 November. Boys return from the mill. Friday, 22 November. Boys out for hay. Bob Munn was in. To Lonsdales and A. Cloustons. Saturday, 23 November. Butcher ox from Thos. Stevenson; sold half to George Gray".

"Monday, 25 November. Up to Michael Fleuries for my cattle . . . Cross at Lepine's ferry. Stay overnight at Francis St. Germains. Got calves and year-olds divided. Home with cows and beef oxen. Leave one just calved. Cross at Morrison's on the ice. . . Home, just as children home from school. Tuesday, 26 November. Kept store. Johnny to town to get groceries. Peter stay overnight on his way down with load of barley. At 11 o'clock the Mistress was delivered of a daughter. All right. Snowed some at night. Wednesday, 27 November. George start up for my beef cattle at Poplar Point. Thursday: Sandy Cameron and I kill 2 oxen; and had Mrs. McLeod to clean the guts. Stormed. Friday: kill 2 oxen. Saturday: put away the beef from the 4 animals killed. Held Committee meeting at B. McKenzie's".

"Sunday, 1 December. Fine. To church in forenoon. A. Clouston and Ben McKenzie had dinner with us. Monday: butcher 3 oxen. Rice Howard and wife and Lonsdale had dinner. . . Had our Committee meeting. . . the two Cloustons, Jim Brown, Sandy Cameron, John Sutherland, A. Murray and Joe Lambert. After . . . to the Hotel. Met Luxton, who was up soliciting votes. He made quite a speech. Tuesday, 3 December. Butcher the last of the cattle . . . down as far as Hall's, electioneering. Wednesday: Round the upper end of the parish; and a meeting at Dauphinais's. Friday: Drive up to Poplar Point. Elections still muddled up. Too many candidates. Sunday. Fine. To church twice. Willie Lumsden was down to church. Magnus and James Brown and Willie Sutherland call; tell of R. McKenzie leaving for the woods. Monday, 9 December. Up as far as Brown's. Called at Sutherland's getting signatures to nomination papers . . . Sworn to by James Brown, before Rod K. MacKenzie. Tuesday: Drive to town. Call at John Gowler's. Call at Murray's, . . . where . . . a committee meeting. Wednesday: Attend nomination and said a few words. Tait did not attend".

So — day after day — doing the farm work; driving over the parish, calling on voters; at Committee meetings. Then: "Wednesday, 18 December. Election day. I was returned by a majority of 17. Monday, 23 Dec. Blowing cold. A good many call: Willie and John Sutherland, Willie and Magnus Brown, his wife and Maggie, Jennet D., Willie Lumsden, Sandy Cameron, Phillip Stevens and James Green. The young people are all up to the wedding at McQuorqudales. Tuesday, 31 Dec. Christmas tree for the Sunday School was success".

On New Year's Day, 1879, a foot of snow falls on the plains. The air breathes softly from the south; veers, strengthens; blows from the West! Soon, the northwest wind, "Kee-way-den", hurls smothering clouds of snow upon the land; and, for 36 hours, raging from the north, blizzards of icy bullets hammer the frozen landscape! Teamsters, caught on the trail, turn their oxen loose; and seek shelter in the timber. Many oxen perish. Homesteaders, fighting their way between stable and shack, are frozen to death!

The last mail from the south, by stage, arrives in St. Boniface on the evening of 8 January; next morning, the first mail — by train — leaves for the south and east. The Winnipeg Snowshoe Club barely completes its big race on 3 March (won by a novice!) when the season's first party of 500 settlers arrive — followed by others, day after day.

Manitoba hard wheat loads the railway to the United States, where Minneapolis millers offer premium prices for its superior milling qualities. To handle the grain, merchants are building 15,000-bushel flat warehouses. The pioneer "elevator" is built at Niverville. "Ten Years in Winnipeg" is published by A. Begg. A "Business Directory" carries 47 pages of advertising; with the Assiniboine Brewery Company, Silver Heights, among the 113 advertisers. On 12 April, a new newspaper, the "Winnipeg Daily Times", begins circulation. Its editor: Chas. R. Tuttle; its politics: Conservative. The flood tide of humanity rolls westward. Ten months, ending last October, see 600,592 acres "located" in Manitoba.

The C.P.R. promoters are true monopolists. Through the Government of Canada, they deny charters to railways in Manitoba which might divert traffic, via United States railroads. An Order-in-Council, of 18 April, rules that "All railway legislation must originate in Ottawa. No charter of a line exclusively in Manitoba should be granted without the Dominion Government assenting thereto". This cancels successive charters granted by the Government of Manitoba. The need for (and profitability of) such connecting lines is indicated by the 17,640 passengers on the Pembina line in its first 5 months of operation. Premier Norquay carries the battle to Ottawa. John Taylor becomes Minister of Agriculture. Clarke, MLA for Ste. Anne, is unseated by Judge Betournay, for personal bribery.

An Eastern editor reports travelling by rail from London, Ontario, to Manitoba in 4 days. A carload of settlers effects costs $220.00. During the last week of March, 395 settlers leave London, for the West.

On 24 May, the "SS Marquette" steams into port *from the West*! She has voyaged up the Assiniboine to Fort Ellice; and back — 1,000 miles in 13 days! However, the railway brings the real boom to Manitoba. Winnipeg, gateway to the Golden West, is to be a second Chicago! Speculators auction land — from maps! Four different railway routes westward, are being surveyed, simultaneously! Donald Smith pulls the strings to draw the main line through Winnipeg, thereby sky-rocketing prices of "Company" land around Fort Garry.

The University of Manitoba — established by the recent union of St. Boniface, St. John's and Manitoba Colleges — holds its first convocation. Sixteen students sit for exams.

And still they come! "With Mr. Patterson's party" (reports our migrant editor) "Tickets; $22.50 . . . London to St. Boniface, with lay-over. Leave midnight, Tuesday . . . Arrive Emerson, Friday. Every passenger allowed 2 seats. At Milwaukee, sleeping car attached, free to ladies and children. . . Fifty men living in the emigrant Emerson sheds. "Some have been here 5 weeks; and no work. Many going to United States. Some walking back to Canada. Leaving daily. Many shamefully used by C.P.R. All not satisfied. Some highly delighted!"

Rev. Daniel M. Gordon, travelling from Ottawa, via San Francisco and Edmonton, sees the C.P.R. building and farmers threshing wheat, between Portage and Winnipeg. Some of that grain may be aboard the stern-wheeler "Marquette" when she steams into "the Forks" from Portage, on 13 August, with 500 sacks for N. H. McMillan's mill; 250 for "the Company"; and 7 tons of general freight. This fall, we harvest another splendid crop.

At Emerson, our Eastern editor reports: "Many farmer's sons come, expecting free land. Good, dry land held by speculators . . . or reserved for Mennonites, Icelanders, English Companies, Hudson's Bay Company, Indians. The only free land. . . wet, low, too far from timber. Canada has lost thousands of good loyal men to the United States. Some have been working on the C.P.R. . . Report shocking conditions. Some die from neglect. Railway conductor tries to make me pay twice. Many are fleeced. Winnipeg M.P.'s, speculators, officials say emigrants 'chicken-hearted'. Many of these have 100,000 acres, cost them 20 to 75 cents; want $3.00 to $10.00. Many settlers, here early . . in high ecstasies.

"Ten miles west on Portage Road. Rain. Meet cart stuck in black, knee-deep mud. Four men push, plastered head to foot. They tie tail of another horse to cart shafts; and pull! They swear 'The Government ought to be hung!' Adjoining Silver Heights and Deer Lodge . . . M.P.P. has dry road through his estate. His wife collects 10 cents per cart for use". In Winnipeg Railway Station: "Lady stands on bottom step of railway car. Stage driver grasp her around the legs;

and carry her through the mud to his muddy hotel bus. Most passengers have a high opinion of the country. Many will return with
families, livestock, etc., Wealthy 'young blades' from England, camp
near Winnipeg . . . They are headed for the foothills . . . big ranches!
Paid guides, managers, etc. Around Winnipeg, many tents . . . Indians,
traders, immigrants. Indians and squaws carry black bottles; drink
freely, even on Main Street . . . but are peaceful . . . and happy".

The buffalo herds disappear. "In the fall of '79, great fires . . . started
by rival bootleg gangs to hamper competitors and police . . . for 500
miles eastward of the foothills". The Great Hunt treks further and
further — for smaller and smaller returns. After 1879, it is only an
"old-timer's" memory. New-comers are excited about the boom in land
prices! Bumper crops in Manitoba and depression in the East — bring
12,000 settlers West this year.

Manitoba's fourth Legislature is elected on 16 December. Hon. John
Taylor is defeated in Headingly. Alex Murray is elected MLA for
Assiniboia. Another delegation heads for Ottawa to fight for "better
terms".

C.P.R. surveys, to the end of 1879, have cost $3,119,617.00; 21 men
killed; and unknown numbers hurt. But the shining new rails extend
from the Lakehead to Selkirk, 409 miles; From Selkirk to Pembina, 84
miles; and from Winnipeg, 100 miles toward the Western horizon.

Donald Smith — hated by so many; deified by others — sees his '79
election upset for corrupt practices. The Supreme Court of Canada
confirms the judgment. He attempts to win the riding, again; but, for too
long he has used the power and personnel of "the Company" to get
elected. Now, new-comers, who do not recognize his dictates, out-
number "Company" supporters. He is defeated! He never forgives
Winnipeg!

It is difficult to free historical writing from the distortion of prejudices
and preferences. Many contemporary records are more hysterical than
historical. Any truly historical record of these days must be distilled from
equal measures of the thinking and actions of Schultz, Riel and Smith —
and all who move around them — tested in equal degree for idealism,
ambition, fear and hate. Few historians have attempted this. Certainly
the time and the "capacity for taking pains" permitted to this writer are
not adequate for such achievement. When successive lifetimes of genius
have, thus, synthesized the truth, we may see that each of these men
contribute to the building of our Canadian nation far more than any
one of them would credit to any other; and far less than countless
unrecorded, unknown men and women whose minds and muscle,
dreams and determination, shrewdness and sweat power the waterways

— tread out the trails — freight the tonnage — harvest the food — raise the buildings — place and displace the governments — and frame the foundations of our vast Nor'West community, as a vital component of a Canadian nation with potential for mankind far beyond that visioned by Smith or Riel or Schultz — or any of their partisans!

Donald Smith

CHAPTER 10

The Great Highway . . . 1880-89

The first train steams eastward, out of St. Boniface, on 10 February, to the Lakehead. Settlers swarm to the booming West! In February, W. B. Hall, of Headingly, is appointed to the new Board of Education.

The Government of Manitoba, in March, divides the Province into 31 Municipalities. One of these is the Rural Municipality of Assiniboia, embracing the parishes of Headingly, St. Charles, St. James and St. Boniface, West; from St. Francois Xavier, eastward, to Sherbrooke Street and, south of the Assiniboine River, to the Red; and covering 124 square miles.

A young girl (to become famous as "Nellie McClung") tells of landing, with the family, at St. Boniface, on 1 May. The steamboat captain is a man of even temper: always in a rage! The deck hands work in torrents of profanity. Living near Deer Lodge, while the men-folks locate land in southern Manitoba, this family finds friends in Mr. and Mrs. Robt. Tait and their children: Herbie, Ellen and Addie. There is some talk of buying Louis Pruden's farm of 108 acres for $1,600.00. The decision is to move "West." Navigating the big swamp beyond Baie St. Paul, the wagons reach Portage la Prairie. There, in Hudson's Bay store, these pioneers buy beans, flour, bacon, salt, nails, duffle, moccasins, a keg of "Golden Drop" syrup, dried apples, soda and Painkiller. Wrapped in blankets, keen-eyed Indians watch. Portage boasts a newspaper: the "Marquette Review"; and a sawmill which ships lumber up the Assiniboine on "SS Cheyenne", "SS Marquette", and "SS Manitoban". The wagons roll 10 miles a day southwestward, along the Yellow Quill Trail. Dogs are "in great demand" among the Settlers. There is much talk of the Nor'West joining the United States.

The tide of Settlers includes families from many lands. On 5 May,

John P. Pennefather, M.D. with his 4 sons, leaves Liverpool, for Manitoba. The good doctor — lured by the "inducements Manitoba holds out as a home for the redundant Anglo-Saxon race"; and holding it "essential that the flag of England should wave over the land of my adoption" — buys 640 acres on the Cypress River. In Winnipeg, he buys, for $150.00, a yoke of oxen . . . and, for $55.00, a yoke of steers; covered wagon, $110.00; cart, $25.00; and 3,000 pounds of supplies. On "the Queen's birthday" his outfit heads West on their great adventure. The 100 miles to their land is traversed in 16 days. Mrs. Pennefather follows: and, in 2 days, does the trip via team and buckboard: elastic boards on 4 wheels, with a spring seat in front. Lumber, freighted by steamboat from Winnipeg to Smart's Landing, is teamed 20 miles across country. The Doctor reports: "What cost me $80.00 per thousand feet, could be purchased in Ontario for $8.00 or $9.00." It is some compensation that "prairie fowl and wild ducks add to our larder."

Adjusting the lens of our History from the wide-angle view of Assiniboia as the hub of our vast Nor'West: and focussing on the newly-created Rural Municipality of Assiniboia, permits more intimate recording of the people who pioneer this 124 square miles as part of Manitoba and Canada.

The first "Council of Assiniboia" is called into session by Miles Macdonnell, in 1812. With various re-organizations, "Councils of Assiniboia" administer the area now called "Manitoba", until 1869. The Council of the Rural Municipality assembles in its first meeting on 3 May, 1880. Called to order by Warden Wm. Tait are Councillors John Taylor, James Green, Duncan McDougall, Antoine Hogue, John Bourke, R. A. McKenzie; and H. J. Arkle, Returning Officer for the first election. W. F. Lane is appointed clerk, being fluent in both French and English. By-laws are passed to regulate Council proceedings; and to legalize wire fencing. In response to Council's appeal for cash assistance, the Government of Manitoba advances $400.00. A Council Chamber is rented in Charles Land's home, at $20.00 for the year. Council discusses taxing dogs; but "lays over" such a contentious issue; and appoints: assessors, W. T. Lonsdale, W. D. McKenzie, Joseph Turcotte, Joseph McMillan and W. F. Fraser; and poundkeepers, James Clouston, Thomas Hogue, Francis Welsh, Philbert Landeronte, Henry Elsey, Joseph Lambert and Frank Ness.

At 2 meetings in June, Council appoints Frank Ness assessor for Ward 4 at $30.00; buys a Municipal seal; accepts Warden Wm. Tait's offer to put a ferry at Headingly; divides the Municipality into 9 road divisions; and names, as road overseers: Cornelius Fidler, James Tait, Geo. Cook,

Joseph Hogue, John Smith, Baptiste Berare, Duncan McQuat and George Gerrie.

York boats, having displaced canoes for heavy freight, are themselves being displaced by steamboats. Increasing tonnages are moved on the Assiniboine River and the Red (and on far distant waters) by steamships. Many of these vessels are built locally. Stern-wheelers — of 200 foot keel; 40-foot beam; and drawing 3 feet of water — are limited by Order-in-Council to 350 passengers, each. Navvies, Chinese, Swedes and Metis are packed below. On upper decks, traders, entrepreneurs and other gamblers luxuriate in magnificent cabins and dining salons. The cart trail southward, which formerly traversed the drier ground, easier grades and prime pasture some miles west of the Red, now hugs the River bank. The cordwood needed to fuel the steamboats is collected at riverside woodyards. These develop into towns. Stretches of trail joining the towns become links in the new "Pembina Trail". Westward, through Assiniboia, the old trail becomes the Great Highway, carrying freight in the cart trains that lurch along its loops to Edmonton, and beyond. Paralleling, and actually part of this Great Highway, the Assiniboine River carries more and more heavy tonnage by steamboat and barge. Already, the "iron horse" begins to take over. In 4 months, ending 30 June, 1880, the new railway between St. Boniface and the Lakehead moves 30,467 tons, including 31,841 bushels of wheat. The basis of our economy is shifting, swiftly, from Buffalo to Bushels.

More and more Settlers follow trail, river and rail to the Western lands and waters, awaiting a new type of use. The homesteaders who "take up" and farm the "open" sections in surveyed townships, give value to the entire area surveyed. In each township of 36 mile-square sections, $16\frac{1}{4}$ sections are "open" to homesteaders; and $19\frac{3}{4}$ go to other owners. "Breaking" new acres builds independence for many pioneers; and profits for the other owners — who "gather where they have not strode."

Settlers of many kinds come to Assiniboia, from many lands. Capt. Edmund Goodridge, his wife, daughter and 3 sons, arrive at Quebec, on "SS Sardinian", 13 May, 1880. They are among 70 cabin passengers; 800 others pack the steerage. The Captain thinks railway fares cheap at a penny a mile; but "Canadian trains poor things; and much overcrowded". At the Windsor Hotel, in Montreal (a metropolis of 140,000) he pays $4.00 per day for his party "including everything but wines" (!) For 6 rail and steamship tickets, Toronto to Winnipeg, he pays $197.12. He finds "meals . . . at unreasonable hours . . . Breakfast, 7 a.m.; dinner, 12; tea, 6 p.m.; and no other refreshment . . . until next morning . . . a period of 13 hours!" Winnipeg hotels are overcrowded; but at the

"Grand Central" they are welcomed — 5,000 miles and 22 days from England — and given "a cold bite".

The Goodridge family finds Main Street "the roughest and rudest of its size and influence in the world." Along the 10-foot boardwalk are really fine shops. The Hudson's Bay Company is erecting a magnificent "edifice of 4 storeys". Dealers in farm implements and livestock, abound. Groceries cost 3 or 4 times as much as in England. Building is booming! Roads are "awful". Murray's swamp is a dreadful bog about 7 miles westward, opposite a Member of Parliament's home. Saloons outnumber churches. Expansion is so rapid "that a description today is not recognizable a year hence."

Capt. Goodridge hires 2 teams "to convey us and our goods," on 7 June, to a farm he has rented south of the Assiniboine, 3 miles below Headingly. In the 5 rutty miles to Silver Heights, the party passes several fair-sized houses, St. James Church and "many fields of growing grain enclosed with wire fencing." At Silver Heights are brewery, flour-mill, store, post office and many attractive houses, with good gardens. After crossing Sturgeon Creek they pass the post office, store, saloon and many farm homes of St. Charles. At Headingly — with its store, post office and roadside inn, the party turns south, to the ferry. How the "scow, guided by a feeble old man and a many-spliced rope, ever gets them across the river — 100 yards wide; and racing 6 miles per hour — is a marvel!" Rain has obliterated the road. A lad, plowing with oxen, shows them to the home of their neighbor-to-be, Mr. Hall. At the "farm", the house is unliveable, the barns "roofless piles of manure"; garden and fields nonexistent! Nothing daunted, they dig and plant a garden; sow barley on land loaned by Mr. Hall; re-roof and repair the house; buy poultry, pigs, cow and calf; and "within 7 weeks, have as good cream and butter on our table as we eat in Devonshire, itself". The Captain marches to Winnipeg; and carries 40 pounds of groceries the 11 miles home (like a good soldier) in his knapsack! Horses, harness, wagon and mower are bought in Winnipeg; and swum across the Assiniboine, since ferries are not running. Stuck in the mud, the Captain takes mower and wagon apart, carries the parts to solid ground; and re-assembles them. This is pioneering!

Hay cutting starts, by law, on 20 July. The Goodridges make hay, on shares. They have 40 acres stacked before rain stops work. In the storm, the horses break away. They are recovered only when a reward of $10.00 is posted. Yes, this is pioneering! Beginning 15 August, the Goodridge boys shoot plenty of prairie chickens and ducks. Everyone shoots! Indians and hybrid hunters sell hundreds of birds to city markets. On 7 September, hard frost kills mosquitoes and black flies; gardens and late barley; as well as the dazzling flower gardens at Silver Heights. It is a bad year for fruit.

As a judge at Winnipeg Fair, the Captain enthuses over the vegetable display. He is critical, however, of current farming methods. "The great need is for drainage of the bottomless bogs". He buys 200 acres, extending from the Assiniboine, 4 miles southward. Self-binders transform harvesting in Assiniboia. Robt. Tait brings in the first self-binder; and also the first threshing machine, run by horse-power. Farmers are fencing bigger fields with the new barbed-wire. Steamboats round the bends of the Assiniboine, to and from Portage and Grand Valley (Brandon).

The Council of Assiniboia calls out statute labor, to straighten the Portage Road, pursuant to petitions from Headingly and St. Charles ratepayers. The first Municipal tax of $2,000.00 is levied — being a rate of 4½ mills on the assessment roll. Council agrees that the Provincial Government grant a railroad right-of-way, along Saskatchewan Avenue; buys 10 road-scrapers; accepts the tender of John M. Tait as collector; and pays the account of James Green for filling holes in the road, near Mrs. Murray's.

Ratepayers demand roads and bridges. Wheel traffic is taking over from water. Settlers are venturing away from streams. November sees Thos. Harrison and Joseph Martel paid for work done on the "Great Highway"; and, following a petition, a road surveyed from John Smith's to J. F. Mulligan's. Cornelius Fidler repairs Omand's Creek bridge, opposite St. James Church; and Charles Land is granted planks for a bridge across a ditch "in front of the Council Chambers". A right-of-way is leased from Mrs. D. Cappelette from St. Charles ferry to the "Highway", for $15.00 yearly. Fifty dollars is voted for year-end elections.

One Manitoba historian writes: "There is a very distinctive group on the White Horse Plain, as Headingly is called in the early days, including graduates of British Universities; and people of sufficient means to live the life of English country gentlemen. These settlers, by their love of good books, art, music, flowers and gentle ways of living" contribute richly to the life of Assiniboia. Among such families, the Goodridges in their rebuilt house, are snugly ready for winter — with piles of dry wood to keep the stoves red hot. Alas! Fire breaks loose! Within an hour, only heaps of glowing embers are left of their home and precious possessions: glassware, heirlooms "and, worst of all, three English saddles." In 2 months, these pioneers build a new home on their new farm. This becomes famous as "the Old Retreat".

Throughout October and November, fires spread destruction far and wide. One farmer loses 300 tons of hay. Fires and bad weather shorten the hay harvest. Last year, hay sold for $5.00 to $7.00 a ton; this fall, "we get $10.00 a ton for 40 tons."

To withstand winter winds, "there is nothing like leather." Leather coats, trousers and boots are worn "with the universal buffalo coat covering all." In November, every sizeable farmer butchers 3 or 4 bullocks and half-a-dozen hogs. This replaces the meat formerly supplied by the Hunt. Poultry and fish are plentiful and cheap. In winter, the River becomes "the Great Highway." Some farmers shut up their farms, and move into town; some hire teams to the railway for $2.50 per day "and keep", for man and team. Generally, farmers haul wood and hay to the city. Hospitality blossoms during winter! Goodridge writes that "Balls . . . masquerade, fancy dress; New Year's Day visiting; Lieut-Governor levees; and surprise parties are the order of the day — and night! A few families, both English and Canadian, of good connections . . . relatives of . . . naval and military officers . . . make society more agreeable. Neither our neighbors nor ourselves . . . mix on social terms with the unsufferable roughness that characterizes . . . so many in Canada!"

The citizens of Assiniboia elect for their 1881 Council: Warden, James Green; and Councillors A. C. Clouston, Joseph McMillan, R. A. Mackenzie, Walter Bourke, John Bourke, D. MacDougall. W. F. Lane is clerk and treasurer, at $240.00 yearly. Edwin Bourke and Charles Gention, are auditors; and H. J. Ackland, assessor, at $125.00. The clerk is instructed to get a map of the Municipality "at least expense". When Councillors Clouston and Mackenzie resign, Messrs. Farmer and Cameron are elected to fill the vacancies. Council calls tenders for bridges at Miry and Omand's Creeks. The original boundaries make Assiniboia a big unit for administration. Citizens in St. Boniface West petition the Manitoba Government to separate from Assiniboia.

The Government of Canada inclines to Selkirk, as the C.P.R. metropolis — but decides on Winnipeg when aggressive 'Peggers build a bridge over the Red River. To get things moving, during the winter Contractor Ryan pumps water, from below to above, the Red River ice. When thick enough, he lays rails; drives a locomotive across the ice; and hauls thousands of tons of material over the River, ready for spring.

Settlers who work for the winter on railway construction, find camps flooded with whiskey. During the winter and spring, 800 gallons of whiskey per month — "taken from Winnipeg concealed in oatmeal, pease, coal oil barrels" — is sold to the 2,000 men working between Whitemouth and Lake Wabagoon, at $15.00 per gallon. The monthly "take" is $12,000.00!

Rev. Cowley follows Rev. W. Pinkham at St. James Anglican church. In Winnipeg, the 130-foot spire of Knox Church is topped by the tower, 250 feet high, built by the Methodists. The new Roman Catholic cathedral, it is said, will point even higher into the heavens! Parliament buildings, governor's residence are projected. New banks, hotels and homes cover the landscape. For free land, new-comers must go 200 miles, West. Prices climb. A 350-acre farm, bought for $2,500.00, re-sells for $5,000.00! Some farmers crop 100 to 300 acres. Mr. Hardy, at Sturgeon Creek, farms several hundred acres.

Spring break-up causes many accidents along the Assiniboine. On 28 April, the first steamboat heads upstream for Fort Ellice; and, on 24 May, "SS Manitoba" docks at Fort Pelly, 120 miles above Fort Ellice. This spring, the railway reaches Brandon; and heads westward. The steamboats fade away!

A Montreal syndicate takes over the C.P.R., together with vast grants of cash and land; and offers to build a branch southwestward — *if* Winnipeg pays $200,000.00 bonus, land for station and tax exemption forever! Citizens vote "Yes!" — 130 to 1! Construction is rushed on workshops, freight sheds, passenger station. Selkirk, with its superlative site, is sidetracked; Winnipeg — on the flooding "Red River flats" — becomes "the Gateway to the Golden West." Real estate booms. Manitoba has 65,000 people. The battle for "better terms" wins enlarged boundaries. A frenzy of speculation sky-rockets land prices. A Provincial Act of 25 May, takes the Fort Rouge area away from Assiniboia; and gives it to Winnipeg.

The Marquis of Lorne, Governor-General of Canada, arrives on 30 July; and takes up residence at Silver Heights. Streets are decorated with flags, bunting and arches. His Lordship lays the cornerstone of Manitoba College. Weeks of picnics, races, garden parties follow. The Governor-General is impressed with Sir Donald A. Smith's farm — with its 800 acres, manorial residence, gardens, fruit trees, cattle, buffalo *and* a special branch of the C.P.R. built right into the farmstead!

Smith (now "Sir" Donald) has transferred his affections from Manitoba. Unseated, for corrupt election practices — he stands as an independent in a by-election. "In spite of large sums spent during the campaign, he is defeated . . . He never forgives Winnipeg". Actually, Smith's political eclipse announces that "the Hudson's Bay Company" — with all its hired and retired servants; wealth, privileges and power; and techniques in manipulation — no longer dominates Manitoba politics.

On 8 August, the Governor-General proceeds, by train, to Portage la Prairie; and, next day, at "track end", 35 miles west of Portage, Premier Norquay and the Marquis lay a rail on the C.P.R. A guard of

"Mounties" under Col. Herchmer, guides the vice-regal party Westward.

When railway service reaches "the Forks", Settlers and traders are ready — with flat warehouses and one standard elevator — to handle the out-turn from the 2.4 million Western acres sown to wheat. Bumper crops lure 12,000 new Settlers, this year, from the depressed East. Each month brings another 1,000 new-comers. Fortunes are made in real estate. Winnipeg's population is 33 times that of 10 years ago! A census counts 65,954 people in Manitoba: 11,503 English; 16,506 Scots; 10,173 Irish; 9,949 French; 9,158 German (including 7,000 Menno-nites); and 1,898 other so-called "white" nationalities — a total of 59,187 "whites". There are, also, 6,767 Indians. The numbers of Canadians and people of mixed parentage are not recorded!

Assiniboia's Council navigates a flood of pressures and petitions demanding roads, bridges and ferries. The Portage Road is graded at James Hallett's and Cameron's swamp; and Wm. Hardie grades from Mrs. Murray's culvert to Doyle's Hotel, for $125.00. In July, G. D. Cook takes the oath, as Councillor. James Hallett and Frank Ness are appointed constables. Roads are rough. Alexander Murray is paid $5.00 for buggy springs broken; and J. B. Auger, $15.00 for damages to his wagon — at railway crossings. The Road, from Silver Heights to Boyle Brothers, is re-located. Louis Capplet is credited $3.00 on his taxes for road-work done; and W. B. Hall "cuts out and scrubs" roads in Ward 1. Henry Elsey, poundkeeper, is re-imbursed $3.00 expenses for a sick horse — which dies on his hands; and, at year-end, the Warden is voted $50.00 for extra services.

Compared with Settlers along the Assiniboine, Winnipeggers are rapidly becoming "citified". During this summer, delivery of water by ox-cart is displaced by water drawn from the Assiniboine. (Our River, for years, provides the water of life; and, later, carries the waste from the people living on its banks.) The first street railway is operating — from Fort Garry to City Hall; with the speed of horse-drawn cars limited to 6 miles per hour; and fares to 10 cents.

A farm paper, printed in Ontario, reports in September, that crops never looked better. Wheat, 25 to 40 bushels per acre; oats, 50 to 60. Imported cattle eat wild hay with relish, especially when well cured . . . The Manitoba Agricultural Exhibition opens in Winnipeg, 4 October. After a week's rain, roads are bad — but attendance is good.

Andrew McDermot dies, at 91. He is Assiniboia's wealthiest citizen. He and Sarah McNab, married at Norway House in 1812, raise 9 daughters and 6 sons. One daughter marries Alexander Logan; and is the mother of Mrs. Willis Bannatyne, of Sturgeon Creek. The fifth daughter, Anne, becomes Mrs. A. G. B. Bannatyne.

The Manitoba Government charters the Manitoba Southeastern Railway. The Government of Canada cancels the charter. Premier Norquay is attacked in local newspapers for "betraying the Province". By March, nevertheless, the Southwestern is bridging the Assiniboine at Headingly; and has track laid 44 miles, beyond. Manitoba voters re-elect John Norquay and his Government. "Gold" at Rat Portage precipitates a boundary war — which Ontario wins; and Manitoba loses.

The Assiniboia Council, elected for 1882, votes $10.00 to Alexis Verrer, who has suffered 2 broken ribs; and $80.00 for a bridge at Boyle's farm. The St. Charles ferry "having floated away" in the spring flood, is recovered; and Thomas Hogue is hired to run it. Council borrows $1,000.00 to meet notes; and passes accounts, to be paid "when funds are available".

In the name of "progress", Winnipeg buys and demolishes, Fort Garry; and grabs big chunks of Assiniboia and Kildonan. The boom collapses — because of world finance and this spring's Red River flood. Many homesteads are abandoned!

Families of Bremners, Sayers and Taylors leave Headingly; and, in Saskatchewan, start the community of "Bresaylor". Joseph Sayer writes, in 1961: "I have been in Bresaylor for 81 years. When I retired I had 15 quarters of good land; and, rather than pay the government income tax, I gave all my children $1,000.00; and shared up all the land. Left enough in the bank to keep us the longest day we live." Again, (on 8 January,1963): "We have a family get-together, Sunday. We are married 73 years. We had 13 of a family; and 8 living. I have split all my winter wood; and my missus, she is 89 . . . I have reached 94 and don't think I am old yet. Just 2 of us living that came out in '82. The others are all gone to rest. My missus was born in Alberta . . . Her Dad was a trader . . . They were taken prisoner by Big Bear. He was the one that saved the 2 white women. One Indian he took Mrs. Gowanlock and want her for his wife. Mr. Pritchard went to the Indian. He want 2 horses to let her go. John Pritchard's horses had all be taken by the Indians. He told Mr. Nolin. Got his horses back; and saved the poor white women. We were prisoners in Poundmaker's Reserve, 2 months; and all our cattle was taken by the Indians; and my Dad and Uncle Charles Bremner was taken as Rebells . . . But they could find nothing on they; And I was only 16; and I kept all my Dad's horses, when he was in jail. We fraited from Swift Current and made good money."

The boom rockets Winnipeg's assessment from $4 million to $30 million in 2 years. In June, gas lights are turned on. Mail is delivered, free. Eight banks, 12 loan companies and 17 insurance companies work overtime. On the distant plain, south of Moose Mountain, several hundred Red River carts head homeward, with robes and pemmican — *from the last Buffalo Hunt!*

By the end of June, the C.P.R. has freighted 3,937,166 bushels of grain and 49,137 cattle. Farmers organize in the "Manitoba and Nor'-West Farmer's Union" — to battle "big financial interests; railway monopoly; and oppressive tariffs; also, to urge building the Hudson's Bay Railway".

This spring, once the flooded Red subsides, 5,000 men, with 1,700 teams and supply trains, build 5 miles of new railway a day — Westward! Gangs work day and night building bridges. Every week, 1,500 Settlers pass through the "Gateway to the Golden West". Thirty-seven "races" contribute to the population of the West. More than 70,000 new-comers arrive during 1882.

New names added to the records of St. Charles parish during the year are: Lamirande, Saintonge, Cloyne, Jacques, Paris, Atkin, Burgess, McLellan, La Frampoise.

Land prices zoom! John Taylor and others buy 38 acres in St. John at $1,200.00 per acre, expecting to multiply their investment by re-selling as lots. Then, suddenly, the boom sags. Depression blankets the West for 5 hard years. Millons of acres "taken up" by 100,000 land seekers are abandoned. However, every furrow "broken", every yard of graded trail, help check the destructive sweep of prairie fires. Even more important, 10,000 Manitoba girls and boys attend 227 schools!

Beginning in '83, 3 dry years, with hard early frosts, submerge the land in ruin. Farmers protest, but pay high tariffs on implements, for the "protection of infant industry" in Eastern Canada. On 23 January, Manitoba voters re-elect John Norquay, with 20 supporters; and 10 Opposition members. Elected in Assiniboia is Alexander Murray — a native son, educated at St. John; and urging accelerated development of Manitoba's resources.

Surveys are pushed at top speed. In 119 parties, 1,200 men "run" 81,300 miles of line to survey 800 Nor-Western townships; and sub-divide 28,000,000 Western acres. Boundaries of 86 existing municipalities are re-defined. The C.P.R. revises its rates — upward. Memories of days a-gone are kept alive, in ageless pemmican — now selling for 15 cents a pound!

Assiniboia's Council for 1883 consists of: Warden James Green; and Councillors C. Fidler, James Tait, Cook, McIntyre, F. Ness, Charles Caron and Taylor. Headingly and St. Charles School Districts ask for cash. Council promises to pay "soon as funds are available". R. J. Lonsdale urges a bylaw to stop pollution of our River. The Clerk is instructed to buy a book to record all bylaws; and McPhillips Brothers make a map of Assiniboia for $280.00. (Could these be found, today, they would be priceless.) Wm. Tait is voted $42.00 for bridging Boyle's Creek. These bills to be paid "soon as funds available". Callicut and Company assessment is reduced by half, since their Silver Heights brewery burned. The Warden offers his personal note for municipal expenses, if necessary. Bylaws are aimed at loose livestock and "all obnoxious weeds". Many citizens bill Council, for scything thistles. W. F. Lonsdale urges Council to straighten the Portage Trail, between St. Charles and St. Francois Xavier. Charles Land's $10.00 claim, for breaking a separator axle at a crossing is relayed to the Southwestern Railway.

Assiniboia loses a famous native son, when J. K. Isbister dies, in London, at age 61. He leaves an estate of $128,766.54. Most of this is bequeathed — with 9,958 books — to the University of Manitoba "for the benefit and improvement of education in the Province, without distinction of race, creed or nationality!" The Free Press eulogizes Isbister as "The Man to whom, more than any other, this country owes whatever prosperity and progress it has experienced."

The Headingly Anglican congregation present their popular rector, Rev. A. G. Pinkham, with a horse and $50.00 cash. At Headingly, too, George Shirtliff begins work for Alexander Bremner — 2 months for $25.00; and, from 24 November to next May, at $15.00 a month. George Broughall is home, after a 310-mile bicycle trip through southeastern Manitoba. The invention of the knotter for self-binders, using twine to tie the sheaves, revolutionizes grain harvesting. Some 5,500 binders cut Canada's crop, this year. On three farms near Indian Head, 39 binders cut 16,000 acres of grain. The Farmers Protection Union meets in Winnipeg on 19 December; and drafts a Bill of Rights — demanding provincial control of public lands; tariffs for revenue only; an end to railway monopoly; and branch railway lines. Young Clifford Sifton, R. P. Roblin and Joseph Martin emerge as leaders in this organization. At the end of 1883, the C.P.R. has sold 3,753,400 acres of its Western lands; and realized, therefrom: $7,482,724.00.

The Farmer's Union collapses. Thomas Greenway and his supporters take up the cry for "Provincial Rights". A new publication is "Waghorn's Guide," which details the Southwest Railway timetable: from Winnipeg to Headingly, 14.2 miles, fare 90 cents; Starbuck, 27.2 miles, $1.50; end of track, 51 miles, $3.00. Stages to Fort Ellice and Calgary; also, from Winnipeg to St. Charles, Headingly, St. Francois Xavier and Pigeon Lake, at 7 a.m. Tuesdays and Fridays. Livery stable tariff: saddle horse, day of 10 hours, $3.00; half-day, $2.00; hour, $1.00. Single rig, day of

10 hours, $4.00; half day, $2.50; hour, $1.00. Double rig, $7.00 per day; half-day, $4.00; hour, $2.00.

The Council of Assiniboia rents the Council room from Charles Land at $30.00 for 1884; warns the Southwestern Railway to stop flooding the lands of Denis Caplette and his neighbors; and sues Winnipeg for $1,541.90 taxes due Assiniboia on property taken by the City. McPhillips and Wilkes are retained as Municipal Solicitors, at $100.00 per year. Bridges are built at Conelley's Creek and near W. B. Hall's farm, in Headingly South. A Court of Revision on 4 June, assesses all lands at $2.00 per acre, or higher. For digging ditches, ratepayers get credit on their taxes; and any balance at $5.00 per day, for man and team. Many owners have large acreages. Frank Ness' assessment is reduced to 450 acres. Council calls tenders for grading the Portage Road, from the eastern boundary to St. Charles. Day workers are paid to scythe thistles; and the land owners charged. D. Foulds is paid $40.00 for accidental injuries at Colony Creek bridge.

In October, Council hires Dr. Crawford, as the first Health Officer, at $100.00 per year. Ferry-man Pat Beauchemin is paid $19.00; James Rickards, $20.00; and Robert Bird, $17.00. Bridges need repair at Miry and McMillan's Creeks. The Reeve canvasses banks, to borrow money for schools. The River Road, south of Headingly, is chopped out by statute labor. Accounts for culverts, cutting thistles and road-work are passed for payment — "soon as funds available". Enthusiastic "boosters" urge our need of "industries". Council asks St. Francois Xavier and Macdonald municipalities to share in a bonus to build a grist mill.

A terrific storm on 28 August, wrecks Holy Trinity Anglican Church and the beautiful grove in which it is situated, east of Headingly. Francis' store and its contents are scattered from the Portage Trail to the Assiniboine. Meantime, George Shirtliff, working for Alex Bremner since last fall, hires for another year, at $180.00. He has drawn on account: 1 pair boots, $1.25; 1 hat, 50 cents; and 3 plugs chewing, 15 cents. Living is simple in these days.

Wm. Brown, 27 years old, takes his bride, of 17, to the farm in the beautiful bend of the Assiniboine where he was born, in 1857. (And where, later, stands St. Charles Country Club House.) They produce some grain and livestock; lots of vegetables; and 11 children. With other farmers, William helps, this fall, to team 700 carloads of sand and piles of cedar blocks to pave Winnipeg's Main Street — already macadamized from the Portage Road to William Street.

Great excitement is generated by the departure, in September, of 100 volunteers, for Egypt! Under Lieut-Colonel Wm. N. Kennedy, they — with 300 Canadian voyageurs — join Maj-General Lord Wolseley, on his Expedition to relieve "Chinese" Gordon at Khartoum.

In Manitoba, the throttling of branch railways by the C.P.R. monopoly, plus crop failure, sparks organization of Farmer's Union locals; and, in the most "loyal" farm homes, there is talk of armed revolt; secession; joining the United States; and: "It's too late for ballots — we must use bullets!" These farmer organizations are charged (by ultra-"loyalists") with starting the rebellion of '85!

The St. Charles parish register records, for the first time, the family names of: Klyne, Adam, Montdirant, L'Febre, Sansregret, Cardinal, Egan, Plante, Caselman and Hooligan. Several deaths are attributed to "consumption". The birth of Marie Louise Bird, on 8 December, records, for the first time, the attendance of a physician: Dr. Brotchie.

James MacKay's "Deer Lodge", for so long a famous stopping place, passes to new owners; and becomes an equally famous hotel. Young and old drive down the Assiniboine to the carnival which, on 15 January, opens the new roller skating rink on Market Street, East. Murray Park station is named for Alexander Murray, MLA, and pioneer settler.

The citizens of Assiniboia elect to their Council, for 1885, Reeve James Green; Councillors: Caron, Laderonte, Gerrie, Cameron, Tait, Land and Ness. Loans of $3,000.00 from the Merchants Bank — as well as $1,000.00 from citizen W. J. T. James and $1,100.00 from Caplette Brothers — are renewed; and another $2,000.00 is borrowed to finance schools. Peter McPherson, unable to move, is granted $24.00. Landowners are invited to do their statute labor for the next 2 years, on vital roads, bridges and drainage; and to accept receipts to apply on their taxes. Headingly, St. Charles, Sturgeon Creek, Morgan and St. Boniface South School Districts, all need money. Council reports: "Banks won't loan money for schools!" Frank Ness earns the thanks of Council for his report on Municipal finances.

Pioneer vital statistics are lost, when the Headingly Anglican log church is destroyed by fire. A new frame church is built to replace the original. Building costs are low. A jag of lumber, including 1,100 feet of 8-inch siding, 550 feet of 6-inch flooring, 28 pieces of 2" x 4" and 6 pieces of 2" x 8" — costs a farmer $43.30. Nails: keg of 4-inch, keg of 3-inch, 50 lbs. of 2½-inch and 40 lbs. of shingle nails cost $7.00!

A farm magazine (March issue) advertises: J. Hingston-Smith & Co: rifles made to order; repairing guaranteed equal to London; Winchesters, 14-shot, .442 calibre, $23.75, 12-shot, 450 calibre, $28.75; Chatham wagons, Massey farm machinery, Vulcan Iron, Steam Plows, Edward L. Drewery; Hudson's Bay Co: 7,000,000 acres of land for sale;

Manitoba & Northwestern Railway, 2,750,000 acres; C.P.R. 25,000,000 acres. From the news columns, readers learn that: 12 "Kinalmeaky" hogs, dressing over 4,000 lbs, net $300.00; "Kinalmeaky Farm", north of Headingly, covers 2,000 acres, 800 acres broken; 600 cropped; 1,000 in natural grass. The English Company owning the Farm plans to market beef, butter, cheese, hogs, sheep and poultry. Four hundred high-grade Shorthorn cows are bought, with calves, at $61.00 each. Steam outfits will speed plowing. This is one of Assiniboia's sizable farms.

Wildlife is still important in supplying food. It is reported that 17 "jumpers" and 8 moose are marketed at Carberry, last fall, at 8 cents per lb.; and the hotel buys 900 pinnated grouse at 25 cents a pair. In April, W. B. Hall, of Headingly, is appointed to Manitoba's new Board of Agriculture.

In a cyclone of Rebellion "news" and rumors, 100 all ranks of the 90th Rifles leave Winnipeg for Qu'Appelle, on 25 March. Next day, the Regiment entrains, headed westward. The 90th Rifles, a cavalry troop and a field battery from Manitoba are the first troops to arrive at Qu'Appelle. The 91st Infantry, organized under Lt. Col. Thos. Scott, is quickly above 400 strong. Companies of scouts are formed, overnight. Major Boulton (now Senator) enlists a Company of Rangers.

On 30 March, General Middleton sends 3 Companies of the 90th Rifles north, to reconnoitre. Already, Capt. "Sam" Bedson is organizing 600 teams, in divisions of 10, to freight supplies furnished by "the Company" and other contractors, between camp sites, sited 20 miles apart. On Monday, 6 April, at 5.45 a.m., the van of the Northwest Field Force moves north from Ft. Qu'Appelle — through blinding sleet and hail. Scouts patrol each side of the trail. One Company of the 90th Rifles, with a field gun, leads; main body, baggage, field gun and rear-guard follow.

Amid bungling excitement in Ottawa, Van Horne, active head of the C.P.R., swears he'll have troops over the new railway to Qu'Appelle in 12 days! There are 1,842 miles of track between Toronto and Qu'Appelle. Several gaps remain unfinished, between the Lakehead and "the Forks". The troops march across some of these; over others, rails are laid on the ice and snow; and trains inch across. Plank walls are spiked onto flatcars — to freight men and material. On the morning of 7 April, the Queen's Own and "C" Company, of the Toronto Infantry School, arrive in Winnipeg; and, that evening, are away on the 324 miles to Qu'Appelle. Next day, 1,000 of the 10th Grenadiers and one Company of the Foot Guards are in Winnipeg; and by 9 April, are in Qu'Appelle.

A schmozzle of incredible inefficiency, duplication and greed is swept forward on the resistless tide of national assertiveness. The entire "show" is Canadian! The first flexing of the muscle of our emerging nationality!

The new railway saves the nation. The nation saves the C.P.R.! The "ribbon of steel" links the Lakehead with Calgary, by May. The promoters, facing failure (with their own pockets full) become examples of "success" for future generations — by simply demanding more Government money! On 11 April, George Stephen writes to the Prime Minister that, without more Government money, the C.P.R. "can not carry on its struggle for life". Within weeks, again, the lament is that the railway is "within 3 hours of bankruptcy for a few hundred thousand dollars." One historian opines that Stephen writes less like a beggar than a blackmailer. John A., who loves to put off to tomorrow, cannot afford to dilly-dally. The Government meets each demand — by shovelling out more cash!

War catches Canada's defence department unprepared. Contractors rush to grab their slice of profits. The Rebellion makes fortunes for some. It, also, puts cash into the hands of many Settlers. Robert Sinton joins the transport column, with 2 good teams and a teamster, on 15 March. With each sleigh carrying 1,400 lbs. of ammunition and 300 lbs. of food, they reach Ft. Qu'Appelle 4 days later. Following the telegraph line, the column halts at isolated mail shacks; and reaches Prince Albert after 7 days — at 45 miles a day! For each team, Sinton earns $6.00 a day in camp; and $10.00 on the trail. He returns to Regina, after 72 days, with (perhaps) $1,200.00 cash; and the suspicion that "Middleton does not want to share the glory with the Mounted Police." The soldiers who die — and the comrades who face death with them — draw 50 cents a day!

In July, the 90th Rifles return to a tumultuous "welcome home" in Winnipeg — after travelling 1,000 miles by boat; 325 by rail; and 575 by "shanks mare". On 1 August, the final day of his trial, at Regina, Louis Riel faces the jury — to hear their verdict of "Guilty!". They recommend mercy. There can be no mercy! Newsmen and politicians who live by the written and spoken word have loosed a duel of verbal fire which they cannot extinguish, even if they would; which may sell some extra papers and sway some elections; but which burns a chasm of hate across our nation that deepens with the years. The Riel-haters gloat in revenge. Rebellion is ended! Or is it?

Against the terrible debit of hatred can be credited some benefits. First, Indians and Metis get some measure of the consideration due them. Second, Canada gets her transcontinental railway built. Third, the surging consciousness of our new Canadian nationality carries our people for 2 generations — until transcended by another and greater wave, after Vimy! Finally, thousands of virile young Canadians, for the first time, see the boundless plains and opportunities of our Canadian West. Some stay. More return, bringing families, friends and neighbors. Typical, is Honore La Fleche, from Louisville, Quebec. As a volunteer soldier, he marches out from Ft. Qu'Appelle. Many days (and 3 pairs of boots) later, he is with his unit at Batoche. Discharged in Winnipeg, Honore locates the land granted him by a grateful Government; and returns home on Christmas Eve. He persuades his father, Jude La Fleche, that Manitoba is the place for his 10 sons; and this family is added to the list of great Assiniboia pioneers.

"To crush the Rebellion", 2,011 soldiers and police are called to arms — as well as home guards. The total enrolled — including staff, transport, medical and "curios" — reaches 7,982. Nearly 4 for each fighting man! The numbers of Metis who take active part may total 500. Dumont is reported to have said 350, of whom 200 are armed. C. V. Alloway told this writer that Metis friends assured him that, at Batoche, no more than a couple of dozen are in the rifle pits at any one time.

In the entire campaign, 70 soldiers are killed; and 130 wounded. The Metis buffalo hunters are trained for short range shooting, from horseback. They have neither training nor arms, for long range accuracy. Some have Winchester rifles; most have old muzzle-loading, smoothbores — accurate at only short range. Their ammunition is counted by rounds, compared with the wagon-loads freighted for the troops. The soldiers carry new Martini-Henry and Snider-Enfield rifles — highly accurate up to long ranges. United States newspapers headline the arms-salesman who grabs the opportunity to demonstrate the Gatling gun. They credit this "drummer" and his 1,000-round-a-minute gun with "winning the war". The truth is: against marksmen in deep, scattered rifle pits, the Gatling has little effect. The field guns win "the fire fight". The decision is completely Canadian.

Gabriel Dumont, the Metis leader, knows that his best weapon is: mobility. He urges that mobility be exploited to decimate the invading columns. (As the Boers do 15 years later.) Had Dumont's will ruled, the wagon trains might have been captured; and the "Field Force" annihilated! Does Riel veto such action because he knows that, even if it succeeds, final victory is impossible? He has travelled in Eastern Canada and the United States; has seen the milling multitudes of people; their countless factories turning out endless supplies; their railways, freighting limitless tonnage. He must know that the hunters can never withstand the manpower and firepower which can be brought against them. He must know, too, that the defeat of his people means death for him! This is not Assiniboia in 1869 — when he leads the population to create a

Provisional Government to fill a vacuum. This is Rebellion! For him, it can have only one end. Why, then, does he return to help his people? Why does he halt the strategy that can win them time? Who knows what impels the mystic to martyrdom? Certainly not the apostles of greed who measure success in dollars and power. It is clear, however, that when Riel says "No!" to Dumont's plan to exploit his advantage in mobility to ambush the troops, he fixes the hour of defeat for his Metis — and death for himself! If martyrdom is his decision, Riel out-manoeuvres all his enemies. His execution hurls him into a more prominent place in Canadian history than is occupied by those who hate and deride him.

Against the Sioux, the Metis hunters could anchor around their laager of carts. In '85, once they give up mobility; and commit themselves to a defensive position, they become a target which artillery blasts at will. Dumont — whose bluff honesty and courageous skill is universally admired; and who fights for a "cause" in which he believes — must flee his country. Middleton, "pompous and paunchy", gets decorations; $20,000.00; and knowing smiles . . . at having collected too many furs as "mementos."

With amazing celerity, "scrip" for 240 acres each, is granted to 6,034 hybrids and early Settlers — totalling 1,448,160 acres. Volunteers in the 1869 Expedition are offered scrip for 160 acres each; 400 of them claim it.

Following a dry, dry summer, prairie fires sweep the country. Grain shipments total 2,429,000 bushels. Farmers beyond railway service have 5,000,000 bushels of wheat for export. Terminal grain elevators are built at Montreal, Lakehead and Owen Sound. The C.P.R. now operates 372 locomotives, 304 passenger cars, 47 sleepers, 8,253 freight cars and 4,668 miles of track. Trains cross the Assiniboine, over a C.P.R. bridge in St. James parish; and the Southwestern Railway bridge at Headingly. Railways revolutionize transport. The trains of carts and Settlers' wagons, bumping westward on Assiniboia's Great Highway, fade into history.

When frost ruins "100 acres of wheat, within 10 days of ripening", Capt. Goodridge states that "More money is made out of hay"; and proposes shipping baled hay, via Hudson's Bay to England! High-priced machinery and high interest rates rob many Settlers of their farms. In Winnipeg, 600 men find employment with the C.P.R.; many more at sawmills and 2 breweries. Improved farms near the City may be bought for $20.00 per acre. Farm produce finds ready sale. Good butter is rare; cream cheese is never seen; eggs and vegetables are scarce. Poultry is imported from Chicago and Eastern Canada! Local hams and bacon are unknown. Beef, by the quarter, is 5 cents per lb; cuts: 10 to 15 cents. Hard coal sells for $10.00 per ton; soft, $8.00; wood, $4.00 to $6.00 per cord. On Sunday, 13 September, the re-built Holy Trinity Church is opened at Headingly. Bishop Pinkham and Rev. A. E. Cowley conduct the service. Rev. Cowley takes services every fort-night at St. Francois Xavier, also. He almost lives in buggy or cutter — composing his sermons en route.

At the Provincial Exhibition, in November, entries from Donald A. Smith's Silver Heights farm win prizes for Highland cattle and Herefords, sheep, poultry, dogs, barley, oats, tobacco and vegetables. W. A. Farmer, of Headingly, shows the winning flax; and W. B. Hall takes firsts for apples, native fruits, pickles and jellies. This year, Kinalmeaky Farm sells 21,000 lbs. of pork, at 6 cents per lb.

When the last spike is driven by Donald Smith, in Eagle Pass, on 7 November, the C.P.R. reaches the Pacific: and "the Forks" of the Assiniboine River and the Red become, in truth, "the Heart of the Continent". This year, despite frost and fires, 7,842,343 bushels of grain is freighted by the C.P.R.; and wheat exports reach 3,455,400 bushels.

Settlers still find moose, caribou, elk, deer, bear, lynx and prairie chicken plentiful. Packs of hounds are kept for wolf hunting. Rheumatism and nasal catarrh are prevalent ailments. Altho much of this year's crop is frozen, fine fall weather speeds threshing. Wheat turns out 20 to 40 bushels per acre; oats, 30 to 50. Wheat prices are 50 to 70 cents; and barley 20 to 30 cents per bushel.

Schools have been operating since the first days of Settlement in Assiniboia. Many early records have been lost. Records available for St. James SD #7 (formed 2 July '71) begin with 1885, when Cora B. Short teaches 25 boys and 31 girls for 74 days. Jessie McGavin, Geo. C. Hill and Chas. A. S. Chapman are successive teachers in the '80's. First available records for Headingly SD #9 (formed 3 July, '71) show F. H. Francis, Secretary-treasurer and John Kelly, teacher. There are 59 pupils at school in 1878. In 1885, 23 boys and 17 girls attend for 95 days. The Government grant is $50.00. Following Matthew Fletcher, M. S. Cameron, F. L. Davis and Nellie F. Braden teach in the '80's. In Sturgeon Creek SD #30, 42 pupils are taught by Alex Acheson for 104 days, in 1885; for which the Government of Manitoba grants $50.00.

Burials, now, are certified by Dr. Brotchie or Dr. Cowan, who list causes of death as: dropsy, palsy, pulmonic disease, heart disease. Successive years of drought and frozen crops; the C.P.R. monopoly; and "the Rebellion", as featured in news media — divert immigration from our Nor'West. Settlements stagnate. "Empire builders" shrink to avaricous predators, fighting to keep what each can salvage. Hard times grip Assiniboia. To finance, Council borrows from citizens — from John Bourke, $3,000.00; John Isbister, $1,100.00; and Roderick Stevenson,

$600.00, at 8%. Special meetings discuss accounting, audit and records. In April, treasurer and clerk W. F. Lane resigns. Frank Ness is appointed Clerk; and, to help keep better records, is instructed to "procure a letter press". Old fur trader methods are no longer adequate. Council resolves that all lands in arrears for taxes shall go to tax sale.

At Kinalmeaky Farm, 3 varieties of wheat are sown: Red Fife, Blue Stem and Black Sea. Arbor Day is 12 May. "The Farmer's Club" elects: President, W. Lomas Harrison; Vice-president, J. G. V. Johnstone, of Kinalmeaky Farm; and, to the Executive: Chas. E. Tizard, St. Charles; Captain Graham, St. James; W. A. Farmer, Headingly; and S. Hardie, St. Charles. An Assiniboia company is formed (Capital Stock: $75,000.00) for raising domesticated buffalo, S. L. Bedson's herd is bought as a nucleus.

On 1 July, the first through train steams into "the Heart of the Continent" (where a three-day celebration is in full swing) and on, Westward. There is history in every puff from her smoke-stack; and triumph in every blast of her whistle! In 137 hours of running time, she rolls 2,905 miles — on Canada's railway; the longest on earth!

In July, Sir John A. and Lady Macdonald visit Manitoba. More significant — for Assiniboia, for Canada and for the hungry world: this crop-year, the Golden West ships 10,960,000 bushels of grain, 1,000,000 barrels of flour and 244,000 cattle! Winnipeg businessmen grab "complete control over the Western grain trade"; and dominate wholesale distribution from the Great Lakes to the Pacific. Flour milling and meat packing boom! Fortunes are made in "land". Entrepreneurs buy scrip from hybrid people for as little as a $2.00 jug of bad whiskey; and re-sell the 240 acres for 500 times that price! Winnipeg grabs acreage from Assiniboia (and other municipalities) for "living room". Nevertheless, the number of Settlers falls far short of expectations. Far more Canadians move to the United States than to our own Nor'West.

At the same time, Settlers from "south of the line" come to Manitoba. The population of Manitoba climbs to 108,640. Nearly 16,000 girls and boys attend 547 public schools. This year, Assiniboia welcomes the Lafleche, Caron and other fine families from Quebec. But the number is tragically inadequate. For each Canadian who comes from Quebec to our Canadian West, hundreds go to the United States. Our in-surge of Settlers is, largely, from Ontario.

All recognize the vital place of education in the new Nation we are building. But, from the beginning, financing our schools is a struggle! Our Municipal Council, this August, must find money for 7 School Districts: Headingly, $500.00; Morgan, $94.00; St. Boniface South, $45.00; St. Charles, $425.00; Sturgeon Creek $475.00; Little Mountain,

$475.00; St. James, $400.00; total $2,414.00. In addition, the Judicial District levies $244.30. Taxes to meet these demands are hard to collect. In our rural economy, cash money is difficult to find. Already, however, there is talk of developing "industry". Convinced that "industry" can improve Municipal income, "a large number of ratepayers" petition our Council to pay a $3,000.00 bonus to Pierre Desganes to build a grist Mill in Headingly.

Drought turns the summer to dust. Waters wither in July's heat. August brings a cyclone! A new problem is: what about overdue taxes on River Lot #39, St. James, now hacked into town-lots? Somehow, accounts are paid, in tax credits for cutting thistles and road work. Cash is found to pay Antoine Hogue $15.00 for a ferry boat; and $38.50 for essential office supplies. In September, David Isbister is elected Councillor, vice Alexander Murray, resigned. The bonus for a grist mill is voted down. Bridges over Sturgeon, McMillan's and Gowler's Creeks must be repaired! Six dollars is voted for a destitute family. (In whatever extremity, pioneer Assiniboia cares for its folks.) For weeks, Council works to untangle records of lands sold for taxes — while owners hold full receipts! (Part of "growing pains" into more complex business.)

Prime Minister Macdonald visits the West, again, in September. The impending Provincial election may have something to do with the visit; and, also, with the announcement that "construction on the Hudson's Bay Railway is being pushed rapidly forward; and 40 or 60 miles will be built this fall!" Construction actually begins; but explodes in scandal! In Manitoba's first hotly partisan election, Liberal candidates are strongly supported in newly settled Western sections; but Norquay is elected — by the old pioneers, "natives" and others who have faith in his honest determination to have branch railways built — to compete effectively with the C.P.R. monopoly.

Out the Southwest Railway, beyond Carman and Glenboro, "Prairie fires cleared 4/5 of the country of grass and bush. Buildings, grain, stock, fodder, implements, homes are burned out." In this year of drought, wheat prices fall lower than for 100 years. Interest is commonly 12% on machine debts; and 10% on land loans. Subscribers to a local farm journal read, in its first issue for 1887, an advertisement by the "Weekly Free Press" of a "Great Prize Drawing" — offering 2,000 prizes, including a Toronto binder, mower, Chatham wagon, sewing machines, shotguns, fanning mills! Just send $2.00 for a subscription!

Throughout 1887, Assiniboia's Council, headed by Reeve Gamble, wrestles with a mounting mass of municipal business — overloaded with the chaos resulting from development out-speeding administration. A salary of $550.00 yearly is voted to Frank Ness, as clerk, treasurer and collector. McPhillips, Wilkes and McPhillips are retained as Municipal Solicitors at $100.00 a year. A special audit, complete from Assiniboia's inception as a Rural Municipality — is ordered; also investigation of sales of lands for taxes in '84 and '85 and the claims of S. Macdonald, Thos. Waddell and Col. Mulligan of properties sold for taxes, improperly. There is talk of action against former clerk and treasurer, W. F. Lane; but none is taken. At the Provincial Exhibition, in June, George Caron, of St. Charles (who last winter built a big new dairy) takes prizes for best butter. And on 28 June, young and old assemble at St. Charles, to celebrate the wedding of Honore Caron, 28, and Claire McKenzie, 17.

July meetings of Council strike off taxes, totalling $337.74. Men and teams, called out to repair the bridge at Gowler's Creek, are allowed $1.50 per man per day; and $3.50 for man and team — to be applied against taxes. On the same basis, work is done on public roads under supervision of the Ward Councillors. For road work and scything thistles, workers are paid "what may be due them, *after* their taxes are paid."

A Manitoba Government charter to the Red River Valley Railway, to meet the Northern Pacific at Pembina, launches that venture on its brief and hectic career. The Macdonald Government, at Ottawa, disallows the charter. But John Norquay is a determined man, too! On 2 July, he turns the first sod; and construction goes ahead — until funds run out! John A. blocks all avenues for loans. George Stephen wires a threat to move the C.P.R. shops out of Manitoba to Ft. William, if the Act passes, incorporating the new Railway. However Westerners resent it, high-handed autocracy rules the day!

Farmers in Assiniboia, as throughout the Nor'West, harvest bumper crops. The out-turn of wheat averages above 25 bushels per acre. Prices, however, are low. Winnipeg wheat is 55 to 57 cents per bushel; barley, 34 cents; oats, 25 cents. Winnipeg grain merchants unite in a Grain and Produce Exchange. Their first office is in the basement of the City Hall. This "Grain Exchange" speedily becomes an efficient mechanism for brokering vast quantities of grain — to the great profit of grain handlers, millers and exporters. Many of these are among the West's first millionaires.

Folks of St. James parish stage a gala Xmas party at Silver Heights. Among those present are: the Misses Bruce; and Messrs. Hill, Taylor, Barrett, Bourke, Copeland and Fortney. As 1887 ends, Assiniboia's

Council pays the good citizens who have done road-work, under path-masters Thomas Beveridge and W. C. Hall, in credits on current and future taxes. Help is voted to 4 needy families; $50.00 is voted to the Reeve; and the 10% rebate for prompt payment of taxes is extended to 10 January.

Charged with advancing money to Hudson's Bay Railway contractors, Premier John Norquay promptly resigns! Hon. D. H. Harrison, of Minnedosa, succeeds as Premier (for a few days); but fails in by-election of proposed Ministers. In Headingly, for example, Hon. Joseph Burke is defeated by Liberal F. H. Francis. So passes from leadership John Norquay — one of Manitoba's great sons! The embryo Harrison government resigns, on 18 January. Thomas Greenway forms an administration. His cabinet decides upon a mid-summer election — to be preceded by "Redistribution". This move, barely mentioned in Manitoba histories, has profound and far-reaching significance!

The political ferment which has wrought changes in so many countries since 1840, has not by-passed Canada. Here — as successive generations of men and women ride the waters, master the mountain passes, range the plains, clear the forests and breathe the free air of this vast land they inherit, direct and sweet-smelling, from the hand of God — a vision of a new Nation takes form. A vision of a new Nation takes form — beyond academic parroting of classical teachings, mouthings of fork-tongued politics and the music of cash registers. The vision takes form among pioneers who know the stink of sweat, the sting of lice, the gnawing of starvation, the terror of the elements; who share the endless work that hardens the hands, disciplines the soul and, from primal raw resources, creates human progress! It is taking form in the souls of men who discipline their days and muscle to ax down forests and shape the timber into farmsteads, towns and roads; who scythe the lush grass of the prairies, with a rhythm in the mowing that is akin to music; who battle stubborn sod into submissive fields; and who master the skills of transport, by land and water. It is taking form in the hopes of women, who — from covered wagons, forest cabins and homestead shacks — see the future in neighbors, schools, churches and secure communities. Vague, confused and contradictory may be the dreaming — felt rather than understood; but — inarticulate — so real it hurts!

The vision is of Canada as a sovereign nation — a Christian democracy; based upon the individual — and the rights and duties that link the individual to family, neighbor, nation and the infinite. In this Canada, shall be no slave, no dictator; no oppressed, no oppressor; no "upper" classes, no "lower" orders; but freedom, equality and opportunity for all. Here, laws — however warped by human fault; and flaunted by conniving greed — shall guarantee every citizen rights; and, from each, demand duties.

The days when Assiniboia is "A Battlefield for Fur" send incredible profits to foreign profiteers; and leave inhabitants a legacy of division. The fur Companies fight each other as "English" and "Canadian". When new-come Ontarioans declare themselves "the Canadians", they tag the original Canadians, and their progeny, white and mixed, as "the French". These, in turn, call all who speak other than French "the English". Such semaisological juggling spawns the myth that Manitoba is a duality: "French" and "English" — like a Red River cart, rolling on two wheels. The historical fact is : for generations, the majority of Assiniboia's people are aboriginals and their offspring; and even now, those born in either France or England are minor fractions of the population. The passing years see an inflow of native-born Canadians, plus pioneers from every corner of the earth (an early census records "37 races in the Nor'West") being moulded (by climate and resources; geography and history) into a new *Canadian* people — as every clan and nation has been formed, throughout mankind's existence. Eventually, even our census-takers may admit our right to call ourselves: "Canadian"!

The Red River cart — supremely useful in its day — gives way to railway trains. The human basis of our Province and our Nation changes in no less degree. In close-coupled unity, running on, not 2, but multiple wheels — we are en route to our destiny! a truly *Canadian* nationality, using our vast resources to serve mankind. Redistribution, in 1888, is a step in this direction. The Province is divided into 38 electoral districts, based upon manhood suffrage and representation by population.

Domestic cattle are replacing buffalo in the West. A Western farm journal reports that Wm. Wright, of Pigeon Lake, south of the Assiniboine, has 75 cattle, 90 sheep and herds of horses. J. A. Ross, Reeve of Belcourt, near St. Eustache, reports a prevalence of abortion among cattle. Forty cows drop only 25 calves. The cause may be the ashes left by prairie fires. Alex. McKinnon started 14 years ago, with 8 cattle; and now has 150, as well as hogs — and a big, solid new log house. After prairie fires burn 200 tons of his hay, he sells 20 steers at $31.00 per head. John McDonald came with 2 cows, 12 years ago; and now has 75. Alex J. and Alex F. McDonald have 90 cattle each; Wm. Sinclair, 175. Wm. Tait, of Silver Heights, with his son, run 200 high-grade cows with Hereford and Angus bulls; and 25 horses, on their ranch at Elm Creek. Cattle winter on swamp hay; a water-hole cut in the river ice; and only bush for shelter. Farmers are up-grading their livestock.

Archibald Wright brings well-bred Holsteins from Ontario to his 1,000-acre farm, south of the Assiniboine. Wright Brothers import a carload of pure-bred Shorthorns. James Walker, Sturgeon Creek farmer, returns from Scotland, bringing two prize Clydesdale stallions.

In March, close seasons on game in Manitoba are announced! Deer may not be taken between 1 January and 1 October; grouse, 1 January to 1 September; plover, 1 January to 1 August; ducks, geese, 1 May to 15 August. Already, Nature needs help for conservation of even a fraction of the wildlife, so long thought to be inexhaustible. Immigration to our Nor'West fell from 65,000 in 1882 to 21,000 last year; and now, dwindles to a trickle.

Council contracts with Antoine Hogue to run the St. Charles ferry for the next 4 years. D. J. Tait agrees to operate the ferry at Headingly — for the fees he can collect. The petition of C. G., Alfred and A. C. Caron for a free ferry to their big, new creamery is "laid over". The Carons do not wait. They build and operate their own ferry to carry customers to their plant; and also to church, free. Councillor Cameron gives notice of a bylaw to stop river pollution. (Oh Lord, how long?) Reeve Tait and Clerk Ness are instructed to buy a safe and "a good office desk" for our Municipal office. In June, Council pays David Isbister $4.25 for repairing Murray's Sturgeon Creek bridge, which has been unsafe for 3 months. Also, $20.00 is voted to get a boat for ratepayers south of the River, to ferry their children to school. On 3 July, Council asks the Manitoba Government to help build the roads and bridges, so desperately needed. Promptly, $1,043.00 is made available. Request and grant may be linked with the Provincial election, on 19 July!

The electors vote sweeping changes in the Government of Manitoba. The tide of new Settlers — particularly in the new districts in Western Manitoba — submerges the older constituencies. Hon. Thos. Greenway becomes Premier, at the head of 33 Liberal MLA's. John Norquay's people re-elect that old warrior; but give him only 4 supporters. The new Government promptly proceeds with work on the Red River Valley Railway — begun under Norquay; but killed in Ottawa. W. F. Alloway negotiates with Prime Minister Macdonald. Greenway and Martin go to the capital. The Prime Minister keeps them waiting. They leave for home. Macdonald asks them to return; and gives in! But the C.P.R. wins a $15 million Government loan. Back in Manitoba, Greenway and Martin are welcomed — as conquering heroes, with bands, bonfires and parades!

The C.P.R. is not given to surrender, however, when its sacred Monopoly is threatened. When a R.R.V. branch to Portage la Prairie would cross the C.P.R. line, the "Battle of Fort Whyte" explodes! Hon.

"Joe" Martin enrolls special police to protect the workers, who build the line at night. Next day, the C.P.R. masses locomotives, flatcars and workers to tear out the new grade! Bloodshed is averted, when a Supreme Court ruling sanctions the crossing.

Among the few immigrants, this year, comes Henry Hilton. He farms at Headingly for many years. Assiniboia's Council finds funds to buy 3 scrapers from James Land for $21.00; and pay 8 citizens $29.25 for cutting thistles! This is the third year of a terrible 11-year drought. The crop is such a total failure that no records are kept! Farm prices drop. Wheat is rarely 75 cents per bushel. Nevertheless, school inspection begins, with 5 inspectors for 600 Manitoba schools.

New Year's Day, 1889, marks the depth of a hard and bitter winter. Assiniboia's Council, in February, votes wood and groceries to 4 families "as they are in need". The list lengthens with the passing weeks. With last year's crop failure; and drought, again, this summer — the flow of export grain dwindles. The lure of "the Golden West" is tarnished! Immigration stops; reverses!

Nevertheless, new homes are building on new streets crossing "the Great Highway" along the Assiniboine, as families press ever westward. Schools are enlarged — and still are over-crowded! Council votes $25.00 to Patrick Smith, to build "a good skiff for . . . crossing children going to the St. James school, from the south side of the Assiniboine." (Typically, another $3.00 is paid, before the skiff is delivered.) Councillors face a new problem: sidewalks! A proposal to spend $250.00 for sidewalks, to serve new homes along Portage Avenue, is debated — amended — debated again; and, finally, against bitter opposition, is passed. Truly, times are changing. Promoters attend Council meetings to sell the idea of telephone service — from Winnipeg to St. Charles!

So — the people of Assiniboia, first Municipality in our great Nor'West, with all the people of our Province, in our well-built canoe, now called "Manitoba" — swing onto the broad waters of Canadian affairs. Along ever-widening ways we voyage, brigaded with our partner-Provinces; running rapids, circling whirlpools, portaging cataracts and paddling, in unison, along deep currents, echoing with song! A unique Canadian brigade; each Province, bigger or smaller, with few or many paddlers, freighting tremendous potential. Each swinging to its own steering; all under command of the "bourgeois" we elect for the entire outfit — onward to the vast ocean of world history; freighting to all mankind the out-pouring of benefits from the unlimited resources of our Canadian lands and waters and nationality!

PART 4

Rails,
Acres
and Millions

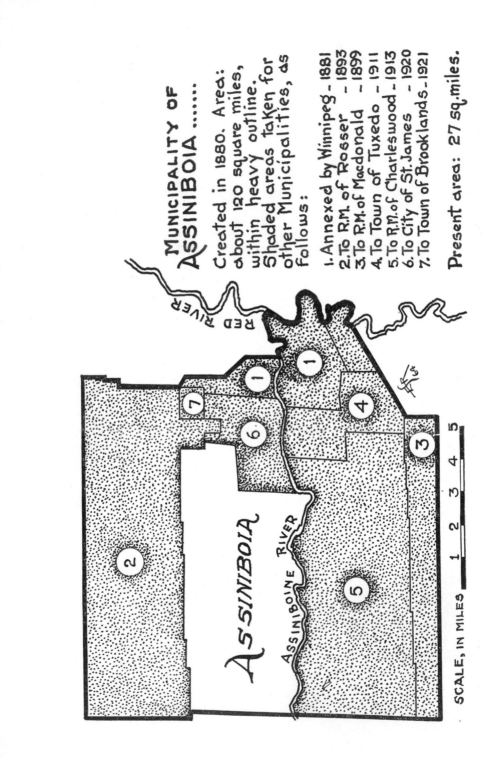

MUNICIPALITY OF
ASSINIBOIA ....

Created in 1880. Area:
about 120 square miles,
within heavy outline.
Shaded areas taken for
other Municipalities, as
follows:

1. Annexed by Winnipeg – 1881
2. To R.M. of Rosser – 1893
3. To R.M. of Macdonald – 1899
4. To Town of Tuxedo – 1911
5. To R.M. of Charleswood – 1913
6. To City of St. James – 1920
7. To Town of Brooklands – 1921

Present area: 27 sq. miles.

RED RIVER

ASSINIBOIA

ASSINIBOINE RIVER

SCALE, IN MILES   1   2   3   4   5

John A. Macdonald

CHAPTER 11

The City Is Coming .. 1890-99

The 90's begin with disaster. If the high McKinley tariff of the United States is designed to starve Canada into annexation (as Canada's leaders suspect) it comes uncomfortably close to succeeding.

In 20 years as a Province, Manitoba's population has multiplied; but recent crop failures halt the inflow of people. The relative numbers of component groups change, dramatically. Whereas, 20 years ago, most Manitobans are home-grown "natives"; and new-comers from Ontario a vocal splinter group — by 1890, recent Settlers are the dominant majority. This change is most startling in the communities which "white" families have created, recently. It is less notable in the Settlements ruled, so long, by the Council of Assiniboia; and particularily, in the Municipality which carries the name "Assiniboia" into the future.

West of Assiniboia, in Portage la Prairie, a politician from "down East", Dalton McCarthy, blows up the fires of hatred lit by Schultz some 20 years ago. He preaches the "McCarthyism" that our new land be exclusively "English"; with all others in subservient status! His lurid oratory barely touches the toughened "natives" of older Settlements; but inflames many who have come together, recently, in new communities. Fired-up crusaders find a "cause" in the vital work of equipping our young Canadians in Manitoba with "the tools of learning".

Assiniboia's people are vitally concerned in "schooling", ever since Miles Macdonnell opens the first classroom for children of his Selkirk Settlers. The mission school in St. Boniface in 1818, is followed, within 2 years, by another in St. John's. When Assiniboia becomes "Manitoba", each of the 24 parishes has schools, operated and financed by its dominant church denomination: 12 Roman Catholic; 12 Protestant. Assiniboia's Bill of Rights does not demand church schools;

but this demand comes into negotiations in Ottawa. The Government of Canada's "Manitoba Act" makes the new Province responsible for education; and provides that customs recognized for Roman Catholic and Protestant schools, shall continue. Subsequently, the new Manitoba Legislature (with "mild" speeches) passes a School Act providing for local administration, under Provincial supervision; with the existing 24 parishes being School Districts, each administered by 3 elected trustees.

When the settled part of the Province is divided into Municipalities, in 1880, each Municipal Council is made tax collector for its School Districts. By 1890, 23,214 Manitoba boys and girls go to 720 schools. This year, responding to general demand, the Greenway Government amends the School Act — creating a Department of Education to administer a unified system of public schools, under uniform regulations; giving religious (not denominational) instruction; and financed from taxes. This action — giving effect to the democratic voice of Manitoba's small population — throws opposing extremists in the populous East into a frenzy of violent attacks upon each other. Politicians, and other apostles of conflict, fire up the ancient engines of prejudice and passion, to generate power for their own designs. They steam up the "Manitoba School Question" into an issue that threatens to explode the political boiler of our new Canadian nation — until, after 6 terrible years, Wilfred Laurier leads Canadians back to sanity.

In Assiniboia, as is to be expected, the back-wash of this nation-testing storm stirs discussion, debate and argument. However, the majority of our people, still, are "natives" — by birth or acclimatizing residence. They may state opinions in direct and forceful speech. Beliefs they hold, unshakeably, through cyclones of controversy. At the same time, pioneer memories are a strong foundation for mutual respect, tolerance and neighborly co-operation. Determined to maintain their own beliefs and opinions, most "natives" expect their neighbors to do the same. There is, also, shrewd speculation on the eagerness of Easterners to take over our affairs when it may promote their purposes — while, eternally, they exact heavy tribute from us via Eastern political and commercial dominance. As the eminent Canadian historian, W. L. Morton, has written: "The . . . controversies were a conflict of extremists only".

As the crops ripen this fall, some 90 standard elevators and 103 flat warehouses, with a total capacity of 4 million bushels, are ready, at 56 points throughout Manitoba, to take delivery of farmer's grain. Settlement is expanding; production is increasing. Twenty years ago, farmers had only a limited market, at "the Forks". All grain was handled by man-power. The elevators of 1890 are operated by horse-power. Some are even installing steam-engines! Transport facilities are transformed. Red River carts and River steamships have given way to Canada's transcontinental railway — with its 484 locomotives, 547 passenger cars and 13,609 freight cars, running on 6,609 miles of track: and grossing revenues, this year, of well above $16 millions. Machinery is also speeding up farm work. The day is gone for harvesting grain with sickle, scythe and cradle. The "Nor'West Farmer" reports that George Sexsmith, farmer on the Boyne, recently cut, between noon and 7 p.m., 12 acres of oats with his binder. without missing a sheaf!

Sir John A. Macdonald, one of the architects of Confederation; and first Prime Minister of Canada — dies on 6 June. A chapter of Canadian history is "finis". Old-time settlers of Assiniboia are willing to forget his share in the Red River troubles; and remember, only, his greatness.

The census of 1891 records 260,573 white people between the Lakehead and the Rockies; 150,000 of them in Manitoba. Of our Western population, farmers, fishermen and miners total 32,473; manufacturers and mechanics, 6,936; and laborers, 9,003. There are an astonishing 8,627 traders; and clergy, lawyers and doctors to the number of 3,786. More than 25,000 people now live in Winnipeg — where only a few shacks stood beside the junction of 2 muddy trails, just 20 years ago. Bursting with growth, the City accepts the offer of Ross, Holt, Mann & McKenzie to build and operate a power plant on our Assiniboine River. A renowned Minneapolis engineer surveys the site; and reports that 10,000 horse-power can be developed: "enough for this growing metropolis *for all time!*" Preliminary work begins; but the deal falls through. Nevertheless, by July the first electric street cars are operating.

This is "the year of the big crop". Forty or 45 bushels of wheat to the acre are common. The plains prove their grain-growing potential. Farmers from Assiniboia and other older Settlements "go West". Bumper yields draw immigrants — like a gold rush. Eager buyers pay the C.P.R. and other big land-holders, $4.50 per acre, and up. Threshing the bumper crop keeps big gangs working through the winter, some of them with horse-powered outfits. As pioneers of Assiniboia have seen so often; and as our Canadian West will see so often, again, the economic wave, cresting this year — is followed by depression.

Families driving from the peace of Assiniboia into the City may be jarred by the clanging bells of 2 competing street railway lines. They may celebrate with a ride all the way out to Elm Park, at 12 tickets for 25 cents!.

Old-timers who, as boys, tripped down the Lakes to York Factory, are interested to know that a fish hatchery is established at Selkirk. Further afield, the C.P.R. operates 3 fine steel steamships on the Great Lakes.

Already farmers who have prospered in Assiniboia, and other Western communities, are visiting "down home" in Ontario; and telling tall tales of Manitoba! Prairie fever (typhoid) is epidemic during the late summer; and claims many victims, particularily among sturdy young single homesteaders. A fine crop is harvested this fall; but prices are sadly depressed. The first offering of "Canadian" wheat is made on the Liverpool Exchange. Silver Heights, landmark in Assiniboia since old "Company" days; and home of great men of the Nor'West like John Rowand and Donald Smith, is destroyed by fire on 25 November. Another link with the past disappears.

The northern-most one-third of Assiniboia is taken to form the new Rural Municipality of Rosser. Even with a reduced area, the Council of Assiniboia faces insistent demands for roads, bridges and drainage, on the one hand; and, on the other, the impossibility of raising money for all the improvements needed. School levies must be paid, totalling $1,409.40! Taxes are imposed for the year, as follows:

	Property Tax	Cut Thistles	Statute Labor
Ward 1	$1,497.37	$99.00	$106.90
Ward 2	1,202.49	16.00	92.50
Ward 3	1,149.16	49.00	157.50
Ward 4	843.11	19.25	58.75
Totals	$4,692.13	$183.25	$414.75

These amounts will be hard to collect. Council appeals to City banks; but already the Municipality has over-reached its bank credit. The need for roads and bridges is partly met by allowing property-owners to apply their Statute Labor for last year, and next, on approved projects.

Many imports from the East, Assiniboia could well do without. Among these are weeds. Our rich, heavy soil is over-run with Canada Thistles. Bravely, the Council attacks these invaders — with pathmasters, inspectors and scythes! At many Council meetings, most of the accounts scrutinized are for cutting thistles. In September, for example, among many others, Thomas Pruden is paid $43.00 for cutting thistles on River Lots 30 and 31, Headingly; S. Minaker gets $37.00 for cutting thistles on River Lots 25 and 26; and these amounts are charged to the owners. The war against the thistles intensifies with the years. It is a losing battle.

Folks who live in Assiniboia are well informed about what goes on, the world over. Three daily newspapers and 8 weeklies published in the City, provide news and views. These report that farmers in Canada's Nor'West, this year, produce 16 million bushels of wheat. Manitoba exports wheat and flour to the value of $8 million; livestock and meat,

$1 million; and hides, etc., $1.5 million. (This last item, old-timers remember, is about the same as fur and hide exports to St. Paul in the old cart train days). Other industries are developing. On Manitoba's big lakes, 954 men sail 452 vessels, valued at $120,567.00, fishing and freighting.

Council appoints Dr. Deschambault, Health Officer — with a yearly salary of $200.00; and instructions to vaccinate all children in the Municipality. Later, Councillor Cameron questions whether Dr. Deschambault's vaccine is worthless; and a December meeting of Council, in view of complaints that he "does not attend to" vaccinating the Municipality's children, cuts the good Doctor's salary in half.

Unable, as yet, to finance bridges, Council operates ferries to carry traffic across the Assiniboine River, in St. James, St. Charles and Headingly. The St. James ferry-man reports a traffic accident! A driver for Mr. Elliott's dairy drives team and milk-wagon onto the ferry. While crossing, the team backs up — with the wagon — overboard; and are swept "down the River". The driver plunges in; cuts the harness; and rescues the horses. Milk bottles are smashed; and the Assiniboine flows white! Mr. Elliott claims $25.00 damages; and gets $20.00.

At the eastern end of Assiniboia, both south and north of the Assiniboine River, people are crowding into more compact communities. The Municipality is still essentially rural, however. Most of our people are concerned, in some degree, with farming. The Council elected for this year includes: Reeve Alexander Murray of River Lot 54, St. Charles; and Councillors: Donald Cameron, who farms River Lots 57 and 59, Headingly; James Good, who owns River Lot 120, St. Charles and Park A in St. James; W. I. Connelly, farmer on River Lot 55, St. Charles; and Edwin Bourke, who owns, along with other lands, River Lots 30 and 31, St. James. About half the area of the Municipality is south of the Assiniboine River; and about half on the left bank. Each of the 4 wards extends to both sides of the River. Council appoints Frank Ness, Clerk, at $500.00 per year. He is to be at the Municipal Office, each Tuesday, through 11 months of the year; and full-time in December. This gives him ample time to work his 500-acre farm. George C. Caron is appointed assessor. Numerous members of the Caron family operate big acreages south of the Assiniboine.

Council reduces the yearly salary of the Municipal solicitor to $75.00; and other officials in proportion "as the revenue of the Municipality is much smaller than it was". At the same time, the Councillors see the need for encouraging industry (as talked of ever since) and ask neighboring Rural Municipalities to share in paying a bonus for building and operating a grist mill. Memories of earlier days are wakened when John Bathie bills Council (duly certified by W. A. Farmer, JP) for killing 16 wolves; and collects the bounty of $2.00 each!

The frostier the air, the further we can hear each other laugh! Our hard climate challenges our capacity for enjoyment. This February, our Legislature cannot assemble a quorum; and must forego sittings. MLA's are at the bonspiel!

Increasing numbers of the City's 34,000 inhabitants are coming westward, along the "Great Highway", into Assiniboia. Council pays the Isbister estate $25.00 an acre for a roadway from the Portage Road to St. Charles ferry. The Department of Agriculture orders that pathmasters cut weedy grain; and have the work charged to land-owners. Nevertheless, livestock still wanders at large. John Taylor, Jr., D. Isbister and N. Else are appointed poundkeepers.

Council demands that the Provincial Government rebuild two bridges, swept away when June rains bring floods raging down Sturgeon Creek, from Municipalities to the north. Every Council meeting echoes demands for roads, culverts, bridges, ferries! The topographical peculiarity which empounds surface water a mile or so from the River requires measures for water management which the Municipality never achieves.

The following tabulation of acreages and assessment of Assiniboia's 6 School Districts, indicates average assessed values of from $6.80 to $18.24 per acre.

School District	Acreage	Assessment	Per Acre
Headingly	18,697	$162,115.00	$ 8.65
Morgan	3.398	25,482.00	7.50
Otto	2,000	13,600.00	6.80
St. Charles	10,738	96,412.00	8.80
Sturgeon Creek	12,533	167,162.00	13.36
St. James	8.633	157,447.00	18.24
	56,000	$622,268.00	

Levies for these schools total $2,392.75. In August, the new School District of Charleswood is formed, from part of St. James parish, south of the Assiniboine.

At an October meeting, Council passes 15 accounts, totalling $398.06, with $169.50 of this amount going for cutting thistles. The Health Officer warns of scarlet fever in St. Charles; calls for general vaccination; and asks for more pay. Dr. Crawford takes over as Health Officer, at $100.00 yearly, including medicines required — except for epidemics! L. Plante takes the 3 ferries out of the River before freeze-up; and is paid $25.00. Ratepayers meet in Headingly, to discuss hiring a second teacher, as more girls and boys overflow the school. From Assiniboia, as from other communities, people crowd to Winnipeg on 3 September, to hear Wilfred Laurier speak; and to share in the great demonstration following his address.

The Anglican congregation of Holy Trinity, Headingly, in their annual meeting, recommend that a roadway along River Lot 54 (the church glebe lands) be given to the Municipality, "so long as the ferry shall be open; the Municipality to bear all expenses". Rev. A. E. Cowley, rector; John Cameron, John Taylor, Robert Fowler and A. G. O'Malley, MPP, are among the leaders of this congregation.

Dr. John C. Schultz is knighted. His well-publicized patriotism pays off. A more modest man — but one of the true greats of Assiniboia's history   goes to his reward, when Tache dies.

The Council of Assiniboia appoints W. F. Lane (first Clerk of the Municipality, 15 years ago) as auditor; succeeds in borrowing $3,000.00; and accepts the hospitality of "Chadwick's Hotel" at Deer Lodge, for monthly meetings — free, as in former years. The offer of the "Nor'Wester" to print Council minutes, gratis, is also accepted. In April, ferry-men are hired: James Rickards, St. James; George Land, St. Charles; and Robert Bird, Headingly, at $18.00 per month.

Everyone economizes. A Court of Revision, in April, reduces assessment on Hon. John Taylor's Hotel, at Headingly, from $3,000.00 to $2,700.00; his blacksmith shop, from $400.00 to $200.00; and store, from $1,100.00 to $1,000.00. Farmlands, fronting the Great Highway, are reduced from $8.00 per acre, to $7.00. Spring comes early. By Easter Sunday, nearly all wheat seeding is completed.

In June, Arthur Creak and Nellie White are married; and go to live on Arthur's farm, north of the "two-mile road" (Saskatchewan Avenue) west of Murray Park. Arthur comes to Canada, from London, in '88. Nellie comes, as a young girl with her mother and brother, 2 years earlier. Landing at Quebec, the mother saves their slim capital from a swindler who robs other passengers. Mr. Creak, like so many farmers, gets a job in the City. He drives a horse-car. Arriving at Sturgeon Creek, the end of the line, at noon, he feeds his horse; shoots prairie chicken along the Creek; and, on the hour, heads back to the City.

A farm journal reports that this fall, up the Assiniboine, rustlers have stolen 100 head of cattle! This may be one result of hard times. The outlook is more hopeful, when Western farmers harvest 35 million bushels of wheat. (Enough to load, to their 1,000-pound capacity, 2 million Red River carts!)

The Council of Assiniboia notifies school teachers that the Municipal Health Officer, Dr. Crawford, will vaccinate all pupils. Every Council meeting debates ditches, roads, bridges; collection of those 1890 seed grain notes; and the need for railway crossings. Prairie fires destroy many farm homes and ranges of timber. Fire guardians are appointed. To build sidewalks, lumber is purchased — at $14.20 per thousand feet. In August, farm families along the Great Highway see the first relay bicycle race in Manitoba — from Winnipeg, through Assiniboia, to Portage la Prairie!

The Government of Canada, in March, orders Manitoba to restore separate church schools. The Government of Manitoba registers a firm refusal; and turning to the people of the Province, calls an election, in December. As nearly as is possible in our type of democracy, the issue of this election is: the School Question. The people of Manitoba speak clearly; and re-elect the Greenway Government. In Ottawa, Wilfred Laurier — opposing Orangemen, ultramontanes and other extremists; and proclaiming that, as Liberal leader, he represents Canadians of all faiths — forces a national election. Thus, as one historian concludes, Laurier "Proves his greatness — as a Canadian".

Alexander Murray continues as Reeve of Assiniboia. New Councillors are Robert Fowler and Jas. N. Elliott. Council advertises a $5,000 bonus to the builder of a 75-barrel grist mill at Headingly. Neighboring municipalities are asked to co-operate. None do. Risk capital is hard to interest. For 8 years, since '88, prices of farm produce are low. Wheat seldom reaches 75 cents per bushel. Council asks the C.P.R. to build a walk across their new bridge at Headingly. The Company replies: yes — if the Municipality pays $50.00 rental, yearly.

Indicating the multiplicity of its concerns, at a single meeting Assiniboia's Council records that nearly all of the 1890 notes for seed grain have been renewed; orders Dr. Crawford to attend cases of mumps at Headingly school; pays Sam Smith $1.50 for saving the St. Charles ferry skiff from the spring ice; demands that the C.P.R. build crossings; fixes tolls for the grist mill (when it is built); and plans co-operation with the R.M. of Rosser, in draining the "4-mile swamp". Antoine Hogue claims payment from Council for a horse, killed by the orders of a "Vet" for "glanders". This dread scourge wrecks the "horse power" of many an Assiniboia farm.

The Headingly Anglican congregation, at their Easter annual meeting, votes thanks to Wm. Tait for long service as people's warden; and to the Ladies Guild for reducing the church debt. The Sunday School reports an average of 33 children, and 5 teachers.

On 11 July, the people of Canada vote in the national election, forced by Laurier's stand on the Manitoba School Question. They elect 118 Liberals; and 95 opposition. "The people of Manitoba had twice elected the Greenway Government on this issue" records historian W. L. Morton. Now, the democratic majority of the voters of all Canada declare clearly, that schools financed by public tax monies shall be public schools, not controlled by any church denomination. Within months, the leadership of Laurier and Greenway, with quiet papal co-operation, achieves a practical compromise — which fails to still raucous extremists, but does satisfy most Canadians, in Manitoba and across the Nation.

The smaller half of the surveyed lands of our Canadian West, left open for homestead, is "taken up" in spurts. Homestead entries reach astonishing numbers during booms and bumper crops; and, in times of depression and crop failure, cancellations often out-number entries. During the 15 years, ending 1896, 56,520 homesteads are taken up; and 16,361 cancelled—leaving a net total of 39,685. This year, the C.P.R. freights out of the "Golden West" 32.5 million bushels of grain and 4.3 million barrels of flour. After years at low levels, wheat prices begin to rise.

Better grain prices may encourage Assiniboia electors to vote for the "Grist Mill" by-law. Of local interest, too, is Headingly's most fashionable wedding, on 29 September, when Flora, daughter of Hon. and Mrs. John Taylor, marries Alexander, son of Hon. and Mrs. Wm. Tait. Thus, 2 of Assiniboia's outstanding pioneer families are united.

This year is the fourth of the deepest slump North America has seen. In Assiniboia — "The Heart of the Continent" — another season of low rainfall is added to the long and destructive drought. Elsewhere in the world, people starve; and the Council of Assiniboia is urged by the Lieut-Governor of Manitoba, to contribute $875.00 for famine relief in India.

Under the necessity of stretching every dollar, Council reduces Dr. Crawford's salary, as Health Officer, to $75.00 for the year. Wm. Pruden is named assessor, at $25.00, half to be applied to his 1890 seed grain note. Former loans are renewed at the Imperial Bank; and another $4,000.00 borrowed.

Every Council meeting is flooded with demands for roads, culverts, bridges. Wheeled traffic is multiplying. Pathmaster Caron uses statute labor to improve the Great Highway, between St. Charles and Headingly. Wm. Beauchemin and Albert Hogue "brush out" the road east of River Lot 60, St. Charles, for $20.00; and another $50.00 is spent on its grading. Two-wheel scrapers are hired at 50 cents a day. The Bicycle Club builds a trail on Portage Road; and horseback riders persist in using it! James N. Elliott resigns as Councillor; and is replaced by George Chapman. Perhaps excited by reports of Klondike gold, Council endorses a petition for a road from Edmonton to the Klondike! Our

Councillors, essentially farmers, also pass a resolution: "As Council believes a combination exists between elevators and grain dealers, giving them monopoly . . . therefore, the Minister of Agriculture and the C.P.R. are urged to take necessary steps to abrogate this monopoly and allow farmers to load grain directly onto box cars".

Gold in South Africa and the Klondike, lower world freight rates and deflated prices push a new prosperity front and centre on the stage of our affairs. Even more vital: rains come again, this summer. Bumper crops circulate prosperity through the Golden West. A decade of booming expansion is underway.

In Assiniboia, our Council must use shrewd dexterity to finance essential municipal services. Wm. Pruden is appointed assessor for the second year, at $25.00 (half of this amount going to clear his 1890 seed grain note to the Province). J. J., A. C. and Alfred Caron, trustees of St. Charles School District ask, "What about last year's levy?"

Husky young men from Assiniboia enlist with the 150 constables going to Dawson City, to reinforce the 80 "Mounties" ordered there last year. An army of goldseekers spreads over the Yukon. Their hardships, sweat and (too often) deaths — pour new gold into the arteries of world finance — to quicken the pulse of trade and development. In addition, the vision and drive of Clifford Sifton's immigration policies bring new people, in thousands, to the "last, best West". Many stay in Winnipeg, the Gateway City. Increasing numbers press westward, along the Portage Road, into Assiniboia.

The old Hudson's Bay "Reserve" is built over, completely. Fine houses grace spacious sites along the Assiniboine. Northward, small homes are packed on narrow lots; and, along the C.P.R., cheap, flimsy shacks are tossed up, amid rickety tenements. South of the Assiniboine, mansions are built by those who skim fortunes from the booming development of the West. "Better times" spread to Assiniboia. The annual meeting of the Anglican church at Headingly learns that the mortgage debt is cleared off, thanks to the Ladies' help; and the Rector's stipend is up to date.

Our Canadian West is carried out of the 19th century, and into the 20th, on a surge of change. (Commonly called "progress"). Last summer, the long drought is rained out. Heavier rains this year, begin 5 years of abundant moisture. Vegetation responds luxuriantly. Prairie fires are forgotten. Meadows become swamps, ponds — even lakes! The pioneer myth that grain must be grown close to rivers or lakes has been exploded, long since. Now, with generous rains, big areas are "taken up" for farms, which have been regarded as pasture, or wastelands. Bumper crops on bigger acreages multiply the out-turn of grain. This year, the

C.P.R. freights 42.7 million bushels of grain; and 4 million barrels of flour. To handle this volume, 447 elevators work overtime. More elevators are needed. The C.P.R. offers — to anyone who builds a 25,000 bushel elevator — a free site; and a monopoly which will force grain growers to use the elevator. In July, Winnipeg grain dealers organize into the Northwest Elevator Association — to make rules and fix prices, handling and storage charges.

Another strip is sliced from Assiniboia's area, this time along the southern side of the Municipality; and transferred to Macdonald Municipality. Originally, "Assiniboia" is the name given by Lord Selkirk to the block of 116,000 square miles which he buys from the "Company" in 1811. In 1818, about half this area is taken by the United States, leaving some 60,000 square miles to his Lordship. The "Company" buys back Assiniboia from the Selkirk estate, about 1835. The Company's governing Committee, in London, re-establishes the Council of Assiniboia (first appointed in 1812) to administer "the Municipal District of Assiniboia" — embracing a 50-mile radius from "the Forks". All the Settlements in this 7,800 square miles are ruled by this Council — until the people of Assiniboia succeed in negotiating with Canada their entry into Confederation, as the Province of Manitoba, in 1870. Our new province sets up a number of municipalities in 1880. Among this number, Assiniboia embraces an area of something more than 120 square miles. The following year, the City of Winnipeg takes 20-odd square miles. In 1893, the northernmost one-third of Assiniboia is taken for the Municipality of Rosser. Thus, with the slice chopped away in 1899, Assiniboia is whittled down to some 60 square miles — a splinter of its original area!

On the other hand, population increases. More and more families are building further and further westward. Streets are sprouting from the Portage Road and even from the River Road, south of the Assiniboine; and homes are budding thereon. At the eastern end of Assiniboia, St. James begins to look like a town. As far westward as Deer Lodge and Silver Heights, the long River Lots of early surveys are being sub-divided into market gardens and building lots.

As pioneer families retire, tenants and new owners (often City business men) take over their old farmsteads. The western part of the Municipality is still, largely, rural. On both sides of the Assiniboine River, thriving centres at Headingly and St. Charles (and eastward, Kirkfield Park and St. James) serve farm communities of well-established, comfortable prosperity. The people of Assiniboia — being near the City; but not of it — enjoy the best of both worlds.

A drive through Assiniboia, on a day in early October, shows the russet leaves of oak trees slashed with the vivid yellows of poplar and ash; and the River running between, rippling clear and cold. We accept the kind offer of Archibald Wright — who farms some 2,000 acres south of the Assiniboine at the eastern end of the Municipality; and goes, daily, to manage the Great West Saddlery business on Market Street — to be driven by one of his men, who can tell us, as we go, about the farms and families that make up Assiniboia. We head westward, along the south River Road. Mr. Wright's lands are River Lots 1 to 11, parish of St. Charles. Up the road, Joseph Chiswell is a tenant on RL 19; and C. White is a neighbor, farming lots 21, 22 and 23. The next 4 River Lots are owned by William and Edwin Bourke, whose home places are in St. James, across the River. George T. Chapman, who farms 28 and 29, is Councillor for Ward 2. T. W. Ashford and W. P. Wallace are tenants on RL 42; Lot 43 is the home of D. B. Chaffey; and Leversidge Brandon farms 49 and 50.

With fine fall weather, the trail is hard and dry. Some patches are gravelled. We whirl along at a spanking trot. Sometimes, the road leads us close to the River; and, through the blazoned foliage, we see the long, lazy loops of the Assiniboine. Then, for a mile or 2, the River is hidden by tall stands of timber. These River Lots — first surveyed by George Taylor about 60 years ago — are 6 chains in width. The farm-steads stand close together; often, within shouting distance. The Lots extend southward to the N. P. & M. Railway, Portage Extension, which marks the limit of their inner 2 miles; and, then, a further "Outer" 2 miles — to dovetail into the square sections, surveyed after 1871.

As we rattle over a rickety bridge across a deep creek-bed, our driver points out the farmstead of J. B. Beauchemin on RL 59. Antoine Hogue's family live on Lots 61 and 62; and Louis Hogue on 64. O. Lamontagne farms 66; Honore Lafleche, 67; and Alfred Caron operates a prosperous dairy farm on RLs 65, 68, 69 and 70. C. T. Caron owns 71 and 72. Our driver tells us that the N. P. & M. Railway has built a siding, which a signboard declares to be "St. Charles Station." . . in the centre of Mr. Caron's farm. On Lot 73 lives the J. B. Braconier family. Their neighbor, on 74, is Pierre Morrissette. Passing A. C. Caron's dairy farm, on Lots 76, 77 and 78; and the farm of I. A. Gamble, on 80 and 81, we pass out of St. Charles parish at River Lot 84; and enter the parish of Headingly.

In this parish, Lot 1 is the original homesite of that great pioneer, W. B. "Ben" Hall. Lots 6 and 7 each have a River frontage of 12 chains. It was about 1859 that W. E. Lonsdale and Herbert Sabine, beginning their work as surveyors, "took up" these Lots. They also, took to wife 2 daughters of the pioneer Cameron clan; and built homes, Lonsdale on

Lot 6 and Sabine on 7. Up the road, Lot 13 (18 chains wide) is farmed by A. G. Parsons. Lot 14 is 36 chains wide. Beyond a bridge over a deep creek is the home of the J. M. Tait family. The C.P.R. — Manitoba South-Western Colonization Branch — after crossing the Assiniboine, runs south, between RLs 16 and 17; and crosses the N. P. & M. Railway and the "two-mile road" at Headingly Station. The big house at the railway bridge is the home of Wm. Tait. Beyond, Lots 18 and 19 are the farm of Robert Irvine. Robert Fowler, S. H. Farmer and Alf Fowler, Ward 1 Councillor, are neighbors on Lots 20 to 24. Crossing Lot 27, the road ventures over a deep creek, on a shaky bridge. G. S. Nordal and Andrew Reykdal are tenants on this big Lot. Richard Powell and James Morgan rent RL 28. At the north end of Lots 30 and 31, between Road and River, lies "Horseshoe Lake" — an ancient loop of the River, now isolated; a favorite spot for swimming, boating and shooting ducks.

Doubling back 2 miles, we cross the C.P.R. railway at the bridge; and, at Lot 15, take the ferry to the north side of the Assiniboine. The crossing gives our horses a "breather"; and gives us a fine view of Holy Trinity Anglican church, overlooking a beautiful sweep of the River. A half-mile north on the Ferry Road brings us to the Portage Trail; and 2 miles west, to the western boundary of the Municipality. Here, we "about turn", for our drive eastward, along the north side of the Assiniboine River. The Portage Road — officially designated "the Great Highway" on maps of the day — has been surveyed and re-surveyed. These re-locations, like R. G. McPhillips' survey of 1879, aim to circumvent such marshes as "Cameron's Swamp". In general, this Great Highway parallels the River, at one-half to a mile distance, for 7 or 8 miles; and, beyond, Road and River run, almost, side by side.

Henry "Doc" Hilton, on River Lot 32, came from England, via Russia, where he managed large estates. From Assiniboia's western boundary we drive across Lots 33, 34 and 35, farmed by Alex C. Bryson. (Fifty years later to be the "Jail farm") His neighbor is F. S. Nugent. Joseph Morgan pioneers the McFee place. At Lot 39, we cross a deep ravine on "Brown's Bridge" — named for the pioneer family of Magnus Brown. Sons Willie and John are the current owners. One of their sisters is wife to Hon. John Taylor. Alex Bremner, coming from the Orkneys, after his term with "the Company", settles here. His sons, James and Charles, farm beside him until, with the Sayer and Taylor families, they move to Saskatchewan; and found the new community of "Bresaylor", in '83. N. F. Layton occupies neighboring acres. Wm. Buchanan is tenant on Lot 45; and Robert McGee farms 46. Then, we drive across the farm of "Johnny Boy" Taylor, long-time secretary-treasurer of the Headingly Agricultural Society; and the farm of the Jack

Willis family. The pioneer Francis family own RL 51. The solid log house is home to successive generations. The C.P.R. angles across River Lots 51, 52 and 53; crosses the Portage Road; and runs south, between Lots 50 and 51, to the bridge. In addition to the railway bridge, 3 others have spanned the Assiniboine, at Headingly. One goes out with the spring ice; a second, of wood, gives way to the steel structure, now building.

In Headingly, we stop at the "Royal Exchange Hotel" for a mid-day snack. Our driver takes the team to J. E. McLean's "Feed and Sales" stables; and asks young Jack Copp (who has taken over the blacksmith shop from Joseph Morgan) to have a look at the shoe on the bay's off forefoot. During noon-hour, we hear about Headingly. This village was a thriving centre, long before "aggressive young men" from Ontario built their first shacks on the Red River flats; and boomed them into the flood-menaced City of Winnipeg.

Long ago, Indian families who set up their teepees for parts of each year, under the towering trees on the banks of our beautiful Assiniboine, are joined by roving free-men. These come and go at will; and camp along the River, wherever whim suggests. The high, dry banks near "the Grand Passage" where north-south traffic crosses, is a favorite stop-ping and resting place. Voyageurs and cart-men — thrown out of work by the merging fur Companies in 1821 — raise snug cabins along these River banks for their Indian wives and families. To escape recurring floods, settlers from the Red River settle along the Assiniboine, where the River Lots are surveyed by Taylor, before 1840. A generation later, come many Old Country "families of means", farm families from Eastern Canada; and, in even greater numbers, the rising generation of "native" pioneers. They made Headingly a centre of culture, education and "gracious living" in rugged pioneer days.

There is great talk, currently, of "industries", to balance our farm economy. The village has a busy cheese-factory, operated by Lester Francis. The grist mill is building on the C.P.R. siding. Local farm boys will team its output to the City, at 10 cents a sack. Best grade flour will sell for $2.10 per 100 pounds. Three miles northward is the giant Kinalmeaky Farm. It is launched as the first of a chain of 10,000-acre farms, strung from the Red to the Rockies, by English capitalists under Sir John Lister Kaye, 20 years ago. Now, it is a big dairy farm — the sole surviving link of the great scheme which was to teach "colonials" how our lands and waters should be used. In the village of Headingly, Black & Francis, general merchants, operate a lumber yard; and have departments dealing in flour and feed, farm implements and contracting.

The 20-acre grounds of Headingly Agricultural Society enclose a pretty fair half-mile race-track. Annual Fall Fairs feature trotting races. The sporting spirit of our racing devotees is as keen as cash is scarce; and bets are, often, made in cattle: "My two-year old red heifer against your brindle steer that's raisin' three!" Assiniboia has a long tradition of horse-racing. The track is rented to a group of sporting men, headed by Messrs. Devlin, Wrigley, Lyons and Dangerfield. The young men of the community develop vigor and skill in a variety of games. Men from the Old Land, serving their time at Kinalmeaky, play football on the River ice, in winter; and, in summer, on the Agricultural grounds. Homeric battles with teams from St. Francois Xavier and Rosser stimulate arguments that are beyond decision. Rev. Cowley organizes cricket matches. Sides of white-clad athletes, through long twilights, field batted balls and swat mosquitoes; and thoroughly enjoy the game. Hunting and fishing put meat on many a table. Prairie chicken, at dawn, line fences and low branches, like blackbirds. Ducks are everywhere. Before the day of locks on the Red River, pickerel and pike, goldeye and sturgeon are abundant in the Assiniboine. Social life includes meetings of a "Lit Society" on Monday evenings, in the school. Old and young gather from near and far. On one occasion, a sleigh-load from St. Francois Xavier starts merrily homeward; sinks through the River ice; returns to the school, to dry out around a roaring fire; and none a whit the worse!

Our noon-time break over — we continue eastward, on our tour. River Lots 52 and 53 are part of the broad acres of Hon. John Taylor and his numerous family. The "glebe" lands of Holy Trinity church are Lot 54. Rev. Cowley, the rector, lives in the eastern end of Assiniboia, where St. James Anglican church is his chief charge. Miss Beatrice Cowley, devoted worker in Holy Trinity, lives in the parsonage, on Ferry Road. Formerly, Mrs. Abigail Corbett owns Lot 55; and in her home, the mysterious and much-discussed "Lord Gordon Gordon" lives — and dies by his own hand — some 30 years ago. R. G. O'Malley, some-time MPP, lives on 56. At his well, boys formerly fill the water-pail for the school. The first school is raised, with log walls and thatch roof, on a grassy glade sheltered by tall elm and ash trees. It is replaced by a frame building; which, when the new school is built in Headingly, is moved and rebuilt into a home.

Trotting briskly eastward, we follow the gravel grade over "Cameron's Swamp". The Camerons may be the first settlers who acquire title to River Lots in this area. An ancestor was a "Company" Chief Factor in 1834. In the current generation, Donald and John Cameron farm River Lots 57, 58 and 59. Donald Cameron is Councillor for Ward 4. John has served on Council, several terms. These families, leaders in community, school and church, build spacious homes; and plant rows of trees that beautify the River bank. Descendants of another family whose roots in Assiniboia reach far back into fur trade days, James and William Clouston, farm RL 60. The Stevensons, on Lot 61, are among those pioneers who seek this "high ground, westward" after the flood of '52; and prosper thereon. From the Portage Road, we can see, between bluffs of October-tinted trees, their fine farm home, built of Minnesota pine, on a curve of the River. The Dennisons farm Lot 62. Donald Dennison is the occupant in 1899. Eastward, past Dave Cook's farm, we cross the bridge on Gowler's Creek. On the sloping banks of this creek-bed, Mary and Oliver Gowler pioneer their celebrated farm; and learn the lessons of successful western farming, which Oliver passes on, in lectures throughout Manitoba.

Our driver points out the Goodridge home on the River bank, as we trot out of Headingly parish; and into St. Charles. (Sixty-odd years later, autos will be crowding into a drive-in theatre on the north side of the Portage Road, here; and, a mile eastward, the Perimeter Highway will cross the Great Highway at River Lot 92.)

St. Charles has been a community since the battling fur Companies escape ruin by uniting, in 1821; and by discharging two-thirds of all the men they had hired to fight each other. Thrown on their own, these ex-employees, with their Indian wives and families, paddle down the waterways to "the Forks". Some go on to Pembina; or merge into the growing population around Fort Garry; or gravitate to the Metis settlement at St. Francois Xavier. Many locate along the Assiniboine. In the sheltering timber, they build log cabins; plant patches of garden and grain in the spring; hunt buffalo or join cart-trains in summer; and, for the winter, return to their cabin "homes".

In the early '50's, Anglican parishes are formed in St. James and Headingly. Midway between, in 1854, Fr. Lafleche builds a log chapel "where the Metis hunters. . could worship on Sundays". There are, then, some 50 families here. The first church — built in 1866; and enlarged in '74 — is wrecked in the great storm of 29 August, '84; and then rebuilt. Fr. Lestance leads in building the first school, in '66. In 1868, Fr. Allard became the first resident priest; and, by '70, has a new school built. The beloved Fr. Dandurand has been parish priest for 24 years. Some of the voyageurs and hunters who first squat along the Assiniboine, get titles to their River Lots. Many of the occupants, in 1899, are descendants of those first settlers — like D. Isbister on Lot 98 and C. Rickard, on 99.

We drive past the St. Charles Post Office, on River Lot 112; and approach Sturgeon Creek. To the high, sloping banks of this stream came people from the flooding Red River — like Alexander Ross, the Scot historian — during the inundations of 1826 and '52. There is talk, now, of Roderick J. McKenzie, and the Manitoba Jockey Club building a giant race-track, north of Sturgeon Creek. Already, south of the Portage Road, the St. Charles Country Club is acquiring 250 acres in a beautiful loop of the Assiniboine; and is developing golf and polo facilities for its 200-and-more members. The Club-house is already building.

How long have people lived on this magnificent site? Nobody knows! The first report of white inhabitants, is that Jean Baptiste Lagimondiere builds a cabin for his family on the River bank, here, about 1815. Before 1840, surveys divide the land in River Lots 113 to 121. Pioneer owners are Billy and Sara Brown; and, soon, their son-in-law, James Good.

James Good is born on a ship sailing from England, in 1836. The Good family — with the Kirtons, Gowlers and others — come to work on "the Company" farm on the flats of the Red River, just north of "the Forks". The contribution made by these pioneer families to Assiniboia and our Canadian West is exceeded by no others, before or since! Alfred Good, son of James, born in '83, recalls being wakened at dawn with the skirl of pipes played by "Scotty" McIntyre, parading in kilts before his Hotel on the Portage Trail. The last word in convenience for Country Club members is a street car operating on a rail line from Portage to the new Club-house. Clubbers alighting from the Portage Road street car, call on their private phone (on Wm. Good's porch) to "Send the car". In minutes they were wafted to the new Club-house; or, if polo enthusiasts, to the stables on the River bank.

As we cross the bridge over Sturgeon Creek, on our right is the triangle of River Lot 122, known as Ashcroft Point. (To become "Woodhaven" — with its homesites of excelling beauty.) Somewhere on Sturgeon Creek, Cuthbert Grant builds a dam and a water-driven grist mill, some 70 years ago. Alas, the builders are better buffalo hunters than engineers! The dam washes out; and the mill is abandoned.

Once over Sturgeon Creek bridge, we are in St. James parish. To our left, on the northeastern bank of Sturgeon Creek, Patrice Caplette and D. Isbister are among the land-owners. River Lot 12, in its great width, embraces 2½ square miles. Within the Inner Two Miles, George Gaffield is one of the tenants. His neighbors include Andrew McDermot (the second), Joseph Benson and others. In the Outer Two Miles of this Lot, a siding on the C.P.R. is named Murray Park, after leading citizen Alexander Murray. Eastward, many River Lots are re-parcelled into blocks "C", "D", "E", etc; and are flourishing market gardens. Silver Heights, property of pioneer John Rowand and, now, of Lord Strathcona, has its manorial farmstead on Lot 18. Alexander Begg, and other enthusiastic entrepreneurs, once finance a brewery in this vicinity; but distance from the City markets proves a handicap. Lot 21 is the site of Deer Lodge. This mansion — long famous as the hospitable home of Hon. James Mackay, plainsman, hunter, freighter, Executive Councillor and natural leader among all classes and conditions of settlers — has been re-built into "Deer Lodge Hotel". It is popular as "Chad's Place". Here, young blades drive by hack; eat, drink and are merry — within quite tolerable limits. Just south of the Portage Road is St. James Post Office; and, nearby, the site of W. F. Lane's first store, as well as of Robert Tait's first steam-driven grist mill, across Portage from his brick house.

We cross River Lot 27, the home of Peter Bruce, where Bruce Creek follows its deepening ravine to the Assiniboine. Edwin Bourke, Councillor for Ward 3, farms Lots 29 and 30. His brother, William Bourke, lives on Lot 34. In earlier times, these lands westward from Omand's Creek, are chosen for a big "Company Farm". In due time, when "Company" farming fails, John Palmer Bourke, emigrant from Sligo, having completed his service with "the Company" begun in 1812, acquires the property; and divides it among his sons: Walter, John, Andrew, William and Edwin. These 5 stalwarts carry on the tradition of pioneering leadership, as true "native sons". The census of 1870 lists 26 members of the Bourke family; all, but the original John Palmer, born in the Nor'West. Edwin is elected MLA for St. James parish (or electoral district) in 1870; and again in 1874. John is elected to the Council of Assiniboia in 1880; and Walter follows him, in '81. Currently, Edwin is Councillor for Ward 3.

Eastward, Alex Speirs, on River Lot 41, has his holding sub-divided into town lots. The City is coming! Before St. James Anglican church, built in the early '50's between the Portage Trail and the Assiniboine, we end our tour, at Assiniboia's eastern boundary. Beyond is historic Omand's Creek; and narrow 4-chain River Lots, which promoters are busily chopping into street on street, with houses packed together on 50-, 40- and (far too many) 25-foot frontages! The broad acres we have seen in today's drive through Assiniboia will, soon, feel the pressure of increasing population — herded together by promoters in the name of "progress" (with profits, of course!) The City is Coming!

In 1899, however, there is still "space" in Assiniboia. The "living room" enjoyed by our people is indicated by our schools. South of the Assiniboine, Charleswood school with 49 pupils, has one teacher: Miss M. L. Caron. At the western end of the Municipality, Headingly school has 76 pupils and 2 teachers: J. H. Arnett and Miss Jemima E. Tait. Mr. Theo J. Watts, the teacher at Sturgeon Creek school, has 51 pupils enrolled. St. James School District, with an annual Government grant of

$78.65, has 31 boys and 36 girls on its roll; and one teacher: Miss Amber L. Glenn. There is still space in Assiniboia!

We thank our driver. He drives over the bridge, southward, to the big Wright farm. It has been a big day. We have seen something of Assiniboia — after 20 years as one of Manitoba's Municipalities; and at the close of an era. We have learned something, too, of the people living here, as the 19th century closes. Lingering along the cool and shady paths of this old churchyard, brings to mind the cemeteries of St. Francois Xavier, Headingly and St. Charles — "Where heaves the earth in many a mouldering heap" over the resting place of pioneers who lived their share of Assiniboia's history in the century gone. Leaving, we close the gate, with a prayerful farewell, upon another chapter in the great story of our Canadian West. We walk away — on the Great Highway, toward the century ahead.

MRS. ISABELLA McQUEEN

CHAPTER 12

Men in Sheepskin Coats .. 1900-1909

Assiniboia — as every community of our Canadian West — feels the impact of the immigration policy put in action by Clifford Sifton, now Minister of the Interior. Like Champlain, 3 centuries ago, Sifton sees that Canada's vast resources of lands and waters can be brought into use only by people; more people; people with the strength to work; asking only opportunity to "make their own way"; and to retain such a share of the wealth they produce, as will mean more abundant living for their families. Donald Smith, now Lord Strathcona, working as Canada's High Commissioner in London (sans salary) may have shared Sifton's ambition to build a new Canadian nation. He is certain that every cargo of "men in sheepskin coats" freighted to our Canadian West, booms the price of the vast acreages held by himself, his Hudson's Bay Company and the C.P.R.

The transfusion of new blood brought by hundreds of thousands of new-comers from the corners of the earth, in these years, pumps new vigor into our Canadian economy and nationality. On its surge, countless new communities are swept into being; and older communities, like Assiniboia, enjoy tremendous change.

In January, Hugh John Macdonald becomes Premier of Manitoba. Sir Daniel McMillan is named Lieut-Governor. The Reeve of the Rural Municipality of Assiniboia is still Hon. Alexander Murray. The Council of Assiniboia, in its narrowed scope, still deals with the multiplicity of affairs of which Municipalities are built. Alfred Caron is paid $4.00 for fishing a dead horse from the River; and burying it. Winnifred Gabriel is paid $2.00 bounty for killing a wolf; the grist mill debentures are sold above par after G. N. Steele inspects the new mill, now operating at full capacity. The bonus for building it is paid to S. P. Hodgson. Reeve

Murray heads a Committee, to urge the Provincial Government to build better highways; and drain swamplands. A resolution of sympathy with the British in South Africa recognizes the ties of Empire. New ferries are ordered for St. James and St. Charles, like that at Headingly; tenders range from $75.00 to $100.00. R. C. McPhillips is instructed to survey land needed to restore the width of the two-mile road (Saskatchewan Avenue) which the CPR has "encroached upon". R. R. Sutherland, Municipal Solicitor, claims $75.00 for extra work in connection with the new grist mill. Council orders that ferries be free to people coming, and going, to church. The Provincial Board of Health, orders that the Health Officer vaccinate all school children. Council pays Thos. Buchanan for building the 2 new ferries, $79.00; and J. E. McLean, for bolts, hinges and ironwork for same: $48.50. Egan Brothers are instructed to refill a hole left on the Cycle Path, opposite River Lot 31, St. James.

The annual meeting of Holy Trinity, Headingly, congregation resolves to "Pledge raising a special . . . 20th Century Fund, as a mark of gratitude to God for blessings vouchsafed during the past century; and . . . start the new century . . . free of debt". Families enrolled include: Brandon, Brooks, Buchanan, Cameron, Clouston, Cook, Cowley, Dennison, Fowler, Francis, Glover, Haggarty, Hall, Johnstone, Lonsdale, Morrice, Rigby, Stevenson, Tait and Taylor. The congregation in St. Charles parish bids farewell to Father Dandurand, parish priest since 1876; and now, succeeded by Fr. Beaudin.

Early Assiniboia farmers cultivate small fields on selected dry spots. Charles Bremner, for example, works some 35 acres in the '90's; and is among the substantial farm operators. Like many of his neighbors, he loses a succession of horses to "swamp fever". In pioneer days, most of the country is under water. No adequate program of water management is ever undertaken in Assiniboia. Nevertheless, piece-meal construction of roads and ditches carries much of the surface water to the River. Big farm operators move in, with power machinery. Aime Benard takes over some 600 acres, west of Headingly. A steam-tractor, pulling a 10-bottom plow, breaks this land 2" deep; and packs it flat. Flax is sown on the breaking. The out-turn is sold for $5.00 per bushel. Then the big steam outfit back-sets the breaking, some 3 inches deep; and the fields are ready for grain production. Other farm operators are doing the same, on varying scale, with horse, and even ox, outfits. This year, 2.5 million acres are sown to wheat in our Canadian West.

Our Municipal Council, in a June meeting, pays 14 accounts: 8 for roads and bridges; 3 for ferries. Jude Lafleche and his sons are permitted to do their statute labor on the road between St. Charles and Headingly. R. C. McPhillips surveys the two-mile road, south of the River. The

Strathcona estate agent is asked for a right-of-way along River Lot 19, from the Portage Trail to the two-mile road; the CPR is urged to build necessary crossings north and south of the River; and John Duffy is paid $150.00 for a horse killed at the Headingly ferry.

A group headed by Roderick McKenzie, president of the Manitoba Jockey Club, is having Kirkfield Park race-track built, northeast of Sturgeon Creek. Trainloads of soil are freighted from far-away Kentucky; dumped at Murray Park siding; and spread by teams and wagons, under the watchful eye of Foreman Alfred Good. Lavish expenditures build palatial stables for 100 horses; and a magnificent mansion!

Young Canadians volunteer for service in the South African war. Some 250 go overseas, through the 90th Winnipeg Rifles. Many enlist in "Strathcona's Horse", a cavalry regiment outfitted by Donald Smith. In all, 7,300 men volunteer from Canada.

Canada's Nor'West is booming into "the Golden West" — where harvest adds 100 million bushels of grain to mankind's food supplies; and whence 60 million bushels of wheat and a million cattle, annually, are shipped to the ends of the earth.

Hitherto, the steam-driven plant which generates electricity to light the City and run its street cars, has closed down each midnight. No lights are switched on, Sunday morning, until church-time. No street cars run, no shops open, to disturb the Sabbath quiet. Now, a Western boom is gathering momentum. Winnipeg numbers 40,000 people. Some 5,000 of them work in industries with annual output exceeding $13 millions. Nearly 2 million passengers, this year, ride the City's street cars. Suddenly, power becomes vital. The battle for the water-power of our Assiniboine River, erupts!

The Government of Canada passes the Manitoba Grain Act, to regulate middlemen. Grain handling, buying and selling is now big business. Milling companies, syndicates and private owners operate 829 elevators throughout the West. The Grand Trunk Railway, leasing lines from Chicago to Winnipeg, becomes a competitor for Western business; and, backed by Canada's Government, is building a third transcontinental railway. Every harvest raises the cry of "box-car shortage!". Main line railways are rushed. Branches race for newly-settled areas. On this expanding frame-work, the new development of the West is shaped — just as the fur trade developed on the frame-work of waterways, trails, canoe, York boat and Red River cart. As the brigades from Assiniboia garnered the wealth of the West's fur harvests to "the Forks" — so, now, railways centralize the flow of the West's new-found farm wealth through this "Heart of the Continent".

On a cold, cold day in mid-December, Mr. and Mrs. Arthur Creak (That good lady relates) with sleigh and pony drive from their farm, north of Saskatchewan Avenue, to a Fort Rouge store to shop for Christmas supplies. While they are in the store, their blanketed horse breaks loose. When they come out — no horse, no sleigh; only the horse-blanket, down the trail! Through the cold, the young couple walk home. Ten miles! Still no horse, no sleigh. Mr. Creak back-tracks, next morning; and finds his steed in the stable of a friend beside Omand's Creek. Jogging along homeward, the horse is lured off the trail by some oats that stick up, thru the snow. The sleigh upsets. Parcels scatter in the deep drifts! Digging deep, Mr. Creak finds his bundles — and others, including bottles of whiskey (unhappily, frozen and broken!) Omand's Creek is long known as a bad spot on the trail — at night or during the winter. This winter, a CPR train is snow-bound near the Creak farm, for 3 days. A succession of engines and rescue crews are imprisoned in the giant snowdrifts! All hands shelter in the Creak home; and enjoy a good visit!

During the season of merriment at Silver Heights, a company of young blades — challenged by the claim that no buffalo was ever tamed — hitch a boisterous 2-year old bull to a toboggan. Eight of the most daring climb aboard. Loosed, the steed stands rock-still; then snorts — bellows — and gallops wildly over the snow — spilling passengers — breaking harness — wrecking the toboggan — then disappearing down the frozen River! The following spring that buffalo is found, still carrying part of his harness — in North Dakota! Old-timers chuckle, knowingly. Reports "in the papers", that buffalo transplanted to Wood Buffalo Reserve have multiplied to 13,000, recall memories of the Great Hunt to former hunters now living out their years along the Assiniboine.

The Council of Assiniboia for 1901 has Reeve C. George Caron presiding; and Councillors: Alfred Fowler, George T. Chapman, Wm. MacFarlane and Donald Cameron. Again, the Council Chamber is in "Chad's" Deer Lodge. Council urges the Provincial Government to improve main roads; pays $300.00 toward improving a mile of the Portage Road, at the eastern limit of the Municipality; abolishes statute labor, that time-honored method of doing road-work; and calls miller Hodgson to account for complaints about over-dockage and under-weights!

The first automobile honks through the City; and out the Portage Road. In their fright, horses smash equipage; and drivers exercise their profanity!

Gold in South Africa and the Yukon make money freer. The inflow of people boosts the population of the Canadian West to 400,000. Nearly 50,000 live around "the Forks." In the general excitement of boom times, the usual multiplicity of big and little cares demands the attention of Assiniboia's Council. A. T. McDermot is hired to move the Bannatyne fence, run new lines on the Portage Road and widen the grade east of Sturgeon Creek. Council buys a road grader, for $260.00 cash; hires men to "brush out" the road between River Lots 59 and 50, in the Outer 2 miles, St. Charles parish; and buys a roadway for $15.00 per acre, from Frank Ness, along the east side of his River Lot 111 — from Portage to the 2-mile road. This fall, our Council threatens to sue the CPR, unless that great Company, within 30 days, restores to Assiniboia the 16½ feet of land chiselled off Saskatchewan Avenue! Giant tractors are prohibited crossing Municipal bridges. Arthur F. Pigott's livery rushes Dr. Burridge to St. James to attend an emergency case of smallpox; Council pays $2.00 for the drive; and $6.00 for necessary medicines.

The congregation of Holy Trinity, Headingly, confirms the transfer to the Municipality of a 50-foot road along Lot 54, from Portage to the River, while the ferry operates. Sale of "glebe lands", excepting south of "the Creek", is approved, at $10.00 per acre.

The first convention of the Territorial Grain Growers' Association, meeting on 1 February, urges sweeping amendments to the Manitoba Grain Act. The air is charged with incipient revolt! The Government of Canada averts an explosion — by accepting the Amendments. Again, in 1902, our Assiniboia Council meets in "Chad's Hotel"; but this year pays $10.00 rent. A roadway along the east side of River Lot 19, St. James, is donated by the Strathcona estate; and within a month, is cancelled, with the advice that the needed right-of-way be acquired from other owners.

A late March blizzard buries Assiniboia under 6-foot snowdrifts; and reduces attendance at the annual meeting of Holy Trinity, Headingly, congregation. The rector reports that "glebe" lands sold, will yield $200.00 annually. Members volunteer to haul 8 cords of foundation stone; plant a windbreak of trees around the parsonage; and build a fence, to keep cattle out.

On 22 June, W. B. "Ben" Hall dies. For this great Assiniboia pioneer and Christian gentleman, no eulogy could be more fitting than the sincere and tender resolution recorded by his friends and neighbors in the congregation of Holy Trinity, Headingly: "His genial kindliness of heart endeared him to the community. For many years he served the church faithfully. We thank God for the grace given our departed friend; and for the example of his blameless life."

In July, Council instructs ferrymen (now paid $20.00 monthly) that, with the present high water, they must operate ferries at a sharper angle; and must not leave small boys in charge! Portage Road in the eastern part of the Municipality is ditched and graded at 11 cents per yard. Council offers $35.00 per acre for a roadway on River Lot 25, St. James; but the owner wants an unheard of $100.00. As more people move into Assiniboia, land prices move up! Sections of the Portage Road are still being re-surveyed and re-located. Our Council hires John and Patrick McMillan to move fences and trees off the Portage Road, eastward from River Lot 16, St. James; and publicly thanks Nurse Ley for helping the James Clouston family, stricken with fever.

For his third consecutive year, C. George Caron is Reeve of Assiniboia. At the first meeting in 1903, Council urges Manitoba's Minister of Public Works (again!) to help build better roads. "Better times" are reflected in a $100.00 raise to the Municipal Solicitor; and $50.00 to the Secretary. Council demands that railway companies pay for damage caused by fires started by locomotives.

On 24 February, a meeting of bee-keepers, chaired by Rev. A. E. Cowley, organizes the Manitoba Bee-keepers Association. Council acknowledges the promise of the C.P.R. to build crossings, bridges, etc; buys piles from McMillan Bros., with 8" tops and up to 30' long, at 12 cents per lineal foot; and votes Dr. Burridge, Health Officer, $40.00, in acknowledgement of his devoted work during epidemics. Council relays to the Attorney-General of Manitoba complaints of disorderliness at Deer Lodge Hospital, making the Portage Road unsafe; and recommends that the bar be closed on Sundays and off hours.

The April annual meeting of Holy Trinity, Headingly, raises the rector's salary from $170.00 to $200.00. Joseph Sayer re-visits Assiniboia, after 21 years absence. As a boy, he had gone to Saskatchewan, in 1883, with the Assiniboia families who found the new community of "Bresaylor".

Municipalities are required to provide all clergymen with registers, wherein to report all births, marriages and deaths, to the Province. The autos honking along our Municipal roads kick up enough dust to cause angry citizens to demand their regulation. An epidemic of "prairie fever" (typhoid) sweeps the plains.

The Headingly Agricultural Society holds its annual Fall Races, in October. J. B. Lewis is starter; C. Halliday and Al McGirr, judges; with S. E. Wrigley, secretary-treasurer; and J. E. McLean, timer. Programs (price 10 cents) list: Ladies Race, pace or trot, 1 mile; "A" Class, 1 mile; and Free-for-all, 1 mile. This is the feature race of the meet — with 19 entries, from Winnipeg, Fort Garry, Moosomin, Norwood, Gladstone, Emo, Darlingford and Murray Park. Among the drivers are: Dangerfield, Morton, Sassroeu, Graham, Hodgson, Banes, Sutherland, Nyon, Campbell and Ronan.

Enthusiastic boosters demand a street railway along the south side of the River, to Headingly. The very air crackles with grandiose schemes! Promoters battle for power, gas, transit and railway properties and franchises! On the tide of Western development, the Hudson's Bay Company sells 350,000 acres of its vacant lands for some $2,000,000.00. Shareholders cash in on Donald Smith's canny "second sight" in getting part of every surveyed township for "the Company", as part of the price for transferring to Canada whatever title it could claim to the Nor'West.

The Council of Assiniboia for 1904 includes: Reeve, Ed. Bourke; Councillors, John M. Tait, George T. Chapman, Robert Bannatyne and Thomas Buchanan. At its first meeting, Council resolves that Clerk Frank Ness "procure a fountain pen for his use". Five weed inspectors are appointed, to carry on the battle against thistles — under R. G. O'Malley, Provincial Inspector. Three loads of wood are delivered to a needy widow. Council is urged to use steel pipe, rather than plank, for culverts. April 30 is a big day for "horseless carriage" addicts. The Winnipeg Automobile Club stages its first run. Five autos navigate all the way from Market Square to Headingly!

The congregation of Holy Trinity, Headingly, annual meeting represents some 29 families, including: Hall, Taylor, Rigby, Layton, Tait, Stevenson, Britton, Lonsdale, Fowler, Brown, Cameron, Cook, Vialoux, Johnstone, Compton, Dennison, Walker, Bremner, Buchanan, Clouston, O'Malley and Gerrard. The Ladies Aid reports receipts of $354.90 from a shower. The Municipality votes $50.00 toward building a "TB" Sanatorium at Ninette. A. W. Good is elected Councillor for Ward 3, when J. W. Tait resigns. The City takes some 300 acres from Assiniboia for "City Park", south of the River.

Wages for Municipal work, currently, are 40 cents an hour for man and team; and 15 cents per hour for the man. A bridge is built over McMillan's Creek. The new mammoth steam tractors, weighing up to 12 tons, cause trouble at Municipal bridges. Ceaselessly, Council demands that the railway Companies build proper culverts, crossings, cattle guards, ditches and roads. Sam Beckett is hired as a second Municipal constable; and is ordered to stop the epidemic of obscene talk; furious driving on the public roads; and shooting on Sundays. He will earn $2.00 a day, while on duty.

This year, rust robs our Canadian West of an estimated 100 million bushels of wheat. In December, Leversidge Brandon resigns as weed inspector, constable and pathmaster. Council warns the Suburban Rapid

Transit officials to stop running cars ahead of scheduled times; and leaving passengers stranded in the cold! Reeve Bourke is authorized to attend the year-end tax sale; and to "bid in" building lots — in River Lot 41, St. James, at $125.00 each; in Lot 9, at $150.00; in plan 245, at $50.00; and in the Outer Two Miles, R. L. 56, St. Boniface, at $15.00 each.

For their 1905 Council, Assiniboia citizens elect W. C. Hall, George T. Chapman, Alex W. Good and Wm. Brown, with Alexander Murray, Reeve. When Portage la Prairie petitions the Government of Canada to battle floods along the Assiniboine River, our Council states that Assiniboia is flood free; but will cooperate in promoting management of the River. A Council room is rented for $12.00, yearly, in Frank Ness' home; and a bylaw to borrow $5,000.00 from the Bank of Commerce is read first, second and third times — and passed — by the usual expedient of suspending the rules. A new ferry is ordered for Headingly; and a new Sturgeon Creek bridge is planned. A Court of Revision assesses building lots in sub-divided River Lot 41, St. James — if facing on Portage Road, at $100.00 each; others, $65.00. The appeal of the City of Winnipeg against assessment of the 300 acres taken from Assiniboia for City Park is refused!

The quickening circulation of money is reflected in reports at Holy Trinity annual meeting: that revenues for the year reach $1,142.69; and, added thereto, the building fund: $446.73; and Ladies Aid earnings: $607.69. Two acres of "glebe" land are offered to the school trustees for $300.00 per acre.

On 1 July, the new provinces of Saskatchewan and Alberta are born!

Assiniboia citizens cry for roads, culverts, bridges. Wm. Stevenson urges that the old Government ditch, west of River Lot 61, Headingly, be deepened from Portage Road to the River. When Denis Kapalet protests that the CPR has flooded his farmstead, our Council orders that mighty corporation to drain all Assiniboia lands flooded by its ditches. After a long battle, Judge Walker rules that Assiniboia cannot assess "City Park". Michele Papineau and Arthur Bourke collect $13.00 in bounties for killing wolves. (Assiniboia is still a "Happy Hunting Ground"). R. D. Waugh, Secretary of the Bicycle Club, gets Council to extend the Portage Road bicycle path from Silver Heights to St. Charles post office.

The St. Charles Roman Catholic congregation open their new, enlarged church. It is a fine structure — 60 x 90 feet; of brick veneer, on a full stone basement; with a tower 108 feet high; and beautiful stained glass windows. Fr. Thibaudeau has provided the energetic leadership in this achievement. In addition, a convent boarding-school is erected by the Oblate Sisters, led by Rev. Mother St. Viateur.

In December the first electric street car clangs over the new line between Winnipeg and Headingly. Daily service is expected to boom trade between Assiniboia dairy-men and City customers. With the first snowfall, the Holly Snowshoe Club is organized. "Snowshoe tramps" by hundreds of the members of this Club, and others, become highlights in the recreational life of Assiniboia; and other communities along the Assiniboine River and the Red.

In 1906, 565 Canadians register those "ridiculous horseless carriages". They blaze trails that lead to transformed living — for all Canadians! Assiniboia's Council legislates regulations designed (hopefully!) to control speeding. Ferrymen are instructed to collect 25 cents for each auto crossing the Assiniboine.

Western farmers harvest above 153 million bushels of grain. Manitoba's wheat out-turn doubles in 5 years. Competing railways race construction to capture freight. Names become towns. Abandoned trading posts become cities. Traders wake up to find themselves millionaires! Big issues crowd the stage of world affairs: Irish Home Rule; autonomy for South Africa; "the ridiculous 8-hour day"; GTP construction; church union in Canada. These, and other, affairs are discussed by the multitudes surging to "the last, best West". Daily trainloads of settlers and their effects follow each other — Westward.

Citizens of Winnipeg, on a third referendum, vote for Sunday street cars; and now have to adjust to the increased traffic and noise, on specified lines. Folks in Assiniboia still enjoy their Sunday quiet. James J. Hill hits town — broadcasting promises of another transcontinental railway; and buying property for terminals. His plans shrink to a connecting branch line, only. Winnipeg traders, controlling the booming grain trade, build the gigantic Grain Exchange, on Lombard Street. The former muddy junction of the River Road and the Portage Trail becomes the financial centre of the West.

In Assiniboia, the annual meeting of the Anglican congregation at Headingly adopts reports of $2,094.47 revenue; $1,197.27 for church extension; and 97 subscribers to pews. Old-timers debate reports that Hon. Frank Oliver, Minister of the Interior, is paying $245.00 a head for 800 buffalo, delivered at Banff. A strike of street railway employees calls out the Winnipeg Rifles in aid of the civil power. Tempers flare; but no untoward incident mars the operation. A contract dated 12 October, 1906, between the trustees of Headingly S.D. #9; John Cameron, John Taylor, Jr. and Thos. Buchanan, and John Black

Morrison, contractor, calls for a new 4-room school building to be completed by 1 February, 1907, "provided that no delay that cannot be avoided occurs to prevent the same". Price: $5,250.00!

On 6 November, the Lieut-Governor of Manitoba, Sir Daniel McMillan, and Premier R. P. Roblin formally open the new Manitoba Agricultural College, which overlooks the Assiniboine River, on land formerly farmed by Archibald Wright. The Council of Assiniboia assembles in a special meeting on 9 February; and decides to attend in a body the Law Amendments Committee of the Legislature "to oppose . . empowering the City of Winnipeg to expropriate . . . lands within 100 miles . . for providing a water supply". A second special meeting discusses with the Provincial Public Works Department, better roads for Assiniboia. Roads, culverts, the grist mill and street railway fares dominate Council meetings in March. Two wells are ordered sunk to serve 300 St. James residents, on Kensington, Bradford, King Edward and Queen Streets.

Reeve Thompson is authorized to divide part of River Lot 22, St. James. Aime Benard, new MLA for Assiniboia, takes Council to ask Hon. Robt. Rogers for help in building roads needed in the Municipality. On 4 April, "Chad's bear", famous Deer Lodge attraction, is killed, "after a struggle with those who seek to prevent him entering into a paw-to-horn battle with an old buffalo bull". Council is busy with plank sidewalks and crossings. Of 37 accounts paid, 18 are for ditches and roads; and 9 for killing wolves. Special meetings warn the Winnipeg Electric Company to stop Sunday cars in Assiniboia, except to City Park; endorse a Provincial Telephone System; approve crossings for Golden Gate sub-division; and confirm 6 more sub-divisions — when these are duly surveyed and certified by H. Patterson, M.L.S.

The 10-year boom has increased Manitoba's population from 150,000 to above 365,000. Roderick McKenzie's Kirkfield Park race-track is taken over by the Manitoba Automobile Racing Association. Crowds pack the Park to see the world's fastest drivers. For 5 years, the craze crescendos. Barney Oldfield (who records the world's first mile in 60 seconds on a dirt track, last year, at Winnipeg's Exhibition), Wild Bob Burman, Leon Devoy, Verne Soules, Jules Ellenboe and Sig Hougdaul head the parade of famous racing drivers in Assiniboia.

An 8-year program of ditching drains the Boyne Marsh; and brings ranges of fine farm lands under cultivation, south of the Assiniboine. A Blue Book, published by Henderson Directories, Ltd., displays 89 advertisements; among them the Walker Theatre, opened last December; the Winnipeg Theatre, home of the Winnipeg Stock Company; the

Bijou Theatre; Manitoba Hall; the St. Charles Country Club (golf and polo for 389 members); and the Manitoba Jockey Club, Roderick McKenzie, President.

The marriage of Miss Helen E. Hall and Montague Vialoux is recorded at Holy Trinity, Headingly. Promoters are buying River Lot farms; and sub-dividing them into building lots. The Council of Assiniboia, in May, approves 6 such sub-divisions, including part of River Lot #95, St. Charles, of which Fr. Thibeaudeau is trustee; McMillan's Inner Two Miles, of 30 and 31; the M. J. H. Daignault acres on Lots 104 and 105, near Sturgeon Creek; the adjoining McPhee properties; Lots 106 and 107 and 4 and 5, all of St. James; and, for Chris O'Kelly, Lot 89, St. Charles, 3 miles west of Sturgeon Creek. So, a new era and new concepts of living replace the pioneer days.

The old era ends — with the announcement that Joseph Good is dead. It is 47 years ago that Joseph and Mary Ann Kirton marry. Seventy years ago, the parents of both, with the Gowlers and others, snowshoe from York Factory, 180 frozen wilderness miles, to Norway House. After 5 years with "the Company", Joseph Good acquires a 4-chain frontage on the Assiniboine (at later Newman Street). Thereon, he builds a log house for his bride. In a work-crowded life, Mary finds time to plant seedling elms and maples. Neighbors ask if she ever expects those tiny things to grow. She replies: "My children will swing from the branches of these trees". They do! So do her grandchildren. Thousands of girls and boys play around those trees which beautify the bank of the Assiniboine, along later Wolseley Avenue.

So a pioneer generation quietly slips away. A bustling new generation, bursting with strength and ideas, takes over. How this generation, in its turn, is displaced, is told in future chapters.

The winter of 1907-08 is hard, cold and stormy. Trainloads of coal are imprisoned in giant snowdrifts. Fuel runs short! Hurriedly, trainloads of wood are rushed from the Interlake country; and doled out, 1 cord per customer. Spring comes at last — and more and more automobiles roar back and forth on the Portage Road, raising more and more dust and racket! Most of the 257 cars licensed in Manitoba travel this Great Highway. Assiniboia families, driving to the City, see men and teams, like myriads of ants, busily "moving dirt" for the new Union railway depot. McKenzie and Mann ("Bill and Dan") two Westerners turned Empire-builders, challenge the great C.P.R. They pour millions of borrowed money into the Canadian West; have crews surveying and building railroads and hotels; and place vast orders with wholesalers and merchants. Thousands of workers eat at their hand; and hundreds of henchmen ride into affluence on the tide of their Empire building! To spur their efforts, the Grand Trunk Pacific Railway, from Moncton, reaches Winnipeg in July.

In Assiniboia Lee Turcotte contracts to brush out and grade Wallasey Street. Increasing traffic over-loads street cars, between Headingly and the City. New home owners petition for wells on Parkview, Ness and Ferry Road, St. James. Levies zoom to above $10,000.00 for the 5 School Districts in Assiniboia. At an August meeting, our Council passes 168 accounts, including 32 for cutting weeds, 151 for roadwork, $10.00 to David Bunting for wolf bounties; and $15.00 for a dozen scythes, for mowing thistles. The 4 ferrymen are now paid $25.00, each; and Frank Ness, Municipal Clerk, $83.35, monthly. A lengthening list of new streets are "brushed out". Headingly Fall Fair, in September, features an "Old-Timers Picnic"; and, of course, the "Farmer's Trot" and other races. From the race-track, visitors see the big new grain elevator on the CPR siding.

Our Municipal Council is called on for an unpredictable variety of decisions. Traffic lanes on the new CNR bridge crossing the Assiniboine are uselessly narrow. How about a pontoon bridge at St. James, from the Portage Road to City Park? Is the two-foot plank sidewalk on Lake Street, good enough? Who piled manure on R. Cunningham's Lot 40, St. James? A Headingly meeting demands better street car service and bridges over the River; and "Mr. Isaacs inquires if a license is needed for practicing as a clairvoyant."

In November, J. H. "Harry" Bremner and Florence Munroe are married, by Rev. A. E. Cowley; and settle on River Lot 40, Headingly. Mrs. Bremner, a City girl, is enthralled by the peace and beauty of life beside the Assiniboine. The sunbeams that flood her home, she weaves into sparkling rhyme; and leaves her happy concept in serene and lilting verse.

Homes and shops leap-frog, westward, along Portage Road. The street railway Company is ordered: to provide lighted and heated waiting rooms and cars in winter; have a car leave the western end of the line at 6 a.m.; and the last west-bound car leave the CPR station, Winnipeg, at 11:30 p.m. Declaring that these demands shall be enforced by legal action, Council votes a bonus to the retiring Reeve of $75.00; a bonus of $200.00 to the Clerk; grants to hospitals; and so concludes the Municipal business of 1908.

The street railway company, having promised a new week-day service: 22 minutes to St. Charles, 60 minutes to Headingly and 75 minutes south of the River — gets Council's approval for "Ys" across Portage at Deer Lodge and St. Charles, with proper waiting rooms. Dr. S. J. Thompson, Reeve, and Councillors Bannatyne and Bourke meet with Aime Benard, our M.L.A., and Provincial officials to apply pressure (political or otherwise) that may improve main highways.

New home-owners protest cattle running at large in Assiniboia; and petition Council for herd law in Wards 3 and 4. Mr. Haynes demands "No cattle watered at Municipal wells!" Municipal business grows, to require postage for March totalling $56.66! At a Court of Revision, the Bank of Commerce and J. C. McLaren declare the Headingly grist mill is now worth only $450.00. An April Council meeting seethes with reports that petitions for better streets met rebuffs; and that costs have been falsified! Apologetic retractions of such statements does little to cool the Municipal atmosphere. Ratepayers petition Council to grade Ferry Road, from Portage, northward; grade Greig Street; put a bridge at Colony Creek; and asphalt the River Road, south of the Assiniboine. Reflecting advancing civilization, a herd law is passed, to keep livestock properly housed at night; wells are sunk on Parkview and Kentyre Streets; and bylaws regulate public health, scavenging, dog taxes and electrical installations.

New names on the roll of Holy Trinity church, Headingly, reported at this year's annual meeting are: Bush, Casey, Cotterall, Cummings, Hale, Turner. Volunteers assemble on 29 June, to clean up the churchyard. Rev. A. E. Cowley resigns, in September. To meet the needs of multiplying population, Britannia School District is formed from part of the original St. James S.D. The "SS Grand Falls" steams into "the Forks" this spring — the last steamship to come down the Red River from the United Stages. In July, citizens vote for Sunday street cars in Assiniboia. Council is bombarded with demands for wells, sidewalks, streets, sanitary closets. Teams are hired — to pick up bottles, cans and other trash, in the eastern end of the Municipality. A bylaw requires that all new houses have cement pit closets. Assiniboia launches on the struggle (which no "civilized" community ever wins!) to survive its own traffic and waste disposal problems!

A new Winnipeg Electric Company sub-station is built on the Portage Road, at R.L. 41, St. James. Major Schuman leads the demand that brush be cut and a well sunk on Brooklyn Street. Other citizens demand a 4-foot plank sidewalk on Kensington Street. The Municipal Commissioner advises that Assiniboia's assessment is equalized at $6,594,000.00. In 1880, assessment totalled $445,000.00. After studying a Provincial Engineer's report, Council decides that a mile of the Portage Road will be gravelled: cost, $2,209.00; and a new bridge built at Gowler's Creek: $1,795.00 — if the Province contributes a proper share. Sidewalks are built on King Edward and Douglas Streets; and wells sunk on Bruce and Inglewood. The first sewer pipe is purchased for $144.00.

In August, work begins on sidewalks north of Miry Creek bridge; on wells in Ward 3; and cutting brush on Madison Street. In September, tenders are called for a sewer on Berlin Street. Some bids are as high as $4,328.00. The contract is awarded for $1,401.00. On petition of W. E. Roscoe and others, Queen Street is graded. Miles of plank sidewalks are built. A well is sunk; and a windmill to pump water, raised — on Berlin Street. An irate citizen reports "the social evil" in Assiniboia. Liquor is sold in a bawdy house in St. James! Constable Hallett is ordered to investigate the disorderly house on Parkview Street; Rev. McColl urges action to keep "houses of ill fame" out of Assiniboia.

Numbers of Assiniboia men are among the 250 working on the construction of the power plant at Pointe du Bois. In a burst of optimism, Manitoba's Government votes $250,000.00 for a World's Fair, in Winnipeg, in 1912! The Reeve of our Municipality, Dr. S. J. Thompson, dies suddenly.

In these years, Assiniboia, like other communities, is swept along on a tide of Western development — powered, largely by Sifton's "Men in Sheepskin coats". They come in swarms, far outnumbering any other inflow into Canada. They come because Canada offers opportunity — free of mythical privilege bequeathed by preceding generations; opportunity for work, homes, independence and equality with every other Canadian.

They come from (does it matter?) every corner of the earth, even Eastern Canada. Wearing sheepskin coats and shouldering "turkeys" of blankets and extra clothing, they build the railways, log the forests, fish the waters and man the mines, sawmills and pulp plants, from the Lakehead, westward. They homestead even "marginal" lands; and build rough, unwanted acres into prosperous farms and communities. They tackle the hard, heavy work of making Canada a vital supplier of bread to mankind; and contribute to the profits checked thru Winnipeg offices to tycoons in Toronto and Montreal.

In the West, they build expanding dimensions into Canadian nationality — far beyond anything the "founding provinces" of Confederation could do, alone. They contribute to material Canada no less than the habitants of Quebec and the Loyalists of Ontario.

More important — in the common opportunity, work, hardship and achievement of pioneering — they establish the fact that there are no "superior" nor "inferior", but only *equal*, Canadians. They confirm that Canadian nationality is not in words entombed in be-ribboned legal documents; not in the ascendancy of some citizens over others; but is the outcome of knowing each other; of working side by side; and, when the time demands, of fighting side by side.

CHAPTER 13

Headingly Parish Church

We Go To War . . 1910-19

The tide of development is at full flood when, on 4 January, Assiniboia's Council for 1910 assembles in its first meeting. Reeve Geo. T. Chapman presides; and Councillors W. C. Hall, Edmund Bourke, Joseph M. McMillan and J. E. McLean attend. The only war thought of, is the battle to provide services demanded by our increasing, changing and impatient population. Council approves sub-division into town lots of J. C. Wilson's property on RL 18 and 19, St. Charles; also RL 95, St. Charles; and RL 32-38, south of the Portage Road and west of Headingly, owned by Gordon Bell. Wm. McIntosh, constable, is provided with handcuffs and billy and is ordered to collect dog licenses; $12.00 rent is paid for Frank Ness' telephone; and Alex Murray's claim for $500.00 damages from deepening the Government ditch, dug about 1882 on RL 41 and 42, St. Charles, is ruled out. When home-owners protest that dairies take too much water from the King Street well, they are advised that any ratepayer is entitled to take all the water he wants from any public well. Complaints re manure, piled at Mr. Fielding's, are referred to the Health Officer.

On a cold January night, fire destroys Headingly School. Only 2 desks and a few books are saved. Ratepayers meet at Headingly to discuss a new school site. R. Taylor, chairman, H. Barrett, J. L. Francis, W. C. Hall and others, debate. After 7 hours, it is agreed to abandon the old site beside the church; and build a new 2-room in Headingly village.

Headingly and St. Charles Anglican congregations undertake to pay $900.00 yearly and use of the Headingly rectory to Rev. L. Smalwell, who takes charge of the Parish when Rev. A. E. Cowley resigns, after 26 years service. New names on the roll are: Chas. Clinch, Seward

McChesney, E. H. Gallagher, J. E. Francis. John F. Nicol, Chas. Stone.

Our "population explosion" dictates more, and better, schools. W. M. Bannatyne, of St. Charles, and W. S. Wrigley, of St. James, arbitrate the division of Britannia S. D. from the former St. James S.D.; and a $40,000.00 debenture is authorized for a fine new school. Bannatyne S.D. is organized from western St. James and the original Sturgeon Creek S.D., formed in 1876. Louden S.D. is set up in Tuxedo and eastern Charleswood; and citizens promptly demand better roads thereto. Pursuant to petitions from W. C. Hall and others, part of Headingly S.D. south of the Assiniboine becomes Phoenix S.D. Phoenix ratepayers meet in Headingly schoolhouse; and elect trustees: C. W. Johnstone, W. C. Hall, A. Lonsdale and D. Rodgers, chairman. Work begins, promptly, on constructing a new school on a full basement, with "modern" hot air heating. The cost — $3,895.00 for the building; $300.00 for site — is to be paid with a $4,200.00 debenture.

Citizens barrage authorities with demands to extend and improve street railway service; and to open, "brush", grade and drain new streets. In June, paving begins on the Portage Road to Kirkfield Park. The street railway, already, is double-tracked. However, most St. Charles Country Club members now ride out in shining motor cars, to play polo, golf or tennis; or to luxuriate in their new $100,000.00 Club house. There is talk of a street railway line to the Agricultural College; and double track to Headingly. "Signs of the times" are: 2 steel culverts replacing the old wooden bridge at Gowler's Creek; and, — on 9 July — the agenda of a Council meeting, for the first time . . . type-written!

One contractor builds 4,000 feet of plank sidewalk for 34½ cents a foot. Black & Francis, of Headingly, contract to build them at 33½ cents a foot! Sewers, wells, ditches are building all over Assiniboia.

The Winnipeg Automobile Club holds a race meet at Kirkfield Park. Ladies attend, attired in the flowing veils, long-peaked caps and voluminous coats proper for motoring. They watch, breathless, while Joe Baribeau lowers the 100-mile world speed record for motor cycles! The Park is loaned to the Auto Club for these races, by owner "Rod" McKenzie. The superb mile race-track has been specially built for the Manitoba Jockey Club — at a cost of above $100,000.00. "One of the best on the continent", it is the mecca for horse-racing all summer; and auto-racing in the autumn. Boat-racing will be added when the flow of Sturgeon Creek is empounded in a mile-long lake!

Whole streets of new homes are mushrooming in Ward 3, the eastern end of Assiniboia. Council buys identifying numbers for owners; and appoints George A. Hallet constable for the Ward. Lengthening lists of sub-divisions are approved at every meeting of Council. Most of the new

home-owners work in Winnipeg offices or factories. Manufacturing now
employs 17,000 workers, who turn out $54 millions, annually, from 267
factories. Local boosters proudly quote visiting Americans, who write
that this is the "most inviting field for settlers and capital to be found in
the world!" It may truly be!

The C.P.R. — double-tracked in 1907 from Winnipeg to the Lakehead — this year, is double-tracked to Portage la Prairie, Brandon and
Regina. In 10 years, grain freighted from "The Golden West" has
increased 340%, to 112,795,000 bushels; and livestock 50%, to
1,381,000 head. The average trainload has grown from 221 tons to
377 tons: full cargo for a train of 754 Red River carts!

Some of the new facilities cause trouble. The Berlin Street sewer
requires a gang of men to thaw the ice which forms at openings;
protect openings with piles of straw; and flush the sewer periodically. All
future sub-divisions must be OK'd by R. C. McPhillips, M.L.S.; and have
streets 60 feet wide; with cross-streets 50 feet wide, 1,600 feet apart.

Our Municipal Council approves sub-division of the former rifle range;
River Lots 26 and 83, St. James; and RL 89, St. Charles; and struggles
to deal with the flood of applications for chopping River Lots into home-
sites and petitions for roads, streets, sidewalks, wells and bridges. Part of
Ward 3 becomes Ward 5; and W. N. Fielding is elected Councillor
therefor.

E. D. Parker, appointed Provincial School inspector in April, has a
Division covering: Assiniboia, St. Francois Xavier, Rosser, Woodlands,
St. Laurent — and northward, to the limits of the Province. He records,
"Not a mile of graded road, except in Rosser. Even Portage Avenue . . .
not graded beyond the Western limits of . . . Winnipeg. A low dirt
trail . . . There was not a doctor or nurse in my whole territory." Councillors, big land owners, Auto Clubs and Golf Clubs of Assiniboia inter-
view Hon. Robt. Rogers — asking that the Provincial Government help
pave Portage Road, from Winnipeg to Headingly, on both sides of the
Assiniboine.

On 18 May, the earth passes thru the tail of Hailey's Comet; and,
"trailing clouds of glory," tycoon Wm. Mackenzie comes home from
London with $40 million — to invest in railway development. There is
intense interest in inland navigation and waterpower. L. Coste, of the
International Joint Waterways Commission, declares: "There will be a
canal right from Lake Superior to Edmonton." Hon. Wm. Pugsley,
Canada's Minister of Public Works, says: "We are considering a waterways system from Winnipeg to Edmonton; and beyond — 1,500 miles.
Along the route . . . 80 million horse-power will be developed to grind
grain and cut lumber."

On the streets and woodland paths of Assiniboia, boys are emulating marathon runners Longboat, Acoost, St. Yves, March and Durando. The equally famous Dr. E. DeForest is in Winnipeg: to install a "wireless" station; and to lecture on — radio! He puts up his apparatus in the Royal Alexandra Hotel; and (wonder of wonders!) talks to people in Eaton's store! Our "wireless" station, in operation by July, will link Chicago with Winnipeg.

Council resolves to pave 2½ miles on the Portage Road; and 1 mile on the south River Road. Reeve George T. Chapman and Councillor P. J. Wright go to Chicago to inspect pavement. Surveyors work to properly locate the Portage Road, from the eastern boundary of Assiniboia to Deer Lodge. This old Trail has been shifted, surveyed and located, repeatedly; and will continue to be, for years! Council awards the contract to build our new Municipal Hall to S. B. Ritchie, for $7,357.00.

Reeve Geo. T. Chapman and trustees Ness, Britton, Lafleche, Caron and Bannatyne are a Committee to organize a giant union picnic for all Assiniboia's school girls and boys on 30 June in Assiniboine Park. Prizes for races and games and 1300 street car tickets are provided. Mrs. A. Williams supplies "sandwiches, cake, tea, ice cream at $20. per 100." (Small hope of profit!)

Among many farm properties sub-divided; and sold for town lots is "Queen Mary Park". This "Park" embraces River Lots 106 and 107, St. Charles, from the Portage Road to Saskatchewan Avenue. It is traversed by Parkdale and Parkhill Streets. Advertisements claim "every lot high and dry!" Fifty-foot lots, 120 feet deep, are offered for $12.50 per foot frontage, at the southern end; and down to $5.50 per foot, northward — with payments of $50.00 to $15.00, cash; and $5.00 to $10.00 a month.

At Phoenix School, this year, 26 pupils average 77 days attendance. The teacher's salary is raised to $600.00. Alex Simpson claims $200.00 damage to his auto at Bruce Creek bridge. Homer Galbraith builds granolithic walks along Portage Road at $1.54 per square yard.

Wm. Mackenzie and Donald Mann, known over the West as "Bill and Dan", become "Sir William" and "Sir Donald". The tempo of expansion quickens. Western newspapers are crammed with ads: buy real estate on the prairies . . . Every gopher hole to be a metro! N. C. Powers, Winnipeg motor enthusiast, is the first airplane passenger to be carried in Canada. He lives to tell about it — although the pilot's name is "Coffyn".

In the area of which Assiniboia is a vital part, this year 71 new companies are chartered; with capital of $8,695,000.00. Cultivated Western acres have increased 400% in 10 years, to 23 million; 5,000 autos struggle bravely on Western trails. Plans for a Selkirk Centennial at "the Forks" collapse, when the Government of Canada refuses to grant $2.5 million. In a national election, the Laurier Government is wrecked, on Reciprocity! But — the census counts 7,206,643 Canadians! Manitoba has 455,614 of them, Saskatchewan and Alberta 867,095. Winnipeg (with Assiniboia and adjoining Municipalities) has grown from 42,340 in 1901, to 136,023 people in 1911.

Assiniboia's magnificent new Municipal Hall is built, and work begins on a fire hall and police station. Sewers, streets, roads, bridges and pavements are rushed, under Municipal Engineer Rogers. Portage Road and River Road, south of the Assiniboine, are declared to be of public importance; and come under the Good Roads Act of Manitoba. Revolver and ammo are issued to Constable Bain; and 2 iron jail cells are bought for $500.00. A by-law to raise $100,000.00 for additions to their big school recently built, is passed by Britannia School District ratepayers. Oakdean Road is "stumped" 36 feet wide, at a cost of $220.00.

Municipal Engineer Rogers hires an assistant: N. Stocker, at $110.00 a month; and an inspector, Mr. Linwood, at $3.00 per day, for concrete work on bridges and sidewalks. The Council Chamber is moved upstairs in the Municipal Hall. The entire downstairs is required for offices. On 10 June, all the pupils of all Assiniboia schools assemble for a great Union Picnic. The Fire Department buys 3 suits, at $19.50; 1 at $22.50; and 6 caps, $4.00 each.

In a brave attempt to solve our problem of waste disposal, the Health Officer gets coal oil; and hires men to burn dead animals at the Municipal Nuisance Grounds and spread loads of lime to disinfect the premises.

Rev. Armstrong, Dr. Houston and Mr. Smith attend Council, representing the St. James Athletic Association; and ask help to build a swimming pool in St. James. Assiniboia Councillors attend a meeting of the "Million for Manitoba League", on 17 July. The eastern end of the Municipality is filling up solidly. Council hires a temporary Fire Chief; buys 2 teams; appoints a temporary fire engineer; buys a bell for a temporary fire hall; also a davenport wagon and double harness. Our Ratepayers' Associations, in the cause of "modern" sanitation, urge Council to have pit closets built on every lot; and charged to owners.

John Delmer contracts to build the Fire Hall and Police Station for $25,622.00. The job of building the sewer on Ferry Road and Ness, for $196,335.00, is let to Guilbault & Company. Many Assiniboia men work on the construction of Winnipeg Hydro, at Pointe du Bois, on the Winnipeg River.

Manitoba — hitherto "the postage stamp Province" — has her boundaries extended northward to the 60th parallel, enclosing 250,000 square miles; and re-establishing the connection of fur-trade days between "the Forks" and "the Bay" sea-coast.

Development booms to a peak along the Assiniboine River and the Red — as across the entire West. A booklet is published extolling the "progress" of Assiniboia. It carries pictures of schools; Municipal Hall; Fire & Police Station; and churches. The Municipality embraces 92 square miles, on both banks of the Assiniboine. Street railway lines run on both sides of the River. Forty classrooms are packed with pupils in Britannia, Bannatyne, St. James, Sturgeon Creek, Headingly, Phoenix, Louden and St. Charles schools. Ten post offices handle mail. In 1907, 637 people lived here; now, more than 6,600. Their property assessment has multiplied from $2.5 million 5 years ago, to $15.2 million. The Portage Road (the Great Highway of pioneer days) is being paved in the eastern half of the Municipality; and will be gravelled, next year, right thru to our western boundary. Assiniboia is paying 80% of the entire cost — half by general levy; half by fronting properties!

Demands for highways sweep the land. The Good Roads League banquets Mr. Thos. W. Wilby, from England — who has driven his auto across Eastern Canada; and come on by rail. Met by H. Maxwell Clarke, stout advocate for a "Trans-Canada Highway", Mr. Wilby heads west, out the Portage Road, on 23 September; and clanks into Regina 4 days later! Thousands of Canadians hail the news of this historic run. More than 50,000 motor vehicles are now registered in Canada.

St. Charles Country Club-house is totally destroyed by fire; and, promptly, raised from its ashes. Claydon Brothers build the magnificent new club-house in record time. Alfred Good is foreman and timekeeper for the dozens of teams and teamsters. Scions of the Montague, Bawlf and other families, play polo on the spacious and beautiful grounds. Horses are stabled on the riverbank (near the later home of Mayor John Belows).

Phoenix School District hires Miss L. O'Neill, as teacher, at $600.00 yearly. On 5 August, Council passes 221 accounts. Seventeen Municipal employees draw $1,304.00 in monthly pay. The air of Assiniboia tingles with "progress"! "Boosters" who see eternal boom as the desirable norm, cannot believe that inter-nation friction threatens a world-economy based on borrowed money; and, already, is braking the inflow of British speculative capital.

In Assiniboia, countless streets are being opened and graded, like Marjorie, Albany and Ness. Miles of sidewalks are building, as on

Oakdean, Rutland, Inglewood, and Albany. Sewers are being installed, as on Silver Street and Thompson Drive. Another motion picture theatre is opened by H. H. Delmer. A great pioneer, C. G. Caron, former Reeve, passes to the "Happy Hunting Ground".

Trouble erupts in Assiniboia's Police Department. Chief Bain resigns. Constables are fired; then, rehired! The fracas drags out for months. Geo. Hill is made Chief; and the force is re-organized. The electors vote to gravel Portage Road; the Province to pay half the cost. Municipal wells are drilled on 30 streets. In December, street lighting is installed in Wards 5 and 3. Many citizens take part in the annual meetings of rate-payers.

Promoters incorporate Tuxedo, as a separate and exclusive residential town, out of part of Assiniboia. Council opposes the separation, until Tuxedo pays 75% of the local improvements under way. Our neighbors living south of the Assiniboine River decide to separate from Assiniboia and form the Rural Municipality of Charleswood.

Wm. Caplette plants trees on the Municipal Hall grounds. The first concrete culverts are used. One at Miry Creek costs $3,138.00. Sewers are laid on Deer Lodge and Bruce Streets. Hon. Alexander Murray, pioneer leader in Assiniboia, on 15 May "joins the majority".

War in the Balkans, climaxing friction and suspicion, halts the flow of British capital to the Canadian West; and ends the boom! Prices of farm products and farmlands, drop. Workers have been short for 10 years. Now, many are thrown out of employment. The Greater Winnipeg Water District starts building a $13.5 million aqueduct, with enough capacity to bring water the 94 miles from Shoal Lake to supply 850,000 people. In a Provincial election, that reeks of scandal and graft connected with building Manitoba's magnificent capitol — the Roblin Government is wrecked! Hon. T. C. Morris succeeds Sir Rodmond Roblin as Premier. An investigating Commission in 2 years of litigation uncovers unbelievable dishonesty in high places. Some of the guilty are imprisoned. Recovery from the financial scare is gaining momentum. Assiniboia invests $2,252.50 in a chemical fire engine and 1000 feet of hose. A $5,021.00 contract is let for granolithic sidewalk on Portage Road. A $375.00 10-ton scale is installed at the Fire Hall; and 3 coonskin coats, at $65.00 each, and 5 lamb caps, at $14.75 each, are purchased for our Police Force. Timothy hay for the Fire Department teams is delivered at $15.50 per ton. Fifty lights are hung to illuminate the Portage Road, from St. James Street to Headingly.

After hearing many salesmen for many Companies, and studying 8 tenders, Council lets the contract to pave Portage Road from RL 113, St. Charles, to the western limit of the Municipality to the Bithuilitic

Company — for $246,258.20. Other bidders kick; and claim their bids are lower! Hon. W. H. Montague, Manitoba's Minister of Public Works, states: the Provincial Government will pay 20% of this cost. Within a month, in the face of the row about tendered bids, the contract for paving Portage Road is rescinded; and new tenders called.

Needy families are given assistance, which is charged to the respective Wards — to be repaid when the recipient is able. Municipal Health Officer Dr. Knipe reports 4 cases of smallpox; and orders general vaccination. In April, a compaign is organized for collection of tins, bottles and rubbish; and disposal in a 40-foot trench, dug in the Nuisance Ground. A contract for scavenging Wards 3, 4 and 5, for $6,992.00, is awarded to M. McMahon. Mr. Sam Budd drills Municipal wells in Wards 4, 5 and 6; and P. McCallum in Wards 1, 2 and 3. Francis & Francis build sidewalks in all Wards. Council passes 6 bylaws calling for expenditure of $49,664.00 in local improvements — 25% of it for laying water pipes. Building booms, particularly in St. James. Land prices soar! S. Mulderoon, is assessed $500.00 per acre for part of River Lots 43 and 44, Headingly; and Plan 1904, embracing 136 acres, is assessed at $1,200.00 per acre!

In May, noxious weeds inspectors, after attending lessons at our Agricultural College, sally forth to fight the good fight against the farmers' eternal foe; and draw $3.00 daily for their efforts. Council votes Nurse Sykes $160.00 for 32 days attendance on smallpox patients at St. Charles Convent.

On 19 May, a new contract is let to pave the Portage Road. It requires that resident workers shall be paid a minimum of 22 cents per hour; and local farmers' teams, 50 cents hourly. The old wooden bridge at Brown's Creek is replaced with a big new steel culvert. Our Council grants the Headingly Agricultural Society $240.00 for its Fall Fair. Ratepayers of St. James S.D. vote to invest $50,000.00 in expansion. A license for a laundry is granted to Sam Wah, *if* the Health Officer OK's his premises. A new worry plagues Council, in successive petitions for widening streets. (Thru Assiniboia's long history, plans are seldom big enough to meet developing needs!) Irate home-owners on Rita, Olive, Vernon and Whytewold Streets demand protection from flooding! The Municipal Commissioner's levy rises to an unheard-of $10,574.19. Petitions pour in to our Municipal Hall for wells, water mains, sewers, sidewalks and new streets.

More than 200,000 of Sifton's "men in sheepskin coats" have come West. Population in Alberta, Saskatchewan and Manitoba has quadrupled since 1900, to total 1,968,000. More than 200,000 people live around "the Forks". Promoters sub-divide; build street railway, water and sewer lines; and map streets, on big acreages held since 1879. Railway construction stampedes over our West. Mackenzie & Mann, since 1896, have stretched 130 miles of track into the "Canadian Northern": a transcontinental system with 10,000 miles of railway serving 7 Provinces; plus hotels, express, telegraph, mines and steamships. The C.P.R., with 18,000 miles of main and branch lines, has 9,000 employees and assets totalling $800 millions. Western farmers survey 10.3 million acres of wheat with swelling optimism!

New housing packs the streets between the Assiniboine River and the C.P.R. — westward, into Assiniboia. Sub-divisions "leap-frog" westward; and become high-priced "city property". Many of these homes are more modest than those on the streets of the wealthy; but more truly "homes" than the crawling slums on Henry, Higgins and adjacent streets.

August brings uneasiness (as on days of shimmering heat the proud optimism of a farmer with a section of Marquis is chilled with fear of hail!) Newspapers headline wild speculation as dire probabilities. Then— their editions of 4 August spread 3 blood-red letters across front pages: W A R!

The Commanding Officer of a local militia regiment parades his unit this evening, to announce that "Canada is at war". Within 2 days the people of Assiniboia see that unit in camp, at St. Charles rifle ranges. By 18 August, in this Military District, 5,500 men volunteer. On 24 August, units entrain for grim training at Valcartier. It is still beyond belief! But, the world's financiers act with incisive swiftness, to shut off credit.

The boom freezes in mid-air! Building halts. Two trans-continental railroads look for traffic, from feeder branch lines not yet built. The flow of settlers is throttled. Men who might have come to Canada next month — are "called up" to enemy armies that we must fight.

Assiniboia's Council notifies the National Paving Company that, on account of war, paving must be suspended. "All works of every nature" are ordered stopped — except the water and sewer mains in the Deer Lodge sub-divisions; and on Albany, Winchester and Bruce Streets. These will be completed with materials already on site. All Provincial grants are ended.

In a surge of patriotic fervor, our Council resolves: "Families left behind by ratepayers . . . at . . . war . . . provided for . . . until the Dominion Government makes arrangements for their support; and that all employees of the Municipality who have volunteered . . . be paid half their regular salary while they are in the service; and their positions be . . open for them". The Reeve calls meetings to organize Home Guard units in each Ward. Council votes $1,500.00 for "relief" in the Municipality. Street cars are ordered to stop only at specified streets.

The first meeting of Assiniboia's Council in 1915 brings together: Reeve D. C. McColl; and Councillors John Taylor, Jr. Ward 1; J. A. Isbister, 2; Ed Dumsday, 3; W. J. Bartlett, 4; A. S. Peldrum, 5; and John Bunting, 6. Frank Ness is clerk; and W. J. Watts, treasurer. Already, families in the Municipality need help. The Provincial Government may advance money for "relief" on the security of Municipal debentures. Public works are halted; but Neil Dow is to dig Municipal wells at $1.50 per foot.

The annual meeting of Holy Trinity, Headingly, brings together not only local folk; but, also, members from other communities, including: Rev. Swalwell, chairman; and Mrs. A. Murray, Charleswood; Mrs. McBette, St. Francois Xavier; Mrs. E. Bewell, Stonewall; Mrs. Flora Cook, Sturgeon Creek; and Wm. Parker, Sanford.

The "St. James Leader" of 12 March, 1915, published by brothers Lewis and Luther Murphy, is an 8-page weekly (including "patent insides"). Its advertisements tell us that the current feature at King's Theatre is "the Million Dollar Mystery"; Keeton autos may be purchased for $1,375 to $1,425; and Keswick's Cash Store has back bacon, at 15c per lb; peas and beans, 3 cans for 25c. From the news columns we learn that auto licenses are up, $5.00 to $10.00 plus $1.00 for plates; F. J. Dixon, MPP for Centre Winnipeg, will speak on "single tax" to Ward 4 Ratepayers Association; a Patriotic Concert is to be held in Britannia School; Assiniboia's Council sells $413,000 in debentures at 89.03; and Edwin Bourke, 79, of Rutland Street, married 52 years, is buried in St. James Cemetery.

In April the St. James Football Club gives a grand concert and dance in Britannia School. Churches in the Municipality, at this time, include: Holy Trinity Anglican, Rev. Swalwell, rector, and the Presbyterian Church, at Headingly; the Roman Catholic Church, St. Charles: curé, Fr. Joseph Therien; St. James Anglican, Roseberry St., Rev., W. G. Nicholson, rector; the Christian Church, Marjorie St.; the Gospel Hall, Ferry Road; St. James Presbyterian, Hampton St., Rev. E. M. McDay, minister; Olivet Baptist, Parkview St., Rev. J. A. Hodgkinson, pastor; King Edward Methodist, Rev. R. G. Pritchard, pastor; the Church of Jesus Christ, 241 Kensington St., Ottis D'Arcy, minister; and the Salvation Army, Capt. and Mrs. Ainslie, leaders.

Reflecting our genteel "suburbia", a Garden Association is formed, in April, in Wards 3, 4 and 5, with Mr. Harry E. England, President. To emphasize our "progress", local pay phones are installed. Then, lest we forget our pioneer roots, coyotes raid chicken roosts; and 1 poultry fancier, on Whytewold Road, loses 57 of his 60 prize birds.

All commonplace trivia are submerged in the terrible news of Ypres — where Canadian men, so lately turned soldier, hold the Allied line against billowing clouds of gaseous death! To Assiniboia, as to communities across our Canadian nation, the wounded begin to come home. Patriotic fervor prompts organization of a Belgium Relief Fund and the Manitoba Patriotic Fund.

The routine of life flows on. A special meeting of Assiniboia's Council, held in the Fire Hall on 5 May, accepts the offer of J. A. Thompson to help finance the Municipality by buying 7-year sidewalk debentures, up to $20,000.00. On 10 May, Councillors discuss garbage disposal with contractor Mr. Ginger Snooks. Problems of new sub-divisions and changing street names demand attention. In June, Council resolves that the jitneys, which are proving so popular, shall each contribute a $5.00 license fee to the Municipal coffers.

Athletic organizations give outlet to the boisterous strength of youth. Contests, sometimes, feature more vigor than finesse. At Melrose Park a near-riot breaks out, when the St. James baseball team loses to the Falcons. Equally exciting are the Manitoba elections, on 6 August. Sir James Aikens, drafted to lend something of the odor of sanctity to a forlorn cause, is smothered with his Conservative followers, by a wave of popular disapproval of recent scandals. Hon. T. C. Norris and the Liberals are returned with an overwhelming majority. John W. Wilton wins a 3-cornered contest, to become Assiniboia's MLA.

Record crowds attend Headingly Fair, in September. Prizes totalling $1,028.00 bring an outstanding exhibit of horses. Alex Gunn, with Mrs. Gunn and daughter Alice, capture many of the prizes. With rising affluence, more and more of the motor vehicles which are to displace the horse, are crowding our streets. On the Portage Road, a speeding auto hits one of our policemen, breaking both his legs. These "gas buggies" are dangerous!

Across our Canadian West, farmers harvest a record crop. Granaries and elevators are bursting with 145 million bushels of Marquis — the finest wheat ever grown. Grain production totals 682 million bushels. The Western maxim is born: "the best crop ever harvested is 1915 — and next year!"

This bumper harvest rockets morale; revives optimism; and generates tremendous activity across our Canadian nation. Assiniboia lets contracts to pave and lay water mains on 10 miles of the Portage Road. Construction is hurried. Dazzled by our greatest crop, few listen to warnings about the tremendous cost. After all, the Province will pay 20%; and the 80% borne by Assiniboia will be carried, half by general taxation; and half by the properties fronting on our Great Highway. In 1915, this worries few; but — in the years that bring rust and drought and crop failure, many families lose the lands they pioneered! Assiniboia is loaded with debt which over-taxes our people for an entire generation.

The Government of Canada takes over the Canadian Northern Railway. None of the promoters has risked a nickel of his own. The *Railway* is bankrupt — not "Sirs" Bill and Dan and Herbert Holt. With swift decision, the Government takes over the Grand Trunk Pacific, also. These rail lines are built into the fabric of a mighty transport system owned by the Canadian people. Thousands of miles of branch lines are constructed. At 10-mile intervals, elevators rise; and towns appear. Wheat, in war-time recognized as a vital commodity, rises in price; and carries farmland prices upward. Orders for war supplies spin the wheels of industry. Everyone is working! The excitement of challenge and achievement is in the air. Population packs eastern Assiniboia — while people in the "West end" still live in pastoral spaciousness. Some 8,568 voters are listed in the Municipality. Ward 5 is home to 3,475 of them — while 171 live in Ward 1.

The Municipality lets contracts for sewers on 10 streets; and requests the Strathcona Estate to donate, or sell, a site for a Municipal Hospital. A carload of tamarac is bought for heating Municipal buildings, at $5.50 per cord. The Municipal staff now comprises 15 clerical; 9 police; and 9 firemen. The Returned Soldiers Manitoba Commission calls a meeting to discuss re-education and employment of Service men, as they come home.

Reeve McColl invites Councillors and Municipal officials to a banquet at "Chad's". During the festivities, the Reeve pulls a fire alarm; and 3 teams, with fire fighting equipment, respond within 4 minutes! In the "Leader" of 21 January, the Karnac Theatre "most emphatically denies" that admission will be raised to 15 cents; "present policy — adults 10 cents, children 5 cents, will *always* be maintained!"

By early February, Reeve McColl announces, 1,300 Assiniboia men have enlisted in Canada's armed services. Council borrows $150,000.00 from the Bank, in February; and votes $100.00 to the Returned Soldiers Association.

The resolution passed in an ecstasy of patriotism, in August, 1914, that the positions of Municipal men who enlist be kept open for them, is rescinded by our Council. The new ruling is that "any Municipal employee who enlists for active service be paid 2 weeks extra wages". A donation of $250.00 goes to the band of the 222nd Battalion. Assiniboia's vital statistics for the last 4 months of 1915 list 182 births, 35 deaths and 37 marriages.

Tragedy stalks Assiniboia — when, on 4 April, Leonard Hallet is jailed for some offense; and hangs himself in his cell! The terrible reality of war is stressed starkly in lengthening casualty lists in local dailies. Deer Lodge Hotel and its 10-acre site are exempted from taxes — when "owner R. J. Mackenzie has loaned it to the Government . . . for returned soldiers". This historic "stopping place" is taken over by the Military Hospital Commission; and, in June, is opened as a soldiers hospital by Princess Patricia and Canada's Governor-General.

After a heated campaign on the issue of "prohibition", in which editorials and advertisements in the "Leader" urge Assiniboia citizens to "vote dry", the Temperance Act is made effective over all Manitoba. Empounded local run-off causes floods that wash out culverts, roads and bridges north of the Portage Road. Municipal Engineer Rogers surveys; and reports. But — no adequate program of water management is put into action; and such local flooding plagues the Municipality throughout its history.

Our newspapers are packed with notices and news of patriotic dances, concerts, socials, whist drives, IOOF, Church Ladies Aids, IODE and Returned Soldiers Association activities. Increasing population emphasizes the need for improved sanitation. Council orders that "garbage must be removed. . . every 2 weeks from homes; and every week from stores." The Patriotic Association reports on 20 July, that it has paid out, monthly, in St. James: $8,400.00. Council pays $200.00 monthly, to the Patriotic Fund; and $50.00 to the Red Cross. In July, also, $400.00 is granted to the Headingly Agricultural Society.

Automobile traffic is no longer a nuisance; it has become a danger. Council orders, for Portage Avenue, 5 signs: "Speed Limit 20 miles"; and 8: "Danger". A grant of $300.00 goes to the Returned Soldiers Association, in September. Some families, whose wage-earner is overseas, are in need. To one such mother, and her 2 children, Council votes $47.00 per month; and forgives a hospital bill of $189.00.

Trouble in the Police force (again!) verges on mutiny! The Municipality discharges all members of the force; and advertises for 9 policemen. A special meeting on 25 October, considers the sworn evidence of former officers. Finally, all are re-appointed. On this same day, in the frightful "fog of battle", a Manitoba Battalion, many of its men from Assiniboia, is decimated at Regina Trench!

With attention rivetted on the battle-line in France, big events happen at home. "Votes for women" agitation leads to the Women's Suffrage

Bill. In Assiniboia, as in the rest of Manitoba, bi-lingual schools are abolished; and the School Attendance Act makes compulsory schooling a fact. Each of these issues generates discussion, debate and (sometimes) bitterness. Out-weighing such over-advertised political issues, another event is unnoticed, except by those who suffer directly from its impact, which has tragic significance for all the multiplying numbers of mankind. The grain crop of our Canadian West is hit by rust! The magnificent Marquis wheat proves susceptible to destruction by migrant spores. The immediate loss to Western farm families is monetized at $243 millions. The loss to mankind is beyond estimate!

Life in Assiniboia, as in all Canadian communities, in ways beyond comprehension, is dominated by far-distant events of war, for whose meaning even those who suffer most can only grope. The Returned Soldiers Association ask that an Honor Roll be inscribed with the names of all enlisted persons from Assiniboia. In the fighting zone, the riddled remnants of Canadian units are wallowing out of the Somme, leaving thousands of their best, buried in its mud. Assiniboia's Council includes $1,000 in the 1917 estimates "for erection of a memorial to the men of the Municipality who give their lives". Next item of business? The Winnipeg Electric Company writes: "cannot supply lighting" to some homes "because of financial conditions".

The Municipal Engineer is worried about localized flooding in St. James; and trouble with wells and pumps. Kindly, earnest men and women wrestle with problems of administering money wisely, to help sufferers who face problems beyond solution. Determined efforts to *do something*, do assist many. The Mother's Allowance Committee of Assiniboia grants $58.47, $38.00, $60.00, to help 3 needy families. So little, compared with the vast sums invested in inflicting misery; yet, so much to needy victims.

Home-owners complain angrily, that the scavenger cleans pits during the day; and spills sewage on the streets! Ratepayers' meetings are called in Headingly Agricultural Hall, St. Charles Church Hall and Linwood, Bannatyne and Britannia schools and Murray Park post office, to discuss Municipal affairs. The day after Christmas, Assiniboia is blanketed with handbills, calling a special meeting in Linwood school — to discuss "National Service".

In January, Assiniboia's police are ordered to collect license fees "from every man driving a team in the Municipality". Seven citizens are paid $16.00 in bounties, for 8 wolves killed. Our fire department floods corner public rinks, free. We now use an average of 26 gallons of water per capita per day. Council grants the St. James Garden Club $150.00 for its fair; and pays W. M. Bannatyne $500.00 yearly, being half his salary as Police Magistrate. Miss Edna Brown, winner of a province-wide spelling contest, is tendered a banquet. To produce more food, the Municipality plows vacant lots, for gardening by responsible citizens. Councillor Bunting reports, in April, that "3 houses of ill-fame" in the Municipality have been vacated. An expert is hired to drill Assiniboia policemen in using motor cycles, to cope with speeding autoists. A Court of Revision, on 26 April, hears 312 protests that property is "assessed too high".

The capture of Vimy Ridge by the Canadian Corps, in April, is headlined in all news media. A feeling of new confidence is generated throughout the Canadian nation. To the half-million Canadians overseas, this action "confirmed, asserted and established Canadian nationality!" Pioneer qualities — with training, experience; and, now, victory — translate the Canadian units from "miscellaneous colonials" into the "Corps d'elite" — the spear-head of victory!

In Assiniboia, April sees the St. James and Britannia School Districts merge in the Consolidated School District of St. James. May sees Francis & Francis, in Headingly, install one of those gas pump contraptions in front of their store. They are responsible for any damage resulting therefrom! Some ratepayers are writing to the "Leader" about "division" of the Municipality. The news columns are heavy with casualty lists. The public response is to buy War Savings Certificates; and embue everything — sewing circles, the Assiniboia Baseball League, everything — with "patriotic" intent. Public meetings discuss "conscription". On 11 June — in a national decision of world significance — the Board of Grain Supervisors takes over all Canada's wheat. "Trading" in grain stops. The Board pays for wheat, to the producer, $2.40 per bushel for the balance of the 1916 crop; and $2.21 for the on-coming 1917 crop.

Rev. Marshall succeeds Rev. Swalwell at Headingly Holy Trinity Church. From Shorncliffe, Pte. G. B. Porteous writes, imploring Council not to sell his home at 362 Woodlawn for taxes, while he is at the front. Deer Lodge becomes a convalescent home for officers. Other ranks are quartered at Tuxedo. Under difficulties, some public improvements are carried out in Assiniboia. August sees by-laws to build sidewalks on 10 streets; wells, on 6; and sewer and water on 30. Headingly Fair, in September, features the band of the 251st Battalion. By October, the Municipality has contributed to the Provincial Government for Patriotic purposes: $47,000.00. The Chief of Police is charged with being intoxicated; and his pay is docked. Mrs. Jane Fogg, of 301 Rutland, suffers a sidewalk accident; and collects $100. damages. The 72 stores and shops in St. James are divided on the issue of early closing.

The former Olivet Baptist Church, in October, becomes the new Methodist church, in St. James. In November, more than 200 veterans come home. The "Leader" carries a banner streaming across a double page of its "patent insides": "Chew Pay Roll Tobacco". In the elections for our 1918 Municipal Council, C. L. Richardson is returned as Reeve, with a record majority. Councillors are: Wm. Buchanan; John A. Isbister; John L. McBride; Wm. H. Champion; Thos. B. Wooler; and John Bunting. A branch of the new Great War Veterans Association is organized in Assiniboia, with W. H. Foster, President.

Our Municipality borrows $200,000.00, to start the year; and doubles licenses for dogs and "jitneys". Then, our Council grants St. James Garden Club $150.00; agrees that veterans shall get preference in employment; and, among many accounts, pays J. A. Isbister $12.00 bounty for killing 12 wolves.

St. James Presbyterian church annual meeting, Rev. Mackay presiding, reports 170 members in the congregation; and 150 names on the Honor Roll, 16 of them killed in action. The Management Board includes J. Sheane, R. Love, J. Reid, J. Jaffery, J. Malcolm, Mr. McEachern, G. A. Graham and P. Rutherford. Pte. James Cooper, in France, remits $52.28 to redeem his home from tax sale. His payment is $2.00 short!

Citizens, meeting in Headingly, urge building a new bridge; and Assiniboia and Charleswood Councils discuss the matter. Miss Rose Hollins, of Sturgeon Creek, winner of a Provincial spelling competition, is presented with a gold medal and watch at St. James School, together with a scholarship for $225.00. As winter ends, Municipal teams prepare to plow lots for "war-time" gardens. Final warnings urge citizens to file income tax returns before 31 March!

Among the 18 members who attend the annual meeting of Holy Trinity, at Headingly, the following names appear for the first time: Mrs. Puddifant, J. McKay and Misses Flossie, Jessie, Fanny, Blanche, Margaret and Doris Taylor. The Rector's salary is increased to $1,200.00 annually. The "Leader" announces a Next-of-Kin organization; and reports a silver medal awarded Pte. J. Wright, 460203, 44th Battalion.

The recently-formed G.W.V.A. branch opens club-rooms at 1840 Portage Avenue. St. James Mission parishioners, at their annual meeting, receive reports that the congregation is debt-free; and has a reserve to move the church building. Rector's Warden is A. Rigby-Jones; people's Warden: W. Hatchinson; and Vestrymen: Messrs. Shelmerdine, Richards, Pildrum, Gordy, Jordon, Goodwin, Champion, Bishop, Coutcha, Garrard, Haines and Williams.

Citizens meet in the Police Station, on 5 April, to organize a campaign to raise $600,000.00 for Red Cross. District Captain, Charles Ezart, has lieutenants for each street. The "Leader" publishes a letter to Mr. and Mrs. Joshua Land, from their son who, recently wounded, is back at the front. A second son is prisoner-of-war in Germany. A third lies in a French hospital, wounded. In May, Municipal salaries are increased "as a war measure": clerks, $5; and firemen, $10 per month.

The intensity of feeling generated by war changes the name of "Frankfort Street" to "Vimy Road". From this street 5 Poole brothers and members of the Glen and other families, join Canada's fighting forces. Nevertheless, the father of a prisoner-of-war is notified that his son's property cannot be kept from tax sale; but must go under the hammer, with the property of other delinquents!

The fact that "it is impossible for the Municipality to sell debentures at present" compounds the difficulties of financing Assiniboia's business. Council manages grants of $300 to the Headingly Agricultural Society, to assist in staging their annual Fall Fair; $150 to the Assiniboia Poultry Association, for a yearly Show; and $500 toward building the new G.W.V.A. headquarters at King Edward Street. Assiniboia's assessment is equalized at $10.4 million — far below the $15.2 million of 1912. Citizens demand that all hog-pens be moved out of Wards 4 and 5. Four teams have re-organized the Assiniboia Baseball League. Citizens are urged to help the Red Cross — by seeing the Dog Show!

Reeve Richardson warns home-owners to buy their winter fuel early. To buy coal, the home-owner fills out a card; and presents it to the Fuel Commissioner for Assiniboia, G. W. Rogers, at the Fire Hall, Berry Street. Newspapers carry Canada Food Board orders; also Department of Justice advertisements, warning that every male must carry documents. With some protests about "a police state", people accustomed to democratic freedoms accept such strictures as dictated by the necessities of war.

On Sunday, 9 June, the St. James Anglican church, on Tylehurst Street, celebrates its 65th anniversary. The first log church raised on this site cost $1,650 in money; and many times that, in contributed cooperation. Five rectors, in succession, have served this pioneer congregation: Rev. W. H. Taylor, Rev. C. Pinkham, Canon Cowley, Rev. G. I. Armstrong and Rev. W. G. Nicholson. The St. James Methodist congregation stage a mammoth picnic, in June; with young and old riding the street cars to Selkirk Park.

In July, Earl Edrowsie, aged 9, and Miss E. S. Janes are drowned, swimming in Sturgeon Creek. The Western plains suffer their second year of drought — bringing "black blizzards" and large-scale soil drifting! At Phoenix School, the trustees apply to the Municipality for coal for next winter. Miss Margaret Taylor, the teacher, has 27 pupils, from 5 to 14 years old, enrolled in 8 grades; with an average of 19 attending. In August, the local weekly carries news of Pte. John Land, prisoner-of-war for 2 years, escaping from a German "stalag". There are notes, too, of lawn socials, Janey Canuck Clubs, festivals, baby shows, Ladies Aids — all "patriotic"! Grocery advertisements list: 4-lb can of jam 90 cents: 1-lb Red Rose tea 55 cents: tomatoes, large tin, 21 cents: 3 lbs apples 25 cents: 5-lb corn syrup 55 cents: 2 tins soup 27 cents: 5 bars Royal Crown soap 25 cents — all delivered. The St. James Garden Club holds its September show at Linwood school. The Club President is Reeve C. L. Richardson; Vice-President, A. W. Wiseman; and Secretary, J. E. MacKenzie.

Although the motor vehicle is beginning to crowd the horse off our trails, Headingly Fall Fair features keen competition in a big exhibit of horses. Winners include: heavy draft stallion, J. E. McLean and Robt. Bell; mare and foal, R. H. Brice, St. Charles; farm horses, J. B. Taylor, John Taylor, Sr. and R. R. McKerracher, Stonewall. Light horses: stallions, S. T. Smith, D. J. McDonald, both of Headingly. Lady rider and driver, Mrs. Florence Hamilton; single driver, Thos. Billington. An outbreak of measles closes Headingly school in September. St. James Consolidated School District #7, now with 4 schools, reports expenditures for the year of $92,980.00; and assets: $254,956.00.

In October "flu" strikes with vicious suddenness! All public assemblies are banned! On 11 November, Armistice! The War is over — between men: but the war against the "flu" is only begun. On this same day, citizens meet to organize for the battle. An emergency hospital and nurses station is opened, in the old St. James School. One hundred and twenty-five cases of "flu" — with 5 deaths — are reported, as at 8 November. The numbers multiply! Nevertheless, the campaign goes on to sell Assiniboia's quota of $124,000.00 in Victory Loans. Within a week, $140,000.00 is subscribed.

Mr. Wilfred Sadler, beloved school principal, takes charge of emergency and volunteer headquarters. Dr. Knipe calls for women, to prepare food and do housework; and for boys to chop wood, carry water and do the manifold chores necessary to keep stricken homes operating. Under Miss B. M. Lang, Public Health nurse, 9 nurses work, day and night. In an average week (13 to 20 November) 176 visits are made to "flu" patients. Bardal's ambulance and Fire Department teams take cases to hospitals. All ambulances are on 24-hour service in other communities. It is the end of November, before the long battle eases; and the ban on church meetings is lifted. On 6 December, citizens go to the polls; and elect Assiniboia's Council for 1919: Reeve: C. L. Richardson; and

Councillors: Peter Brown, John L. McBride, W. H. Champion, Thos. B. Wooler and John Bunting.

Rather wearily, folks get back on the trail of routine living. The final meeting of the 1918 Council, on 17 December, has no minutes to read. "Flu" has so reduced the Municipal clerical staff that none are prepared.

During 1918, under the impetus of "$2.00 wheat", the Hudson's Bay Company sells 400,000 acres of the lands got when the Nor'West was yielded to Canada — at above $15 per acre. Long since, all agree that canny Donald Smith was right: the real wealth is "land"! "The Company" harvest far more profit from the lands they claimed, than ever from furs and trade. Land is the basis of an abundantly expanding economy which the fur-trade, so mistakenly, strove to throttle. The old fallacy that farm use of lands and waters must wipe out fur, always was false!

Municipal salaries are increased. A bank loan of $250,000.00 is negotiated. Assiniboia, like most public bodies, finances on borrowed money — thereby doubling costs to citizens; but, of course, adding to bank profits.

On a crisp January Sunday morning, church bells announce, not religious services, but the burning of St. James Methodist church. The congregation, led by Rev. T. G. Bethell, last year purchased this magnificent edifice from the Baptists. Fire fighting is hampered. Many firemen are a-bed with "flu". This virulent virus attacks again. Schools are closed. Once more, Linwood school is fitted up as a nursing centre.

"Improvements" planned include sewer and water on 14 streets. Tax penalties against veteran's homes are remitted. Assiniboia's Council buys medallions (at $15 each) for school teachers who serve during the "flu" epidemic. The Government of Canada announces a National Housing Plan, whereunder funds will be loaned to Provinces — to be retailed to Municipalities and builders. Assiniboia asks for $1.5 million in loans. Many homes are built. Perhaps too many! Streets of houses rise in Ashcroft Point, re-named "Woodhaven"; and in St. Charles.

Municipal finances improve. Since the surplus will meet 1919 general expenditures, no general rate is levied this year. On 7 May, a letter tabulating wage demands is laid before Council by the "Assiniboia Municipal Employees Federal Union, Local 33". Council resolves that salaries shall be increased. On 17 May, Assiniboia citizens vote (232 to 39) for the Housing Bylaw, which makes loans available up to 70% of the value of land and building. On this same day, Reeve Richardson reports to an incredulous Council that our Municipal employees have struck!

Ten days later, Council records its resolution that "whereas Municipal employees on 15 May . . . struck in sympathy . . . broke contracts . . . endanger property and life . . . no union of fire, police or waterworks employees subject to commands other than Council" can be tolerated! Work stops! Families store water in pails, barrels, bath-tubs. Wild rumors circulate. Men roam the streets, hoe their gardens, play baseball on corner lots. Some hitch-hike or walk, to see what is happening "down town". Reeve Richardson reports, in June, that 2 policemen are on the job in Assiniboia. Bread and milk are delivered "by Permission of the Central Strike Committee". Skeleton staffs and volunteers maintain essential services. As always, people prove amazingly resourceful, resilient and downright neighborly. Being separated, by distance and outlook, from the core of conflict, the people of Assiniboia are less influenced by the terrific heat and frictions generated thereat. By early July, many Municipal employees are back on their jobs.

The machinery of life grinds ahead. The Municipal Commissioner demands that the Municipality pay his $38,775.00 levy. Lady Strathcona declines (again!) to provide the requested site for a War Memorial Hospital, even at $1,200.00 per acre. On 5 July, T. L. Roberts, E. S. Pildren and W. M. Bannatyne, chairman, are appointed a Board to pass on Housing Loans, along with Municipal Engineer Rogers. Additional loans are offered for plumbing. The Municipal Engineer hires more staff to process such loans. By mid-July, 48 applications go to the Provincial Government, under the new Soldiers Taxation Relief Act; 8 Housing loans, up to $4,500.00 each, have been OK'd; and V. C. Maddock asks loans to build 18 houses in St. Charles.

There is wide interest and an insistent demand for some fitting Memorial to the men from Assiniboia who gave their lives in the War. Council, on 22 July, resolves that a Park shall be built, with space for a General Hospital, playgrounds, sports and picnics. Also approved are: arc lights on 21 streets; 11 Housing loans; 19 plumbing loans; and 27 applications under the Soldiers Taxation Relief Act. A monster "Next-of-kin" picnic is staged by St. James Anglicans and the Assiniboia G.W.V.A. on the Bourke property, along our beautiful Assiniboine.

Differences between urban and farm people widen, following the War. The folks who live in northeast Assiniboia, separate from the Municipality; and form the Village of Brooklands. The Western end of Assiniboia witnesses a spectacular fire, when the Headingly boarding house — formerly the "Royal Exchange Hotel" — goes up in flames, in 40 minutes! The Municipal fire brigade rushes to the catastrophe; but, without water, is powerless! The building, owned by Hon. John Taylor, has been a landmark of Assiniboia history since 1887.

Farm families — who still occupy the great part of Assiniboia; and earn their bread in the sweat of farming — hail the announcement on 31 July, that the Canadian Wheat Board is, now, the sole marketing agency for grain. The Board makes an initial payment, on wheat, of $2.15; and total payments of $2.63 per bushel. Above 19 million Western acres now grow wheat, more than double the pre-war acreage.

With a $300.00 Municipal grant, the Headingly Agricultural Society holds its big Fall Fair, in August. At every meeting, Assiniboia's Council reviews applications for Housing loans, Plumbing loans and Soldiers Taxation Relief, recommended by the various Boards; and forwards these to the Provincial Government for action. For example, on 3 September, 35 such applications are processed; and, 2 weeks later, another 41. The Municipal clerk writes to the Provincial Treasurer, asking for the balance of $500,000.00 for Housing loans this year; and advising that, in 1920, $1.5 million will be required!

At a concert in Linwood school, on 9 October, medals are presented to 37 nurses and teachers, in recognition of devoted public service during the "flu" epidemic. Dudley Ward demands electrical lighting for homes in the "Soldiers' Settlement" on River Lot 61. Our Police Chief reports 52 hens stolen from roosts in Headingly! Turning from this item, Council buys a motor fire engine for $8,500.00; passes 25 bylaws for installing sewer and water mains; and wrestles with claims for accidents on aging plank sidewalks.

November — and "freeze-up" — bring the annual crop of demands for rinks. The St. James Athletic Association, Kirkfield Park Athletic Association, Sturgeon Creek Tecumseh Club, and many others, clamor for club and community skating, hockey and curling facilities. By December, a Municipal rink at Lyle and Portage is humming with all these winter activities. Future stars buy hockey sticks at 35 cents each; the very best for 60 cents! A joint meeting of Assiniboia's G.W.V.A., Council and clergy resolves to build a Soldiers' Memorial Hall! Council records 262 applications OK'd for Soldiers Taxation Relief; and approves a by-law for Phoenix School District to raise $5,000 to enlarge their school.

A petition, calling for the separation of St. James from Assiniboia is presented to Council by H. Lee, on 19 November; is debated at successive meetings; and, finally, on 12 December, is accepted by Council, for presentation to the Government of Manitoba.

CHAPTER 14

Pere
Joseph Provencher

St. James Leaves Home 1920-29

A new bridge, built at Headingly over the Assiniboine, may symbolize great changes in Assiniboia's history. Our 1920 Municipal Councillors are: Wm. Buchanan, Peter Brown, Thos. Stockdale, W. H. Champion, Jos. A. Buchanan, George A. Graham, and John Bunting; with Chas. L. Richardson, Reeve. Municipal employees now number 32. Secretary-Treasurer Frank Ness is paid $275.00, and Chief Clerk, Chas. Dalton, $150.00, per month. Nine Municipal phones are in use. One Council meeting processes 32 by-laws for water supply, sewer service and wells; and considers the claims of H. Soutar of St. Charles, for $25.00 damage to his cows caused by a stag in pound!

The night of 27 January is aflame, as "The Hermitage" burns! W. C. "Billy" Hall dies, vainly trying to save his 5-month old son. John Marigold, age 70, and 15-year old William Rodgers, son of Mr. and Mrs. Wm. Rodgers, of Headingly, also perish in the flames. Mrs. Hall escapes with her baby girl, who later becomes Mrs. Ernie Vialoux. This famous home — with its heirlooms, pictures and books — is totally destroyed. Pioneer and new-come families, along both sides of our Assiniboine River, are shocked.

In Assiniboia, last year, 298 building permits are issued, valued at $396,892.00. Portage is paved from Kirkfield to Headingly. Scavenging wastes from homes and shops, cost the Municipality $25,000.00, for horses, wagons and stables. Early this year, the Municipal Health Officer calls for volunteers, to fight another threatened epidemic of "flu". In March, reports that Dominion Government horses stabled at the Kirkfield Race track are starving, raise an outcry.

Life in Assiniboia is to the staccato rag-time tune of hammers nailing houses together! By mid-March 64 new houses are built, inspected and sold in Ashcroft Point, now "Woodhaven". By July, 110 are to be built; and, by October, 500! Under the Housing Scheme, the Government of Canada loans, via the Province and Municipality, up to $4,500.00 to the builder of a new home. Promoters will loan another 30% of the building cost. A citizen can build a $6,000.00 to $7,000.00 home for $200.00 cash; and $50.00 per month! North of Portage Avenue, 300 houses are planned for this summer. Already, 60 are completed. Priced at $2,700.00 to $3,450.00, these can be bought for $50.00 down and $30.00 per month! Assiniboia is a salesman's paradise. Beneath all the hip hoorah, however, begins to stir uneasy apprehension. Early in April, Council names a Committee to investigate this entire Housing Loans business.

The big Municipal Rink — which cost $3,698.69; and earned $921.90, last winter — is torn down; and the lumber used in other Municipal construction. The Assiniboia Branch of the Great War Veterans Association urges our Council to take a lead in building a Memorial Hall. Our Municipal steam roller surfaces Melrose football field for the Assiniboia Athletic Association. A Gun Club busily bangs at clay pigeons, north of Silver Avenue. There is much talk, and inspection, of sites along Sturgeon Creek for swimming pools, beaches and parks. In a single meeting, our Council passes 9 by-laws for culverts, water, sewer, drainage, police and fire protection. And, our Municipal Engineer gets a self-starter for his auto; cost — $120.00!

The building boom rattles ahead, "in high". In one week, in June, the Loans Board considers 47 housing loans; and Council passes 19 more by-laws for sewers, paving, street lighting, schools, fire protection and waterworks. Late in the month, the Provincial Treasurer yanks the brake! He advises Council that the amount of $250,000.00 already approved for Housing Loans is OK'd; but — no more! A Provincial election brings 92% of Assiniboia's voters to the polls. R. D. Bayley is elected our MLA, with 113 majority over Capt. Jack W. Wilton. Manitoba's new Legislative Buildings, under construction since 1913, are opened on 15 July.

The congregation of St. James Methodist church assembles in a monster marquee at Portage and Parkview, to celebrate the 25th wedding anniversary of Rev. and Mrs. T. G. Bethell; and to bid "Farewell" to this devoted couple, who are transferring to Weyburn, Saskatchewan. Assiniboia's Council grants St. James Garden Club $300.00; and is billed for the Municipal Commissioner's levy: $41,400.00! Winnipeg's Grain Exchange resumes trading. The Secretary proclaims: "If farmers forget the Wheat Board; and go back to the open market, they will get $3.00 a bushel — or more!" Alas, average prices for wheat sink, in

September, to $2.73½; and, in December, to $1.93½. As quotations continue to sag, agitation mounts for revival of the Wheat Board.

Municipal financing becomes difficult. Our Council options 20-year debentures at 90! The debate about widening Wallasey Street drags on for years. Early Headingly pioneer, D. M. Dennison, passes on. Harry Bremner, on the Headingly School Board, reports getting 30 or 40 applications from teachers for positions that pay $350.00 yearly; and "they turned out good students". At Phoenix School, 44 pupils, from 6 to 18 years, are taught by Miss Margaret A. Taylor, principal ($800.00 annually) and Miss Blanche Taylor, assistant ($82.50 monthly).

Mr. Wrigley, hired by the Municipality, gets a 2-page story in a Winnipeg daily, "boosting" Assiniboia. Readers learn that ours is "the first Municipality in Western Canada". We have stores, banks, schools, bridges, sewers, water mains, pavements, sidewalks, parks, fire, police and health protection; industrial sites with ample trackage, cheap power and soft water. The Portage Trail is the longest highway in Canada: 800 miles to Edmonton. More than half of Assiniboia is divided into building lots. Portage is electric-lighted and paved, to Headingly; with a street railway all the way. We have 10 miles of asphalt paving, 2 miles of cement walks, 100 miles of graded streets and lanes, 100 miles of plank walks, 24 miles of sewer and 26 miles of water mains; and "the best lighted Rural Municipality in Canada".

On duty at our Police Station, Berry Street, are a Magistrate and 9 policemen, 2 of them motor cyclists. The Municipal Hall has a staff of 22. Assiniboia has the only cancer hospital in western Canada: the Russell Institute, at Sturgeon Creek. Seven post offices, 1,200 telephones and 2 local newspapers — the "Leader", edited by the Murphy brothers; and the "Assiniboia News", by Mr. Pickering — serve the population of 12,000. The first commercial aerodrome in Manitoba is at Kirkfield Park. Eight dairies, with 66 cows, supply local needs and a large share of the milk, cream and butter marketed in the Winnipeg area. A flour mill, at Headingly, has turned out a fine grade of flour for 30 years. Of long standing, too, is the Headingly Fair — with its outstanding yearly meet of harness racers on a fine half-mile track. A new concrete bridge carries the Portage Trail over Sturgeon Creek. A dam, just below, will empound a 3-acre lake. Work is well under way to enlarge this lake, for boating and swimming; and, in winter, skating and tobogganing. "The bright, sparkling waters of the Lake, with its semi-circle of beautiful oak and elm trees make a picture" (we read) "as delightful to the eye as the cooling, shady lawns will prove to the tired mothers and children, with whom this delightful resort will become instantly popular".

In a beautiful loop of the Assiniboine River, the St. Charles Country Club devotes 245 acres of sward and park-land to golf, polo and tennis. Among the visitors is the Prince of Wales. Just north of the Portage Trail, Kirkfield Park boasts the fastest dirt race-track in Canada; and is served by a spur from the C.P.R. line. Enthusiastic Athletic Associations are active in St. James, Sturgeon Creek and Kirkfield Park. The Assiniboine Golf Club, at Ness and Mandeville, provides club-house, dining room and spacious verandas. The Assiniboine Curling Club is building a 6-sheet rink. Another curling rink, in Headingly, invites devotees of "the roarin' game". The cultural life of Assiniboia is no less active. The Salvation Army Band, G.W.V.A. orchestra, St. Patrick's orchestra and the Kirkfield Park Choral Society, under W. Newbold, are among the musical organizations. Eight public halls are busy throughout the year.

The claim is made that Assiniboia sent more men to World War 1 than any other Rural Municipality in the West, if not in all Canada. Records, admittedly incomplete, list the names of 1,302 men and women who enlist for overseas service from this Municipality. Of these, 72 are killed in action. Veterans maintain St. James Club Rooms at 280 King Edward Street; and are organized at Sturgeon Creek and Kirkfield Park. A Memorial Park, Sport Centres and Hall are proposed. New military Rifle Ranges at St. Charles, developed at a cost of $200,000.00, provide 1,200 acres for army camps and annual Manitoba Rifle Association competitions. Public schools in Kirkfield, Headingly, St. James, and the Convent school in St. Charles, are all crowded — as is the new High School opened this year on Linwood Street. Glasses are provided free to children needing them. Great progress is noted in music.

Assiniboia, in 1920, records more buildings, more prosperity, than ever before. Dominion-Provincial loans for the Housing Scheme total nearly $1,500,000.00. Seven banks are busy in St. James, Sturgeon Creek and Headingly. The Portage Road — "the Great Highway" — traverses five prosperous business and residential districts: St. James, Sturgeon Creek, Kirkfield, St. Charles, and Headingly. This year, building will double the total for the last 10 years; and local improvements, valued at above $1,400,000.00, will reach twice that total. A new bridge at Headingly has been completed. A new bridge opposite Sharpe Boulevard will be added to the railway and traffic bridge at St. James Street; and the pontoon bridge to City Park at Deer Lodge.

As Assiniboia is the historic hub of waterways and trailways, so, now, Assiniboia is the centre of Canada's pioneer airways! On 7 October, the "first trans-Canada air mail" takes off from Halifax, on the Atlantic. Three days later, Lt-Col. Robert Leckie and Major Basil D. Hobbs land their seaplane, after dusk, on the Red River, at Selkirk. By street car, they carry the mail-bag to Assiniboia's St. Charles Aerodrome; and, at dawn, on 11 October, Lt-Col. Tylee and Capt. Home-Hay take off in a 2-seated, wheel-equipped De Haviland biplane, with 400 HP engines, to "carry the mail" westward — to the Pacific! A high mark in the history of mankind!

V. C. Maddock gets a license to run buses between Deer Lodge and Headingly; and launches "The People's Bus Service". He runs a 15-minute service between Deer Lodge and Sturgeon Creek; and 3 buses to Headingly. At 25 tickets for $1.00, his vehicles are packed! Tenders are called for sewer and water mains on 10 streets, in mid-October. Two contractors offer to take Municipal debentures in payment — at 87! Tenders for Police and Firemen's coon coats are from $324.50 to $434.50. In 1912, these cost $65.00.

The booming diapason of prosperity rides disturbing undertones! Assiniboia citizens are asking whether the substance of our affairs really measures up to the statistics, so ecstatically advertised. Our Municipal auditors tell a mass meeting of ratepayers, at Linwood School, that "Municipal offices are weeks behind in records and accounting". After charges "by a few . . . whose whole aim . . . is to further their own interests", our Council orders the Municipal auditors to get out an up-to-date financial statement; and asks the Municipal Commissioner for an independent audit. The Commissioner appoints auditors on 6 November; and, on the 17th, the financial statement prepared by the Municipal auditors is advertised in area dailies. Manitoba's Building Superintendent reports that the "life of Municipal houses . . . will not exceed 10 years". Paint that peels before it is well dried, shows shoddy construction, using "sand instead of concrete". Cracks in the gilding of prosperity expose growing dissatisfaction.

Council orders Engineer Rogers to have stumps removed from lanes, so that autos may navigate; passes by-laws for sidewalks on 15 streets; and accepts a bid of 85, less 1% commission, for debentures of $75,000.00.

The new St. James Methodist Church is opened on 5 November, with Rev. D. H. Telfer, pastor. Judge Patterson is appointed to enquire into Housing Loans in Assiniboia. Increasing numbers of needy families call for "Relief". By November, applications for Soldier's Taxation Relief number 425. By-laws are passed to build: sidewalks on 13 streets and a Fire Hall; to buy a fire engine; and to dig 15 wells. Finances improve; and, on 15 December, $80,000.00 in 6% bonds are sold at 95. The next week, 17 families demand "Relief"; and 17 cases of flu are reported. Nevertheless, The Assiniboia Poultry Association show, in Britannia School, draws big crowds.

Throughout the year, the citizens of Assiniboia have been carrying forward the process of separating the eastern "citified" half of the Municipality from the rural, western part. Now, the divorce is final. Wards 3, 4 and 5 become the Municipality (and in due course, the City) of St. James. Westward from Sturgeon Creek continues as the Rural Municipality of Assiniboia. Thus, the 116,000 square miles ruled by the original Council of Assiniboia is finally whittled to the 32 square miles remaining in Assiniboia.

The good citizens of both Municipalities in December, 1920, go to the polls; and elect their respective 1921 Municipal Councils; for the new St. James Council: Reeve, J. W. Godkin; and Councillors C. S. Ezart, Geo. Smith, Jas. Potter, W. H. Champion, C. A. Boultebee, Thos. Stockdale; and, for the 108-year-old Council of Assiniboia: Reeve, J. H. Black, with Councillors: J. Taylor, H. Lee, Peter Brown, John Bunting.

Frank Ness remains Secretary-Treasurer, with 2 office men. The new Council appoints Dr. G. W. Knipe, Health Officer; and pays accounts — from $1.00 for a typewriter ribbon, to $10,300.00 for a fire engine. Housing Loans are debated wherever people gather. Judge Patterson is urged to speed up his investigation. W. D. Bayley, our MLA, charges that the investigation is a "narrow, circumscribed whitewash". The annual meeting of Phoenix School ratepayers elect A. E. Lonsdale, Chairman; and Capt. Max Meinke, secretary-treasurer. There are 53 pupils in 10 grades; and an average attendance of 46. St. Charles United Church congregation begins to meet in a converted cottage called "the church". Petitions are circulated both for, and against, a new school in St. Charles.

Before Judge Patterson's report on Assiniboia Housing is submitted, in April, 58 of the houses are vacated; and become Municipal property. Since last November, collections have totalled $23,809.00; arrears are $22,532.00; and, of 300 Loans, 145 are paid. The Housing Loan Board is dissolved.

In Headingly, Mrs. John Taylor suffers serious burns, when her clothing catches fire from overheated stovepipes. She is saved when her daughter, Mrs. Britton, runs to her; and beats out the flames! Assiniboia and St. James Councils meet jointly; and divide assets and liabilities. The Municipal Commissioner rules that St. James shall pay Assiniboia $551,764.00; and Assiniboia shall assume liabilities totalling $727,-773.00.

Citizens clamor for better highways. On 7 June, J. C. W. Agnew writes to Manitoba's Highway Commissioner, that the Portage Road, from Headingly westward, is the "most prominent in the Province". "I

live just west of Headingly. . Observe enormous traffic. . . Thousands of
cars weekly. . . Need gravel". A. C. Emmett writes the Minister of Public
Works: "The condition of Portage from Headingly to St. Francois Xavier
is deplorable . . . Dozens of cars stuck; and compelled to hire teams to
get them through". Engineer G. W. Rogers transfers to St. James.

Constable Dixon hires special constables at $5.00 a day, for the 22nd
annual Headingly Fair, during the last week in July. Baby show; livestock judging; auto races; sports program; produce and dairy exhibits,
all record the biggest entries in the long history of the Fair. John Bunting
and Wm. Dumbrill win many prizes for outstanding vegetable exhibits. In the hotly contested baseball tournament, Garrison defeats
Charleswood; and, then, meets Headingly in the final game. Rain post-
pones a decision; but the big crowds go home happy. They have had
their money's worth. Our Fair is the recognized Mecca for horse exhibits from a wide area. Over the West, farmers now use 179,000 cars,
trucks and tractors; but still own 2,500,000 horses.

Until records and affairs are in proper order, Assiniboia's finances
are put in charge of the Municipal Commissioner. Each item must be
O.K'd by Deputy Commissioner E. M. Wood. He stops paying Municipal
workers each 2 weeks; but approves sidewalks and street lights for
Buchanan and Stewart Streets. The Minister of Public Works agrees that,
since Portage is the most travelled Road, the Province will do the work
of gravelling it; Assiniboia to pay one-third now, and the balance when
able. In September, Alfred Good and Robideau and Daignault, contractors, grade and gravel 2 miles of the Portage Road, west of Headingly. Seven steel culverts are allowed by Mr. Wood. But he stops all
wood cutting. Further gravelling is not done "owing to financial conditions relating to the Municipality".

A new School District, No. 2071, is created in St. Charles. A fine
2-room brick school-house is built by contractor P. H. Hedges. The
corner-stone is laid by Dr. Robert Fletcher, Deputy-Minister of Education, on 22 July. The school opens in October, with Misses Annie
Cameron and Regina Campagne teaching 46 pupils—in 10 grades! The
first Secretary of St. Charles School District is Ralph Goodridge.
Trustees are: V. C. Maddock, P. Brown and Joseph Cachat, chairman.

With no Wheat Board, cash prices for wheat drop $1.63 in one year!
Western farmers organize for political action. In the National Election
on 9 December, Progressives take every rural seat in the Canadian West.
Members of Parliament elected are: Liberals, 117; Progressives, 63;
Conservatives, 48; total 235.

The long struggle is underway for "Relief", for needy citizens. Under
a Federal Relief plan, unemployed workers register; get a certificate; and

draw advances thereon. The Municipality bills Provincial and National Governments for one-third of the expense. It is a terrible business; but it brings hope to many families. Unemployed are put at useful work "grubbing out" Grove Avenue. E. M. Wood stops a $25.00 cheque to Knowles Boys' Home. The Relief Committee of Council meets every week; and tries to stretch every dollar to cover every situation. For example, a worker lives on Buchanan Street, with his wife and 6 children under 10; his earnings go to make payments on the house; his brother, a veteran, living with them, gets $5.50 in groceries, weekly, and $18.00 pension, monthly. This family needs help. Another — with wife and 1 child, 10 years old; with $10.00 a month to pay rent, can manage. A third, whose wife is ill, must care for 3 children, aged 7, 9 and 13; and needs assistance. Cordwood is delivered to keep homes liveable through a bitter winter.

The carefully calculated Relief schedule for a family of 5 for a month, lists 30 items, including 48 pounds of flour, 48 of meat, 20 of potatoes and 28 quarts of milk; totals 255½ pounds of food, plus yeast, soap and matches; and costs $4.98 per person. Or, per day: 1.7 pounds of food, costing 16½ cents per person. Regulations allow consideration only after a man is out of work for 2 weeks; and has applied for work to the Municipality. Relief is issued in kind — after a detailed means test.

Mrs. John Taylor, of Headingly, dies, in February. Widely beloved, she is recorded "a very energetic and helpful woman" by Holy Trinity Rector, Rev. T. Marshall.

In June, the Provincial Treasurer is asked to release the Municipality from control of finances. Two months ago, Council sent a cheque to the Manitoba Government, to clear off the 1920 $100,000.00 loan. Nevertheless, Assiniboia does not win its administrative freedom for another 40 years!

The fourth year of drought, 1923, forces families off farms in southwestern Manitoba; and blankets the homes along the Assiniboine and the Portage Road with "anxiety and want".

Manitoba's "Farmer" Government, under Premier John Bracken, pursues one policy: Economize! Actually, the money lenders rule Municipality, Province and Nation! Our Assiniboine, like other Western rivers, shrivels to a trickle. At City Park, the tops of piles in the riverbed are exposed, where preliminary work began on a power plant in 1883, which, according to the imported engineering authority, would generate power "enough to supply Winnipeg for all time!"

A City Directory, of this date, advertises Maxwell, Chalmers and

Overland cars; and, among "Parks", lists: "Assiniboine" and "Kirk-field". "Suburban Municipalities" include: Assiniboia, Reeve, J. L. McBride; secretary-treasurer, Frank Ness; and Councillors Geo. Catheralle, Peter Brown, J. A. Spenard and John Bunting. "Clubs and Associations" include: Alcrest Golf Club, St. Charles Country Club, Assiniboine Golf Club and 20 Snowshoe Clubs — stag, Ladies and Mixed.

Many real estate developers "get out from under" Housing Scheme commitments. Harrison & O'Kelly, with 59 "Loan" houses, carry on contracts for 17; and "turn back" 42, to the Municipality. Assiniboia vehemently protests the Municipal Commissioner's division of "Housing Scheme" assets and liabilities with St. James. Veterans in the Soldiers' Settlement, on River Lot 61, Headingly, build 2-foot side-walks, with lumber supplied by the Municipality. Plank sidewalks are built on Portage, from Sturgeon Creek School to Muriel Street; and Portage Road is gravelled to Headingly. Council grants Headingly Agricultural Society, $300.00; withdraws from Engineer Rogers' plan for draining the whole country north of the lower Assiniboine; and urges Winnipeg to buy Kirkfield Park from Rod McKenzie, at $250,000.00, for an Exhibition site.

Ratepayers who apply for work, cut cordwood at the Municipal Hall, by hand, for $1.50 a cord. Our Municipal Health Officer reports an outbreak of measles; and, also, 14 smallpox cases in Kirkfield Park. In Sturgeon Creek School, a public presentation is made to Miss May McMillan, Manitoba champion speller, on 7 May.

Many of the Municipal houses in St. Charles must have the water pumped out of their basements, before they can be rented. Forced to take over homes built under the Housing Scheme and subsequently abandoned by builders or buyers, Assiniboia inherits all the troubles of an unwilling landlord, plus heavy financial losses. Some of these "Loan" houses cost more than $20.00 per month in carrying charges; and earn only $10.00 in rent. Only 4 are up-to-date in their payments!

School trustees appeal to Dr. Robert Fletcher, to have the Government advance money to pay school debts. In Phoenix School, 50 girls and boys are enrolled; 12 of them in Grades 7 to 11. The senior teacher is Mrs. Hazel Laycock; and her assistant, Miss Clara Rindfleisch. Families supplying the pupils include: Hann, Randall, Block, Barnes, Living-stone, Robinson, Ruttle, Anders, Skinner, McIntosh and Hatfield.

The Strathcona estate appeals their assessment; and has it lowered by 50%. At the end of August, the Municipality pays the 1923 Municipal Commissioner's levy; and $41,000.00 on notes held by the bank. A

grant of $100.00 goes to Kirkfield Park Boys and Girls Club. All prop-
erty assessments are cut by 50%. In November, John Bunting resigns,
after many years as Ward Councillor.

Multitudes of citizens attend the funeral of Hon. John Taylor, oldest
Assiniboia resident. This great pioneer, aged 91, dies on 6 March, 1925.
Through the long span of his life, John Taylor contributes leadership in
school, church, Municipal and Government affairs. He leaves the stamp
of his own strong, self-reliant and progressive character on the early
history of Assiniboia; and a numerous family to carry these qualities into
the future.

Returning confidence begins to thaw the financial currents, so long
frozen by fear; and money begins to circulate. Our Council is able to
advance Headingly School District, $2,000.00; St. Charles, $2,000.00;
and Sturgeon Creek, $1,200.00. J. Gagnon, loses 100 bushels of pota-
toes; and P. Morris, his crop of chicks, when basements flood because
ditches are not cleared of snow. Both demand damages!

Assiniboia's assessment for 1925 is equalized at $1.6 million; and
Municipal estimates total $17,053.00. Those Municipal houses cause
more trouble! Many, particularly on Vimy Road, are reported in "very
bad condition". Some buyers have to spend $1,000.00 on repairs or
rebuilding. Many demand that cracked walls be fixed by the Municipality! Some of our streets, also, are sadly in need of improvement.
T. Corbett, driving Mrs. Blane and her baby to hospital, in his car, on
2 July, strikes a post "stuck in . . a soft spot" on Isbister Street. The log
is thrown through the windshield! Council pays $10.40 damages. (With-
out prejudice!)

After 1925, "better times" renew home building. Families with autos,
select riverside and other spacious sites; build substantial homes
thereon; and enjoy peace, comfort and privacy. This year, John A.
Isbister and his wife, Mary, move back to 371 Isbister Street. Born Mary
Bruce, on Christmas day, 1880, near the later site of St. Paul's church,
Mrs. Isbister is educated at St. Boniface Convent. Her father is Peter
Bruce: her mother, a daughter of Wm. McMillan, who treks to Assiniboia from Oregon, about 1850. John's father, James Isbister, from the
Orkneys, works for "the Company"; and, like so many Assiniboia
pioneers, afterwards settles along the Assiniboine. John and Mary
drive by horse-and-buggy to be married, in St. Charles church, by the
revered Father Dandurand. Mary's mother's mother, Margaret Dace, an
Irish colleen, comes to Assiniboia via Minneapolis; marries Wm.
McMillan; and lives to be 98. William imports goods via Hudson's Bay;
and loses all, when the "Company" ship is wrecked. He lives to be 104,
as attested by his gravestone in St. Charles cemetery.

John and Mary Isbister farm for 20 years beside Wm. Brown, on part of that beautiful loop of the River occupied by St. Charles Country Club. Their snug log home — often visited by Uncles Pat, Joe and John — is circled by small fields of wheat, oats, barley; and pasturing cattle. John serves as Justice of the Peace and Assiniboia Councillor. His boys go to school at St. Charles; the girls go to St. Boniface Convent. From their home, Mary sees "stern-wheelers" and loaded barges, plow up and down the Assiniboine; and, on one occasion, waves to Pat Caplette and his bride, on their honeymoon trip up the River. Just eastward, Andrew McDermot, Junior, lives on a farm which extends from the River to Saskatchewan Avenue; and "the Pines", on the Portage Road, is the home of Mrs. Russell, specialist in the treatment of cancer.

The population of Winnipeg reaches 191,931; but Assiniboia numbers only 1,200 people — having lost the bulk of our citizens when "St. James Leaves Home", 5 years ago. Many of our workmen go to Pine Falls, to help build the new pulp mill. Others are "down North", on construction of the Hudson's Bay Railway to Churchill. A late, wet spring in 1927 delays seeding, until mid-June. The crop is a failure.

With typical Western unpredictability, 1928 is "the year of the big crop!" Prosperity floods the land with automobiles. Beer parlors flourish. Flin Flon develops as a gigantic copper producer. In Headingly, Holy Trinity Anglican Church awakens to new life. After 1920, when members number 49, the congregation battles difficult years. Rev. T. Marshall is succeeded, as rector, by Rev. A. W. Neale, in 1925. New names on the church records of these years include: G. F. Shrive, G. Kenny, G. B. Franklin, Mrs. McLaren, Mrs. Monorgan, T. Kidd, H. Newton, Mrs. Scutchings and Miss Elsie Clouston. This year, the congregation tries to buy the Headingly United church building; and contributes $40.00, to buy a new battery and licence for Rev. Neale's auto.

Assiniboia horse-men try to revive horse-racing at Kirkfield Park; but the Provincial Government refuses a license. Meantime, the facilities of Kirkfield are used by Walter Kane, to break Montana mustangs. Citizens cooperate to build the "Assiniboia War Memorial Curling Rink"; and, also, to block the Provincial Government purchase of Whitegates Farm, for "the Jail Farm". Headingly Agricultural Society leases their race-track to the Winnipeg Driving Club for 10 years, for annual meets. Traffic problems develop at Kirkfield Park Airfield. Citizens demand that airplanes be kept off the Portage Avenue pavement; that autos speeding into the "wee sma' hours", be stopped; that others, parked with lights out, on Portage, to 2 a.m., "smoking, drinking, petting" be properly dealt with; and that livestock be prevented roaming at large all night!

This year, St. Charles parish is put in the care of the Oblate Fathers of St. Mary's Province, with Fr. Schaller, Parish Priest. In August, the Oblate Fathers open St. Charles Novitiate; and Fr. K. Mayer, OMI, takes over the Parish. In December, the church is destroyed — totally — by fire. Immediately, a new building of the same dimensions, is begun; and, for the third time, the church is re-established!

In December, too, a bronze plaque is unveiled in Assiniboia's Municipal Hall, bearing the inscription:

"1914- 1918 . . . Erected to the Honor and memory of men from the Municipality of Assiniboia who bravely faced Peril and Hardship in the Great War of 1914-18 . . . and who finally laid down their lives in the cause of Liberty, Justice and Humanity . . .

Garnet V. Ness	8th Bn.	Henry H. Dahl	16th Bn.
Andrew Bird	8th Bn.	James J. Buchanan	78th Bn.
James C. Tyrie	8th Bn.	George Bremner	179th Bn.
Joseph H. Jones	8th Bn.	William S. Heatley	179th Bn.
John Ballentyne	8th Bn.	William D. Heatley	179th Bn.
Peter T. Anderson	8th Bn.	E. Ford Abell	8th F.A.
Clement Cachat	11 Chasseurs	David Bunting	1st CMR

In Holy Trinity Anglican Church, Headingly, 2 plaques bear these additional names of Honored Dead in World War 1: Frances H. Whittaker, 7th Bn.; W. R. Fowler, D. A. N. Acheson, C. W. Tait, F. L. Tait.

Some of these names are included in, and some omitted from, a great Honor Roll which Reeve C. L. Richardson unveils on 14 June, 1920 — before St. James separates from Assiniboia. This Honor Roll, assembled with tremendous effort and infinite care, is incomplete. Today it hangs in reverent pride, in the St. James Legion Board Room, 1755 Portage Avenue, blazoned with the names of 1,302 Canadian service personnel; and inscribed: "The following men enlisted from the Municipality of Assiniboia for Overseas service from August, 1914, to November, 1918." Stars mark these 72 "killed in action":

Andrews, E. A.	27 Bn.	Barnes, A. J.	78 Bn.
Akehurst, C. E.	27 Bn.	Brown, W. J.	46 Bn.
Arnold, N. J.	—	Ballentyne, John	8 Bn.
Atha, W.	205 Bn.	Coupland, A.	144 Bn.
Abell, E. Ford	8 F.A.	Campbell, S. F.	8 Bn.
Almond, J. R.	8 Bn.	Cameron, R.	45 Bn.
Ainsworth, J.	52 Bn.	Clifford, H. J.	4 F.A.
Atkinson, W.	43 Bn.	Convery, P.	79 Bn.
Brown, E.	—	Davidson, R.	8 Bn.
Bethel, J. O.	106 Bn.	Davey, W. R.	8 Bn.
Brown, G.	10 Gar Bn.	Desauleux,	76 Bn.
Bruce, G. A.	8 Bn.	How, J. D.	43 Bn.

Irwin, G. C.	222 Bn.	Pascoe, A.	43 Bn.
Jones, J. H.	90 Bn.	Park, J.	144 Bn.
Kelly, T. A.	27 Bn.	Parsons, R. C.	D.A.C.
Lane, F. B.	45 Bn.	Robertson, F. G.	43 Bn.
McColl, A. B.	79 Bn.	Reid, Geo.	27 Bn.
Gilholm, J. T.	183 Bn.	Reid, Adam	44 Bn.
Griffity, J.	8 Bn.	Russell, James	16 Bn.
Lamb, J.	17 F.A.	Russell, H.	10 Bn.
Laird, P. T.	190 Bn.	Rogers, C. W.	101 Bn.
Lakey, J.	1. C.E.	Rogers, W. G.	101 Bn.
Lightfoot, J.	79 Bn.	Smallacombe, F. I.	C.E.
Houston, J.	15 Bn.	Smith, J.	10 F.A.
Hunter, H.	44 Bn.	Shelmerdine, G.	14 Bn.
Harrison, T.	44 Bn.	Sefton, D.	1 CMR
Meyer, A. W.	8 Bn.	Taylor, S. H.	244 Bn.
Meyei, E. S.	144 Bn.	Tyrie, J. C.	90th Bn.
Murdock, A. S.	1 Can. Cav.	Tye, E. S.	16 Bn.
Murray, A.	43 Bn.	Vosper, J.	43 Bn.
Maitland, Wm. J.	8 Bn.	Williams, H.	27 Bn.
Mawn, Geo.	61 Bn.	Weir, J.	43 Bn.
Miller, A.	8 Bn.	Wilbur, N.	61 Bn.
McBeth, P.	12 F.A.	Weaver, W. J.	78 Bn.
Ness, V. W.	90 Bn.	Wright, J.	44 Bn.
Neary, F.	78 Bn.	Webb, W. A.	144 Bn.

With the utmost care, a complete list is not possible. Many names are omitted. Two come to mind as I write: Harry Woodsworth and S. S. Smith, 44th Battalion. Listed or omitted, however, the men who volunteer from Assiniboia earn the proud gratitude of *this truly typical* Canadian community.

Councillors elected by our citizens, for 1929 — 117 years after the appointment of the original Council of Assiniboia — include Harry Bremner, James Glen, Joseph Cachat, Wm. S. Craig and John Bunting, Reeve. Our police seize a still at Whitegates Farm. At a tax sale, in August, building lots on Parkdale Street sell for $55.00; and, on Buchanan, for $25.00.

Geography decrees that Assiniboia — "The Heart of the Continent" and historic hub of waterways and trailways — shall be the pioneer centre of Canada's aviation development. Since the first trans-Canada air mail takes off from St. Charles Aerodrome, on 11 October, 1920, our local airfields have become "the largest and busiest in Canada." One airfield operates at Whittier Street. Western Canada Airways (the embryo Air Canada) and Berryhill Airways have airfields on David Street. Last year, planes are banned from Portage Avenue pavement. This summer, motorists are prohibited parking, to watch the aerial activities. Stevenson Field, begun in 1925, in Assiniboia and St. James, as the Northland aviation base, rapidly becomes the Airport for the entire region.

One of the great folk movements in the history of mankind takes shape, in the 3 Western Wheat Pools. In this co-operative action by primary producers, 142,000 farm families contract with each other to deliver the annual out-turn from 50% of Western wheat acreage and 33% of acreage sown to oats and barley, to the 1,636 country elevators and 12 terminals which they, jointly, own and operate; and through which, in 5 crop-years, they handle a billion bushels of grain. Naturally, all this is to the tune of violent struggle — in which Assiniboia farmers share, enthusiastically.

The people of our Canadian West need all their organized strength to survive the tide of disaster which engulfs the world! On 29 October, the loss of $14 billions in a single session on the New York Stock Exchange, heralds the crash of the world's financial structure! Within 3 years, stocks listed on that Exchange, drop in price from $89 billions to $15 billions! Of total listed values, 83% are swept away!

More disastrous to our economy (based on production of food which gives Stock Exchange prices whatever meaning they possess) drought cuts grain production to fractions of average out-turn. Rust robs our Western crops of hundreds of millions of dollars of *real* value. Fear stalks the land! Unemployment smothers confidence; and numbs initiative. Wheat prices fall to lowest levels in 300 years! Depression condemns all to despair — from which none knows the escape. Eventually, the bitter lesson of sane management of land and water resources begins to force itself upon our attention. In 1929, however, this is still far in the future.

The routine of living occupies our people of Assiniboia, as of all communities. At Phoenix School, a second room is added, to accommodate the 44 pupils of 1920. Miss Blanche Taylor is the junior teacher. Miss Margaret Taylor leaves, after 7 years as principal; and Miss Shepherd succeeds. Annual costs total $9,719.00. Mrs. Laycock is principal in 1925, with Miss T. O. Long, assistant; and the trustees buy an Encyclopedia Britannica, on $10.00 monthly installments. In 1929, Miss Cook is hired as senior teacher at $1,100.00 per annum. (Teachers' salaries begin to rise from starvation levels!) This September, Miss A. Sonnischen is awarded a medal for courage and decision in rescuing young Gordon Taylor from drowning, in Sturgeon Creek.

When "St. James Leaves Home", in 1921, Assiniboia loses not only 75% of our population; but, also, all the schools which have been racing to build new class-rooms for the multiplying numbers of their girls and boys. For example, Bannatyne School has 295 pupils in 8 rooms in 1920; 12 class-rooms in 1922; and, with 378 pupils, in 1925 consolidates in the St. James School District.

The remnant of our people who "stand fast" in the Assiniboia community, strive valiantly to meet strange conditions and solve unforeseen problems imposed by our changing community status.

Slow increase in our population is reflected, subsequently, in our school attendance. In 1921, 49 pupils occupy 2 class-rooms in Headingly School; Miss Margaret Taylor transfers from Phoenix to complete 12 years of teaching Assiniboia's girls and boys. By 1929, Misses Aileen Gunn and Joyce Freer are teaching 66 pupils in this School. St. Charles School opens, in 1921, with 46 pupils. Four years later average attendance is 51; and the Provincial Government grant is $177.14. By 1929, some 74 girls and boys attend. At Sturgeon Creek School, Miss Catherine Dohaney completes 34 terms of teaching; Miss Jessie Taylor, 32; and Miss Mary Davies, 21 terms. Pupils average 160 throughout the '20's.

Through the hard years of this grim decade our people in Assiniboia work and fight to survive as families and as a community. They work and fight with all the ingenuity, tenacity and jollity which are the inheritance of pioneers, who can

".... Watch the things you gave your life to broken,

And stoop and build 'em up with wornout tools."

The community of Assiniboia survives—to head into its tremendous future.

PART 5

The Sun
Rides West

CHAPTER 15

Sunsets Black and Dawns Aflame . . . .
1930-1939

Sunset red and morning gray
Will set the traveller on his way;
But — sunset Black and Dawn Aflame
Will cancel travel, work and game!

Old Weather Adage.

Following trails that criss-cross Assiniboia's history since 1811 (after scouting ancient paths that wind into the long before) we come to 1930 — within a generation of Canada's Centennial Year. One generation is small time to assess current happenings, as they flow together into our History. Nevertheless, this brief span is packed with extremes that test our community and our nation.

The panic of last fall spawns Depression. Fear freezes enterprise. Blindly, we try to fight an enemy — unseen, nebulous, pervasive, unknown. Exasperated, we "starve in the midst of plenty". Frustrated, we see the tools of production rust, while willing workers are denied their use. On many Assiniboia streets, half the workers have no work, no wages. To keep body and soul together, we develop "Relief". Clumsy, shameful and destructive, this make-shift gnaws into the vitals of individual, community and nation; and fastens itself upon our History.

Over our Canadian West, drought and rust wreck primary production. The grain we do produce cannot be moved into use, since, over the so-called "civilized" world, fear immobilizes the machinery of trade. Year after year dawns bright with hope — to be buried in dust!

Beyond all this, in Assiniboia, our people are over-loaded with debt. With pioneer daring, early in World War 1, our Municipality paves the Portage Road; and, in the flush of Victory, builds streets of houses for in-coming families. Later years teach that such works for the general good are properly financed by Province and Nation. Trail-blazing Assiniboia saddles the future with debt; and, in addition, learns hard lessons about building highways and houses in our soils and climate. By May, 1930, engineers report that the Portage pavement is a broken mass of cracks, holes and faulty drainage. Many of the houses built in the first days of Peace, are long since abandoned. Thus, we have: crushing debt; plus a highway that must be rebuilt and streets of houses not worth rebuilding!

Back in 1921, supposedly differing interests impell Assiniboia's people to separate. Capital commitments are divided between the new suburban Municipality of St. James and the remaining Rural Municipality of Assiniboia. As families, factories and warehouses move westward from the crowded City, St. James becomes metropolitan; and old debts dissolve in booming expansion.

Assiniboia withers. By 1930, our population is barely 25%, and assessment 6%, of pre-war levels. This June, the vestrymen of Holy Trinity church, in Headingly: Messrs. Bremner, Kenny, Williams, Stevenson, Kidd and Jones, report that the dwindling congregation cannot pay the rector's stipend. A break of 17 years follows, in the records of this pioneer congregation.

Promoters, who "boosted" us into over-expansion, take their schemes and salvaged profits elsewhere. Farmers fronting on Portage Road cannot pay the taxes levied. Pioneer families lose their homesteads. Drought, rust and 'hoppers drive other families from farming. Fertile fields revert to primal prairie. Homes built with Municipal loans are abandoned, when buyers are thrown out of work. With all these on its hands, our Municipality becomes the biggest owner of Assiniboia properties. Successive Councils strive to restore farms and homes to use, on whatever terms; and, meanwhile, to make sure that every family survives; and every child gets "schooling".

In summer, many families shed worries and raiment; and "cool off" at Tony Scalena's "Easy Reach Beach", on our River. In August, a new Government, under Prime Minister R. B. Bennett, takes up the task of moving into use the grain we harvest. There is talk of "blasting our way to world markets". J. I. McFarland, made czar of grain marketing, too soon reports: "The bottom fell out of world markets". Wheat brings 32 cents a bushel at country elevators. Many a farmer teams a wagon-load to town; and, for it, nets too little to buy groceries for his family. Many have no grain to sell.

Even in Depression, the automobile extends its rule over our lives. When Assiniboia paves the Portage Road, in 1914, horse-power is on the hoof; and only 7,000 of Canada's 69,000 motor vehicles pollute the air of Manitoba — at 15 miles-per-hour in towns; and 10, crossing bridges. By 1931, 80,000 cars and trucks kick up dust on Manitoba trails; and more than a million are registered in Canada.

Hon. W. R. Clubb, early in 1933, warns of the "alarming increase in Relief". Our Assiniboia Councillors grimly agree. They are in the front line, battling an unknown foe. Work stops on opening new streets. Even wolf bounties are suspended. For our community, as for its families, financing becomes a nightmare. Municipal houses are rented for $8.00 a month. Provincial School loans are rationed: Headingly, $1,127.00; Sturgeon Creek, $2,851.00; St. Charles, $1,440.00; Little Mountain, $182.00; and St. James school, $400.00 — for the year! Municipal salaries are cut 40%; wages are fixed at: man, 30 cents per hour; man and team, 50 cents. Few are hired. More are fired.

Our farms have been famous for fine livestock; and well-fenced fields. Drought forces farmers to abandon livestock; and buries fences under banks of drifted soil, which sprout weeds and buck-brush; and come alive with grasshoppers. The Headingly Fair barns are headquarters for yearly campaigns to spread tons of poison (along with rumors that the 'hoppers fatten on it!)

Municipal lands north of Headingly are sold to Wm. Nicol at $5.00 per acre, on time. J. R. Wilkins buys 170 acres of RL 61 for $10.00 an acre, over 10 years; taxes to begin next year; and 100 acres to be re-broken this summer. Nine acres go at $30.00, no cash down. Unemployed ratepayers paint our Municipal Hall, at 30 cents an hour — half in cash; half credited on taxes. School teachers are paid $55.00 to $90.00 per month; caretakers, $30.00 to $80.00. Our Council fixes prices for grits, meat, flour and milk; and buys 30 quarters of beef at 3 cents a pound and 2½ tons of oatmeal and flour at $1.90 per 100 pounds for families on Relief. Two cords of wood per month is the winter fuel ration.

To begin 1934, our Council votes to "leave in abeyance" the Provincial Treasurer's demand for $47,700.00 interest on Assiniboia debentures; accepts $200.00 for 11 lots in St. Charles; and, backed by the Province, borrows $5,000.00 for our schools. In March, Frank Ness, after "long and distinguished services" to Assiniboia, goes to his reward. R. R. Kirby becomes Municipal Secretary-Treasurer.

Spring revives interest in Municipal real estate. Building lots sell for $30.00, $15.00 and even for $5.00, each. J. Land buys a house and 4 lots for $800.00. Eighteen families are cut off Relief. With free seeds, unemployed families raise acres of fine gardens. Our people respond with true pioneer spirit to appeals for vegetables needed in communities more drought-damaged than our own. Few people can afford to play golf; and Royoumont becomes a pasture.

A Relief Committee is formed in 1935, representing Municipality, Province and Nation. Kort Feculak buys 35 Municipal acres at $16.00; W. W. Shaver pays $200.00 for 6 River lots; and market-gardener Gibson tenders potatoes, at 30 cents a bushel, to pay his taxes. The Municipal houses in St. Charles are up for sale and removal. Several are bought at $250.00, each. The Governments of Canada and Manitoba build the new bridge needed at Headingly. Assiniboia pays $\frac{1}{3}$ the cost of maintenance.

In October, Canadians elect a new Government. The Canadian Wheat Board is established; and the requisite foundation of stability is laid, upon which to rebuild our Canadian West, by fixing the price of wheat at $87\frac{1}{2}$ cents a bushel. More vital: rains fall, again! Our farms, so long wizened by drought, burst into productivity. Water unlocks fertility. Crops flourish. Slowly, confidence returns. Assiniboia doubles Relief rations and adds a cord of wood, for each family, during December.

Our 1937 Council — Wm. M. Taylor, P. A. Beauchemin, James Glen, Wm. S. Craig; and John S. Lamont, Reeve — sells part of River Lot 12, St. James, at $10.00 per acre; buys relief milk from G. E. Murphy at $1.50 per 100 pounds; grants $20.00, each, to Assiniboia and Headingly Curling Clubs and St. Charles Community Rink; cuts Relief rolls by 25 families; and begins to grade and gravel long-neglected roads.

In March, George Stevenson dies, aged 78, on River Lot 61, which has been farmed by this pioneer family for 85 years.

Amazingly, in these depression years, Canadian aviation expands. From 1926 to 1936 air freight increases 2500% and passenger traffic 3500%. This miracle is cradled in Assiniboia. From a local airfield, in 1931, an air service is scheduled to Calgary and Edmonton. In 1935, Western Canada Airways, flying from one of our aerodromes, becomes Canadian Airways, Limited. This year, the Government of Canada creates Trans-Canada Airways, to serve our nation, from sea to sea and around the globe. In Assiniboia and neighboring Municipalities, TCA builds facilities employing hundreds of highly-skilled workers.

Ceaselessly, our Council works to get lands back into family ownership, producing and paying taxes. Sub-divisions are cancelled; and the land sold at $10.00 per acre. Fur "ranches" flourish in Assiniboia. The world fur market, after years in foreign centres, comes back home to "the Forks" of the Assiniboine River and the Red, its native habitat! Pioneers of the old fur trade pass away. James Omand goes to "the Happy Hunting Ground," early in 1938. Born at York Factory, in 1856, he lives his life in Assiniboia; and leaves 11 children, 56 grand-children, 8 great-grandchildren and the Creek bearing his name. This year, also, Mrs. Barbara Dilworth dies. She is the last survivor of the Stevenson family. Barbara and Wm. Dilworth, Wolseley Expedition volunteer, marry in 1872; trek, by covered wagon, to Prince Albert; and, later, farm at High Bluff.

Parkhill Street lots are rented for the taxes, as gardens. Slowly, family and community finances improve. Our Council donates $25.00 to the St. Charles Hockey Club; and $500.00 to Headingly Fair. More streets are opened, where families have already built homes: Vimy, Muriel, Kirkfield, Whittier and Woodlands. Assiniboia's 1939 budget totals $38,715.00. Relief rolls are cut to 8 families. In April, 75 excited paddlers start from Headingly in the first Winnipeg Canoe Club annual race. Old echoes waken at every bend of our River as they pass.

Suddenly, on 3 September, German armies invade Poland! Once again, Canadians "stand on guard" to defend our freedom — where it is attacked!

The financial stream — so long frozen from bank to bank — surges into circulation. Workshops hum! Wages rocket! Cash registers tingle with the music so adored by our monetized society. Remembering World War 1, we know that "war is hell". But, grimly confident, we organize to make, and man, the machinery of Victory.

We are a more mature, cohesive and solid nation than in 1914. In the generation since then, the proud certainty of sovereign nationhood — born in the 100,000 Canadians who "confirmed, asserted and established Canadian nationality" at Vimy Ridge — is become the basic faith of all Canadians. We are a people set apart by Destiny to render historic service to mankind, by using our vast resources for the greatest good of the greatest number of humans. No-one — in whatever time or place; by whatever strength or stratagem — shall take from our Canadian nation any fraction of the lands, waters and resources entrusted to all Canadians. Threatened — we go to war!

Not all our heroes are at the battle-fronts. This November, Wm. E. Catton, of Headingly, is named to the Hall of Fame of Canadian Aviation, for "one of the greatest mercy flights ever made in North America", to bring out "a badly injured missionary from Repulse Bay, 1,300 miles northward, on . . . Hudson's Bay". Capt. "Bill" Catton, pilot in World War 1 and now superintendent at Canada Airways' Lac du Bonnet base,

A. J. Hollingsworth and "Red" Terpenning volunteer for this mission, on 15 November. In a single-engined Junkers, with fuel for 300 miles, they head into a blinding blizzard; and buck fog, icing, cold and invisibility — flying "by the seat of their pants" and the grace of God, to land at Repulse on 9 December. Fr. Buliand, the injured man, is suffering agonies from frozen arms and legs. Capt. Catton and crew get him to hospital at Chesterfield Inlet. The log of the Lac du Bonnet base, for 20 December, 1939, records: "SN and crew return from Repulse Bay trip today . . . Held at God's Lake by . . . weather since the 15th. Fr. Buliard sent immediately to St. Boniface Hospital".

Less exciting, but basically vital, Canadian farm families harvest 520 million bushels of wheat this fall. Upon Western farm prosperity, our Canadian economy rebuilds. Assiniboia, primarily, is still a farm community; but our population is growing. Schools call for more class-rooms, more teachers, to care for the inflow of girls and boys.

Assiniboia is "the truly typical Canadian Community". All the multiple components of our coalescing Canadian nationality are recorded in the family names in our school, church and Municipal records. For example, Phoenix school enrolls girls and boys from the Friesen, Sawatzsky, Seekings, Druse, Coates, Hamill, Schoph, Toews, Bergenstein, Bloomer, Brown, Alexander, Molyneaux, McIntosh, Kilworth, Masters, Robinson, Lyons, Beattie, Yeager, Walker, Stacey, Evans, Broen, Bartley and Sonnichesen families. Among all who live, labor and are laid to rest in Assiniboia, families listed in St. Charles parish records during the 1930's include: Kotschaw, Zimmerman, Varga, Sagas, Dessing, Hoelscher, Brooks, Kyper, Shwinsky, Hearst, Lumsden, Brodeux, Demeyer, Leyer, Pinvedic, Papnfuss, Mousette, Diers, Schmitt, Rosiat, Piche, Bowsboom, Mihaychuk, Koepowich, Kiffmeyer, Holtmann, Thomas, Hotscher, Bentler, Turney, Keith, Drysdale, Goldstone, Forsythe, Baroni, Susans, Patry, Hammer, Ellman, Morrisseau, Swansky, Halpenny, Ketter, Sinclair, Broerken, Todd, McClay, Holsberg, VanVleet, Dufault, Holt, Suskowski, Swaranowsky, Masylaskev, Muller, Latrail, Street, Dineen, Kennedy, Anderson, Dijolte, Szewczyk, Daniels, Wheatcroft, Holmes, Holiday, Brunn, Creak, Couture, Malloy, Deegan, Burgoyne, Thompson, Gowing, Botchain, Hogue, Caron, Allard, Branconnier, Lafleche and many more. Some of these family names are more native to Assiniboia than much of our written history. Others come from far-away tribal, national and racial backgrounds. Now, all are Canadians — proud to share, equally, in the multi-partnership of all the "founding peoples" of our Canadian nationality. Having, together, come through a dire decade of sunsets, black with drought and depression — we now face a long succession of dawns, aflame with bloody war!

Our Municipality (like business and governments, generally) is ready to let the dead past bury its debts, for whatever cash can be salvaged. One estate settles tax arrears of $1,893.48 for $500.00 cash. A debenture debt of $2,804.00 for Sturgeon Creek SD is paid with $1,500.00. A liability to St. James, fixed by Manitoba's Municipal Board at $13,788.28, is paid with $3,000.00. Our Municipality writes off $14,272.67 in over-due hospital and other accounts. Henceforth, Relief grants are to be repaid in work done, at 30 cents an hour. Charles Land rents Kirkfield Golf Course for 10% of gross earnings. Among local golfers, Alan Boes emerges as one of the greats.

Overseas, the German war machine roars across Europe, grinding nation after nation into subjection. Denmark and Norway are lost. May sees the British army back from Dunkirk, minus its armaments. France falls. On 9 December, 1941, Assiniboia men with the Winnipeg Grenadiers at Hong Kong, are among the first Canadians engaged in World War 2; and, under Japanese mass attacks, become prisoners-of-war, on Christmas Day.

With distant defences crumbling, home defences are hurried. A giant airport is built at Goose Bay, Newfoundland; the Reserve Army trains in earnest; convoys struggle through, to supply the Fortress of Britain, where Canada's overseas Divisions train. In Assiniboia, registration for National Service calls young men to our Municipal Hall.

Parcel by parcel, citizens buy and restore to production, lands which have become Municipal property through tax sale. John Airey rents the old Kirkfield race-track, as pasture, for $100.00. J. W. Alderson buys 47 acres of Lot 51, Headingly, at $12.00 per acre. Part of Lot 92, St. Charles, is bought for $24.00 per acre. This winter, Relief vouchers are increased by 15%, to meet rising living costs. An extra week's Relief is provided at Christmas. As 1941 ends, the Municipal Commissioner's levy of $1,512.05 is paid, plus arrears of $2,701.41. We are working, slowly, back to solvency.

In January, 1942, Madame Sara Peltier dies, aged 95. Our Council raises Municipal wages to 40 cents per hour; and enlists the RCMP to police Assiniboia. Military District engineers cooperate to grade Isbister Street and Saskatchewan Avenue to the new Rifle Ranges.

In August, we are stunned by the news of Canadians slaughtered at Dieppe!

Demands for wheat and meat bring big speculative land holdings (which have "gone back" to prairie or have never been cleared of their timber) into productive cultivation, as family farms. Our economy moves ahead in high gear, to meet the life-and-death challenge of war.

On the battle front, it is July, 1943, when our Canadian Divisions, integrated in the great Allied counter-offensive, smash into Sicily; and, in September, into Italy. At home, the machinery of production hums!

Food and munitions load an endless chain of shipping; and, despite terrific losses, immense tonnages get through to vitalize the Fortress of Britain. The terrible price of war comes home to all — as we anxiously scan the lengthening casualty lists; and see the gigantic extensions to our Military Hospital at Deer Lodge.

In Assiniboia's battle against bankruptcy, eternal vigilance in spending and everlasting diligence in generating income are whittling down our overload of debt. Our Council is able to invest $30,000.00 in Victory Loans; grant $25.00 to Grace Hospital; and bonus Municipal Clerk Gabe and his assistant, Miss O'Malley, $50.00, each, for 1943.

After 20 months fighting in Italy, our Canadian Divisions return to "Blighty"; and, on "D day", 6 June, share in the greatest attack ever mounted — to batter through the strongest defences ever built. In 380 days of battle, as a vital part of the Allied forces, Canada's Army fights across Northern Europe, yard by yard; engages 60 German Divisions; and takes 192,000 prisoners before "VE day", 8 May, 1945. In this War, Canadians fight on 4 continents; on all the seas between; and in the skies above — "always opposed", writes General Crerar, "by the best forces available to the German High Command". In World War 1, from our population of 7.8 millions, 628,462 Canadians serve in Canada's active defence forces. Of these, 51% are born Canadians. In World War 2, more than a million of our population of 11.2 million share in the active defence of our Canadian nation. In this War, 84% of all who fight for Canada are native sons and daughters.

More than 41,000 Canadians are killed in Action with our Army, Navy and Air Force. How many of these are from Assiniboia is not known. The following list, admittedly fragmentary, is supplied by Hon. Roger J. Teillet, Minister of Veteran Affairs:

P/O Duncan S. Brown	S/Sgt. Donald A. Taylor
Sgt. Magnus Brown	F/L J. A. L. Couture
Pte. Robt. G. Findlay	Pte. Wm. Eluke
F/S Ronald F. Glass	P/O R. G. Kelly
Pte. James D. McIntosh	P/O F. E. Joynson
F/O Geo. W. Parliament	Pte. Geo. LaPeyre
Pte. Marcel Robidoux	P/O R. G. Madge
F/S M. S. McKellar	F/S J. W. Markle
S/Sgt. D. A. Wither	

In addition, these Assiniboia men are found among the 497 killed in action, with the Royal Winnipeg Rifles:

Lieut. L. J. McQueen	Pte. F. Boivin
Pte. F. M. Findlay	Pte. P. Zastre

In two World Wars, 100,000 Canadians give their lives for Canada. Their names, on grave-stones across Europe and around the world, are signatures to a pact (none the less real and sacred, none the less clearly understood, because unwritten, even unspoken) that: all Canada belongs to all Canadians; our history, geography and future are an inviolate, inseparable entity; and our Canadian nationality is indivisible and different from all its ancestral components. Our Assiniboia community is a symbol, perhaps unique in all Canada, of this wordless, eternal covenant that binds together all Canadians of all origins for all time.

CHAPTER 16

"Westward, Look, the Land is Bright"

"And not by Eastern windows only,
When daylight comes, comes in the light.
In front, the Sun climbs slow, so slowly;
But — Westward, Look, the Land is Bright!

— Arthur Hugh Clough

The War thunders to its climax; and ends — in stunning silence!
Families flood Westward, into Assiniboia. Thousands own autos; and
join the traffic jam on Portage Avenue. Others pack into already over-
loaded street cars; and reinforce demands for better transit service. Sturgeon Creek School, over-crowded, opens class-rooms in our Municipal
Hall. In April and May, 1946, 72 buyers inquire about Municipal lands;
and purchase 52 properties. The new "Kirkfield Hotel" opens at Portage
and Parkdale, in August.

Glendale Country Club takes over the old Royoumont property; and
builds magnificent club-houses, thereon. The St. James—Winnipeg
Airport Commission plans expansion of Stevenson Field. Our Council
contributes necessary lands (more than any other Municipality) on
condition that such lands revert to Assiniboia should this use terminate;
and that the Government of Canada "shall provide adequate drainage
of all lands in the area". Regrettably, such wise and needful water
management is never carried out.

Assiniboia citizens urge MP's and MLA's to "do something" to provide
water supply to the people of our Municipality. Our Council demands
return of lands taken for the Veterans' "Rehab Centre", in Kirkfield;
but is not interested in the spread of buildings, never completed. Licenses

for commercial kennels are granted to A. H. Good, F. Owens, R. T. Aconley and K. A. Sadlier. A Mecca for generations of horse-racers, Assiniboia is becoming a noted centre for breeding and training hunting and show dogs.

In the spring of 1950 (as periodically throughout our History) the Red River brings flood-waters from its upper drainage basin, to inundate the flood-plain along the River's main stem. Later, a gigantic ditch is dug, to protect the high-priced properties of Winnipeg real estate owners. This monumental "dirt-mover's dream" may promise protection, until cancelled out by silt-and-water dynamics. Meantime, the vast investment therein yields some sense of security; and, perhaps best of all, provides tremendous scope for recreation.

In any case, the flood moves more people to the "High Ground, Westward", up the Assiniboine River. (As did the great flood of 1826, according to Historian Alexander Ross; and, again, the flood of 1852.) River Lots pioneered a century ago, by families since scattered, and fine old manorial homes (like the "Cameron place", on RL 59, Headingly, walled by trees; spacious, sturdy and beautiful, even in dis-integration) are taken over by new families. Some such Lots are sites for new homes. Others are farmed by families who live in Kirkfield, St. Charles or Headingly. Still others are bought by speculators and rented to producing farmers; or bent to commercial use, like Assiniboia Downs and the Odeon Drive-in Theatre.

In this flood of change, islands of our History stand out, still occupied by families who pioneered and brought these lands into farm production. On these farms, strong, square and balanced homes (like the Taylor's, Keith's and many more) reflect the characters of the pioneers who built them.

Pioneers pass on. Madame Charles Caron, nee Amandine Lafleche, dies at 88, on 5 April, 1950; and, within 28 days, Charles Caron, himself, passes on, at 92. In 1952, Wm. J. McMillan, 74, dies in an accident at Kirkfield. On 13 January, 1954, Madame Honore Lafleche, nee Claire McKenzie, goes to rest at 84 years of age.

With the increase of our native population reinforced by the tide of new-comers, land prices in Assiniboia climb. In 1962, $1,000.00 per acre, cash, is paid for 270 acres of the original homestead of Oliver and Mary Gowler. Assessed at $9.50 per acre in 1945, this historic farm on Gowler's Creek is built into a magnificent public park and golf course. The need for parks and open spaces multiplies, as Assiniboia's population doubles and re-doubles, by Centennial year.

Real estate operators, much like those we knew before World War 1, return under the name of "developers". These entrepreneurs buy old

River Lot farms; sub-divide them into entire communities; and sell new homes in new neighbourhoods, complete with all "modern" facilities and conveniences.

Whereas, a former generation realized, with some concern, that "the City is coming" — now, the Eastern fraction of our Municipality explodes in a "high-rise boom". By 1962, Assiniboia breaks free from the shackles of Province-monitored financing. On the rushing tide of inflated prices and wages, prosperity roars into "high", with the accelerator on the floor-board!

Wildwood areas, Sturgeon Creek, "the big Slough" (where, just yesterday, ornithologists B. W. Cartwright and Angus and Terry Short study our wealth of winged wildlife) are displaced by street on street of homes, facing miles of concrete, studded with forests of poles carrying phone and power lines. School-boys who played "hookey" to trail these famous "bird-men", now sweat out taxes to build and staff palatial schools, as "shades of the prison-house begin to close" about their own growing families.

Our school population multiplies. At St. Charles School, the 70 pupils of 1940 increase to 135 in 5 class-rooms in 1950; and to 612 girls and boys, with 12 teachers (plus 9 teachers at the new Buchanan School) before Centennial Year. At Kirkfield Park School (old Sturgeon Creek re-named) pupils increase from 161 in 6 class-rooms in 1945, to 380 in 14 class-rooms in 1955; and to 526 girls and boys in 20 rooms by 1958. In 1965, part of this School becomes administrative offices for the magnificent system of schools being built to give all of Assiniboia's girls and boys opportunity to acquire "the tools of learning."

The tide of families moving to flood-free Assiniboia is dammed at the Perimeter Highway, some 3 miles east of Headingly, by the dictum of authorities who favor other communities. Margaret McWilliams, in her fine history: "Manitoba Milestones", names Headingly one of 2 centres in pioneer Manitoba where culture and gracious living flourish. Now, denial of normal essential services sentences this historic pioneer community to slow decline. Attendance at Headingly School dwindles from 70 pupils in 1940, to 44 in 1945. In 1955, Headingly and Phoenix School Districts are re-united (after a separation of 45 years). The old Headingly school-house is demolished; and a fine new structure is built at Phoenix, where, by 1956, 146 scholars fill 5 class-rooms. In Headingly — pioneer community up the Assiniboine River; where John Taylor taught the first school 117 years ago — no school-house exists in Centennial Year.

Here, this writing of the History of Assiniboia comes to rest. Vast research and many books are needed, to tell the full story of the people who, here, set the corner-stone for the building of Western Canada.

Assiniboia — earliest experiment in civil administration on the European model; and designated a Municipality generations before any other in our great Nor'West — in 1811 embraces 116,000 square miles. By Centennial Year, this area is home to 3 million people, populating a score of cities and hundreds of towns; and producing tremendous wealth. Thru 156 years, politics and economics have divided the original Assiniboia among 3 of the United States and 3 of Canada's Provinces; and sub-divided it into a multitude of counties and Municipalities. Of these, only our present Municipality of 32 square miles carries the original name: "Assiniboia".

Nevertheless, not politics, not economics, "nor any other creature" shall erase the History of Assiniboia's people. They shape the building of our Canadian West. (Without which Canada must wither, economically and politically.) They sow the sweat and courage, endurance and daring, from which others ("reaping where they have not sown; and gathering where they have not strode") harvest wealth and power — first, in Paris and London; since then, in Montreal and Toronto.

Far beyond setting in motion the vast stream of production which is the stuff of Canadian affluence, however, the men and women who people the History of Assiniboia indelibly influence our Canadian nationality.

The trails of Mankind's History are strewn with the wrecks of nations, grown briefly mighty by exploiting resources to sate the greed for possessions and the craze for dominance by mythical "master races". Canada's History — on the warp of unmatched resourses — weaves all the strength, worth and beauty brought from the ends of the earth by our myriad component peoples, into the fabric of a new Canadian nationality. Our emerging nationality refutes any myth of "master races"; and, reflecting contributions from all, is distinctly different from any, of our ancestral contributors.

The History of Assiniboia — thru generations menaced by hardship, freezing, starvation and war, when any cart separating from the defensive circle brings destruction to all — fixes in our folk-memory the lesson that survival is thru competitive cohesion, disciplined difference and shared mutual benefits.

So, Assiniboia is *the truly typical* Canadian community — prototype of the nationality which all we Canadians, together, are building. From the long folk-memory of our History, we know it is right that we use all the boundless resources entrusted to us within Canada's bounds for the good of all Humanity. Thus, Canada establishes valid title to these resources. Thus, our Canadian nationality makes its full contribution to the History of Mankind.

SELECTED BIBLIOGRAPHY

A Canadian People, by Lorne Pierce. Ryerson Press, Toronto, 1945

Agriculture in Red River Colony, by W. L. Morton. Canadian Historical Review, 1949

A History of Transportation in Canada, by G. P. deT. Glazebrook. Ryerson Press, Toronto, 1938

A History of the Canadian Pacific Railway, by Harold A. Innis. McLelland & Stewart, Toronto, 1923

A Saga of the St. Lawrence, by D. D. Calvin. Ryerson Press, Toronto, 1945

A Short History of Prairie Agriculture, by H. G. L. Strange. Searle Grain Co., Ltd., Winnipeg, 1954

An Historical Atlas of Canada, by Laurence J. Burpee. Thos. Nelson & Sons, Ltd., Toronto, 1927

A Historical Atlas of Canada, by D. G. G. Kerr. Thos. Nelson & Sons, Ltd., 1959

A Pictorial History of the American Indian, by Oliver La Farge. Crown Publishers, Inc., New York, 1956.

Assiniboine Basin, The, by Martin Kavanagh. The Public Press, Winnipeg, 1946

A Year in Manitoba, by Capt. Edmund Goodridge. W & R Chambers, London, 1882

Between the Red and the Rockies, by Grant MacEwan. University of Toronto Press, 1952

Birth of Western Canada, by G. F. C. Stanley. Longman's, Green & Co., New York, 1936

Blankets and Beads, by James G. MacGregor. The Institute of Applied Art, Ltd., Edmonton, 1949

Builders of the West, by F. W. Howay. Ryerson Press, Toronto, 1929

Canada's Century, by D. M. LeBourdais. The Methuen Co. of Canada, Toronto, 1951

Canada Moves North, by Richard Finnie. The MacMillan Co. of Canada, Toronto, 1942

Canadian Spring, by Florence Page Jacques. University of Minnesota Press, Minneapolis, 1938

Canadian Army, The, by Col. C. P. Stacey, OBE. King's Printer, Ottawa, 1948

Canadian History Readers, (Vol. 1-7), edited by Lorne Pierce. Ryerson Press, Toronto

Canadian Northwest, The, by E. H. Oliver. Government Printing Bureau, Ottawa, 1914

Canadian Northwest, The, by G. Mercer Adam. Rose Publishing Co., Toronto, 1885

Canadians in the Making, by Arthur R. M. Lower. Longman's, Green & Co., Toronto, 1958

Carlton Trail, The, by R. C. Russell. Modern Press, Saskatoon, 1955

Canada Unlimited, by Gerald Anglin. O'Keefe Foundation, Toronto, 1948

Canoe Country, by Florence Page Jacques. Harper & Bros., Publishers, New York, 1947

Champlain Road, The, by Franklin Davey McDowell. MacMillan Company of Canada, Toronto, 1949

Champlain, Northwest Voyageur, by Louise Hall Thorp. Little, Brown & Co., Boston, 1946

Church Beginnings in Western Canada, by Rev. Francis Armstrong. MSS. Winnipeg, 1966

Clearing in the West, by Nellie McClung. Thomas Allan, Toronto, 1935

Colonist at Home Again, The, by Capt. Edmund Goodridge. Wm. Dawson & Sons, London, England, 1889

Colony to Nation, by Arthur R. M. Lower. Longman's, Green & Co., Toronto, 1946

Cuthbert Grant of Grantown, by Margaret Arnett MacLeod and W. L. Morton. McClelland & Stewart, Toronto, 1963

Deeper Roots of Oakville, The, by A. J. Moore. Vopni Press, Ltd., Portage la Prairie, 1963

Deep Furrows, by Hopkins Moorhouse. Geo. J. McLeod, Ltd., Winnipeg, 1918

Diary, of Hon. John Taylor, Headingly, Assiniboia, 1876

Early Life in Canada, by J. W. Chafe and Sybil Shack. Ryerson Press, Toronto, 1943

Essays on Wheat, by A. H. Reginald Buller. MacMillan Company, New York, 1919

Geologists & Prospectors, by Margaret Mason Shaw. Clarke, Irwin & Co., Toronto, 1958

Great Company, The, by Beckles Willson. Copp, Clark Co., Toronto, 1899

Greater Winnipeg Investigating Commission Report and Recommendations, Queen's Printer, Manitoba, 1959

Face of Canada, The, by C. L. Bennett, Gerard Filion, Gregory Clark, Roderick Haig-Brown, Marjorie Wilkins Campbell. Clarke, Irwin & Co., Toronto, 1959

First Furrows, by Rev. A. C. Garrioch

Flanders Fields. Prints of 17 CBC Radio Broadcasts, 1967

Forest, Lake and Prairie, by John McDougall. Ryerson Press, Toronto

From Sea Unto Sea, by W. C. Hardy. Doubleday & Co., Inc., New York, 1960

Henderson's Directory. Winnipeg, 1923

Historical Diary of Winnipeg, by F. C. Lucas. 1923

History of the Canadian West, to 1870-71, by A. S. Morton. Thos. Nelson & Sons, Toronto

History of the Northwest, The, by Alexander Begg (Vol. 1-3). Hunter, Rose & Co., Toronto, 1895

Honourable Company, The, by Douglas Mackay. McLelland & Stewart, Toronto, 1936

Hunters of the Great North, by Vilhjalmer Stefansson. Harcourt, Brace & Co.

Incomplete Canadian, The, by G. R. Stevens. 1965

Indian Days on the Western Plains, by Marius Barbeau. National Museum of Canada, 1960

Indians of Canada, The, by Diamond Jenness. National Museum of Canada, 1932

In Scarlet and Plain Clothes, by T. Morris Longstreth. The MacMillan Co., New York, 1944

SELECTED BIBLIOGRAPHY

Kelsey Papers, The, edited by Arthur G. Doughty & Chester Martin. Public Archives of Canada, 1929

Lake Erie, by Harlan Hatcher. The Bobbs-Merrill Company, New York, 1945

Lake Huron, by Fred Landon. The Bobbs-Merrill Company, New York, 1944

Lake Michigan, by Milo M. Quaife. The Bobbs-Merrill Company, New York, 1944

Lake Ontario, by Arthur Pound. The Bobbs-Merrill Company, New York, 1945

Lake Superior, by Grace Lee Nute. The Bobbs-Merrill Company, New York, 1944

Life of the Rt. Hon. John A. Macdonald, by Lt. Col. J. Pennington MacPherson ADC

Looking Backward, by Robert Sinton, MSS.

Lord Selkirk of Red River, by John Morgan Gray. The MacMillan Co. of Canada, 1963

Lord Selkirk's Colonists, by Dr. George Bryce.

Louis Riel, Patriot or Rebel, by G. F. C. Stanley.

MacKenzie, The, by Leslie Roberts. Rinehart & Co. Ltd., New York, 1949

Manitoba—a History, by W. L. Morton. University of Toronto Press, 1957

Manitoba as I Saw it, by Dr. J. H. O'Donnell.

Manitoba Milestones, by Margaret McWilliams. J. M. Dent & Sons, Toronto, 1928

Manitoba: The Birth of a Province, by W. L. Morton. D. W. Friesen & Sons, Altona, Manitoba, 1965

McLoughlin and Old Oregon, by Eva Emery Dye. Doubleday, Page & Co., New York, 1924

Memories Along the Badger, Cartwright Historical Committee. Derksen Printers, Ltd., Steinbach, Manitoba, 1966

Mere Living, The, by Hazel McDonald Parkinson. D. W. Friesen & Sons, Ltd., Altona, Manitoba, 1957

Minutes of Councils of Red River Colony—Publication of the Canadian Archives #9 "The Canadian Northwest, Vol. 1, by E. H. Oliver. Government Printing Bureau, Ottawa, 1914

Mounties, The, by Anne I. Grierson. Ryerson Press, Toronto, 1947

Mound Builders, The, by Henry Clyde Shetrone. Appleton Company, New York, 1930

Northwest Company, The, by Marjorie Wilkins Campbell.

Ocean to Ocean, by Rev. Geo. M. Grant. The Radisson Society of Canada, Toronto, 1925

Oregon, by Rev. Gustavus Hines. Geo. H. Derby & Co., Buffalo, 1851

Oregon Trail, The, Federal Writer's Project. Hastings House Publishers, 1939

People of Red River, The, Harper's New Monthly Magazine, December, 1858

Peter Fidler, by J. G. MacGregor. McLelland & Stewart, Ltd., Toronto, 1966

Pioneers and Prominent People of Manitoba, Historical Introduction by W. J. Healy. Bulman Bros. Ltd., Winnipeg, 1925

Pioneers in Agriculture, by Elizabeth Waterston. Clarke, Irwin & Company, Toronto, 1957

Pioneer Sketches in the Bathhurst District, by Andrew Haydon. Ryerson Press, Toronto, 1925

Place Names in Canada, by G. H. Armstrong. MacMillan Company of Canada, Toronto, 1930

Prairie Settlement, The Geographical Setting, by Wm. A. Mackintosh. MacMillan Company, Ltd., Toronto, 1934

Progressive Party in Canada, The, by W. L. Morton. University of Toronto Press, Toronto, 1950

Quick-Stepping Pioneers, by James McCook. "The Beaver," Spring, 1960

Rainy River Country, by Grace Lee Nute. The Minnesota Historical Society, Minneapolis, 1953

Range Men, The, by L. V. Kelly.

Red Indians of the Plains, The, by Rev. J. Hines. Society for Promotion of Christian Knowledge, London, England, 1915

Red River Settlement, by Alexander Ross. Smith, Elder & Co., London, England, 1856

Red River Shadows, by Olive Knox. MacMillan Company, Toronto, 1948

Red River Runs North, by Vera Kelsey. Harper & Bros., Publishers, New York, 1951

Reminiscenses of Northwest Rebellions, by Major Boulton. Grip Printing & Publishing Co., Toronto, 1886

Rockwood Echoes, Rockwood Historical Society. Derksen Printers, Ltd., Steinbach, Manitoba, 1960

Romance of the Canadian Canoe, The, by John Murray Gibbon. Ryerson Press, Toronto, 1951

Riel, Defender of the Past, by George Woodcock. "The Beaver," Spring, 1960

Romance of Western Canada, by R. G. MacBeth. Ryerson Press, Toronto, 1920

Saddle, Sled and Snowshoe, by John McDougall. Wm. Briggs, Toronto, 1896

Saint Among the Hurons, by Francis Xavier Talbot, S. J. Harper & Bros., Publishers, New York, 1949

Saskatchewan, The, by Marjorie Wilkins Campbell. Rinehart & Company, Inc., Toronto, 1950

Saskatchewan History, published by the Saskatchewan Archives Board.

Settlers of the Plains, by O. E. A. Brown & C. Finnen. The Maple Leaf Press, Gilbert Plains, Manitoba, 1953

Seven Rivers of Canada, by Hugh McLennan. MacMillans of Canada, Toronto, 1961

Six Thousand Canadian Men, by E. S. Russenholt. De Montfort Press, Winnipeg, Manitoba, 1932

Shooting the Stars and Chaining the Land, by Marjorie Forrester. "The Beaver," Spring, 1960

Sodbusters, The, by Grant MacEwan. Thos. Nelson & Sons, Ltd., Toronto, 1948

Story of Manitoba, Vol. III, S. J. Clarke Publishing Co., Winnipeg, 1913

Story of Stony Mountain, by Edward R. R. Mills. De Montfort Press, Winnipeg, 1960

Strange Empire, by Joseph Kinsey Howard. Swan Publishing Co., Ltd., Toronto, 1965

Substance of a Journal, by Rev. John West. L. B. Seeley & Son, London, 1824

Tales and Trails of Western Canada, by Nell McVicar and Irene Craig. School Aid Publishing Co., Ltd., Regina, 1947

Tales of the Mounted, by William Brockie. Ryerson Press, Toronto, 1949

Ten Years in Winnipeg, by Alexander Begg and Walter Nursey. Times Printing and Publishing House, Winnipeg, 1879

Trade Guns of the Nor'West Company, by Gordon T. Howard. Canadian Journal of Arms Collecting, August, 1964

Thirteen Years on the Prairies, by John Pennefather. Kegan, Paul, French, Truber, London, England, 1892

SELECTED BIBLIOGRAPHY

Three Centuries of Canadian Story, by J. E. Wetherell. The Munson Book Company, Ltd., Toronto, 1928

Vanishing Frontier, The, by Phillip Godsell. Ryerson Press, Toronto, 1930

Voyageurs, 1957 and 1958, by Eric Morse. Reprinted from Ottawa "Journal."

West by South, by J. C. Strothers & Elva Armitage. Ryerson Press, Toronto, 1938

White and the Gold, The, by Thos. B. Costain. Doubleday Canada, Ltd., Toronto, 1954

Winnipeg Blue Book, 1907

Women of Red River, by W. J. Healy. Russell, Lang & Co., Ltd., Winnipeg, 1923

Women Pioneers of North America, The, by Sophy L. Elliott. Garden City Press, Ltd., Gardenvale, P.Q. 1941

Additional information sources include: "Manitoba Pageant" and "Transactions" published by the Historical & Scientific Society of Manitoba; diaries, scrapbooks and letters; the "Farmer's Advocate", 1879-85, the "Nor'West Farmer", 1885-90, the "Canadian Historical Review", "Winnipeg Tribune", Winnipeg "Free Press", St. James "Leader", "The Nor'Wester", and "The New Nation". Also drawn upon: Census reports, "Waghorn's Guide" and Parliamentary Guide; minutes of School Districts and the Rural Municipality of Assiniboia, 1880-1940; St. Charles and Headingly parish records; and files of the Manitoba Highway Service and the Historic Sites Advisory Board. Research in the Public Archives of Canada, in Ottawa, tapped Hudson's Bay Company micro-film records, including: Headquarters records, Post records, Governor's papers, Correspondence, as well as Minutes of the London Committee, General Courts and the original Council of Assiniboia.

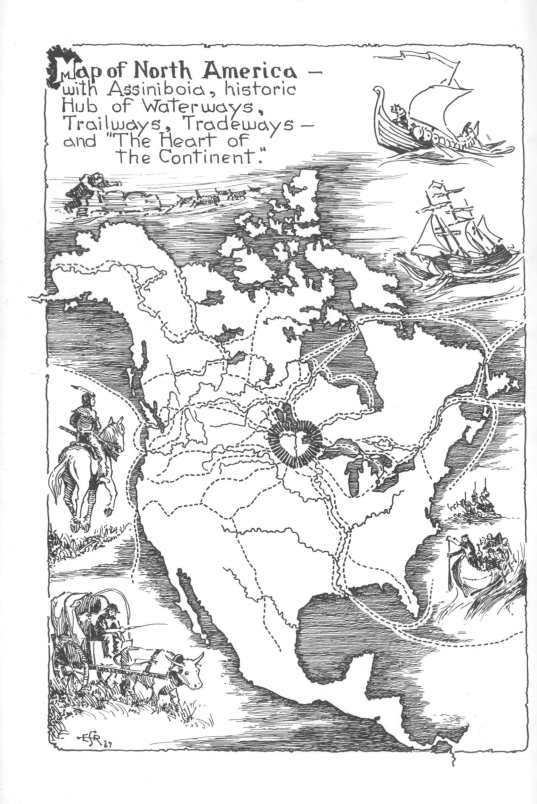

Map of North America — with Assiniboia, historic Hub of Waterways, Trailways, Tradeways — and "The Heart of the Continent."